ROAD TRIP

The Road Traveler's Complete Guide
To America's Best Scenic Drives

Published by:
Roundabout Publications
2767 S. Parker Rd., Suite 240
Aurora, Colorado 80014

Includes an Extensive
Road Traveler's Resource Guide

Unfortunate - But Necessary

Every effort has been made to make this book as complete and as accurate as possible. However, there may be mistakes both typographical and in content. Therefore, this text should be used as a general guide to the scenic drives covered. Although we regret any inconvenience caused by inaccurate information, the author and Roundabout Publications shall have neither liability nor responsibility to any person or entity with respect to any loss or damage caused, or alleged to be caused, directly or indirectly by the information contained in this book.

Published by:
Roundabout Publications
2767 South Parker Road, Suite 240
Aurora, Colorado 80014-2701
Phone: 800-800-6727

First Printing August 1994

Road Trip USA Copyright © 1994 by Roundabout Publications

Printed and bound in the United States of America.

All rights reserved. No part of this book may be reproduced in any form or by any electronic or mechanical means including information storage and retrieval systems without permission in writing from the publisher, except by a reviewer, who may quote brief passages in a review.

Library of Congress Catalog Card Number: 94-67023

ISBN: 1-885464-24-X

TABLE OF CONTENTS

TABLE OF CONTENTS (CONT.)

FOREWORD

If we Americans have a common denominator, it is a love of driving. No other society is so passionate about hitting the road.

Blame Henry Ford. Back at the turn of century, the Michigan man had a dream — of a speedy, mass-produced, motorized vehicle — no horse up front, just a motor! Americans, tired of traveling behind slow animals, and by the railroads' strict time tables, soon responded to Ford's "better idea."

Before long, they were driving from town to town, and, as roads improved, from coast to coast along famous highways like the Lincoln and, later, Route 66.

In the '50s, everybody was being pleasantly brainwashed by a pretty blonde singer named Dinah Shore. In brilliant black and white, on TVs across America, she stood before the camera, and belted out "See the USA in your Chevrolet."

And everybody did, although not just in Chevys, of course. The Sunday drive became the national pastime.

Then, in the 1960s, President Eisenhower got another "better idea" — a seemingly brilliant one: to build a giant web of wide and fast superhighways called Interstates, designed to move the troops and the masses as well. A decade later, we proudly sped along these multi-laned miracles of pavement. However, we were so impressed at how fast we were going we failed to notice that something was missing — scenery!

Luckily, something has come along to help us combat the boredom of the Interstates — our Scenic Byways, the most gorgeous, photogenic roads in America — mostly two-laners through mountains, along the ocean, across deserts, through lava fields and wheatfields — through the most knock-out beautiful terrain any motorist could expect in a single world, not to mention a single country!

The best part is that these roads are here for all of us. There's lots to see, and admission is free.

So come along, and let this book be your guide.

Enjoy the scenery.

Chuck Woodbury
Nevada City, California
July, 1994

Chuck Woodbury is the editor and publisher of Out West, an acclaimed quarterly newspaper about travel along the back roads of the American West. For subscription information, call 1-800-274-9378. Additional information about Out West may be found in the resource guide, listing number 93 on page 248.

INTRODUCTION

America's Best

In the United States today, there are approximately four million miles of roads criss-crossing the country. Found in the pages that follow, you will discover those roads that represent America's best scenic drives. The roads described travel through a beautifully diverse landscape, as diverse as the people that make up this great land of ours.

Driving these roadways will take you through lush green forests, past glistening lakes and rivers, into sheer-walled, red-rock canyons, and across desert landscapes with unique geologic formations. These scenic drives provide you with the chance to pull off the interstate, slow down, and discover America's scenic countryside and the treasures within.

A wide array of recreational opportunities await you along these beautiful roadways. You can camp alongside the road in a spot offering a spectacular view or choose a developed campground with the amenities of home. Enjoy a hike or horseback ride through dense wilderness areas to peaceful and secluded areas. You'll have the opportunity to fish in a mountain stream or lake, four-wheel on a rugged, bumpy road to nowhere, canoe down a meandering river, or picnic under the shade of trees.

In addition to the recreational opportunities, many scenic drives offer glimpses into the past. Ghost towns await your inspection, the Pony Express trail can be followed, ancient Indian rock art may be studied, and wagon wheel ruts of the pioneers traveling west can be seen. You'll discover historical sites and museums, National Monuments and Memorials, and treasures of America's past preserved in the National Park areas.

So whether you are traveling by car, motorcycle, or recreational vehicle, this is your invitation to come and experience the America we are proud to call home.

About The Scenic Drives

On January 28, 1985, President Ronald Reagan established the *President's Commission on Americans Outdoors*. The commission was to review public and private outdoor recreational opportunities and make recommendations to ensure the future availability of outdoor recreation for the American people.

The results of this study found that 43% of American adults identified driving for pleasure as a favorite leisure pursuit, second only to walking.

As a result of the commissions findings, the National Forest Service and the Bureau of Land Management started two new scenic byway programs. In 1988 the National Forest Service began designating routes as *National Forest Scenic Byways* and in 1989 the Bureau of Land Management (BLM) started the *Back Country Byways* program. The routes that were officially designated into the programs represent the very best scenic routes from the thousands of miles of roads that travel across the Nation's public lands.

National Forest Scenic Byways

The National Forest Service administers 190 million acres of public lands in 156 forests across the country. The officially designated *National Forest Scenic Byways* represent the very best scenic routes from over 100,000 miles of roads that run through the national forests. The scenic byways primarily travel over two-lane paved roads that are suitable for travel by all vehicles.

The recreational opportunities found along these byways are numerous. Developed recreation areas and campgrounds are located along most of the routes. Camping may also be permitted anywhere within the national forest for those interested in a more primitive setting. Many of the national forests also have areas designated for off-road vehicle use, mountain biking, hunting, hiking, horseback riding, boating, fishing, and backpacking.

BLM Back Country Byways

The 342 million acres of public lands managed by the U.S. Bureau of Land Management provide unique opportunities for traveling the more remote areas and back roads of America.

Recreational opportunities found along the routes are in the form of primitive camping, bicycling, four-wheeling, fishing in lakes and rivers, or simply enjoying an afternoon picnic and the solitude. Many of the byways provide developed campgrounds, however, camping is permitted anywhere on BLM administered lands.

Since many of the BLM *Back Country Byways* travel through remote countryside it is always a good idea to be prepared for your journey. Carry plenty of water for you and for your vehicle's radiator. Be sure to start each trip with enough gasoline to drive the entire route. It is also a good idea to have a spare tire, jack, shovel, blanket, and tools for emergency road repairs.

Many of these byways become impassable during winter or after periods of heavy rainfall so it's a good idea to inquire about the current road conditions and any possible limitations for your type of vehicle before attempting to travel the route.

The *Back Country Byways* have been classified into four types for determining the level of difficulty, road surface, and type of vehicle required to travel them. Listed below are descriptions of each classification.

Type I - Roads that are paved or have an all weather surface and have grades that are negotiable by a normal touring car. These roads are usually narrow, slow speed, secondary roads.

Type II - These roads require a high clearance type vehicle such as a truck or four-wheel drive. These roads are usually not paved but may have some type of surfacing. Grades, curves, and road surface are such that they can be negotiated with a two wheel drive high clearance vehicle without undue difficulty.

Type III - These are roads that require a four-wheel drive vehicle or other specialized vehicle such as a dirt bike or all-terrain vehicle (ATV). These roads are usually not surfaced, but are managed to provide for safety considerations and resource protection needs. They have grades, tread surfaces, and other characteristics that require specialized vehicles to negotiate.

Type IV - These are *trails* managed specifically to accommodate dirt bikes, mountain bikes, snowmobiles, or all-terrain vehicles. These are usually single track trails.

State Scenic Drives

Some of the scenic drives found in this book have not been officially designated by the National Forest Service or the Bureau of Land Management but offer such scenic or historical qualities that they warrant inclusion in this book. Such routes are found in New York, Pennsylvania, Texas, and Alaska. Since the routes in Alaska can travel over remote countryside, it is advisable to contact the addresses listed for more detailed information on the current road conditions and any vehicle limitations.

About This Book

This book was designed to provide you with a wealth of information on traveling America's scenic drives. Understanding how to read and use the information presented will help you fully reap the benefits this information provides.

The first page for every state provides an alphabetical listing of the scenic drives and National Park Areas in that state.

The scenic drives are plotted on the state map with the corresponding number in a "square" while the National Park Areas are identified with the corresponding letter in a "circle". An alphabetical listing of all the scenic drives can be found on page 236. More information on the National Park Areas is found starting on page 273.

The pages that follow the state page describe each scenic drive in that state. The information has been divided into 5 subheadings for easy reference. Following is a brief description of each subheading. *Route Location:* Provides the general location of the route, usually in perspective to a major city and provides the location of a starting and ending point. *Roads Traveled:* Details the length, road numbers, surface and width, vehicle limitations, and any official designation of the route. *Travel Season:* Provides information on road closures due to weather restrictions. *Description:* Provides a brief overview of the attractions and recreational opportunities traveler's will encounter along and nearby the route. Keep in mind this is not a complete listing of all the opportunities available. The additional information sources were provided so you can receive more in depth information than was possible to provide in this book. The opportunities are numerous and the information on them is free from the sources provided. *Other Nearby Routes:* Provides the approximate location of other routes described in this book that are close by.

The last section of the route description pages lists the information sources where you can receive free brochures, maps, and additional information on the scenic drives and the communities around the routes.

Road Traveler's Resource Guide

The resource guide at the end of the book is an extensive listing of information on outdoor recreation and travel related services, products, newsletters, magazines, directories, clubs and associations. The listings include the address and phone number along with a brief description of the product or service offered. You will also find the addresses and phone number for State Tourism Offices, National Forests, Bureau of Land Management, and the National Parks.

Helpful Tips

Please note that some of the attractions found along the routes are located on private property. Please respect the landowners and receive permission before crossing their land to inspect the sites located on their property. Only take photos and memories with you.

Many of these scenic drives travel across mountainous land. Keep in mind that mountain driving courtesy always gives the right-of-way to uphill traffic. Use caution when approaching blind turns, especially on narrow roadways, and be prepared for another vehicle around the turn.

LEGEND

Using The Scenic Drive Maps

Following are the symbols used on the maps and their meanings. Please note that the maps are not to scale.

———	Scenic Drive		70	Interstate Highway
———	Other Roads		69	U.S. Highway
○	City or Town		12	State Highway
▪	Point of Interest		12	County Road
▲	Campground		123	Forest Service Road or BLM Road
�	Body of Water			
🚶🚶	Hiking, Backpacking Trail			
🌲🌲	Wilderness Area			

Using the Recreation and Attraction Bars

The recreation and attraction bars were designed to give you information about the scenic drives at a glance. Listed below are the icons used and their meaning.

RECREATION		
▲	•	Camping
🚶🚶	•	Hiking / Backpacking
🚶	•	Nature Trail / Walk
🐎	•	Horseback Riding
🦆	•	Hunting
🐟	•	Fishing
🛶	•	Boating / Canoeing / Rafting
🦅	•	Wildlife Viewing
⛷	•	Cross-Country / Downhill Skiing
🛷	•	Snowmobiling
🚲	•	Bicycling / Mountain Biking
🚙	•	Off-Road Vehicle Use
⛱	•	Picnicking

ATTRACTIONS		
🦌	•	Wildlife Refuge / Area
🌲🌲	•	Wilderness Area
〰〰	•	National Wild and Scenic River
💧	•	Waterfall
🔫	•	Historic Area / Site
🏛	•	Historic Monument / Memorial
🏛	•	Museum
🏠	•	Ghost Town
⛏	•	Mining Ruins
N᚛F	•	National Forest
⛰	•	National Park
↑	•	Park, State / City / County
⛺	•	Recreation Area / Site

ALABAMA

□ *Scenic Drives*

1. Talladega

○ *National Park Areas*

A. Horseshoe Bend National Military Park
B. Little River Canyon National Preserve
C. Russell Cave National Monument
D. Tuskegee Institute National Historic Site

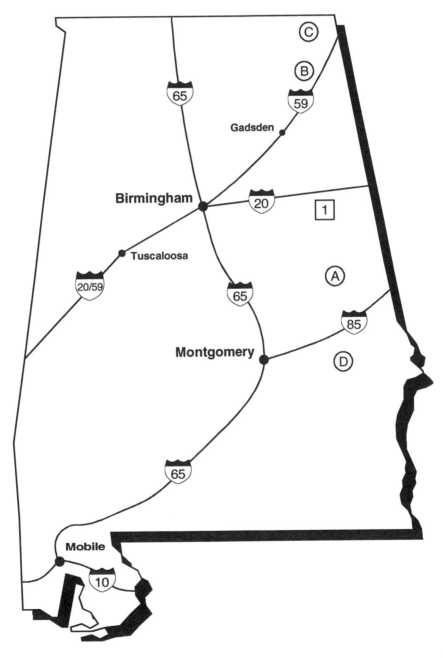

Road Condition Number: 205-242-4378

TALLADEGA

Alabama

- *Route Location:* Located in east-central Alabama, east of Birmingham. The northern access starts just west of Heflin off U.S. Highway 78 and travels south to the town of Lineville.
- *Roads Traveled:* The 34 mile route follows Alabama State Highway 49/281 which is a two-lane paved road suitable for all vehicles. Twenty-three miles of this route has been designated a National Forest Scenic Byway.
- *Travel Season:* The route is open year-round.
- *Description:* This scenic drive travels across the Talladega National Forest and offers spectacular views of the surrounding Appalachian Mountains. The highest point in Alabama, Cheaha Mountain at 2,407 feet above sea level, is crossed at approximately midway along the route. The Pinhoti National Recreation Trail runs along the scenic drive and several access points to the trail are provided. The Cheaha Wilderness area offers camping, hiking, backpacking, hunting, and fishing. Motorized vehicles and bicycles are prohibited from this area. There are two areas within the national forest that have been designated for off-road vehicle use, the Ivory Mountain and the Kentuck Mountain Off-Road Vehicle Areas. Also located within the national forest are several developed recreation areas including the Coleman Lake, Lake Chinnabee, and Pine Glen Recreation Areas. These areas provide opportunities for camping, picnicking, fishing, hiking, and hunting. Cheaha State Park is located approximately midway along the scenic drive.
- *Other Nearby Routes:* The Ridge and Valley scenic drive, located in Georgia, is approximately 75 miles northeast from Heflin, Alabama.

RECREATION	
⛺	•
🧗	•
🚶	•
🐎	•
🎣	•
🐟	•
🛶	
🥾	•
⛷	
🛷	
🚲	•
🚙	•
⛱	•

ATTRACTIONS	
🦌	
🌲	•
〰	
💧	
🔫	
🏛	
🏛	
🏠	
🛒	
N F	•
⛰	
⬆	•
⛴	•

Information Sources:

National Forests In Alabama, 2950 Chestnut, Montgomery, AL 36107-3010 / 205-832-4470
Cleburne County Chamber of Commerce, P.O. Box 413, Heflin, AL 36264 / 205-463-2222
Alexander City Area Chamber of Commerce, 100 Tallapoosa St., Alexander City, AL 35010 / 205-234-3461
Calhoun County Chamber of Commerce, 1330 Quintard, Anniston, AL 36202 / 205-237-3536

ALASKA

□ *Scenic Drives*

Road Condition Number: 907-243-7675

1. Dalton Highway
2. Denali Highway
3. Richardson Highway
4. Seward Highway
5. Taylor Highway

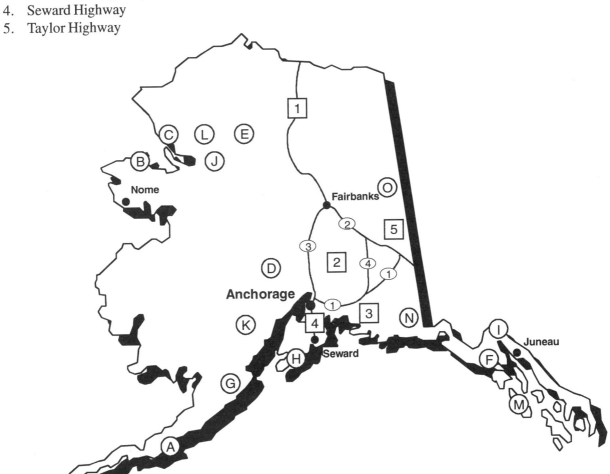

O *National Park Areas*

A. Aniakchak National Monument and Preserve
B. Bering Land Bridge National Preserve
C. Cape Krusenstern National Monument
D. Denali National Park and Preserve
E. Gates of the Arctic National Park and Preserve
F. Glacier Bay National Park and Preserve
G. Katmai National Park and Preserve
H. Kenai Fjords National Park

I. Klondike Gold Rush National Historical Park
J. Kobuk Valley National Park
K. Lake Clark National Park and Preserve
L. Noatak National Preserve
M. Sitka National Historical Park
N. Wrangell - St. Elias National Park and Preserve
O. Yukon - Charley Rivers National Preserve

DALTON HIGHWAY

Alaska

- *Route Location:* Located in north-central Alaska, north of Fairbanks. The southern access starts in Livengood and travels north to Prudhoe Bay on the coast of the Arctic Ocean.
- *Roads Traveled:* The 304 mile route travels across a rough two-lane gravel surfaced road but is suitable for all vehicles. The route can be very dusty or slippery, depending on the weather. Private vehicles may be driven from Livengood to the Disaster Creek turn-around point (milepost 211) north of Big Lake. A road use permit is required from the Alaska Department of Transportation for travel beyond this point. There are tour companies that offer bus tours of the highway between Fairbanks and Prudhoe Bay.
- *Travel Season:* The route is generally open year-round although winter driving conditions can be hazardous and delays are possible.
- *Description:* This scenic drive travels north alongside portions of the Arctic and Yukon Flats National Wildlife Refuges and the Gates of the Arctic National Park and Preserve. It is the only highway in Alaska where you can cross the Arctic Circle. Most of the land along the route is undeveloped and offers a wealth of unusual and seldom-seen wildlife. Muskoxen may be seen from the highway north of the Brooks Range, the northernmost extension of the Rocky Mountains. Alaska natives call these animals "oomingmak," which means "the animal with skin like a beard." Please note: there are no services available along the route between the Yukon River crossing and Coldfoot, a distance of 119 miles.
- *Other Nearby Routes:* The Richardson Highway scenic drive is approximately 80 miles south of Livengood.

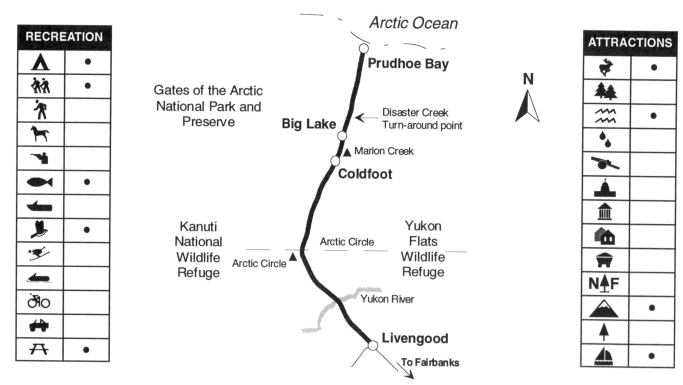

Information Sources:

BLM, Arctic District, 1150 University Avenue, Fairbanks, AK 99709-3844 / 907-474-2302
Alaska Department of Transportation, 2301 Peger Rd., Fairbanks, AK 99707 / 907-451-2200
Big Lake Chamber of Commerce, P.O. Box 520067, Big Lake, AK 99652 / 907-892-6109
Greater Fairbanks Chamber of Commerce, 709 Second Ave., Fairbanks, AK 99701 / 907-452-1105

DENALI HIGHWAY

- *Route Location:* Located in central Alaska, south of Fairbanks. The eastern access starts in Paxson off Alaska State Highway 4 and travels west to Cantwell near the boundary of the Denali National Park and Preserve.
- *Roads Traveled:* The 135 mile route follows Alaska State Highway 8 and is suitable for all vehicles. The first 21 miles west of Paxson travel over a paved surface and the last 114 miles travel over a gravel surfaced road.
- *Travel Season:* The route is generally open from about late May to early October and then closed by heavy winter snows.
- *Description:* The Denali Highway is the highest road in Alaska as it crosses the Maclaren summit at 4,086 feet. Traveling this route offers views of a variety of wildlife, spectacular scenery, and a glimpse into Alaska's past. Wildlife seen in this area includes cari-

bou, moose, bears, ptarmigan, and trumpeter swans. Spectacular views of Mt. McKinley to the west, the Wrangell Mountains to the east, and the many peaks of the Alaska Range to the north are all offered along this route. Recreational opportunities exist in the 455,000 acre Tangle Lakes Archaeological District. Numerous trails are found in this area for hiking, mountain biking, and off-road vehicle use.

Alaska

- *Other Nearby Routes:* The eastern terminus of this route in Paxson is at about the mid-point of the Richardson Highway scenic drive. The Seward Highway scenic drive starts about 210 miles south in Anchorage. Approximately 220 miles to the north is Livengood, which is the starting point for the Dalton Highway scenic drive.

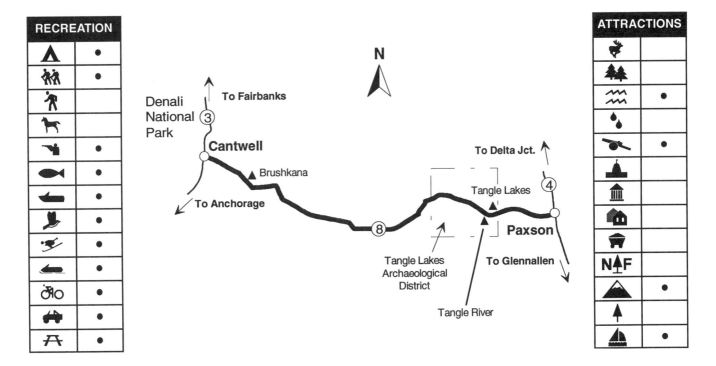

Information Sources:

BLM, Glennallen District Office, P.O. Box 42, Glennallen, AK 99588 / 907-822-3217
Delta Junction Chamber of Commerce, P.O. Box 987, Delta Junction, AK 99737 / 907-895-5068
Greater Copper Valley Chamber of Commerce, P.O. Box 469, Glennallen, AK 99588 / 907-822-5555

RICHARDSON HIGHWAY

- *Route Location:* Located in central Alaska with the northern access starting in Fairbanks. The route travels south to the town of Valdez near the Gulf of Alaska.
- *Roads Traveled:* The 365 mile route follows Alaska State Highways 2 and 4 which are two-lane paved roads suitable for all vehicles.
- *Travel Season:* The route is open year-round although winter driving conditions can be hazardous and delays are possible.
- *Description:* The Richardson Highway was the first road in Alaska and the original north-south route from Valdez to the Klondike gold fields. Portions of the route follow the boundary of the Wrangell-Saint Elias National Park and Preserve, and offers spectacular views of the surrounding mountains. The Sourdough Roadhouse, located just south of Paxson, was built in 1903 and is the oldest roadhouse still op-

erating in its original structure. The building was placed on the National Register of Historic Places in 1974. Recreational opportunities are found all along the route at several state recreation areas. The Big Delta and Harding Lake State Recreation Areas offer camping, picnicking, hiking, and fishing opportunities as does the Paxson Lake Recreation Site. A portion of the scenic drive travels alongside the Delta National Wild and Scenic River which offers rafting and floating.

- *Other Nearby Routes:* The Denali Highway scenic drive can be accessed along this route in Paxson and the Seward Highway scenic drive is about 190 miles west of Glennallen. The Dalton Highway is approximately 80 miles to the north from Fairbanks.

Alaska

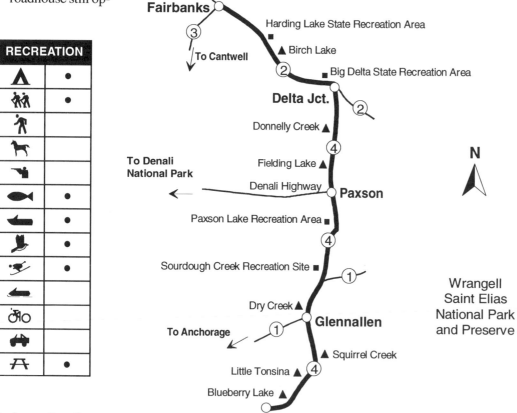

Information Sources:

Greater Fairbanks Chamber of Commerce, 709 Second Ave., Fairbanks, AK 99701 / 907-452-1105
Delta Junction Chamber of Commerce, P.O. Box 987, Delta Junction, AK 99737 / 907-895-5068
Greater Copper Valley Chamber of Commerce, P.O. Box 469, Glennallen, AK 99588 / 907-822-5555
Valdez Chamber of Commerce, 208 N. Harbor Dr., Valdez, AK 99686 / 907-835-2330

SEWARD HIGHWAY

- *Route Location:* This scenic drive is located in south-central Alaska, with the northern access starting in Anchorage and traveling south to Seward.
- *Roads Traveled:* The 127 mile route follows Alaska State Highways 1 and 9 which are two-lane paved roads suitable for all vehicles although some sections are narrow and winding. The entire route has been designated a National Forest Scenic Byway.
- *Travel Season:* The entire route is open year-round although winter driving conditions may be hazardous. Snow avalanches can temporarily close sections of the highway.
- *Description:* The route parallels the Kenai National Wildlife Refuge as it travels through the Chugach National Forest to the boundary of the Kenai Fjords National Park at Seward. Spectacular scenery and a variety of wildlife are offered along this drive. Beluga whales are occasionally seen rolling at the surface of

the Turnagain Arm as they chase salmon and searun smelt. Tracks of the Alaska Railroad are visible along the Turnagain Arm. This railroad was completed in 1923 and linked the port of Seward to the gold fields.

Alaska

Portage Glacier lies at the end of Turnagain Arm and is Alaska's most visited recreation site. Exit Glacier, outside of Seward, is also a great place to experience a glacier first-hand. Bald eagles may be spotted soaring in the skies above as Dall sheep scale the rugged mountain sides. Moose, bear, and mountain goats also inhabit the area along the route.

- *Other Nearby Routes:* The Richardson Highway scenic drive is about 190 miles west of Anchorage while the Denali Highway scenic drive is approximately 210 miles north of Anchorage.

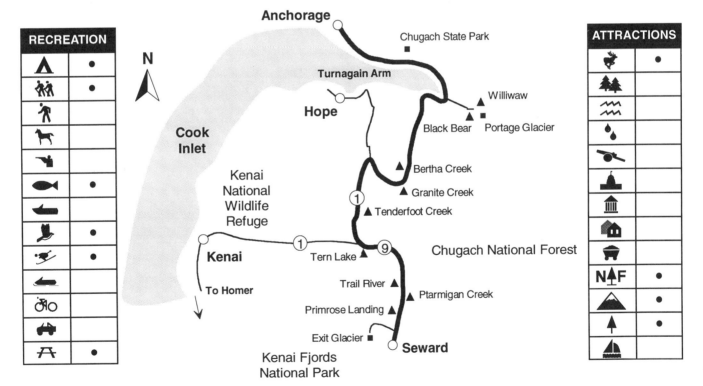

Information Sources:

Chugach National Forest, 201 East 9th Ave., Suite 206, Anchorage, AK 99501 / 907-271-2500
Anchorage Chamber of Commerce, 441 W. 5th Ave., 3300, Anchorage, AK 99501-2365 / 907-272-7588
Seward Chamber of Commerce, P.O. Box 749, Seward, AK 99664 / 907-224-8051
Kenai Chamber of Commerce, 402 Overland, Kenai, AK 99611 / 907-283-7989

TAYLOR HIGHWAY

Alaska

- *Route Location:* Located in east-central Alaska, southeast of Fairbanks. The southern access starts in Tetlin Junction off Alaska State Highway 2 (Alaska Highway) and travels northeast to the town of Eagle near the boundary of the Yukon Charley Rivers National Preserve.
- *Roads Traveled:* The 160 mile route follows Alaska State Highway 5 over a two-lane gravel road that is suitable for all vehicles. The road ends in Eagle so you will need to retrace the route back to Tetlin Junction or to the junction of highways 5 and 9, which runs into Dawson, Canada.
- *Travel Season:* The entire route is closed in the winter from heavy snows.
- *Description:* The Taylor Highway travels through the rolling hills of the historic Fortymile country, an area noted for its colorful mining history. Located about 5 miles north of Tetlin Junction is a short ½ mile trail that leads to Four Mile Lake which offers good rainbow trout fishing. Taylor Creek is an all-terrain vehicle trail, accessed along the drive, that leads to Taylor and Ketchumstuk Mountains. The trail also leads you to the abandoned village of Ketchumstuk. Portions of the scenic drive travel alongside the Fortymile National Wild and Scenic River. The BLM offers two brochures, *"Fortymile River Access Points and Float Times,"* and *"Fortymile River Rapids"* for those interested in floating the river. Historic Fort Egbert is located in Eagle.
- *Other Nearby Routes:* The Richardson Highway scenic drive is approximately 120 miles northwest of Tetlin Junction and an additional 180 miles to the southern access in Livengood for the Dalton Highway scenic drive.

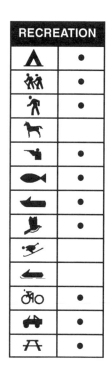

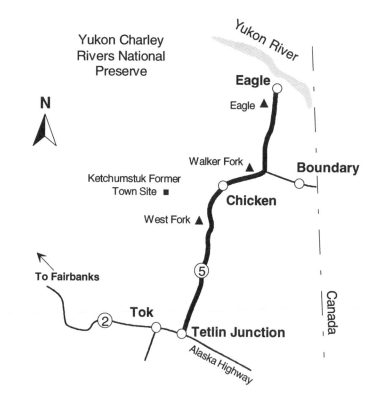

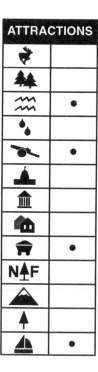

Information Sources:

BLM, Steese-White Mountains District Office, 1150 University Ave., Fairbanks, AK 99709-3844 / 907-474-2352
BLM, Tok Field Office, P.O. Box 309, Tok, AK 99780 / 907-883-5121
Tok Chamber of Commerce, P.O. Box 389, Tok, AK 99780 / 907-883-5775 (summer)

ARIZONA

☐ *Scenic Drives*

1. Apache Trail
2. Black Hills
3. Coronado Trail
4. Diamond Bar Road
5. Historic Route 66
6. Kaibab Plateau -
   North Rim Parkway
7. White Mountain
   Scenic Highway

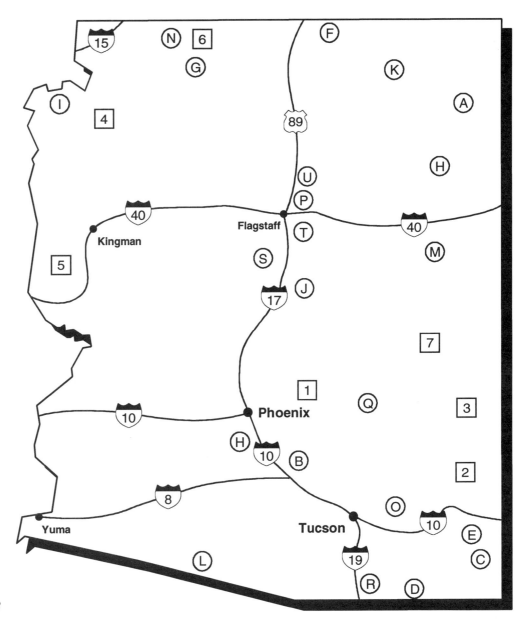

○ *National Park Areas*

A. Canyon de Chelly National Monument
B. Casa Grande National Monument
C. Chiricahua National Monument
D. Coronado National Memorial
E. Fort Bowie National Historic Site
F. Glen Canyon National Recreation Area
G. Grand Canyon National Park
H. Hubbell Trading Post National Historic Site
I. Lake Mead National Recreation Area
J. Montezuma Castle National Monument
K. Navajo National Monument

L. Organ Pipe Cactus National Monument
M. Petrified Forest National Park
N. Pipe Spring National Monument
O. Saguaro National Monument
P. Sunset Crater Volcano National Monument
Q. Tonto National Monument
R. Tumacacori National Historical Park
S. Tuzigoot National Monument
T. Walnut Canyon National Monument
U. Wupatki National Monument

APACHE TRAIL

- *Route Location:* Located in central Arizona, east of Phoenix with the southwestern access starting in Apache Junction off U.S. Highway 60/89. The scenic drive travels northeast to the town of Roosevelt near the Theodore Roosevelt Lake.
- *Roads Traveled:* The 46 mile route follows Arizona State Highway 88 to the junction with Arizona State Highway 188. The route travels over dirt and paved roads with numerous sharp curves and an occasional narrow stretch of road. The last 20 miles of this route are not recommended for vehicles pulling trailers. Thirty-eight miles of this route has been designated a National Forest Scenic Byway.
- *Travel Season:* Generally open year-round although portions of the route are subject to temporary closure due to heavy rains.
- *Description:* The Apache Trail winds through some of the most awe-inspiring country in Arizona as it trav-

els across the Tonto National Forest. The scenic drive is bound on the north by the Canyon, Apache, and Roosevelt Lakes, and on the south by the rugged Superstition Mountains. Several hiking trails into the Superstition Wilderness area can be accessed from along the route. Opportunities for camping, picnicking, hiking, boating, and fishing are found all along this scenic drive. Located at the eastern terminus of this route is the Theodore Roosevelt Dam. Built from 1906 to 1922, this dam was the first Federal Reclamation Project in the west and is the highest masonry structure in the world.

Arizona

- *Other Nearby Routes:* The White Mountain, Coronado Trail, and Black Hills scenic drives are located approximately 120 miles east of Roosevelt.

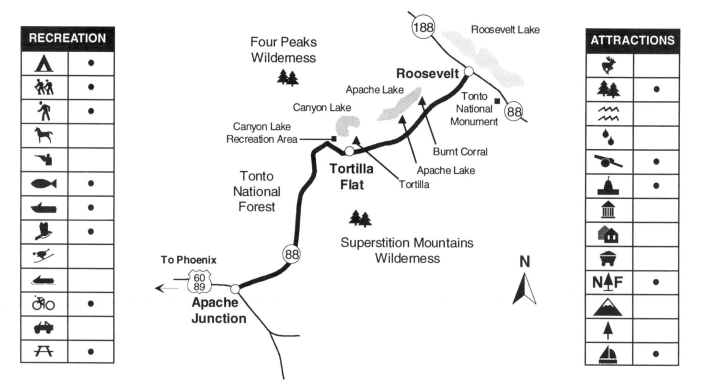

Information Sources:

Tonto National Forest, 2324 E. McDowell Rd., Phoenix, AZ 85010 / 602-225-5326
Apache Jct. Chamber of Commerce, 1001 N. Idaho Rd., Bldg. H, Apache Junction, AZ 85217 / 602-982-3141
Greater Globe - Miami Chamber of Commerce, 1360 N. Broad St., Globe, AZ 85502 / 800-448-8983
Superior Chamber of Commerce, 151 Main St., Superior AZ 85273 / 602-689-2441

BLACK HILLS

- *Route Location:* Located in southeastern Arizona, east of Safford near the New Mexico border. The northeastern access starts south of Clifton off U.S. Highway 191 (milepost 160) and travels southwest back to U.S. Highway 191 (milepost 139) near U.S. Highway 70.
- *Roads Traveled:* The 21 mile route travels the Old Safford-Clifton Road over an unpaved surface along a narrow and winding road. Do not attempt this route if you have a travel trailer or any vehicle more than 20 feet long. Motor homes and trailers can be left at parking areas on each end of the route. The route has been designated a BLM Type II Back Country Byway.
- *Travel Season:* Open year-round, although sections may become impassable during and after heavy rains.
- *Description:* This route offers sweeping views of the scenic Black Hills as it follows alongside the Gila River. The Gila Box Riparian National Conservation Area offers 21,000 acres of scenic desert canyon surround-

Arizona

ing rivers and creeks that provide opportunities to raft, hike, horseback ride, and camp. A developed picnic area is located on each side of the Old Safford Bridge, which has been placed on the National Register of Historic Places. This area also serves as a launch point for those floating the Gila River and is a prime spot for catching catfish. Found on the southern end of this route are the ruins of a prisoner camp where prisoners once slept in tents during the construction of portions of this route between 1917 and 1919.

- *Other Nearby Routes:* The Coronado Trail scenic drive is located about 10 miles to the north. In New Mexico, the Inner Loop-Gila Cliff Dwellings scenic drive is located about 55 miles from the New Mexico border.

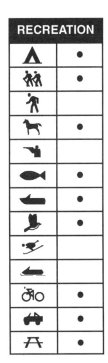

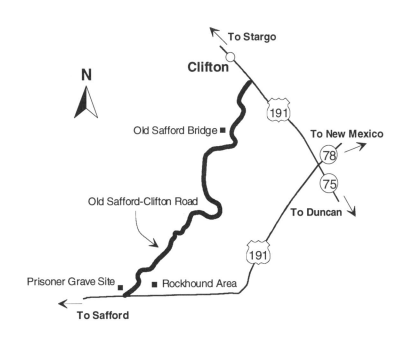

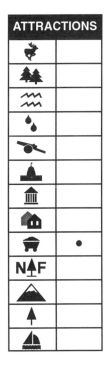

Information Sources:

BLM, Safford District Office, 711 14th Ave., Safford, AZ 85546 / 602-428-4040
Graham County Chamber of Commerce, 1111 Thatcher Blvd., Safford, AZ 85546 / 602-428-2511
Greenlee County Chamber of Commerce, 251 Chase Creek, Clifton, AZ 85533 / 602-865-3313

CORONADO TRAIL

Arizona

- *Route Location:* Located in east-central Arizona, northeast of Safford. The southern access starts in the town of Morenci and parallels the Arizona-New Mexico border as it travels north to Springerville.
- *Roads Traveled:* The 123 mile route follows U.S. Highway 180/191 which is a two-lane paved road. There are sharp curves and steep drop-offs along several sections of narrow road with no guardrails. The route is not recommended for vehicles towing a trailer or motor homes over 20 feet long. The entire 123 mile route has been designated a National Forest Scenic Byway.
- *Travel Season:* The route is generally open year-round with the exception of possible temporary closure during the winter for snow removal.
- *Description:* This scenic drive travels through steep canyons and across high, rolling mountains with spectacular views of the surrounding lakes and meadows. The route travels across the Apache-Sitgreaves National

Forests, which have the largest stand of ponderosa pines in the nation. The Bear Wallow and Escudilla Mountain Wilderness Areas can also be accessed from along this route. Trails leading into the wilderness areas offer opportunities for hiking, backpacking, and horseback riding. Several developed national forest campgrounds are also located along the route, each offering various amenities. The K.P. Cienega Campground offers a three mile hiking trail along a lush canyon bottom that leads to small twin waterfalls.

- *Other Nearby Routes:* The White Mountain Scenic Highway is to the west of this drive and may be accessed in Alpine on Forest Service Road 249. The Black Hills scenic drive begins south of Morenci and Clifton.

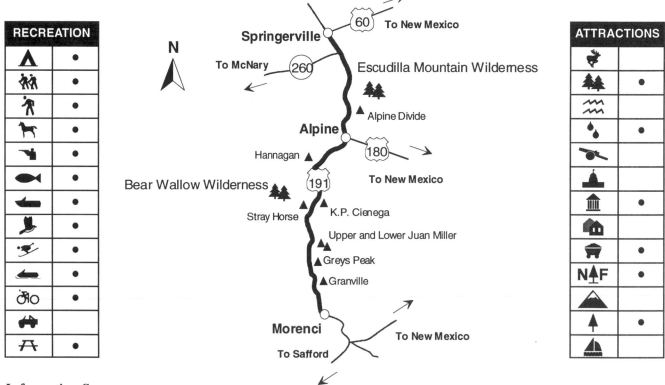

Information Sources:

Apache-Sitgreaves National Forest, 309 S. Mountain Ave., Hwy. 180, Springerville, AZ 85938 / 602-333-4301
Greenlee County Chamber of Commerce, 251 Chase Creek, Clifton, AZ 85533 / 602-865-3313
Round Valley Chamber of Commerce, 418 E. Main St., Springerville, AZ 85938 / 602-333-2123
Alpine Chamber of Commerce, P.O. Box 410, Alpine, AZ 85920 / 602-339-4330

DIAMOND BAR ROAD

Arizona

- *Route Location:* Located in northwestern Arizona, north of Kingman. The southwestern access is off of the Pearce Ferry Road northeast of Dolan Springs and travels northeast to the boundary of the Hualapai Indian Reservation.
- *Roads Traveled:* The 15 mile route travels the Diamond Bar Road which is a county maintained dirt/gravel surfaced road suitable for passenger cars. To enter upon reservation lands, travelers must first obtain a permit from the Hualapai Indian Reservation; the phone number is listed below. The 15 mile route has been nominated as a BLM Back Country Byway, but has not officially been designated.
- *Travel Season:* The route is open year-round but can become impassable during periods of heavy rainfall.
- *Description:* As you travel along this scenic drive, you will pass through one of the best stands of Joshua trees in Arizona. The views of the Joshua tree forest

and the Grand Wash Cliffs in the background is quite impressive. These two areas have been proposed for designation as an "Area of Environmental Concern," which will help ensure that the scenic character of each area would remain unchanged for future generations to enjoy. Recreational opportunities are found in the Lake Mead National Recreation Area, which is located to the west of this scenic drive.

- *Other Nearby Routes:* It is about 50 miles south to the northern access in McConico for the Historic Route 66 scenic drive.

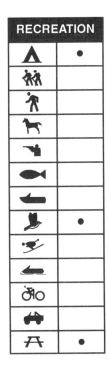

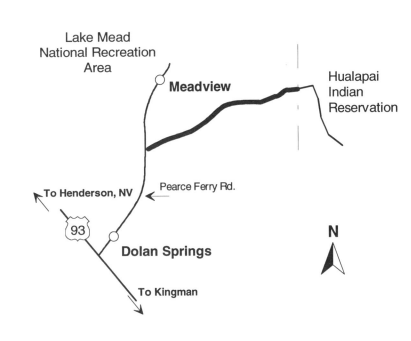

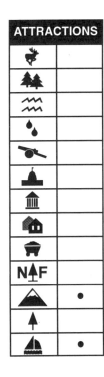

Information Sources:

BLM, Kingman Resource Area, 2475 Beverly Ave., Kingman, AZ 86401 / 602-757-3161
Dolan Springs Chamber of Commerce, Pierce Ferry Road, Dolan Springs, AZ 86441 / 602-767-3530
Hualapai Indian Reservation, Hualapai Tribal Wildlife Department / 602-769-2227

Historic Route 66

Arizona

- **Route Location:** This scenic drive is located in northwestern Arizona, south of Kingman. The northeastern access starts in McConnico off Interstate 40 and travels southwest to the town of Golden Shores at the junction with Arizona State Highway 95 near the California-Nevada border.
- **Roads Traveled:** The 42 mile route travels over a paved two-lane road suitable for most vehicles. There are sharp curves along this route and it is not recommended for vehicles over 40 feet long. The entire 42 mile route has been designated a BLM Type I Back Country Byway.
- **Travel Season:** The entire route is open year-round.
- **Description:** The Black Mountains section of historic Route 66 is preserved here along this scenic drive. There are famous sites to be discovered or revisited, including the Sitgreaves Pass tri-state overlook which provides a spectacular view into the state of California, Nevada, and Arizona. Also found along this scenic drive is the vintage Cool Springs Gas Station which was in operation during the 1930s. All that remains today of the stone structure is located on private property, please take only pictures. Footings, rock formations, and mine shafts are all that remain of the once bustling gold mining community of the Gold Road Townsite. It too is located on private property. Wild burros walk freely among the streets of Oatman, which is located about midway along the route.
- **Other Nearby Routes:** The Diamond Bar Road scenic drive is located about 50 miles north of McConico. In California, the eight scenic drives in the East Mojave National Scenic Area are approximately 40 miles west of Topock, Arizona along Interstate 40.

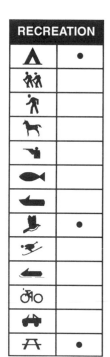

Information Sources:

BLM, Barstow Resource Area, 150 Coolwater Lane, Barstow, CA 92311 / 619-256-3591
Golden Valley Chamber of Commerce, 4305 Hwy. 68, Kingman, AZ 86402 / 602-565-3311
Oatman - Goldroad Chamber of Commerce, P.O. Box 423, Oatman, AZ 86433 / 602-768-4603
Bullhead Area Chamber of Commerce, P.O. Box 66, Bullhead City, AZ 86430 / 602-754-4121

KAIBAB PLATEAU - NORTH RIM PARKWAY

Arizona

- *Route Location:* Located in north-central Arizona about 35 miles south of the Utah-Arizona border, south of Fredonia. The northern access starts in Jacob Lake off U.S. Highway Alt. 89 and travels south to North Rim.
- *Roads Traveled:* The 44 mile route follows Arizona State Highway 67 which is a paved two-lane road suitable for all vehicles. The route ends in North Rim where you will need to retrace the route back to Jacob Lake. The entire route has been designated a National Forest Scenic Byway.
- *Travel Season:* Due to heavy winter snow cover, this route is normally closed from mid to late November through mid-May.
- *Description:* The Kaibab Plateau travels across the Kaibab National Forest through dense forests of pine, fir, and aspen, and ends in the Grand Canyon National Park. Located within the national forest are two wilderness areas, the Saddle Mountain and Kanab Creek Wilderness areas. Each area offers opportunities for the hiking and backpacking enthusiast. Several other trails located throughout the national forest offer challenges to the hiker, backpacker, mountain biker, and cross-country skier. Camping opportunities are provided by three developed national forest campgrounds found along the route. Camping is not limited to these developed areas, however, as camping is permitted nearly anywhere within the boundaries of the forest.
- *Other Nearby Routes:* The Smithsonian Butte scenic drive in Utah is about 55 miles northwest of Fredonia. Also in Utah, the Markaguant scenic drive is located approximately 50 miles north of Fredonia.

Information Sources:

Kaibab National Forest, 800 S. 6th St., Williams, AZ 86046 / 602-635-2681
Fredonia Chamber of Commerce, P.O. Box 547, Fredonia, AZ 86022 / 602-643-7241
Page - Lake Powell Chamber of Commerce, 638 Elm St., Page, AZ 86040 / 602-645-2741

WHITE MOUNTAIN SCENIC HIGHWAY

- *Route Location:* The scenic drive is located in east-central Arizona, northeast of Globe. The southwestern access starts in Whiteriver on the Apache Indian Reservation and travels north to Hon Dah, then east to the junction of highway 180/191 north of Alpine.
- *Roads Traveled:* The 123 mile route follows Arizona State Highways 73, 260, 273, and 373 and Forest Service Roads 87 and 249 to the junction of U.S. Highway 180/191 near Alpine. The series of connecting roads travel over a combination of two-lane paved and gravel surfaced roads that are suitable for all vehicles. The entire 123 mile route has been designated a National Forest Scenic Byway.
- *Travel Season:* Arizona routes 73 and 260 are open year-round. The remaining portions of the route are subject to closure due to winter snows.
- *Description:* This scenic drive travels through the Fort Apache Indian Reservation and the Apache-Sitgreaves

Arizona

National Forests, offering views of colorful rimrocks and the majestic peaks of the White Mountains. Recreational activities on the Indian reservation require a tribal permit which may be obtained at the tribal Game and Fish Office in Whiteriver, or in Hon Dah, McNary, Horseshoe Lake, and Sunrise. Other recreational opportunities may be found along the scenic drive and within the national forest. Wildlife inhabiting the area along the route includes deer, elk, pronghorn, foxes, and turkeys. Bald and golden eagles can also be seen.

- *Other Nearby Routes:* The eastern terminus of this route connects with the Coronado Trail scenic drive in Alpine. Approximately 100 miles to the south of Alpine is the Black Hills scenic drive.

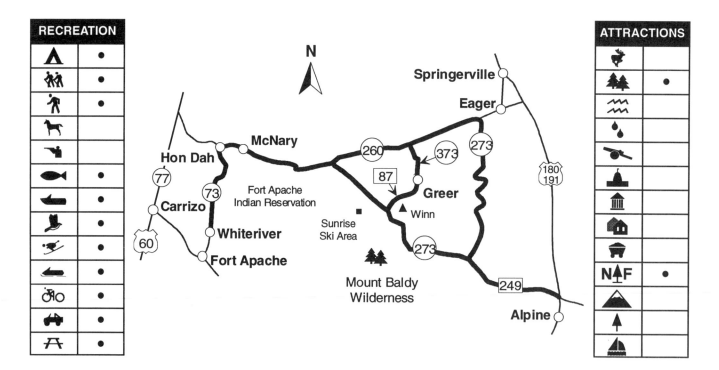

Information Sources:

Apache-Sitgreaves National Forest, 309 S. Mountain Ave., Hwy. 180, Springerville, AZ 85938 / 602-333-4301
Alpine Chamber of Commerce, P.O. Box 410, Alpine, AZ 85920 / 602-339-4330
Pinetop - Lakeside Chamber of Commerce, 592 White Mountain Blvd., Pinetop, AZ 85935 / 602-367-4290
Round Valley Chamber of Commerce, 418 E. Main St., Springerville, AZ 85938 / 602-333-2123

ARKANSAS

□ *Scenic Drives*

1. Arkansas Highway 7
2. Mount Magazine
3. Ozark Highlands
4. Pig Trail
5. St. Francis
6. Sylamore

○ *National Park Areas*

A. Arkansas Post National Memorial
B. Fort Smith National Historic Site
C. Hot Springs National Park
D. Pea Ridge National Military Park

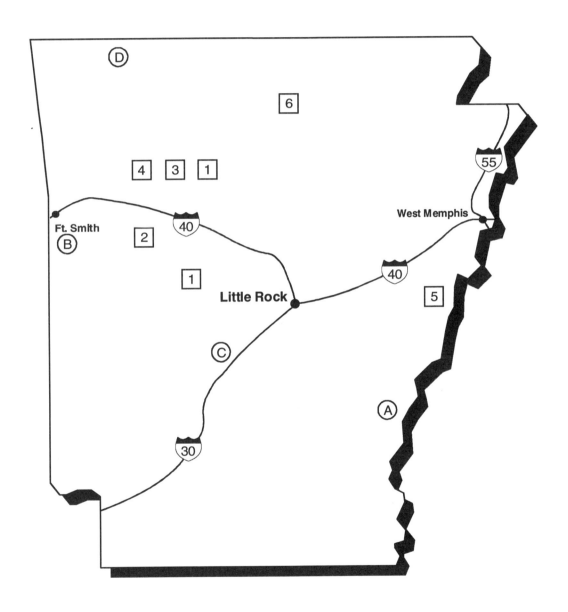

Road Condition Number: 501-569-2227

ARKANSAS HIGHWAY 7

- *Route Location:* This route consists of two separate sections of Highway 7 located in central Arkansas, east of Fort Smith. The northern access for the north section starts south of Jasper and travels south to the national forest boundary. The northern access for the southern section starts just south of Fourche Junction and travels south to the national forest boundary.
- *Roads Traveled:* The entire route from Jasper to Fountain Lake is 132 miles and travels on Arkansas State Highway 7 which is a two-lane paved road suitable for all vehicles. Thirty-six miles on the north section and 24 miles on the south section has been designated a National Forest Scenic Byway.
- *Travel Season:* Year-round.
- *Description:* The northern section travels through the Ozark National Forest while the southern sec-

tion travels across the Ouachita National Forest. Outstanding scenery of forested hills, valleys, cliffs, bluffs, and waterfalls are offered along the entire length of the route. Two national recreation trails can be accessed along the scenic drive. Numerous campgrounds and state parks provide opportunities to camp, picnic, fish, boat, and hike. Hot Springs National Park is located near the end of the route.

- *Other Nearby Routes:* The Mount Magazine scenic drive is approximately 30 miles northwest from the southern section of Arkansas Highway 7. The Ozark Highlands scenic drive is about 25 miles west of the northern section and an additional 30 miles west to the Pig Trail scenic drive.

Arkansas

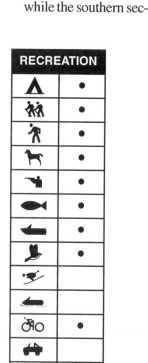

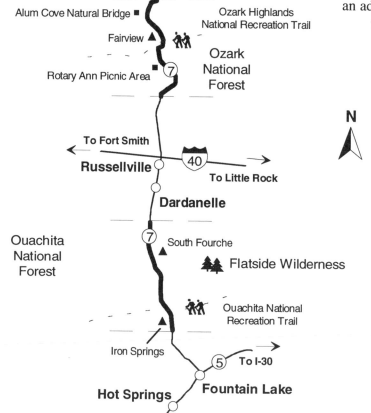

Information Sources:

Ozark - St. Francis National Forest, 605 W. Main St., Russelville, AR 72801 / 501-968-2354
Harrison Chamber of Commerce, 621 E. Rush, Harrison, AR 72602-0939 / 501-741-2659
Russellville Chamber of Commerce, P.O. Box 1777, Russellville, AR 72801 / 501-968-2530
Dardanelle Chamber of Commerce, 510 N. 2nd St., Dardanelle, AR 72834 / 501-229-3328
Greater Hot Springs Chamber of Commerce, 659 Ouachita, Hot Springs, AR 71902 / 501-321-1700

MOUNT MAGAZINE

Arkansas

- *Route Location:* Located in west-central Arkansas, southeast of Fort Smith. The northern access starts south of Paris off Arkansas State Highway 109 and travels southeast to Havana at the junction with Arkansas State Highway 10.
- *Roads Traveled:* The 25 mile route follows Arkansas State Highway 309 and Forest Service Road 1606. The entire route travels over two-lane paved roads that are suitable for all vehicles. Twenty-three miles of this route has been designated a National Forest Scenic Byway.
- *Travel Season:* The entire route is open year-round.
- *Description:* This scenic drive travels through the Ozark National Forest and takes you to the highest point in Arkansas, Mount Magazine. At 2,753 feet above sea level, this mountain is considered the tallest between the Rocky Mountains in the west and the Appalachian Mountains in the east. This scenic drive offers a winding mountain drive with sharp curves and switchbacks and offers views of timber-covered mountains, rugged rock bluffs, and beautiful blue lakes. Several scenic overlooks along the north slope of Mount Magazine offer panoramic views of the surrounding countryside. Signal Hill Trail is a short hike to the top of Mount Magazine while Magazine Trail leaves the Mt. Magazine Recreation Area and ends up in the Cove Lake Recreation Area. Both recreation areas also offer camping and picnicking facilities.
- *Other Nearby Routes:* The Pig Trail scenic drive is about 40 miles to the north of Paris. The southern section of the Arkansas Highway 7 scenic drive is approximately 30 miles southeast of Havana.

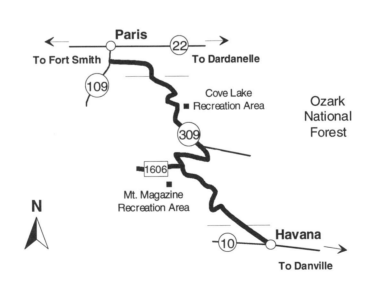

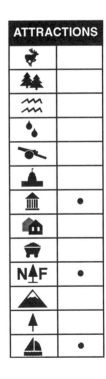

Information Sources:

Ozark - St. Francis National Forest, 605 W. Main St., Russelville, AR 72801 / 501-968-2354
North Logan County Chamber of Commerce, 301 W. Walnut, Paris, AR 72855 / 501-963-2244
Booneville Chamber of Commerce, Second & Bennett Sts., Booneville, AR 72927 / 501-675-2666
Dardanelle Chamber of Commerce, 510 N. 2nd St., Dardanell, AR 72834 / 501-229-3328

OZARK HIGHLANDS

- *Route Location:* Located in northwestern Arkansas, northeast of Fort Smith. The southern access starts just east of Clarksville off U.S. Highway 64 and travels north just past the town of Mossville.
- *Roads Traveled:* The 45 mile route follows Arkansas State Highway 21 which is a two-lane paved road suitable for all vehicles. Thirty-five miles of this route has been designated a National Forest Scenic Byway.
- *Travel Season:* The entire route is open year-round.
- *Description:* The scenic drive travels through the Ozark National Forest and alongside the Upper Buffalo Wilderness area. Wonderful views of the rugged terrain, colorful fields and forests are offered along this route. Wildlife is abundant along the route and it is not uncommon to see deer, turkeys, and black bears. Bald eagles and golden eagles can also be seen occasionally. The Upper Buffalo Wilderness, located near the scenic drive's northern end, encompasses hardwood forest with rock outcrops and a mountainous terrain. Hiking, picnicking, camping, and wildlife viewing opportunities are offered here. The Buffalo National River also runs through this area and offers opportunities for fishing and floating. Access along the route to the Ozark Highlands National Recreation Trail is also provided. The Ozone Recreation Area, located near the southern end of the route, was originally the site of a Civilian Conservation Corps camp during the late 1930s and early 1940s. Camping is available here.
- *Other Nearby Routes:* Approximately 30 miles to the west is the Pig Trail scenic drive and about 25 miles to the east is the northern section of the Arkansas Highway 7 scenic drive.

Arkansas

RECREATION	
⛺	•
🚶‍♂️	•
🧗	
🐎	
🦆	•
🐟	•
🛶	•
🎿	•
🏂	
🛷	
🏍️	
🚙	
⛱️	•

ATTRACTIONS	
🦌	
🌲	•
⛰️	
💧	
🔫	
🏛️	
🏦	
🏚️	
⛏️	
N↑F	•
🔺	
↑	
⛵	•

Information Sources:

Ozark - St. Francis National Forest, 605 W. Main St., Russelville, AR 72801 / 501-968-2354
Huntsville Chamber of Commerce, P.O. Box 950, Huntsville, AR 72740-0950 / 501-738-6000
Johnson County Chamber of Commerce, Main St., Clarksville, AR 72830 / 501-754-2340
Harrison Chamber of Commerce, 621 E. Rush, Harrison, AR 72602-0939 / 501-741-2659

PIG TRAIL

- *Route Location:* Located in northwestern Arkansas, east of Fort Smith. The southern access is off Interstate 40 north of Ozark and travels north to the junction of Arkansas State Highway 6, south of St. Paul.
- *Roads Traveled:* The 28 mile route follows Arkansas State Highway 23 which is a two-lane paved road suitable for all vehicles. Nineteen miles of this route has been designated a National Forest Scenic Byway.
- *Travel Season:* The entire length is open year-round.
- *Description:* This route travels across the Ozark National Forest and a unique portion of Arkansas. Views of spectacular panoramas of timber-covered mountains, rugged landscapes, clear mountain streams, colorful spring flowers and autumn foliage, and isolated farms and ranches. Seasonal waterfalls may also be seen along the route. The Ozark Highlands National Recreation Trail may be accessed from this route. This hiking trail extends for 160 miles through the Boston Mountain range. Access to the Mulberry River is provided along the route and offers a challenge to both canoeing enthusiasts and fishermen alike. Camping and picnicking opportunities are found along this route as well as throughout the national forest. Four wilderness areas within the boundaries of the forest, the Upper Buffalo, Hurricane Creek, Richland Creek, and East Fork Wilderness areas, all offer opportunities for camping, hiking, and backpacking.
- *Other Nearby Routes:* From the northern terminus of this route, the Ozark Highlands scenic drive is approximately 20 miles east, and an additional 25 miles east to the northern section of the Arkansas Highway 7 scenic drive. The Mount Magazine scenic drive is about 20 miles south of Interstate 40.

Information Sources:

Ozark - St. Francis National Forest, 605 W. Main St., Russelville, AR 72801 / 501-968-2354
Fayetteville Chamber of Commerce, 123 W. Mountain St., Fayetteville, AR 72701 / 501-521-1710
Ozark Area Chamber of Commerce, P.O. Box 283, Ozark, AR 72949 / 501-667-2525
Huntsville Chamber of Commerce, P.O. Box 950, Huntsville, AR 72740-0950 / 501-738-6000

St. Francis

- *Route Location:* Located in eastern Arkansas, south of Forest City. The northern access starts in Marianna and travels south to the junction of Arkansas State Highway 242 north of West Helena, near the Arkansas-Mississippi border.
- *Roads Traveled:* The 23 mile route follows Arkansas State Highway 44 and Forest Service Road 1900. The route travels on a combination of paved and gravel roads that are suitable for all vehicles. Twenty miles of this route has been designated a National Forest Scenic Byway.
- *Travel Season:* The entire route is open year-round although the gravel portion can become slippery after heavy rains.
- *Description:* The St. Francis scenic drive travels through the St. Francis National Forest, its land divided between the fertile bottom lands along the river and Crowley's Ridge. Crowley's Ridge spans north

Arkansas

and south for 200 miles from southern Missouri down to the Mississippi River at Helena and is one of the state's most unusual features with an irregular surface of broad valleys, narrow gullies, steep slopes, and hills. Legend has it that a tribe of Indians known as the "Mound Builders" lived in the St. Francis area long before the American Indian. The tribal name came from the custom of burying their dead with the tools considered necessary for existence in another world. Some of these mounds can still be found in this area. Located along the scenic drive are two lakes, Bear Creek and Storm Creek, that offer opportunities for boating, fishing, camping, swimming, hiking, and picnicking.

- *Other Nearby Routes:* There are no other close routes.

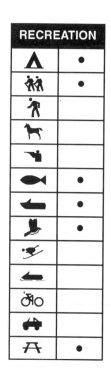

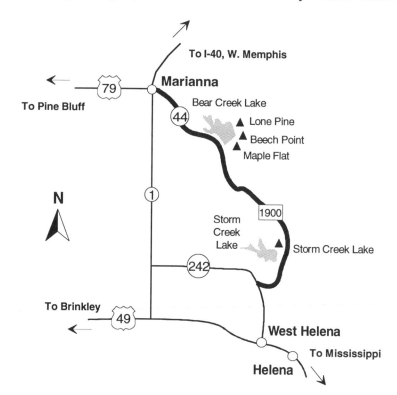

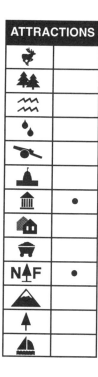

Information Sources:

Ozark - St. Francis National Forest, 605 W. Main St., Russelville, AR 72801 / 501-968-2354
Marianna - Lee County Chamber of Commerce, 67 W. Main St., Marianna, AR 72360 / 501-295-2469
Phillips County Chamber of Commerce, P.O. Box 447, Helena, AR 72342 / 501-338-8327

SYLAMORE

Arkansas

- *Route Location:* Located in north-central Arkansas, southeast of Mountain Home. The northern access starts just south of Calico Rock and travels south to Allison and then west to the Blanchard Springs Caverns.
- *Roads Traveled:* The 26 mile route follows Arkansas State Highways 5 and 14 and Forest Service Road 1110 to Blanchard Springs Caverns. The entire route travels on two-lane paved roads suitable for all vehicles. All 26 miles have been designated a National Forest Scenic Byway.
- *Travel Season:* The entire route is open year-round.
- *Description:* This route travels through a beautifully scenic portion of the Ozark National Forest, through White Oak and Hickory forest, stands of shortleaf pine, and across rugged, rocky outcrops. A stream parallels a portion of the byway offering glimpses of rushing water and calm pools. Blanchard Springs Caverns is the main attraction along this route. Managed by the national forest, the Blanchard Springs Caverns are one of the most beautifully decorated show caves in the world. Nestled under high rock cliffs is the nearby Blanchard picnic area, campground, swimming beach, and amphitheater where regularly scheduled summer night programs highlight the folklore and culture of the Ozark National Forest. Also located in this area is the Sylamore Trail. Located west of this route is the Leatherwood Wilderness which offers hiking, backpacking, and camping.
- *Other Nearby Routes:* Approximately 75 miles to the north in Missouri is the Glade Top Trail scenic drive and about an additional 35 miles to the Blue Buck Knob scenic drive, also in Missouri.

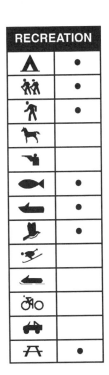

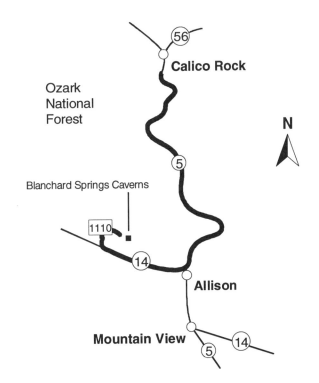

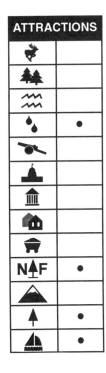

Information Sources:

Ozark - St. Francis National Forest, 605 W. Main St., Russelville, AR 72801 / 501-968-2354
Mountain Home Area Chamber of Commerce, 1023 Hwy. 62 E., Mountain Home, AR 72653 / 800-822-3536
Calico Rock/Pineville Trade Area Chamber of Commerce, P.O. Box 245, Calico Rock, AR 72519 / 501-297-8868
Mountain View Area Chamber of Commerce, P.O. Box 133, Mountain View, AR 72560 / 501-269-8068

CALIFORNIA

□ *Scenic Drives*

1. Ancient Bristlecone
2. Angeles Crest
3. Barrel Springs
4. Black Canyon Road
5. Bradshaw Trail
6. Buckhorn
7. Carson Pass Highway
8. Cedar Canyon Road
9. Cima Road
10. Essex Road
11. Feather River
12. Jacinto Reyes
13. Judy Andreen Sierra Heritage
14. Kelbaker Road
15. Kelso-Cima Road
16. Kings Canyon
17. Lanfair-Ivenpah Road
18. Lassen
19. Lee Vining Canyon
20. Owens Valley To Death Valley
21. Palms to Pines
22. Rim of the World
23. Saline Valley
24. Sierra Vista
25. Smith River
26. State Of Jefferson
27. Sunrise
28. Trinity
29. Trinity Heritage
30. Wild Horse Canyon
31. Yuba Donner

*Road Condition
Number, Northern:*
916-445-7623

East Mojave
National
Scenic Area
4,8,9,10,14
15,17,30

○ *National Park Areas*

A. Cabrillo National Monument
B. Channel Islands National Park
C. Death Valley National Monument
D. Devils Postpile National Monument
E. Eugene O'Neill National Historic Site
F. Fort Point National Historic Site
G. Golden Gate National Recreation Area
H. John Muir National Historic Site
I. Joshua Tree National Monument
J. Kings Canyon National Park
K. Lassen Volcanic National Park
L. Lava Beds National Monument
M. Manzanar National Historic Site
N. Muir Woods National Monument
O. Pinnacles National Monument

P. Point Reyes National Seashore
Q. Port Chicago Naval Magazine National Memorial
R. Redwood National Park
S. San Francisco Maritime National Historical Park
T. Santa Monica Mountains National Recreation Area
U. Sequoia National Park
V. Whiskeytown-Shasta-Trinity Nat'l. Recreation Area
W. Yosemite National Park

ANCIENT BRISTLECONE

California

- *Route Location:* Located in east-central California, south of Bishop near the Nevada border. The southwestern access starts in Big Pine off U.S. Highway 395 and travels northeast to the roads end at Patriarch Grove on the Inyo National Forest.
- *Roads Traveled:* The 36 mile route follows California State Highway 168 and Forest Service Road 4S01, also known as the White Mountain Road. The route travels over a paved surface to Schulman Grove and then travels on a graded dirt road to Patriarch Grove. Because of the grade and tight curves, motor homes or vehicles pulling trailers are not recommended beyond the paved section. Travelers will need to retrace the route back to highway 168. The entire 36 mile route has been designated a National Forest Scenic Byway.
- *Travel Season:* The route is generally open year-round although sections are subject to closure in the winter months.
- *Description:* Traveling this scenic route through the Inyo National Forest provides the visitor access to an unusual high desert community, the Ancient Bristlecone Pine Forest. Bristlecone pines exist at elevations above 11,000 feet and are the oldest known living trees on earth. A visitor center at Schulman Grove provides information on the ancient trees and two nature trails offer the opportunity to view the trees up close. Camping is available throughout the national forest except within the boundaries of the Ancient Bristlecone Forest
- *Other Nearby Routes:* The Saline Valley and Owens Valley To Death Valley scenic drives are in the same area as this scenic drive.

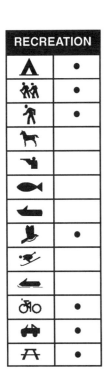

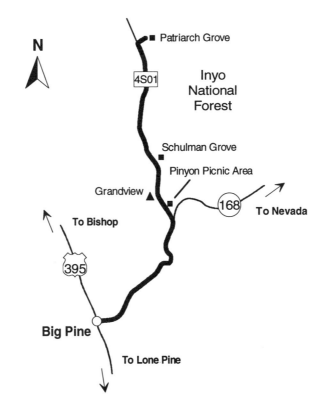

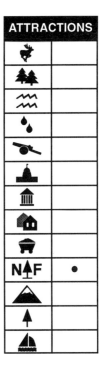

Information Sources:

Inyo National Forest, White Mountain Ranger District, 798 N. Main St., Bishop, CA 93514 / 619-873-2525
White Mountains Ranger District, 798 N. Main St., Bishop, CA 93514 / 619-873-2525
Bishop Chamber of Commerce, 690 N. Main St., Bishop, CA 93514 / 619-873-8405

ANGELES CREST

California

- *Route Location:* Located in southwestern California, northeast of Los Angeles. The western access starts in the town of La Canada off Interstate 210 and travels east to the junction of California State Highway 138, northeast of Wrightwood.
- *Roads Traveled:* The 70 mile route follows California State Highway 2 which is a two-lane paved road suitable for all vehicles. Sixty-four miles of this route has been designated a National Forest Scenic Byway.
- *Travel Season:* Most of the route is open year-round except for a small segment closed by winter snows from late December through early April.
- *Description:* This scenic drive travels on the Angeles National Forest and along the boundaries of the San Gabriel and Sheep Mountain Wilderness areas. Wildlife inhabiting this area includes bighorn sheep, mountain lions, coyotes and badgers. Opportunities exist along the drive for mountain biking and four-wheel driving. There are several ski and snowplay areas along the route offering winter activities. The Pacific Crest National Scenic Trail crosses the route near Buckhorn and the first National Historic Trail, the Gabrielino, runs adjacent to the route near Red Box junction. The famous 100 inch telescope of the Mount Wilson Observatory is located a short drive off the scenic drive. Surrounding the observatory is the Fern Canyon Natural Research Area.
- *Other Nearby Routes:* About 10 miles from the eastern terminus is the Rim Of The World scenic drive and approximately 100 miles to the northeast is the Jacinto Reyes scenic drive.

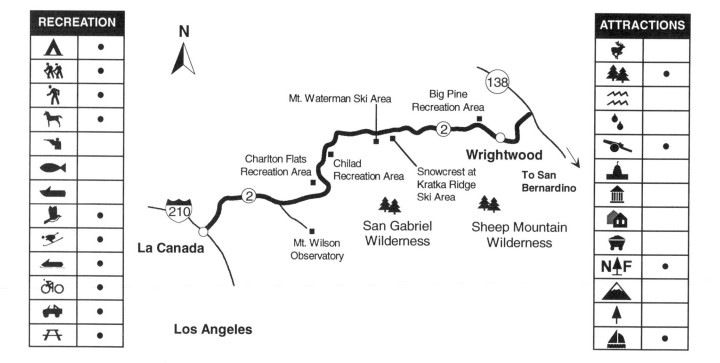

Information Sources:

Angeles National Forest, 701 N. Santa Anita Ave., Arcadia, CA 91006 / 818-574-5200
La Canada Flintridge C of C, 4529 Angeles Crest Hwy., #102, La Canada Flintridge, CA 91011 / 818-790-4289
Wrightwood Chamber of Commerce, P.O. Box 416, Wrightwood, CA 92397 / 619-249-4320

BARREL SPRINGS

California

- *Route Location:* Located in the northeastern corner of California, northeast of Alturas, and the northwestern corner of Nevada. The western access starts 5 miles east of Fort Bidwell, California off Modoc County Road 6 and travels east into Nevada to the junction with Mosquito Valley Road.
- *Roads Traveled:* The 20 mile route follows the Barrel Springs Road which is a single-lane gravel surfaced road that can safely be driven in a two-wheel drive, high-clearance vehicle. Note that the route travels across remote country where other vehicles may not pass through for one or two days at a time, so be prepared for any road emergencies. This 20 mile route has been designated a BLM Type II Back Country Byway.
- *Travel Season:* The route is generally open from May through mid-November and then closed due to heavy winter snows. The eastern access (Mosquito Valley Road) may also become impassable after heavy rains.
- *Description:* A maze of rocky rims alternates with sagebrush and juniper along rolling hills as you travel across the high plateau of Great Basin country. Golden eagles, red-tailed hawks, deer, and antelope are often seen in the area. Coyotes can also occasionally be seen and heard serenading the moon, should you choose to stay overnight.
- *Other Nearby Routes:* The Lakeview To Steens scenic drive is approximately 25 miles to the north in Oregon which also leads to the Steens Mountain and Diamond Loop scenic drives. Less than 100 miles to the south is the Buckhorn scenic drive.

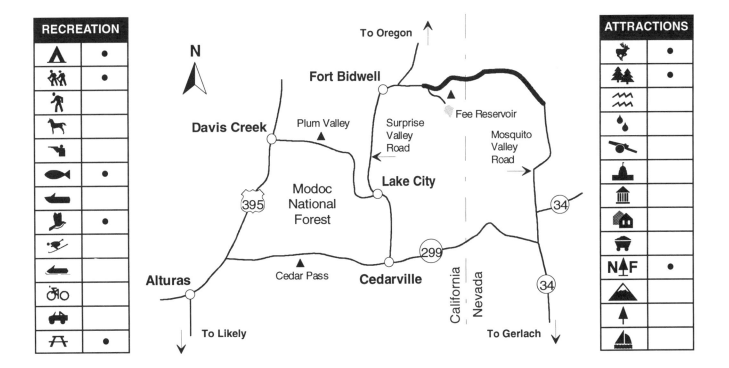

Information Sources:

BLM, Susanville District Office, 705 Hall St., Susanville, CA 96130-3730 / 916-257-5381
Modoc County Chamber of Commerce, 522 S. Main St., Alturas, CA 96101 / 916-233-2819
Lake County Chamber of Commerce, 513 Center St., 97630, Lakeview, OR 97630 / 503-947-6040

BRADSHAW TRAIL

California

- *Route Location:* Located in southeastern California, west of Blythe near the Arizona border. The eastern access starts in the town of Mesa Verde off Interstate 10 and travels west to the junction of California State Highway 111, south of North Shore.
- *Roads Traveled:* The 70 mile route follows the Bradshaw Trail Road which is a county maintained graded dirt road. The route travels across remote country and requires a four-wheel drive vehicle or other specialized vehicle such as a dirt bike or all-terrain vehicle. The entire route has been designated a BLM Type III Back Country Byway.
- *Travel Season:* The route is generally open year-round with possible temporary closures at times due to severe storms and heavy rainfall.
- *Description:* Traveling across the southern end of the Mule Mountains, the route parallels part of the Chocolate Mountain Gunnery Range and ends near the Salton Sea and the Salton Sea National Wildlife Refuge. Views of the Chuckwalla Mountains to the north and the Chocolate Mountains to the south can be seen along the route as well as the distant mountains of Arizona. A variety of wildlife can also be seen along the scenic drive, including desert burro mule deer, bighorn sheep, and coyotes. Lying near the western terminus is the Salton Sea State Recreation Area which offers opportunities for boating, fishing, hunting, and camping.
- *Other Nearby Routes:* Approximately 30 miles to the northwest is the Palms To Pines scenic drive. Traveling about 85 miles southwest leads to the Sunrise scenic drive.

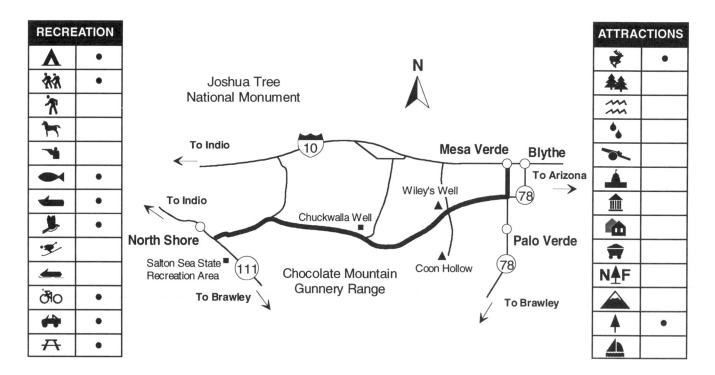

Information Sources:

BLM, Indio Resource Area, P.O. Box 2000, North Palm Springs, CA 92258-2000 / 619-251-0812
Indio Chamber of Commerce, 82-503 Highway 111, Indio, CA 92202 / 619-347-0676
Thermal Chamber of Commerce, P.O. Box 284, Thermal, CA 92274 / 619-399-0080
Coachella Chamber of Commerce, 1648 Sixth St., Coachella, CA 92236 / 619-398-5111
Blythe Chamber of Commerce, 201 S. Broadway, Blythe, CA 92225 / 619-922-8166

BUCKHORN

California

- *Route Location:* Located in northeastern California, northeast of Susanville, and in northwestern Nevada. The western access starts east of Ravendale off U.S. Highway 395 on Lassen County Road 526 and travels northeast into Nevada to the junction with Nevada State Highway 81.
- *Roads Traveled:* The 31 mile route follows the Buckhorn Road which is a single-lane gravel surfaced road that can safely be driven in a two-wheel drive, high-clearance vehicle. Note that the route travels across remote country where other vehicles may not pass through for one or two days at a time, so be prepared for any road emergencies. This 31 mile route has been designated a BLM Type II Back Country Byway.
- *Travel Season:* The route is generally open from mid-May through mid-November and closed during the winter. Heavy rains can also make the route impassable.

- *Description:* The scenic drive passes through scattered juniper, sagebrush, and small valleys. A walk to the edge of a narrow canyon will reveal mountain mahogany and small stands of aspen. Opportunities to explore the narrow canyons are available to bicyclers and backpackers. This is also an excellent area to view small herds of wild horses roaming free on the range. Pronghorn antelope, deer, hawks, and coyotes may also be seen.
- *Other Nearby Routes:* The Barrel Springs scenic drive is less than 100 miles north and the Lassen scenic drive is approximately 75 miles southwest. About 100 miles south of Gerlach, Nevada is the Fort Churchill To Wellington scenic drive.

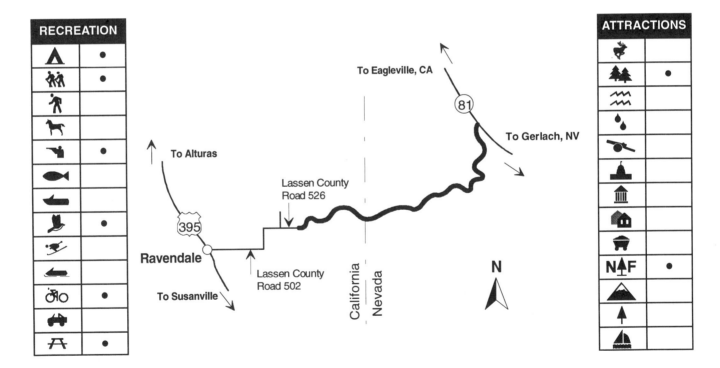

Information Sources:

BLM, Susanville District Office, 705 Hall St., Susanville, CA 96130-3730 / 916-257-5381
Lassen County Chamber of Commerce, 34 N. Lassen St., Susanville, CA 96130 / 916-257-4323
Modoc County Chamber of Commerce, 522 S. Main St., Alturas, CA 96101 / 916-233-2819

CARSON PASS HIGHWAY

California

- **Route Location:** Located in east-central California, east of Sacramento. The southwestern access starts in the town of Dewdrop and travels northeast to Woodfords near the Nevada border.
- **Roads Traveled:** The 58 mile route follows California State Highway 88 which is a two-lane paved road suitable for all vehicles.
- **Travel Season:** The route is open year-round except for occasional closures in the winter for snow and ice removal.
- **Description:** The scenic drive travels through the Eldorado and Toiyabe National Forests. The drive winds its way through the western slope of the Sierra Nevada, reaches the summit at Carson Pass, and ends up on the eastern slope of the Sierra Nevada. The road travels through rugged volcanic skylines, lush green meadows, mountain lakes surrounded by timber-covered slopes, and rock valleys. This highway was one of the first trans-Sierra routes into California and was first explored in 1844 by John C. Fremont and mountain man Christopher "Kit" Carson. The Pacific Crest National Scenic Trail, among other trails, can be accessed from the route. Several lakes along the drive offer opportunities for boating, fishing, camping, and picnicking. Winter brings recreation in the form of cross-country skiing, downhill skiing, snowmobiling, and sledding.
- **Other Nearby Routes:** Approximately 100 miles to the south is the Lee Vining Canyon scenic drive while the Yuba Donner scenic drive is about 60 miles to the north. About 50 miles to the east in Nevada is the Fort Churchill To Wellington scenic drive.

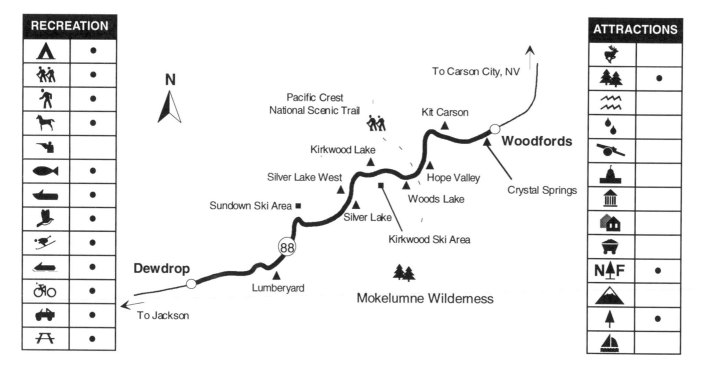

Information Sources:

Eldorado National Forest, 100 Forni Rd., Placerville, CA 95667 / 916-622-5061
Toiyabe National Forest, Carson Ranger District, 1536 Carson St., Carson City, NV 89720 / 702-882-2766
Amador County Chamber of Commerce, 125 Peek St., Jackson, CA 95642 / 800-649-4988
Alpine County Chamber of Commerce, P.O. Box 265, Markleeville, CA 96120 / 916-694-2475
El Dorado County Chamber of Commerce, 542 Main St., Placerville, CA 95667 / 800-457-6279

EAST MOJAVE NATIONAL SCENIC AREA

① Black Canyon Road
② Cedar Canyon Road
③ Cima Road
④ Essex Road

⑤ Kelbaker Road
⑥ Kelso-Cima Road
⑦ Lanfair-Ivenpah Road
⑧ Wild Horse Canyon

California

N

To Las Vegas

Searchlight

Nipton

Baker

To Barstow

Cima

Mid Hills

Nevada
California

Kelso

Hole-In-The-Wall

Goffs

To Barstow

Providence Mountains
State Recreation Area

To Needles

RECREATION

ATTRACTIONS

- **Route Location:** The following eight scenic drives are all located in southeastern California, east of Barstow between Interstates 15 and 40, near the Nevada border. All of the routes travel through the East Mojave National Scenic Area. All eight routes are interconnecting, giving you the option to choose those you wish to explore.
- **Travel Season:** All of the routes are open year-round except after severe thunderstorms which can make the routes impassable due to flash flooding.
- **Description:** The East Mojave National Scenic Area is a unique 1.5 million acre desert region full of scenic, historic, and natural wonders. Table Mountain is a flat topped mesa visible from many of the scenic drives

as are the Providence Mountains. The scenic drives travel through pinon-juniper woodlands, sage-covered hills, cactus gardens, and the colorful volcanic Cinder Cones and Lava Beds while offering outstanding views of the surrounding rugged mountains.

A variety of recreational opportunities are available in the East Mojave National Scenic Area. Camping is offered in two developed campgrounds, the Mid Hills and Hole-In-The-Wall, as well as primitive camping which is permitted anywhere on BLM administered lands.

Old mining roads in the New York, Castle, Clark, and Providence Mountains provide

East Mojave National Scenic Area (Cont.)

plenty of opportunities for hiking and mountain biking. Several developed trails can be found in the Piute Range, Providence Mountains, and between the two developed campgrounds.

There are two off-road vehicle trails crossing the region, the Mojave Road and the East Mojave Heritage Trail. The Mojave Road is a 130 mile historic Native American trade route, later developed into a wagon trail, and crosses east to west through the heart of the national scenic area. The East Mojave Heritage Trail is a 700 mile loop beginning and ending in Needles, with much of this trail passing through the East Mojave region.

Listed below are descriptions and conditions of the roads travelled for each scenic byway.

Black Canyon Road

This scenic drive is a 20 mile route that travels over a graded dirt road suitable for all vehicles as long as caution is used on the occasional rough or sandy segments. The entire route has been designated a BLM Type I Back Country Byway.

Cedar Canyon Road

This is a 25 mile long route that travels over a graded dirt road suitable for all vehicles as long as caution is used on the occasional rough or sandy segments. The 25 mile route has been designated a BLM Type I Back Country Byway.

Cima Road

This 17 mile route travels over a paved road suitable for all vehicles. The entire route has been designated a BLM Type I Back Country Byway.

Essex Road

The 16 mile route travels over a paved road suitable for all types of vehicles and has been designated a BLM Type I Back Country Byway.

Kelbaker Road

All but 5 miles of this 60 mile route travels over a paved road. The route is suitable for all vehicles. The entire route has been designated a BLM Type I Back Country Byway.

Kelso-Cima Road

The 20 mile route travels over a paved road suitable for all vehicles and has been designated a BLM Type I Back Country Byway.

Lanfair-Ivenpah Road

This 55 mile route travels over a combination of paved and graded dirt road suitable for all vehicles. The entire route has been designated a BLM Type I Back Country Byway.

Wild Horse Canyon

This 12 mile route travels over a dirt surfaced road that can be safely driven in a two-wheel drive, high-clearance vehicle. The entire route has been designated a BLM Type II Back Country Byway.

• *Other Nearby Routes:* About 50 miles south of Barstow on Interstate 15 are the Angeles Crest and Rim Of The World scenic drives. Approximately 50 miles north on Interstate 15 across the Nevada state line is the Red Rocks scenic drive and less than 75 miles more on Interstate 15 is access to the Gold Butte and Bitter Springs scenic drives. About 12 miles southeast of Needles on Interstate 40 is access to the Historic Route 66 scenic drive in Arizona.

Information Sources:

BLM, Needles Resource Area, 101 W. Spikes Rd., Needles, CA 92363 / 619-326-3896
BLM, California Desert District Office, 6221 Box Springs Blvd., Riverside, CA 92507-2497 / 714-697-5219
Barstow Area Chamber of Commerce, 408 E. Fredricks, Barstow, CA 92311 / 619-256-8617
Needles Area Chamber of Commerce, 100 G St., Needles, CA 92363 / 619-326-2050
Laughlin Chamber of Commerce, 1725 Casino Dr., Laughlin, NV 89029 / 800-227-5245

FEATHER RIVER

California

- *Route Location:* Located in northeastern California, north of Sacramento. The western access is north of Oroville off California State Highway 149 and travels northeast to the town of Hallejujah Junction on U.S. Highway 395, near the Nevada border.
- *Roads Traveled:* The 130 mile route follows California State Highway 70 which is a two-lane paved road suitable for all vehicles. The entire 130 mile route has been designated a National Forest Scenic Byway.
- *Travel Season:* The entire route is open year-round although winter driving conditions can be hazardous.
- *Description:* This scenic drive follows a route that is the dividing line between the Sierra Nevada and Cascade Mountain Ranges and provides the lowest pass in the Sierras. The route travels across the Plumas National Forest through steep canyon walls covered in places with moss and ferns, past large rock outcrops, and waterfalls. The Bucks Lake Wilderness area can be accessed from this scenic drive and offers opportunities for back country camping, picnicking, hiking, horseback riding, and backpacking. The Pacific Crest National Scenic Trail may also be accessed as it crosses the route in Belden. Several recreation areas found along the drive offer camping and picnicking, as does the Plumas Eureka State Park and Jackson Creek Campground.
- *Other Nearby Routes:* From about the mid-point on this route in Paxton, the Lassen scenic drive is located about 25 miles north. Approximately 20 miles south of Blairsden is the Yuba Donner scenic drive. Traveling about 50 miles across the Nevada border leads to the Fort Churchill To Wellington scenic drive.

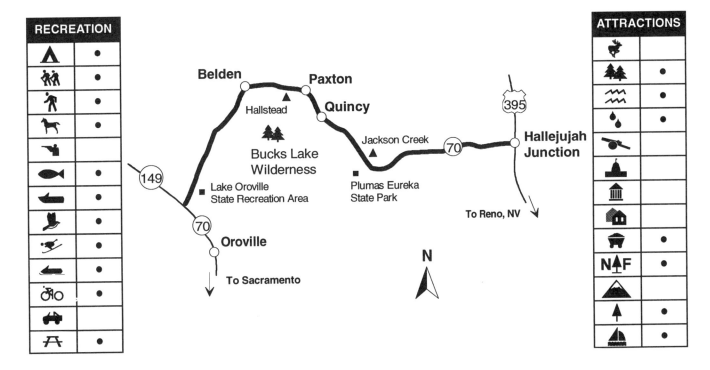

Information Sources:

Plumas National Forest, 159 Lawrence St., Quincy, CA 95971-6025 / 916-283-2050
Eastern Plumas Chamber of Commerce, P.O. Box 1379, Portola, CA 96122 / 916-832-5444
Quincy Main Street Chamber of Commerce, 522 Lawrence St., Quincy, CA 95971 / 916-283-0188
Oroville Area Chamber of Commerce, 1789 Montgomery St., Oroville, CA 95965 / 800-655-GOLD

JACINTO REYES

California

- **Route Location:** Located in southwestern California, east of Santa Barbara. The southern access starts on the national forest boundary northwest of Ojai off California State Highway 150 and travels north, ending west of Scheideck.
- **Roads Traveled:** The 37 mile route follows California State Highway 33 which is a two-lane paved road suitable for all vehicles. The entire route has been designated a National Forest Scenic Byway.
- **Travel Season:** The entire route is open year-round.
- **Description:** This route travels across the Los Padres National Forest and begins almost at sea level, winds upward through the coastal mountains to an elevation of 5,020 feet, and then makes a dramatic descent into the Cuyama Valley. At times along the route, views of the Pacific Ocean and the distant Channel Islands are possible. The Sespe, Dick Smith, and Matilija wilderness areas surround the scenic drive and provide numerous opportunities for camping, hiking, backpacking and horseback riding. A 31.5 mile long segment of the Sespe Creek has been designated a Wild and Scenic River and offers outstanding opportunities for fishing, swimming, camping, and hiking. A popular spot for rock climbing is the Sespe Gorge which has steep rock walls dotted with fir trees. Bellyache Springs offers the thirsty motorist a place to stop for a cool drink of spring water at the foot of a cascading waterfall.
- **Other Nearby Routes:** Located approximately 85 miles to the east is the Angeles Crest scenic drive which also leads into the Rim Of The World scenic drive.

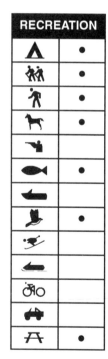

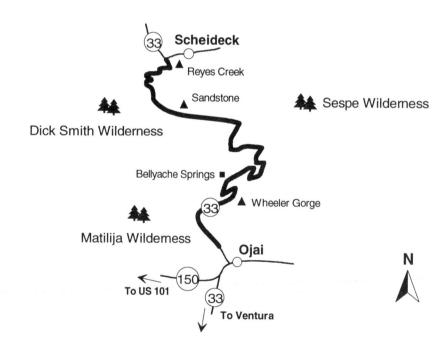

Information Sources:

Los Padres National Forest, 6144 Calle Real, Goleta, CA 93117 / 805-683-6711
Ojai Valley Chamber of Commerce, 338 E. Ojai Ave., Ojai, CA 93024 / 805-646-8126
Santa Barbara County Chamber of Commerce, 504 State St., Santa Barbara, CA 93101 / 805-965-3023
Greater Ventura Chamber of Commerce, 785 S. Seaward Ave., Ventura, CA 93001 / 805-648-2875

JUDY ANDREEN SIERRA HERITAGE

California

- *Route Location:* Located in east-central California, northeast of Fresno. The southwestern access starts in Clovis off California State Highway 41 and travels northeast ending near the town of Mono Hot Springs.
- *Roads Traveled:* The 70 mile route follows California State Highway 168 which is a two-lane paved road suitable for all vehicles except the last segment from Huntington Lake to Kaiser Meadows which is paved but narrow. The road ends in Mono Hot Springs and travelers will need to retrace the route. The entire route has been designated a National Forest Scenic Byway.
- *Travel Season:* Mose of the route is open year-round. The road from Huntington Lake to Kaiser Meadows is closed in the winter due to heavy snows.
- *Description:* The scenic drive travels across the Sierra National Forest through oak, ponderosa pine, and mixed conifer forests between Yosemite and Kings Canyon National Parks. A beautiful display of wildflowers are offered in the foothills in spring and in the mountains during summer months. Huntington Lake is ranked as one of the top sailing lakes in the state of California and several sailboat races take place here during the summer. Fishing, canoeing, and waterskiing are also offered on this alpine lake. The wilderness areas surrounding the scenic drive offer numerous opportunities for hiking, backpacking, camping, and horseback riding. A variety of wildlife inhabits this region and includes golden eagles, flying squirrels, deer, bears, and hawks.
- *Other Nearby Routes:* A short drive off this route will lead to the Sierra Vista scenic drive and less than 50 miles east of Fresno is the Kings Canyon scenic drive.

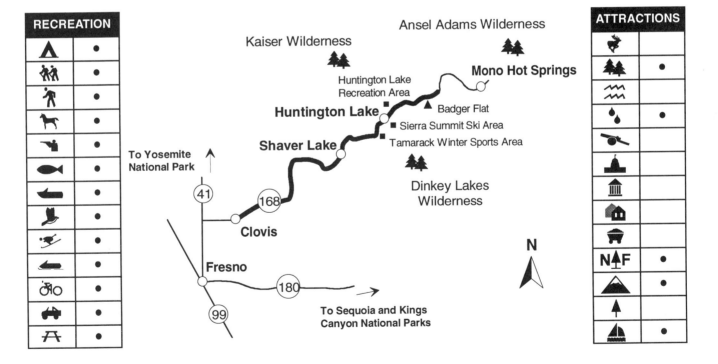

Information Sources:

Sierra National Forest, Pineridge Ranger District, P.O. Box 300, Shaver Lake, CA 93664 / 209-841-3311
Fresno Chamber of Commerce, 2331 Fresno St., Fresno, CA 93716 / 209-233-4651
Clovis District Chamber of Commerce, 325 Pollasky Ave., Clovis, CA 93612 / 209-299-7273

KINGS CANYON

- *Route Location:* Located in central California, east of Fresno. The western access starts on the national forest boundary east of Squaw Valley on California State Highway 180 and travels east into the Kings Canyon and Sequoia National Parks.
- *Roads Traveled:* The 50 mile route follows California State Highway 180 which is a two-lane paved road suitable for all vehicles. The road ends in the national park where you will need to retrace the route back to the junction of California State Highways 180 and 198. The entire 50 mile route has been designated a National Forest Scenic Byway.
- *Travel Season:* The entire route is generally open from mid-April through early November then the eastern section is closed from heavy winter snows.
- *Description:* The route travels on the Sequoia National Forest to its end in the Sequoia and Kings Canyon National Parks. This scenic drive passes through the

California

largest species of tree on earth, the giant sequoia, and one of the deepest canyons in North America, the Kings Canyon. Dramatic changes in vegetation, wildlife, and geology are experienced as you climb 4,000 feet through the foothills of the Sierra Nevadas, descend 3,700 feet into Kings Canyon and then climb again 2,000 feet to Zumwalt Meadows. Recreational opportunities along this scenic drive include fishing, boating, hunting, camping, mountain biking, and picnicking. Winter recreation includes cross-country skiing and snowmobiling.

- *Other Nearby Routes:* Approximately 50 miles to the northwest is the Judy Andreen Sierra Heritage scenic drive which is also close to the Sierra Vista scenic drive.

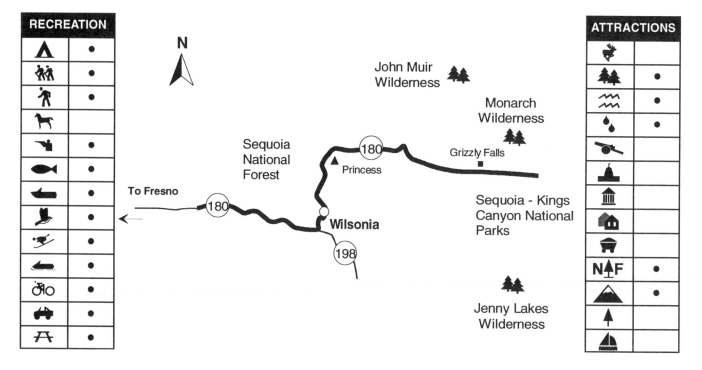

Information Sources:

Sequoia National Forest, 900 W. Grand Ave., Porterville, CA 93257-2035 / 209-784-1500
Fresno Chamber of Commerce, 2331 Fresno St., Fresno, CA 93716 / 209-233-4651
Visalia Chamber of Commerce, 720 W. Mineral King, Visalia, CA 93291 / 209-734-5876

LASSEN

California

- *Route Location:* Located in northeastern California, east of Redding. The eastern access starts west of Susanville off U.S. Highway 395 and travels northwest, forming a loop drive back to Susanville.
- *Roads Traveled:* The 172 mile route follows California State Highways 36, 44, 89, and 147 which are all two-lane paved roads suitable for all vehicles. The entire route has been designated a National Forest Scenic Byway.
- *Travel Season:* The route is generally open year-round with temporary closures in the winter possible.
- *Description:* This scenic drive travels through the Lassen National Forest and the Lassen Volcanic National Park, into deep forests, through expansive meadows, around numerous lakes, and scenic wetlands. Lake Almanor is located at the southern end of the route and provides plenty of opportunities for boating, sailing, water-skiing, and fishing. Many hiking and backpacking trails are accessed along the drive, including the Pacific Crest National Scenic Trail. In addition to hiking and backpacking, horseback riding is offered in the Thousand Lakes and Caribou Peak Wilderness areas. Winter sport enthusiasts are offered cross-country skiing and snowmobiling opportunities throughout the forest.
- *Other Nearby Routes:* To the west, approximately 50 miles, is the Trinity scenic drive and an additional 45 miles along the Trinity leads to the Trinity Heritage scenic drive. The Feather River scenic drive can be accessed off of this route about 25 miles south of Canyondam. Less than 75 miles northeast is the Buckhorn scenic drive.

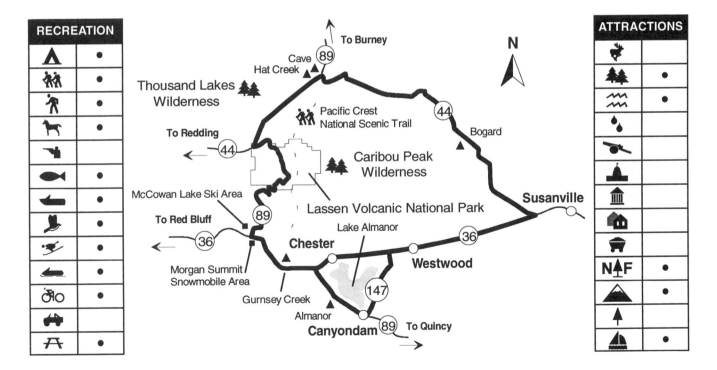

Information Sources:

Lassen National Forest, Almanor Ranger District, P.O. Box 767, Chester, CA 96020 / 916-258-2141
Chester - Lake Almanor Chamber of Commerce, 529 Main St., Chester, CA 96020 / 916-258-2426
Westwood Area Chamber of Commerce, P.O. Box 1235, Westwood, CA 96137 / 916-256-2456
Lassen County Chamber of Commerce, 34 N. Lassen St., Susanville, CA 96130 / 916-257-4323
Burney Chamber of Commerce, 37477 Main St., Burney, CA 96013 / 916-335-2111

LEE VINING CANYON

California

- **Route Location:** Located in east-central California between Mono Lake and Yosemite National Park. The eastern access starts in Lee Vining off U.S. Highway 395 and travels west to the entrance of Yosemite National Park.
- **Roads Traveled:** The 12 mile route follows California State Highway 120 which is a two-lane paved road suitable for all vehicles. The 12 mile route has been designated a National Forest Scenic Byway.
- **Travel Season:** The route is normally open from Memorial Day through early November then closed by heavy snows during the winter.
- **Description:** The scenic drive travels through the Inyo National Forest and leads to the Yosemite National Park entrance. The route climbs through the spectacular and rugged Lee Vining Canyon and the high country of the Sierra Nevada Range offering views of numerous meadows and high mountain peaks. Autumn brings a golden color to the area as large stands of Aspen prepare for the winter. This route is the highest crossing of the Sierra Nevada Range as it crosses the 9,945 foot high Tioga Pass. Several campgrounds are located along the route and within the national park. Two wilderness areas provide opportunities for hiking and backpacking and the Lee Vining Creek offers fishing for rainbow trout.
- **Other Nearby Routes:** The Carson Pass scenic drive is located approximately 100 miles to the north and about 85 miles to the south is the Ancient Bristlecone scenic drive. Approximately 75 miles through the Yosemite National Park and south past Sugar Pine is the Sierra Vista scenic drive.

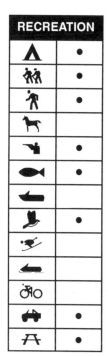

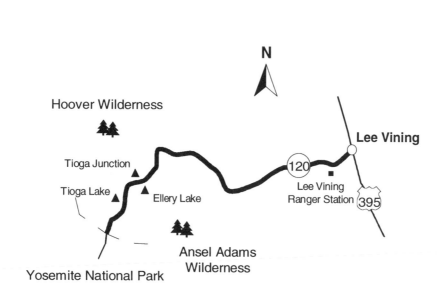

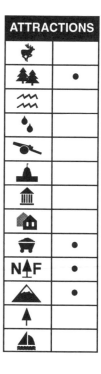

Information Sources:

Inyo National Forest, White Mountain Ranger District, 798 N. Main St., Bishop, CA 93514 / 619-873-2525
Lee Vining Chamber of Commerce, P.O. Box 130, Lee Vining, CA 93541 / 619-647-6627
Mono County Chamber of Commerce, P.O. Box 247, Bridgeport, CA 93517 / 619-932-7500
Mariposa County Chamber of Commerce, 5158 Hwy. 140, Mariposa, CA 95338 / 209-966-2456

OWENS VALLEY TO DEATH VALLEY

California

- *Route Location:* Located in east-central California, south of Bishop, near the Nevada border. The western access starts east of Big Pine off U.S. Highway 395 and travels east to the northwest entrance of Death Valley National Monument.
- *Roads Traveled:* The 63 mile route follows the Big Pine Death Valley Road which is a county maintained road. The first 32 miles are paved with the remaining 31 miles traveling over a graded dirt surface. You can safely drive this route in a two-wheel drive, high-clearance vehicle. The entire route has been designated a BLM Type II Back Country Byway.
- *Travel Season:* The route is generally open year-round, but is subject to closure at times of heavy rainfall or winter snowfall.
- *Description:* This route travels through portions of the Inyo National Forest and the California Desert Conservation Area, winding through narrow canyons, high plateaus, and vast desert valleys. Views of the 700 foot high Eureka Sand Dunes, ten miles south of the route, and the Eastern Sierra Nevada Mountains are offered along this desert scenic drive. Camping and day use facilities are located near the sand dunes as well as throughout the Inyo National Forest. Within the Death Valley National Monument is Scotty's Castle and the lowest point in the Western Hemisphere.
- *Other Nearby Routes:* The Saline Valley scenic drive is accessed off of this route. The Ancient Bristlecone scenic drive is just north, starting in Big Pine. Approximately 80 miles to the north is the Lee Vining Canyon scenic drive.

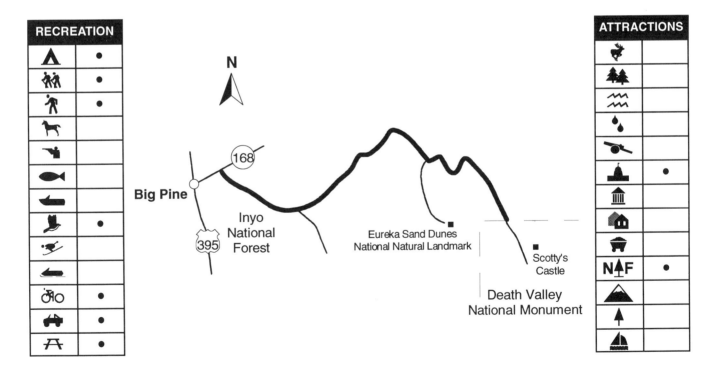

Information Sources:

BLM, Ridgecrest Resource Area, 300 S. Richmond Rd., Ridgecrest, CA 93555 / 619-375-7125
Bishop Chamber of Commerce, 690 N. Main St., Bishop, CA 93514 / 619-873-8405

PALMS TO PINES

- *Route Location:* Located in southern California near Palm Springs. The northwestern access starts in Banning off Interstate 10 and travels an open loop southeast to the town of Palm Desert on California State Highway 111.
- *Roads Traveled:* The 67 mile route follows California State Highways 74 and 243 which are two-lane paved roads suitable for all vehicles. The entire route has been designated a National Forest Scenic Byway.
- *Travel Season:* The entire route is open year-round.
- *Description:* The scenic drive winds through the San Jacinto Mountains of the San Bernardino National Forest and through the Santa Rosa Indian Reservation. The mountains provide a drastic contrast to the surrounding desert landscape. There are over 150 miles of hiking trails to be explored, including a portion of the Pacific Crest National Scenic Trail. Hiking, backpacking, camping, and horseback riding are offered in the

San Jacinto and Santa Rosa Wilderness areas. A short ¼ mile trail at the Cahuilla Tewanet overlook offers spectacular views into the Santa Rosa Wilderness. Hunting, rock climbing, and off-road vehicle use are other recreational pursuits found along this scenic drive. The San Jacinto Ranger District Office is located in Idyllwild and provides information on the scenic drive and the surrounding area to visitors 7 days a week during the summer months.

California

- *Other Nearby Routes:* The Rim Of The World scenic drive is about 30 miles north which also leads to the Angeles Crest scenic drive. The Sunrise scenic drive is located approximately 70 miles to the south.

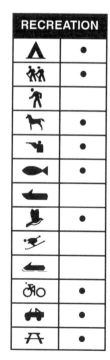

Information Sources:

San Bernardino National Forest, 1824 S. Commercenter Cir., San Bernardino, CA 92408-3430 / 714-383-5588
Palm Desert Chamber of Commerce, 72-990 Hwy. 111, Palm Desert, CA 92260 / 800-873-2428
Idyllwild Chamber of Commerce, 54274 N. Circle Dr., Idyllwild, CA 92349 / 714-659-3259
Banning Chamber of Commerce, 123 E. Ramsey St., Banning, CA 92220 / 714-849-4695
Palm Springs Chamber of Commerce, 190 W. Amado Rd., Palm Springs, CA 92262 / 619-325-1577

RIM OF THE WORLD

- *Route Location:* Located in southwestern California, north of San Bernardino. The northwestern access starts at the Mormon Rocks Fire Station on California State Highway 138, just west of Interstate 15, and travels southeast to the national forest boundary east of Redlands.
- *Roads Traveled:* The 115 mile route follows California State Highways 138, 18, and 38. The entire route travels over two-lane paved roads suitable for all vehicles. All but 8 miles of this route has been designated a National Forest Scenic Byway.
- *Travel Season:* The entire route is open year-round.
- *Description:* The route travels through the San Bernardino National Forest with portions following alongside the San Gorgonio Wilderness area, offering some of the most naturally beautiful areas in southern California. Many spectacular and panoramic views of the surrounding countryside is offered along the route.

California

Many opportunities for camping and picnicking are offered in the numerous campgrounds located along the scenic drive. Big Bear Lake offers fishing opportunities as well as camping. Hiking opportunities can be found along the Pacific Crest National Scenic Trail and in the wilderness area, which is a 56,000 acre high mountain wonderland of granite ridges, subalpine meadows, and placid lakes. Winter recreation activities are found in the many ski areas located along the route.

- *Other Nearby Routes:* Approximately 10 miles from the northwestern terminus is the Angeles Crest scenic drive while about 30 miles to the south from the southwestern terminus is the Palms To Pines scenic drive.

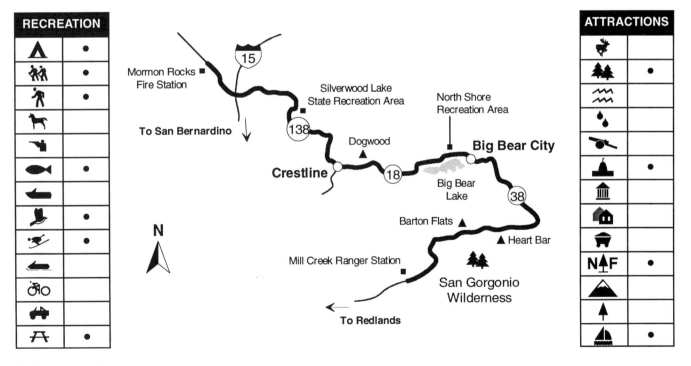

Information Sources:

San Bernardino National Forest, 1824 S. Commercenter Cir., San Bernardino, CA 92408-3430 / 714-383-5588
Crestline Resorts Chamber of Commerce, 607 Forest Shade, Crestline, CA 92325 / 909-338-2706
Lake Arrowhead Chamber of Commerce, 28200 Hwy. 189, Bldg. J, Lake Arrowhead, CA 92352 / 909-337-3715
Running Springs Area Chamber of Commerce, 31974 Hilltop Blvd., Running Springs, CA 92382 / 800-332-1166
Big Bear Chamber of Commerce, 630 Bartlett Rd., Big Bear Lake, CA 92315 / 909-866-7000
Redlands Chamber of Commerce, 1 E. Redlands Blvd., Redlands, CA 92373 / 909-793-2546

SALINE VALLEY

California

- **Route Location:** Located in east-central California, near the Nevada border. The southern access starts southeast of Keeler off California State Highway 190 and travels north to the junction of the Owens Valley To Death Valley scenic drive, east of Big Pine.
- **Roads Traveled:** The 82 mile route follows the Saline Valley Road which is a county maintained graded dirt road. The route can safely be traveled in a two-wheel drive, high-clearance vehicle. The entire route has been designated a BLM Type II Back Country Byway.
- **Travel Season:** The route is normally open year-round, but may occasionally close due to heavy summer rains or winter snowfall.
- **Description:** This route passes through sweeping vistas of the Panamint and Saline Valleys, through sage scrubland, joshua tree woodland, and sand dunes while offering views of the towering Inyo Mountains. The historic Saline Valley Salt Works and Tram, which was in operation between 1911 and 1913, is located along the drive. This was the steepest tramway in the United States, rising from 1,100 feet in the Saline Valley floor to 8,500 feet at the Inyo Crest, then dropping to 3,600 feet at Swansea in the Owens Valley. The lowest point in the Western Hemisphere can be accessed along the route in the Death Valley National Monument.
- **Other Nearby Routes:** The Owens Valley To Death Valley scenic drive is accessed from the northen terminus of this route. The Ancient Bristlecone scenic drive is just to the north with access in Big Pine. The Lee Vining Canyon scenic drive is about 80 miles to the north of Big Pine.

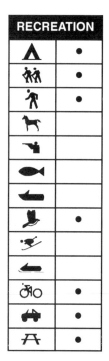

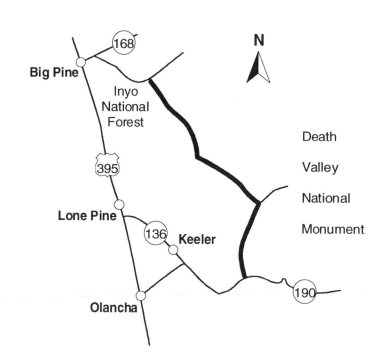

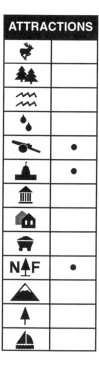

Information Sources:

BLM, California Desert Information Center, 831 Barstow Rd., Barstow, CA 92311 / 619-256-8617
Bishop Chamber of Commerce, 690 N. Main St., Bishop, CA 93514 / 619-873-8405
Lone Pine Chamber of Commerce, 126 S. Main St., Lone Pine, CA 93545 / 619-876-4444
Ridgecrest Chamber of Commerce, 400 N. China Lake Blvd., Ridgecrest, CA 93555 / 619-375-8331

SIERRA VISTA

California

- *Route Location:* Located in east-central California, south of Yosemite National Park. The southern access starts southeast of North Fork on the Minarets Road (Forest Service Road 81) and travels an open loop to the northeast ending at the junction of California State Highway 41, north of Oakhurst.
- *Roads Traveled:* The 100 mile route follows Forest Service Roads 81, 7, and 10. Approximately 75% of the route is paved with the remaining portions a combination of gravel and dirt roads that are rough in spots, however, they are suitable for all vehicles. The entire route has been designated a National Forest Scenic Byway.
- *Travel Season:* The route is generally open from mid-May through mid-November and then is closed the remainder of the year by winter snows.
- *Description:* This scenic drive offers spectacular views of the surrounding mountain peaks, meadows, and varied wildlife as it travels through the Sierra National Forest. In Nelder Grove, you will find the Shadow of the Giants National Recreation Trail which is a one mile, self-guided trail through giant sequoia trees. Bass Lake is a popular summer resort area offering fishing, swimming and water-skiing as the major activities. Globe Rock is a unique geological oddity of a large balanced rock.
- *Other Nearby Routes:* About a 75 mile drive through Yosemite National Park will lead to the Lee Vining Canyon scenic drive. Approximately 40 miles south of Oakhurst is the Judy Andreen Sierra Heritage scenic drive and an additional 35 miles southeast leads to the Kings Canyon scenic drive.

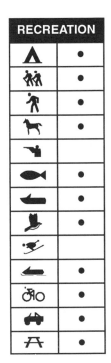

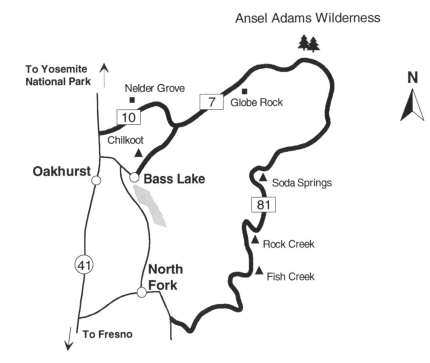

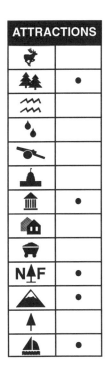

Information Sources:

Sierra National Forest, Minarets Ranger District, P.O. Box 10, North Fork, CA 93643 / 209-877-2218
Eastern Madera County Chamber of Commerce, 49074 Civic Cir., Oakhurst, CA 93644 / 209-683-7766
North Fork Chamber of Commerce, P.O. Box 426, North Fork, CA 93643 / 209-877-2410
Bass Lake Chamber of Commerce, P.O. Box 126, Bass Lake, CA 93604 / 209-642-3676

SMITH RIVER

California

- **Route Location:** Located in the northwest corner of California, north of Eureka. The southwestern access is off U.S. Highway 101 north of Crescent City and travels northeast ending near the Oregon-California border.
- **Roads Traveled:** The 39 mile route follows U.S. Highway 199 which is a two-lane paved road suitable for all vehicles. Thirty-three miles of this route has been designated a National Forest Scenic Byway.
- **Travel Season:** The route is open year-round although poor driving conditions can exist in the winter.
- **Description:** The route travels through the Redwood National Park and the Six Rivers National Forest, offering a variety of changing landscapes, from large rock outcrops to miles of panoramic vistas. Wildlife seen along the byway also varies from otters, ducks, osprey to an occasional bald eagle. The Smith River is the only undammed river system in California and is designated a Wild and Scenic River. Fishing, swimming, kayaking, rafting, and tubing are popular activities along this river. The Smith River National Recreation Area provides numerous opportunities for camping, picnicking, hiking, horseback riding, and mountain biking. Rare and endangered species such as the bald eagle and Peregrine falcon make their homes within this area.
- **Other Nearby Routes:** The Trinity scenic drive is about 90 miles south of Crescent City and the State of Jefferson scenic drive lies about 10 miles to the north in Oregon. Approximately 75 to 100 miles across the Oregon border are the Rogue Umpqua, Galice-Hellgate, Grave Creek to Marial, and Cow Creek scenic drives.

Information Sources:

Six Rivers National Forest, 500 Fifth St., Eureka, CA 95501 / 707-442-1721
Crescent City-Del Norte County C of C, 1001 Front St., Crescent City, CA 95531 / 800-343 8300
Illinois Valley Chamber of Commerce, 201 Caves Hwy., Cave Junction, OR 97523 / 503-592-3326
Grants Pass/Josephine County Chamber of Commerce, 1501 N.E. 6th St., Grants Pass, OR 97526 / 800-547-5927

STATE OF JEFFERSON

California

- *Route Location:* Located in the northwestern corner of California near the Oregon border. The southeastern access starts in the town of Yreka off Interstate 5 and travels northwest across the Oregon border, ending with the junction of U.S. Highway 199 south of Cave Junction, Oregon.

- *Roads Traveled:* The 108 mile route follows California State Highways 263 and 96 and Forest Service Road 40S07, also called the Grayback Road. All the roads travel over a two-lane paved surface suitable for all vehicles. The entire route has been designated a National Forest Scenic Byway.

- *Travel Season:* The route is generally open year-round with possible closures for snow removal in the winter.

- *Description:* This route travels across the Klamath and Siskiyou National Forests along much of the Klamath National Wild and Scenic River. Excellent opportunities for hiking and backpacking exist in the three wilderness areas and the Pacific Crest National Scenic Trail which crosses the route at Seiad Valley. Several developed campgrounds are located along the scenic drive as well as picnic areas. Excellent cross-country skiing and snowmobiling can be found along the Grayback Road. Wildlife seen along the route includes deer, otters, geese, ducks, osprey, bears, and bald eagles.

- *Other Nearby Routes:* From the northern terminus of this route in Oregon, head south to begin the Smith River scenic drive. Continuing north in Oregon, the Rogue Umpqua, Galice-Hellgate, and Cow Creek scenic drives are all nearby. About 30 miles south of the eastern terminus is the Trinity Heritage scenic drive.

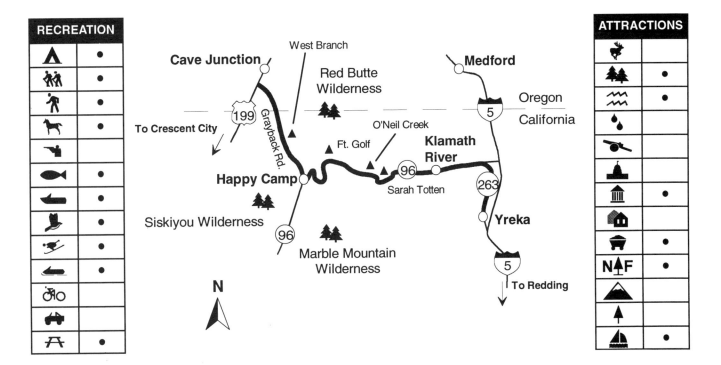

Information Sources:

Klamath National Forest, 1312 Fairlane Rd., Yreka, CA 96097 / 916-842-6131
Yreka Chamber of Commerce, 117 W. Miner St., Yreka, CA 96097 / 916-842-1649
North Klamath River Chamber of Commerce, P.O. Box 25, Klamath River, CA 96050 / 916-465-2366
Illinois Valley Chamber of Commerce, 201 Caves Hwy., Cave Junction, OR 97523 / 503-592-3326

SUNRISE

California

- *Route Location:* Located in southwestern California, east of San Diego. The southern access starts 1 mile east of Pine Valley off Interstate 8 and travels north to the junction with California State Highway 79, south of Julian.
- *Roads Traveled:* The 24 mile route follows County Road S1 which is a two-lane paved road suitable for all vehicles. The entire 24 mile route has been designated a National Forest Scenic Byway.
- *Travel Season:* The route is open year-round except for temporary closures in the winter for snow removal.
- *Description:* The Sunrise scenic drive travels on the Cleveland National Forest and is adjacent to the Anza Borrego Desert State Park. Views offered along the drive are mountain meadows, pine and oak forests, and breath taking views of the Anza Borrego Desert State Park. Blacktail deer, coyotes, red-tailed hawks, and many other birds and small mammals may be seen from

along the scenic drive. The Pacific Crest National Scenic Trail and the Noble Canyon National Recreation Trail are accessible from the route. Within the nearby Cuyamaca Rancho State Park are over 100 miles of hiking and nature trails. This state park also offers camping and picnicking opportunities. Developed campgrounds and picnic areas are also located along the drive. The visitor center located in Mount Laguna offers wildlife exhibits and information on the scenic drive and surrounding area. The center is open on weekends during the summer. A nature trail is also located here.

- *Other Nearby Routes:* The Palms To Pines scenic drive is approximately 70 miles to the north.

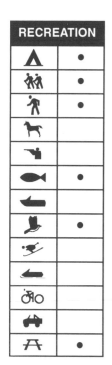

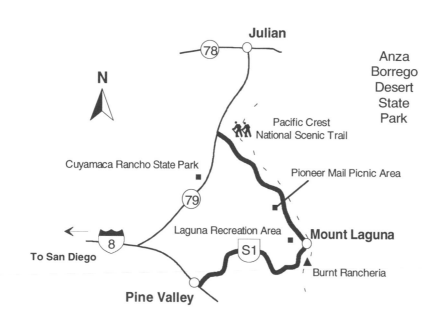

Information Sources:

Cleveland National Forest, 10845 Rancho Bernardo Rd., San Diego, CA 92128 / 619-557-5050
Julian Chamber of Commerce, P.O. Box 413, Julian, CA 92036 / 619-765-1857
Alpine Chamber of Commerce, 2157 Alpine Blvd., Alpine, CA 91903 / 619-445-2722

TRINITY

California

- *Route Location:* Located in northwestern California, starting in Redding. The eastern access starts in Redding off Interstate 5 and travels northwest to the junction of U.S. Highway 101, north of Eureka near the coast.
- *Roads Traveled:* The 140 mile route follows California State Highway 299 which is a two-lane paved road suitable for all vehicles. The 140 mile route has been designated a National Forest Scenic Byway.
- *Travel Season:* The entire route is generally open year-round although winter driving conditions may be hazardous.
- *Description:* The scenic drive crosses the Trinity National Forest through the spectacular mountain scenery of the Trinity Alps and winds along the crystal waters of the Trinity River gorge. The scenic drive provides access to California's largest wilderness area, the Trinity Alps Wilderness, which offers over 500,000 acres of pristine wilderness in which you can hike, backpack, camp, fish, and ride horseback. Located a short distance off this route is the Clair Engle Lake, also known as Trinity Lake, which offers opportunities for camping, fishing, and boating. Several campgrounds and picnic areas are also located along the route. The ghost town of Helena is located west of Weaverville, just north of the route on East Fork Road. Most of the buildings that remain are on private property and may not be entered.
- *Other Nearby Routes:* The Trinity Heritage scenic drive is accessed along this route in Weaverville which also leads to the State of Jefferson scenic drive about 30 miles to the north.

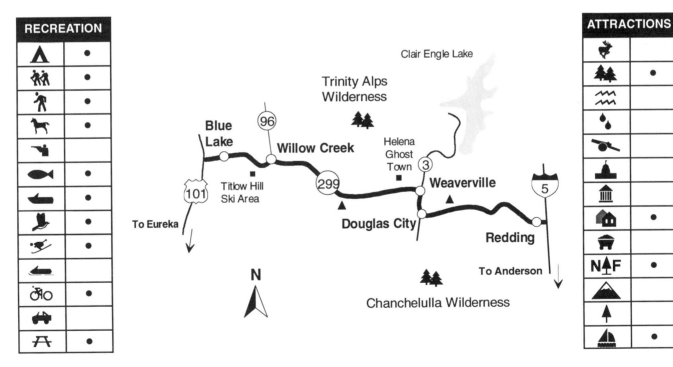

Information Sources:

Shasta - Trinity National Forests, 2400 Washington Ave., Redding, CA 96001 / 916-246-5152
Greater Redding Chamber of Commerce, 747 Auditorium Dr., Redding, CA 96001 / 916-225-4433
Arcata Chamber of Commerce, 1062 G St., Arcata, CA 95521 / 707-822-3619
Greater Eureka Chamber of Commerce, 2112 Broadway, Eureka, CA 95501-2189 / 707-442-3738
Willow Creek Chamber of Commerce, P.O. Box 704, Willow Creek, CA 95573 / 916-629-2178
Trinity County Chamber of Commerce, 317 Main St., Weaverville, CA 96093 / 800-421-7259

TRINITY HERITAGE

California

- *Route Location:* Located in northwestern California, northwest of Redding. The southern access starts in Weaverville off State Highway 299 and travels northeast to the junction of Interstate 5, north of Weed.
- *Roads Traveled:* The 120 mile route follows California State Highway 3 and Forest Service Road 17. The entire route travels over two-lane paved roads suitable for all vehicles. The 120 mile route has been designated a National Forest Scenic Byway.
- *Travel Season:* The route from Weaverville to Forest Service Road 17 is open year-round with the remaining section closed by winter snows from around late November through the end of May.
- *Description:* This route passes through a mountainous landscape as it travels through the Shasta-Trinity National Forests alongside the Trinity Alps Wilderness area. A major portion of the scenic drive follows the path of early miners and settlers. The Clair Engle Lake, also known as Trinity Lake, is the third largest man-made lake in California. Several campgrounds, picnic areas, boat ramps, beaches, and restaurants are located here. The wilderness area offers back country camping, hiking, horseback riding, and fishing in any of its 60 alpine lakes. The Bowerman Barn is one of the last of its kind, with a foundation of hand-laid stone, mortise and tenon framework, and whipsawn pine boards attached with hand-forged square nails.
- *Other Nearby Routes:* The Trinity scenic drive is located at the southern end of this drive and the State Of Jefferson scenic route is about 30 miles north from the northern terminus of this scenic drive.

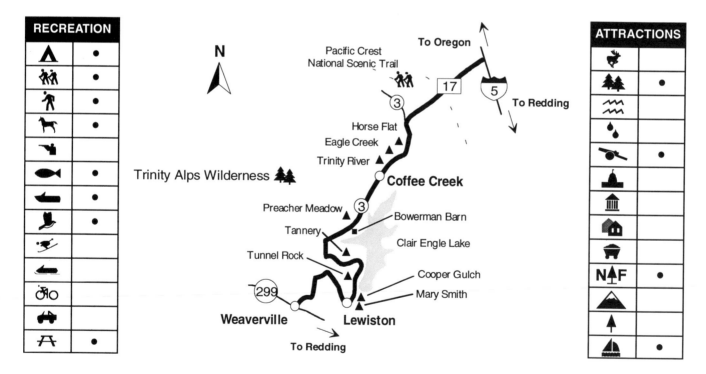

Information Sources:

Shasta - Trinity National Forests, 2400 Washington Ave., Redding, CA 96001 / 916-246-5152
Trinity County Chamber of Commerce, 317 Main St., Weaverville, CA 96093 / 800-421-7259
Yreka Chamber of Commerce, 117 W. Miner St., Yreka, CA 96097 / 916-842-1649

YUBA DONNER

California

- *Route Location:* Located in east-central California, northeast of Sacramento near the Nevada border. The southeastern access starts just north of Truckee off Interstate 80 and forms a loop drive northwest back to Truckee.
- *Roads Traveled:* The 170 mile route follows California State Highways 20, 49, and 89 and Interstate 80. All of the routes travel over two-lane paved roads suitable for all vehicles. The entire route has been designated a National Forest Scenic Byway.
- *Travel Season:* The entire route is open year-round although winter driving conditions may be hazardous.
- *Description:* The route travels on the Tahoe National Forest through the foothills and mountains of the Northern Sierra Nevada. It climbs through miles of forests and valleys with meandering rivers and streams. This area is also rich with gold mining history and emigrant and transportation history, including Native American

trade routes, and the campsites of the ill-fated Donner Party. There are a large number of campgrounds located along the route and within the national forest. Several scenic vistas and pullouts provide opportunities for picnicking and photographing the surrounding wilderness. Museums, mining sites, and historical mining towns can also be found along the route.

- *Other Nearby Routes:* The Feather River scenic drive is about 20 miles to the north which is also close to the Lassen scenic drive. Approximately 60 miles to the south is the Carson Pass Highway scenic drive. Less than 100 miles east in Nevada is the Fort Churchill To Wellington scenic drive.

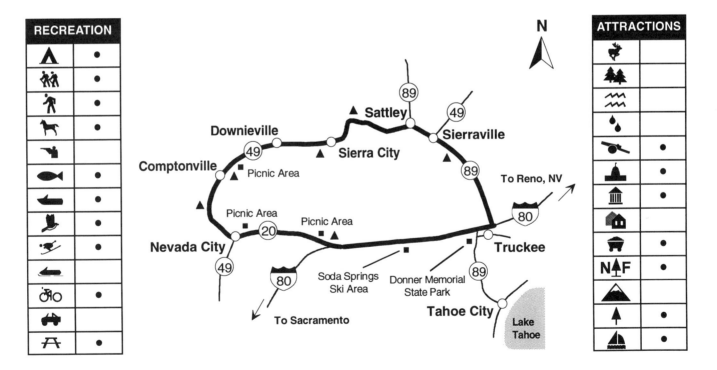

Information Sources:

Tahoe National Forest, 631 Coyote St., Nevada City, CA 95959-6003 / 916-265-4531
Truckee - Donner Chamber of Commerce, P.O. Box 2757, Truckee, CA 96160 / 916-587-2757
Nevada City Chamber of Commerce, 132 Main St., Nevada City, CA 95959 / 916-265-2692
Eastern Plumas Chamber of Commerce, P.O. Box 1379, Portola, CA 96122 / 916-832-5444

COLORADO

□ *Scenic Drives*

1. Alpine Loop
2. Flat Tops Trail
3. Gold Belt Tour
4. Guanella Pass
5. Highway of Legends
6. Mount Evans
7. Peak To Peak
8. San Juan Skyway
9. Silver Thread Highway
10. Unaweep / Tebeguache

○ *National Park Areas*

A. Bent's Old Fort National Historic Site
B. Black Canyon of the Gunnison National Monument
C. Colorado National Monument
D. Curecanti National Recreation Area
E. Dinosaur National Monument
F. Florissant Fossil Beds National Monument
G. Great Sand Dunes National Monument
H. Hovenweep National Monument
I. Mesa Verde National Park
J. Rocky Mountain National Park

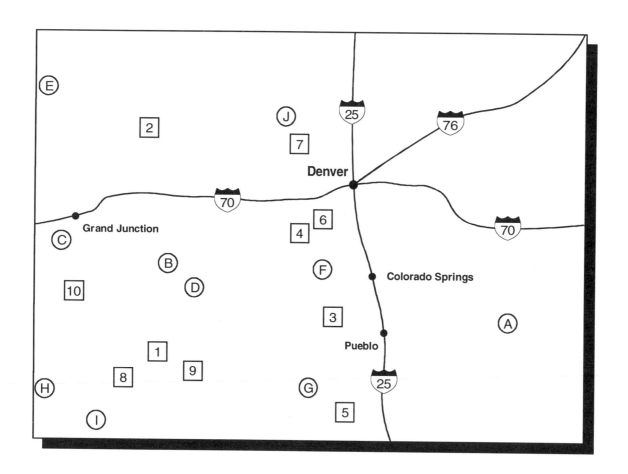

Road Condition Numbers: 303-757-9228 (construction); 303-639-1234 (conditions)

ALPINE LOOP

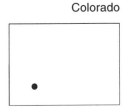

Colorado

- *Route Location:* Located in southwestern Colorado, southwest of Gunnison. The northeastern access is located in Lake City off Colorado State Highway 149 and travels to the towns of Ouray and Silverton, forming a loop drive back to the junction of highway 149, south of Lake City.
- *Roads Traveled:* The 65 mile route follows a series of old mining roads that are marked with "Alpine Loop" signs. About two-thirds of the route travels over dirt roads that are suitable for two-wheel drive vehicles. A four-wheel drive vehicle is needed to travel the entire route. The entire 65 mile route has been designated a BLM Type III Back Country Byway.
- *Travel Season:* The entire route is generally open from late June through October. Heavy snow closes the route for the remainder of the year.
- *Description:* This route was originally constructed by prospectors in the late 1800s for mineral exploration access. The scenic drive winds its way through the San Juan Mountains to elevations as high as 12,800 feet, crossing Engineer and Cinnamon passes. Views of high mountain peaks, many over 14,000 feet, meadows of wildflowers, ghost towns, and deep blue lakes are all offered on this back country route. Animas Forks is one such ghost town with many buildings remaining that await inspection. Four-wheel drive vehicles and tours are available in the surrounding communities. Mountain biking, hiking, backpacking, camping, and fishing are all popular activities along this scenic drive.
- *Other Nearby Routes:* Both the Silver Thread Highway and San Juan Skyway are accessed from this route. The Unaweep / Tebeguache scenic drive is only about 35 miles to the west from Ouray.

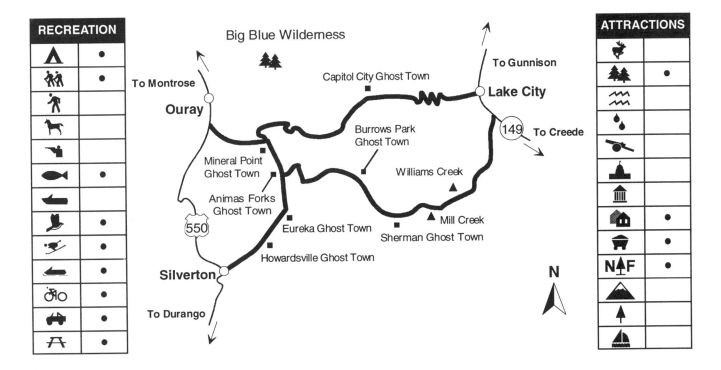

Information Sources:

BLM, Gunnison Resource Area, 216 N. Colorado Ave., Gunnison, CO 81230 / 303-641-0471
Uncompahgre National Forest, Ouray Ranger District, 2505 S. Townsend, Montrose, CO 81401 / 303-249-3711
Silverton Chamber of Commerce, 414 Greene St., Silverton, CO 81433 / 800-752-4494
Ouray Chamber Resort Assn., 1222 N. Main St., Ouray, CO 81427 / 800-228-1876
Lake City Chamber of Commerce, 306 N. Silver St., Lake City, CO 81235 / 800-569-1874

FLAT TOPS TRAIL

- *Route Location:* Located in northwestern Colorado, north of Glenwood Springs. The western access is located in Meeker off Colorado State Highway 13 and travels east to the junction of Colorado State Highway 131, in the town of Yampa.
- *Roads Traveled:* The 82 mile route follows Forest Service Roads 8 and 16 over a combination of paved and gravel surfaced roads that are suitable for most vehicles. The 82 mile route has been designated a National Forest Scenic Byway.
- *Travel Season:* The route is open year-round except for the winter months when the roads are not plowed.
- *Description:* The scenic drive passes through sage-covered rolling hills, hay meadows, and working ranches as it travels across the Routt and White River National Forests. As you travel this scenic route, views of sheer escarpments and deep canyons change into forests of lodgepole pine, spruce, fir, and aspen mingled with

grassland parks and meadows. Sheriff Reservoir is a popular fishing and primitive camping spot as well as providing trail access to the Flat Tops Wilderness. The scenic beauty of Trappers Lake, known as the "Cradle of Wilderness," is often referred to as the birthplace of the wilderness area concept which ultimately led to the Wilderness Act in 1964. Recreational opportunities found in this area includes camping, picnicking, horseback riding, and fishing. Several other developed campgrounds are found along this scenic drive.

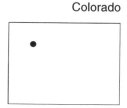

Colorado

- *Other Nearby Routes:* Approximately 100 miles to the east are the Peak To Peak, Guanella Pass, and Mount Evans scenic drives. About 100 miles southwest is the Unaweep/Tebeguache scenic drive and about 110 miles west in Utah is the Flaming Gorge-Uintas scenic drive.

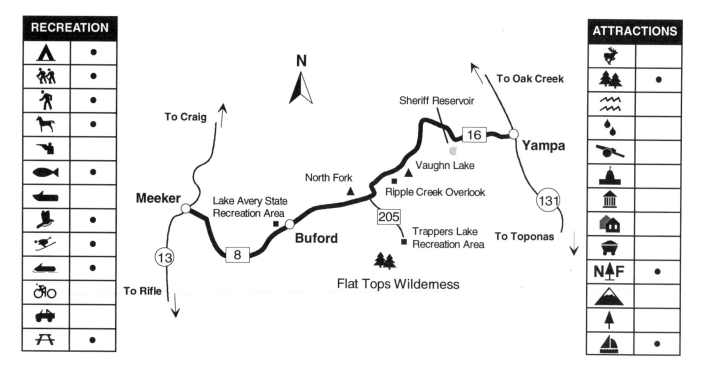

Information Sources:

Routt National Forest, Yampa Ranger District, P.O. Box 7, Yampa, CO 80483 / 303-638-4516
Meeker Chamber of Commerce, 710 Market St., Meeker, CO 81641 / 303-878-3510
Steamboat Springs Chamber Resort Assn., P.O. Box 774408, Steamboat Springs, CO 80477 / 303-879-0880

GOLD BELT TOUR

- *Route Location:* Located in central Colorado, northwest of Pueblo. The southeastern access is located in Florence on Colorado State Highway 115 and travels northwest across three historic routes, forming a loop drive back to Florence.
- *Roads Traveled:* The 122 mile route follows the Phantom Canyon, Shelf, and High Park roads. All are unpaved, but are accessible by normal passenger cars during dry weather. The Phantom Canyon Road and the upper portion of the Shelf Road should not be traveled by motor homes or vehicles pulling trailers since these routes are confined by canyon walls and narrow in many places to one lane. The entire route has been designated a BLM Type I and II Back Country Byway.
- *Travel Season:* The route is generally open year-round although heavy snows may temporarily close portions of the route.
- *Description:* This historic route

once linked the Cripple Creek District gold camps with the towns of Florence and Canon City during the gold mining boom. Now the route offers a recreational drive through rolling mountain parklands and deep rocky canyons offering opportunities to view mountain lions, elk, mule deer, and golden eagles. Many recreational opportunities can also be found along this back country drive including camping, hiking, fishing, whitewater rafting, and hunting.

- *Other Nearby Routes:* Less than 100 miles to the north is the Guanella Pass scenic drive and a few more miles north to the Mount Evans and Peak To Peak scenic drives. Approximately 80 miles to the south is the Highway of Legends scenic drive.

Colorado

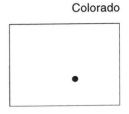

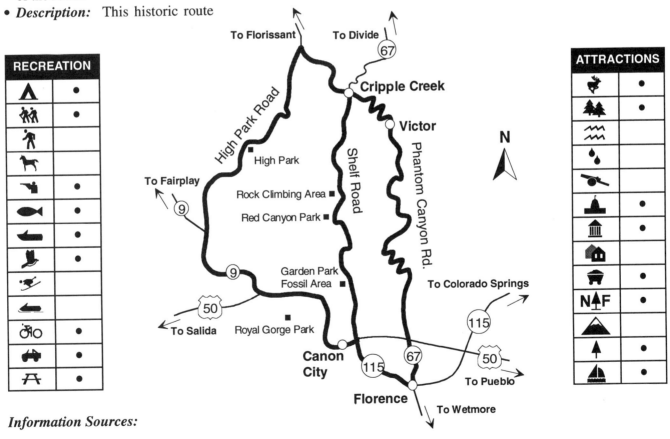

Information Sources:

BLM, Royal Gorge Resource Area, 3170 E. Main St., Canon City, CO 81215 / 719-275-0631
Florence Chamber of Commerce, 117 S. Pikes Peak Ave., Florence, CO 81226 / 719-784-3544
Greater Canon City Chamber of Commerce, 1032 Royal Gorge Blvd., Canon City, CO 81215 / 800-876-7922
Cripple Creek Chamber of Commerce, P.O. Box 650, Cripple Creek, CO 80813 / 800-526-8777
Victor Chamber of Commerce, P.O. Box 83, Victor, CO 80860 / 719-689-3211

GUANELLA PASS

- *Route Location:* Located in central Colorado, west of Denver. The northern access starts in Georgetown off Interstate 70 and travels south to the town of Grant on U.S. Highway 285.
- *Roads Traveled:* The 22 mile route follows the Guanella Pass Road. The first 10 miles from Georgetown are paved with the remaining segment to Grant a gravel surfaced road. This route is not recommended for large recreational vehicles or vehicles pulling trailers. The entire 22 mile route has been designated a National Forest Scenic Byway.
- *Travel Season:* The route is generally open year-round except after heavy winter snows. Caution should be exercised while traveling this route in the winter months.
- *Description:* This scenic drive travels through the spectacular mountain scenery of the Arapaho and Pike National Forests. A portion of the route parallels the western boundary of the 73,000 acre Mount Evans Wilder-

ness area, providing outstanding views of Mount Evans, Mount Bierstadt, and the Sawtooth Range. The Waldorf cutoff follows the Argentine Central roadbed to the top of Mount McClellan where views of 176 mountain peaks are possible, including Pike's Peak. Several back roads and trails along the route offer horseback riding, mountain biking, hiking, and four-wheel driving. Snowmobiling and cross-country skiing are popular winter activities along the route.

- *Other Nearby Routes:* Approximately 15 miles to the east is the Mount Evans scenic drive and an additional 15 miles northeast to the Peak To Peak scenic drive. Less than 100 miles to the south is the Gold Belt Tour scenic drive. About 110 miles to the northwest lies the Flat Tops Trail scenic drive.

Colorado

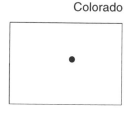

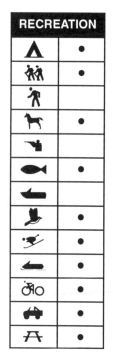

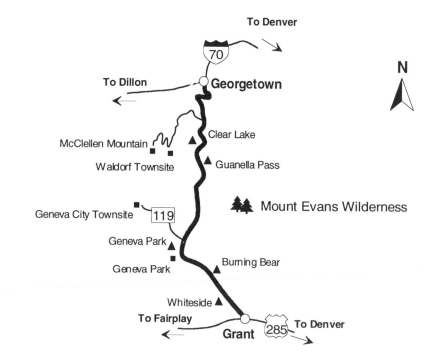

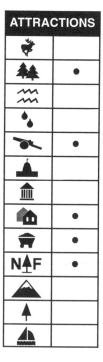

Information Sources:

Arapahoe and Roosevelt National Forest, 240 W. Prospect Rd., Fort Collins, CO 80526-2098 / 303-498-1100
Park County Tourism Office, P.O. Box 220, Fairplay, CO 80440 / 719-836-2771
Georgetown Chamber of Commerce, P.O. Box 444, Georgetown, CO 80444 / 303-569-2888
Idaho Springs Chamber of Commerce, P.O. Box 97, Idaho Springs, CO 80452 / 303-567-4382

HIGHWAY OF LEGENDS

- *Route Location:* Located in southern Colorado, south of Pueblo, near the New Mexico border. The northern access starts in Walsenburg off Interstate 25 and travels southwest forming an open loop drive back to Interstate 25 in Trinidad.
- *Roads Traveled:* The 82 mile route follows U.S. Highway 160 and Colorado State Highway 12. Both highways are two-lane paved roads suitable for all vehicles. The 82 mile route has been designated a National Forest Scenic Byway.
- *Travel Season:* The entire route is open year-round.
- *Description:* This scenic drive passes through a portion of the San Isabel National Forest and provides spectacular views of the Sangre de Cristo Mountains, the Spanish Peaks, and a variety of unique geological formations. A variety of wildlife inhabits this region and includes deer, elk, mountain lions, black bears, and bighorn sheep. Monument Lake received its name from the rock formation in the middle of the lake that rises 15 feet above the water and is said to represent two Indian chiefs. Camping, picnicking, fishing, and boating are offered here. Hiking and backpacking trails can be found in the national forest and along the route. One trail leads to the top of the West Spanish Peak, offering fabulous views of the surrounding countryside.
- *Other Nearby Routes:* Approximately 80 miles northwest is the Gold Belt Tour scenic drive and about 90 miles to the west is the Silver Thread Highway scenic drive. About 75 miles southwest across the New Mexico border is the Enchanted Circle scenic drive and the Wild Rivers scenic route is a few additional miles west from there.

Colorado

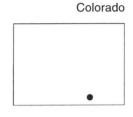

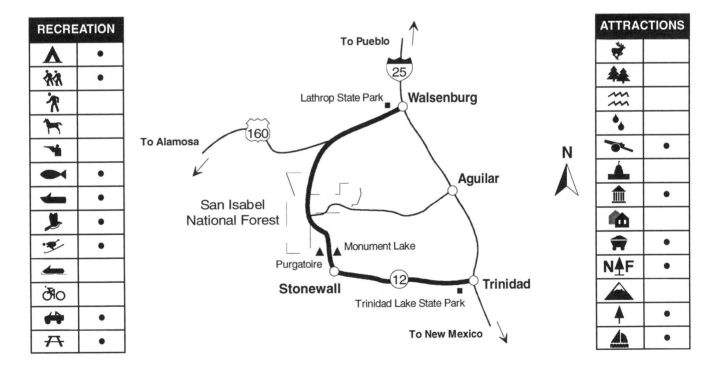

Information Sources:

Pike and San Isabel National Forests, 1920 Valley Dr., Pueblo, CO 81008 / 719-545-8737
Huerfano County Chamber of Commerce, 112 E. 4th St., Walsenburg, CO 81089 / 719-738-1065
Trinidad - Las Animas County Chamber of Commerce, 309 Nevada Ave., Trinidad, CO 81082 / 719-846-9285
LaVeta / Cuchara Chamber of Commerce, P.O. Box 32, LaVeta, CO 81055 / 719-742-3676

MOUNT EVANS

- *Route Location:* Located in central Colorado, west of Denver. The northern access is located in Idaho Springs off Interstate 70 and travels south to the summit of Mount Evans.
- *Roads Traveled:* The 28 mile route follows Colorado State Highways 103 and 5 which are two-lane paved roads. Highway 103 is well suited for all vehicles including those with small trailers (25 feet or less). Highway 5 is not recommended for large RVs or vehicles pulling trailers. The entire 28 mile route has been designated a National Forest Scenic Byway.
- *Travel Season:* Colorado State Highway 103 is usually open year-round with possible temporary closures in the winter for snow removal. Highway 5 is open from Memorial Day through Labor Day
- *Description:* Traveling through the Arapaho National Forest, this scenic drive rises almost 7,000 feet in elevation to 14,150 feet above sea level, making this the

highest paved auto road in North America. The view from the summit of Mount Evans is incredible as you are provided a 360 degree view of over 100 miles of Rocky Mountain peaks as well as the plains to the east.

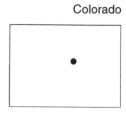

Colorado

Two glistening alpine lakes located along this high mountain road are stocked with trout. Developed picnic areas, shelters, and a hiking trail to fishing piers and scenic overlooks is also provided. Three trailheads into the surrounding wilderness area are accessed along this route. A visitor center is located in Idaho Springs and offers a self-guided tape tour of the drive.

- *Other Nearby Routes:* The Guanella Pass scenic drive is about 15 miles west and the Peak To Peak scenic drive is approximately 15 miles northeast. The Flat Tops Trail scenic drive is about 120 mile northwest.

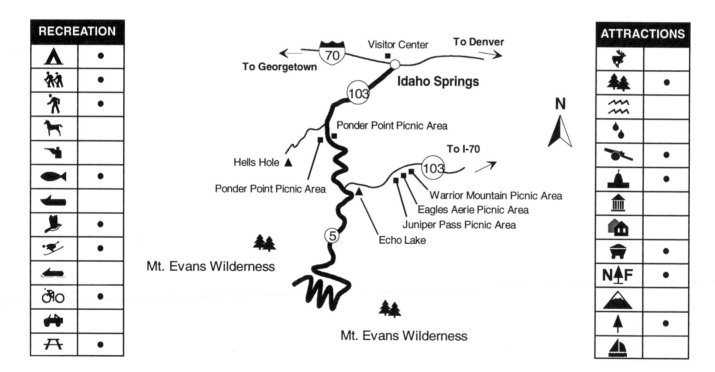

Information Sources:

Arapahoe and Roosevelt National Forest, 240 W. Prospect Rd., Fort Collins, CO 80526-2098 / 303-498-1100
Arapahoe N.F., Clear Creek Ranger District, 101 Chicago Creek, Idaho Springs, CO 80452 / 303-567-2901
Idaho Springs Chamber of Commerce, P.O. Box 97, Idaho Springs, CO 80452 / 303-567-4382

PEAK TO PEAK

- *Route Location:* Located in north-central Colorado, west of Loveland. The northern access starts in the town of Estes Park off U.S. Highway 36 and travels south to the junction of U.S. Highway 6 in the town of Blackhawk.
- *Roads Traveled:* The 55 mile route follows Colorado State Highways 7, 72, and 119. All are two-lane paved roads suitable for all vehicles. The entire 55 mile route has been designated a National Forest Scenic Byway.
- *Travel Season:* The entire route is open year-round with delays possible in the winter for snow removal.
- *Description:* Views of the snow covered Continental Divide, high mountain valleys, and the golden color of aspen trees in autumn are offered along this route as it crosses the Arapaho and Roosevelt National Forests. Central City and Blackhawk are historic mining towns established in the late 1800s. They are now historical districts with much of that

period's architecture preserved. Casino style gambling has also been legalized there. Access to the Rocky Mountain National Park lies at this routes northern terminus. Trailridge Road, within the park, crosses the Continental Divide and offers magnificent views of the Rocky Mountains. The Indian Peaks Wilderness area is accessed along this drive and offers horseback riding, hiking, and back country camping opportunities. Elk, bighorn sheep, and mule deer can occasionally be seen.

- *Other Nearby Routes:* The Mount Evans scenic drive is approximately 15 miles to the southwest and an additional 15 miles west leads to the Guanella Pass scenic drive. The Flat Tops Trail scenic drive is about 120 miles west of Estes Park.

Colorado

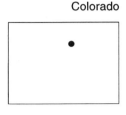

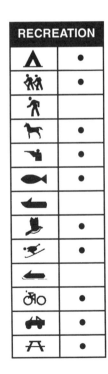

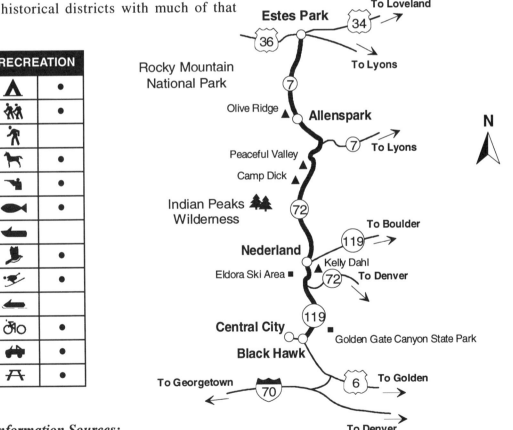

Information Sources:

Arapahoe and Roosevelt National Forest, 240 W. Prospect Rd., Fort Collins, CO 80526-2098 / 303-498-1100
Estes Park Chamber of Commerce, 500 Big Thompson Hwy., Estes Park, CO 80517 / 800-44-ESTES
Nederland Chamber of Commerce, P.O. Box 85, Nederland, CO 80466 / 800-221-0044
Gilpin County Chamber of Commerce, 440 Lawrence, Black Hawk, CO 80422 / 303-582-5077

SAN JUAN SKYWAY

- *Route Location:* Located in the southwestern corner of Colorado near the New Mexico and Utah borders. The southeastern access starts in Durango and forms a loop drive through Cortez, Placerville, Ridgway, Ouray, Silverton, and then back to Durango.
- *Roads Traveled:* The 236 mile route follows U.S. Highway 160 and 550 and Colorado State Highways 145 and 62. All of the routes travel over two-lane paved roads suitable for all vehicles. The entire 236 mile route has been designated a National Forest Scenic Byway.
- *Travel Season:* The entire route is generally open year-round although winter driving conditions can be hazardous and sections may temporarily close for snow removal.
- *Description:* This scenic drive passes through millions of acres of the San Juan and Uncompahgre National Forests, offering views of cascading waterfalls in spring, fields of wildflowers ablaze with color in summer,

mountain sides glistening a brilliant gold in autumn, and a wintery wonderland. The historic toll road, "Million Dollar Highway," is traveled across along this route, winding through the Red Mountains, along the sheer sides of the Uncompahgre Gorge, and through tunnels above waterfalls.

Several designated wilderness areas are accessed along this scenic route and offer opportunities for back country camping, hiking, backpacking, and horseback riding. Hiking trails that lead into the national forests can be found all along the route and at Trout Lake, Haviland Lake, and Molas Lake. These lakes also provide campgrounds, picnic areas, and fishing for rainbow trout. The Dolores River Valley also offers great fishing spots

continued

Colorado

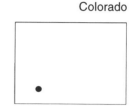

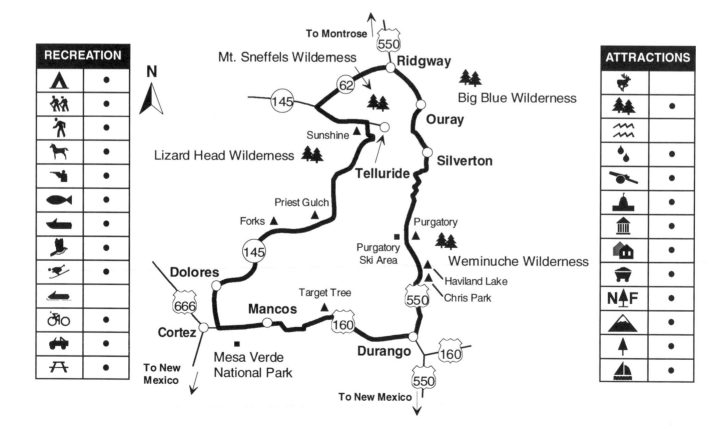

SAN JUAN SKYWAY (CONT.)

and four-wheel drive roads that lead to campgrounds and more hiking trails. Located nearby in this area is the McPhee Reservoir, which boasts fishing, boating, camping, and picnicking, and the Escalante Ruins Historical Site. The "Galloping Goose" which is part train, part bus, and part car, is found in the town of Dolores. The town of Cortez is located south of Dolores and is known as the "Archeological Center of the United States." Located in this area is the Mesa Verde National Park, showcasing the cliff dwellings once inhabited by the Anasazi Indians. Guided tours, a museum, camping, and lodging are available here. Lying to the southwest is the famous Four Corners Monument where you can stand in four states at once.

Durango was founded in 1880 and served the once booming mining industry. Many restored historic landmarks line the streets of downtown. Also found here is the historic Durango and Silverton Narrow Gauge Train. Visitors can ride the train, from May through October, for a unique sight-seeing trip through the rugged mountains. The station is located downtown at the south end of Main.

The town of Telluride is a Victorian mining town founded in the late 1800s and is now an international ski resort. Butch Cassidy's first bank robbery took place here. Located in the area are four-wheel drive roads that lead to other historic mining towns within the forest.

- *Other Nearby Routes:* The Unaweep / Tebeguache scenic drive can be accessed off this route in the town of Placerville. The Alpine Loop can also be accessed off this route just south of Ouray, which also leads to the Silver Thread Highway scenic drive.

Information Sources:

San Juan National Forest, 701 Camino del Rio, Room 301, Durango, CO 81301 / 303-247-4874
Grand Mesa - Uncompahgre and Gunnison National Forest, 2250 Highway 50, Delta, CO 81416 / 303-874-7691
Durango Area Chamber Resort Assn., 111 S. Camino del Rio, Durango, CO 81302 / 303-247-0312
Cortez Area Chamber of Commerce, 928 E. Main St., Cortez, CO 81321 / 303-565-3414
Dolores River Valley Chamber of Commerce, P.O. Box 620, Dolores, CO 81323 / 303-882-4018
Rico Chamber of Commerce, P.O. Box 176, Rico, CO 81332 / 303-967-2861
Telluride Chamber Resort Assn., P.O. Box 653, Telluride, CO 81435 / 800-525-3455
Ouray Chamber Resort Assn., 1222 N. Main St., Ouray, CO 81427 / 800-228-1876
Silverton Chamber of Commerce, 414 Greene St., Silverton, CO 81433 / 800-752-4494

SILVER THREAD HIGHWAY

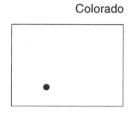

Colorado

- *Route Location:* Located in southwestern Colorado, northwest of Alamosa. The southeastern access starts in the town of South Fork off U.S. Highway 160 and travels northwest to Lake City.
- *Roads Traveled:* The 75 mile route follows Colorado State Highway 149 which is a two-lane paved road suitable for all vehicles. The 55 mile route has been designated a National Forest Scenic Byway.
- *Travel Season:* The route is open year-round except for possible temporary closure for snow removal during the winter.
- *Description:* Traveling through the Gunnison and Rio Grande National Forests, this scenic route offers spectacular views of the San Juan Mountains, cascading waterfalls, and historic mining towns. Wildlife inhabiting the wilderness along the scenic drive include bighorn sheep, elk, mule deer, coyotes, and bears. Colorado's second largest natural lake, Lake San

Cristobal, offers excellent fishing opportunities as do the waters of the Rio Grande River and Rio Grande Reservoir. Numerous hiking and backpacking trails may be accessed along the drive and throughout the national forests. Two wilderness areas offer back country camping, horseback riding, and hiking opportunities. Winter brings enthusiasts of cross-country skiing and snowmobiling to this scenic drive. Camping and picnicking opportunities are found in the many national forest campgrounds along the route.

- *Other Nearby Routes:* From the western terminus of this route, the Alpine Loop scenic drive can be accessed which also leads to the San Juan Skyway. To the east, approximately 100 miles is the Highway of Legends scenic drive.

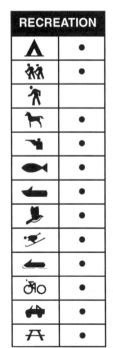

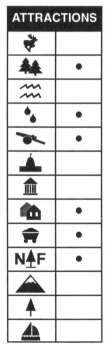

Information Sources:

Rio Grande National Forest, Creede Ranger District, 3rd and Creed Ave., Creede, CO 81130 / 719-658-2556
South Fork Chamber of Commerce, P.O. Box 116, South Fork, CO 81154 / 719-873-5512
Creede - Mineral County Chamber of Commerce, P.O. Box 580, Creede, CO 81130 / 800-327-2102
Lake City Chamber of Commerce, 306 N. Silver St., Lake City, CO 81235 / 800-569-1874

UNAWEEP / TEBEGUACHE

Colorado

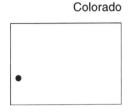

- *Route Location:* Located in western Colorado, south of Grand Junction. The northern access is located in Whitewater off U.S. Highway 50 and travels southeast to the town of Placerville.
- *Roads Traveled:* The 133 mile route follows Colorado State Highways 141 and 145 which are two-lane paved roads suitable for all vehicles. The entire 133 mile route has been designated a BLM Type I Back Country Byway.
- *Travel Season:* The entire route is open year-round with possible delays in the winter for snow removal.
- *Description:* This scenic drive circles the boundary of the Uncompahgre National Forest as it travels through 1,200 foot granite walls rising from lush green fields. Eagles can be seen in the cottonwoods along Westcreek, and Peregrine falcons nest along the cliff edges of the Dolores Canyon. The Unaweep Seep is a marshland that is home to the rare Nokomis Fritilary butterfly.

Abandoned mines and mills are also a scenic attraction found along this route. Attached to the sheer canyon walls above the Dolores River are portions of the Hanging Flume, which was built in the late 1800s to carry water from the San Miguel River to placer mines in the canyon. Many side roads from the route lead into the national forest and offer challenges to four-wheel drive and mountain bike enthusiasts. Primitive camping is allowed anywhere on BLM administered lands and developed campgrounds can be found within the national forest.

- *Other Nearby Routes:* The southern terminus of this route connects with the San Juan Skyway scenic drive which connects with the Alpine Loop scenic drive that connects with the Silver Thread Highway.

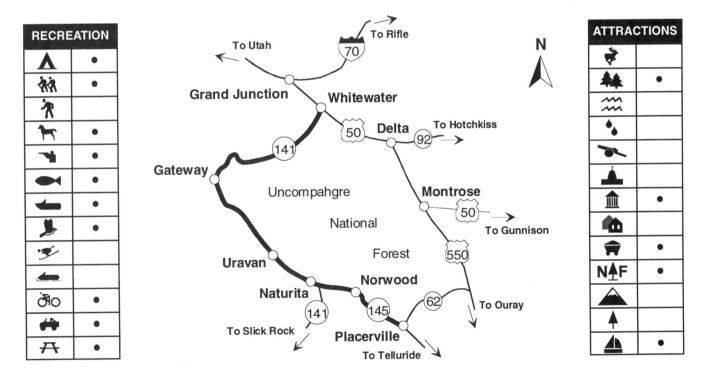

Information Sources:

BLM, Uncompahgre Basin Resource Area, 2505 S. Townsend Ave., Montrose, CO 81401 / 303-249-6047
Norwood Chamber of Commerce, P.O. Box 116, Norwood, CO 81423 / 303-327-4406
Grand Junction Area Chamber of Commerce, 360 Grand Ave., Grand Junction, CO 81501 / 303-242-3214
Telluride Chamber Resort Assn., P.O. Box 653, Telluride, CO 81435 / 800-525-3455

FLORIDA

□ *Scenic Drives*

1. Apalachee Savannahs

○ *National Park Areas*

A. Big Cypress National Preserve
B. Biscayne National Park
C. Canaveral National Seashore
D. Castillo de San Marcos National Monument
E. De Soto National Memorial
F. Dry Tortugas National Park
G. Everglades National Park
H. Fort Caroline National Memorial
I. Fort Matanzas National Monument
J. Gulf Islands National Seashore
K. Timucuan Ecological and Historic Preserve

APALACHEE SAVANNAHS

Florida

- *Route Location:* Located in northwestern Florida, west of Tallahassee. The northern access starts on the national forest boundary south of Bristol and travels south to the national forest boundary, south of Sumatra.
- *Roads Traveled:* The 32 mile route follows County Roads 12 and 379 and Florida State Highway 65 which are two-lane paved roads suitable for all vehicles. The entire 32 mile route has been designated a National Forest Scenic Byway.
- *Travel Season:* The entire route is open year-round.
- *Description:* Traveling this scenic drive through the Apalachicola National Forest offers views of gentle slopes, longleaf pine flats, savannahs, cypress bogs, and many sloughs and creeks. A growing attraction among the local sight-seers is the seasonal color offered by the spectacular array of wildflowers. Over one hundred species are interspersed among the grasses and sedges of the savannahs. The Florida National Scenic Trail can be accessed along this scenic drive and offers opportunities for hiking and backpacking through the national forest. Several creeks and the Apalachicola River, which follows alongside much of this route, provide opportunities for boating and fishing. Several recreation areas and campgrounds are located along the route and throughout the national forest. Fort Gadsden State Park is located near the southern terminus of this route and offers interpretive exhibits depicting the history of the fort and the part it played in Florida's history.
- *Other Nearby Routes:* There are no other routes within a close distance.

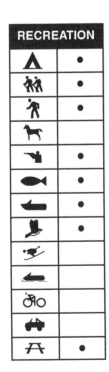

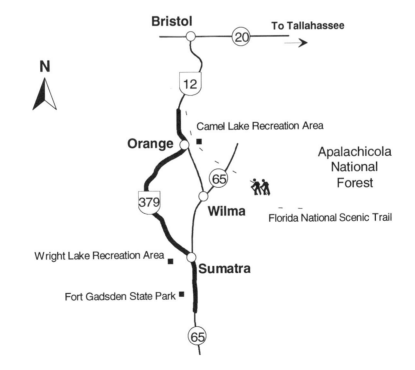

Information Sources:

National Forests In Florida, 325 John Knox Rd., Suite 200S, Tallahassee, FL 32303 / 904-681-7265
Liberty County Chamber of Commerce, P.O. Box 523, Bristol, FL 32321 / 904-643-2359
Apalachicola Bay Chamber of Commerce, 128 Market St., Apalachicola, FL 32320 / 904-653-9419

GEORGIA

1. Ridge And Valley
2. Russell-Brasstown

Road Condition Numbers: 404-656-5267
In Georgia 800-722-6617

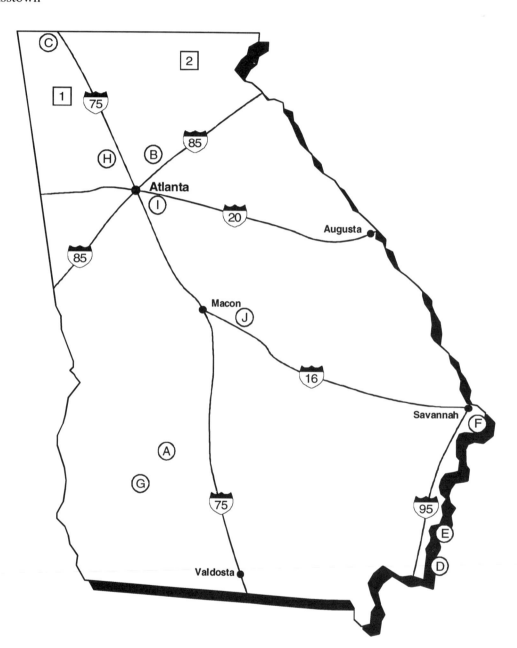

O *National Park Areas*

A. Andersonville National Historic Site
B. Chattahoochee River National Recreation Area
C. Chickamauga & Chattanooga Nat'l. Military Park
D. Cumberland Island National Seashore
E. Fort Frederica National Monument

F. Fort Pulaski National Monument
G. Jimmy Carter National Historic Site
H. Kennesaw Mountain National Battlefield Park
I. Martin Luther King, Jr. National Historic Site
J. Ocmulgee National Monument

RIDGE AND VALLEY

- *Route Location:* Located in the northwest corner of Georgia, north of Rome. The northern access is located in Villanow off U.S. Highway 136 and travels southeast, forming a loop drive back to Villanow.
- *Roads Traveled:* The 47 mile route follows U.S. Highway 27, Georgia State Highway 156 and the Armuchee, Thomas Ballenger, Floyd Springs, Johns Creek, Pocket, and Furnace Creek Roads. All of the routes are two-lane paved roads suitable for all vehicles. The entire route has been designated a National Forest Scenic Byway.
- *Travel Season:* The entire route is open year-round.
- *Description:* As you travel this scenic route across the Chattahoochee National Forest, outstanding views of long parallel ridges with broad valleys situated in between are offered. Two waterfalls are located in the 218 acre Keown Falls Scenic Area, which also has a picnic area and short hiking trail leading to the falls.

Georgia

The Johns Mountain Overlook is the site of an old fire tower that has been removed but provides spectacular views of Alabama and Tennessee. Lake Marvin and Lake Arrowhead provide warm water fishing opportunities in a beautiful wooded setting. Hunting is a popular activity found in the John's Mountain Wildlife Management Area, through which the scenic drive travels. This is also an excellent area for viewing white tailed deer and wild turkeys.

- *Other Nearby Routes:* Approximately 70 miles northeast in Tennessee is the Ocoee scenic drive. About 65 miles southwest of Rome is the Talladega scenic drive in Alabama.

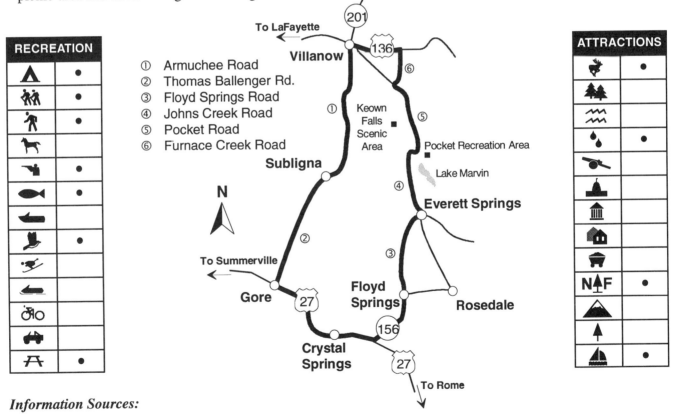

RECREATION	
▲ (camping)	●
👫 (hiking)	●
🚶 (walking)	●
🐎 (horseback)	
🦆 (hunting)	●
🐟 (fishing)	●
🛶 (boating)	
🦅	●
🚤	
🛷	
🚴 (biking)	
🚙	
⛩ (picnic)	●

① Armuchee Road
② Thomas Ballenger Rd.
③ Floyd Springs Road
④ Johns Creek Road
⑤ Pocket Road
⑥ Furnace Creek Road

To LaFayette
201
136
Villanow
⑥
Keown Falls Scenic Area
①
⑤
Pocket Recreation Area
Lake Marvin
Subligna
④
N
Everett Springs
②
③
To Summerville
Floyd Springs
Rosedale
Gore
27
Crystal Springs
156
27
To Rome

ATTRACTIONS	
🦌	●
🌲	
〰	
💧	●
🔫	
🏛	
🏛	
🏠	
🛒	
N⚡F	●
⛰	
⛺	
⛵	●

Information Sources:

Chattahoochee and Oconee National Forests, 508 Oak St. NW, Gainesville, GA 30501 / 404-536-0541
Chattooga County Chamber of Commerce, P.O. Box 217, Summerville, GA 30747 / 706-857-4033
Walker County Chamber of Commerce, P.O. Box 430, Rock Spring, GA 30739 / 706-375-7702
Dalton - Whitfield Chamber of Commerce, 524 Holiday Ave., Dalton, GA 30720 / 706-278-7373
Greater Rome Chamber of Commerce, One Riverside Pkwy., Rome, GA 30161 / 706-291-7663

RUSSELL-BRASSTOWN

Georgia

- *Route Location:* Located in the northeastern corner of Georgia, north of Gainesville. The southeastern access is located northwest of Helen off Georgia State Highway 75 and travels northwest, forming a loop drive back to Helen.
- *Roads Traveled:* The 38 mile route follows Georgia State Highways 17/75, 66, 180, and 348 which are all two-lane paved roads suitable for all vehicles. The 38 mile loop has been designated a National Forest Scenic Byway.
- *Travel Season:* The route is generally open year-round with occasional temporary closures for winter snow removal.
- *Description:* Traveling this scenic drive of forested hills, mountains, and valleys through the Chattahoochee National Forest offers some of the most spectacular and diverse scenery in Georgia. The highest point in Georgia, Brasstown Bald, is accessed along the route.

An observation tower located here offers a wonderful view of the surrounding countryside. A visitor information center, theater, and hiking trails may also be found here. Two wilderness areas also provide opportunities for hiking as well as camping and picnicking. Located on the southern end of this route are the Dukes Creek Falls and a trail that leads to the base of the falls. Several access points to the Appalachian National Scenic Trail can also be found along the route.

- *Other Nearby Routes:* Approximately 50 miles to the east in South Carolina is the Oscar Wigington scenic drive. About 40 miles northeast in Tennessee is the Ocoee scenic drive. The Forest Heritage scenic drive is about 80 miles northeast in North Carolina.

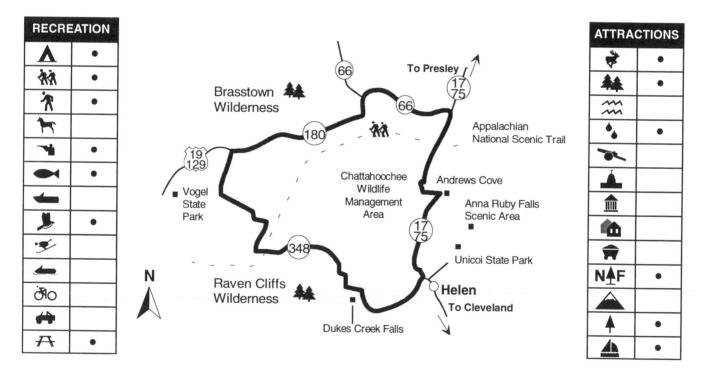

Information Sources:

Chattahoochee and Oconee National Forests, 508 Oak St. NW, Gainsville, GA 30501 / 404-536-0541
Greater Helen Area Chamber of Commerce, P.O. Box 192, Helen, GA 30545 / 706-878-3677
Blairsville / Union County Chamber of Commerce, 385 Blue Ridge Hwy., Blairsville, GA 30512 / 706-745-5789

IDAHO

☐ *Scenic Drives*

1. Bear Lake-Caribou
2. Lewis And Clark
3. Mesa Falls
4. Owyhee Uplands
5. Ponderosa Pine
6. Salmon River
7. Sawtooth
8. Teton

○ *National Park Areas*

A. City of Rocks National Reserve
B. Craters of the Moon National Monument
C. Hagerman Fossil Beds National Monument
D. Nez Perce National Historical Park

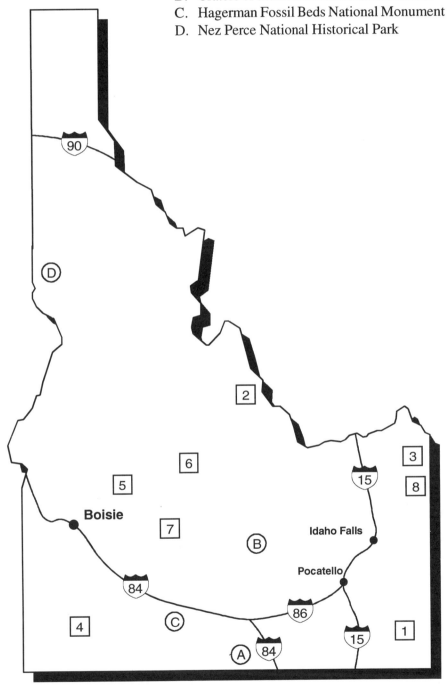

Road Condition Numbers: 208-336-6600 (winter); 800-334-8888 (summer)

BEAR LAKE-CARIBOU

Idaho

- **Route Location:** Located in southeastern Idaho, east of Pocatello. The northeastern access is located on the Wyoming border, near the town of Freedom off U.S. Highway 89 and travels southeast to the Utah border, south of Fish Haven.
- **Roads Traveled:** The 115 mile route follows Idaho State Highway 34 and U.S. Highways 30 and 89. All of the routes are two-lane paved roads suitable for all vehicles. Approximately 57 miles of this route has been designated a National Forest Scenic Byway.
- **Travel Season:** The route is generally open year-round although heavy winter snows can temporarily close the route for snow removal.
- **Description:** This route travels through farm lands, open livestock ranges, along a wildlife refuge and the shores of Bear Lake. A portion of this route also travels through the Caribou National Forest. Bear Lake is a 20 mile long, 8 mile wide lake on the Idaho-Utah

border offering numerous opportunities for camping, fishing, boating, swimming, and hiking. The Blackfoot Reservoir, located near Henry, also offers camping, fishing, swimming, and hiking. Located north of this reservoir is the Grays Lake National Wildlife Refuge which is the summer home to the largest concentration of sandhill cranes in the United States.

- **Other Nearby Routes:** Approximately 40 miles to the north is the Teton scenic drive which also leads to the Mesa Falls scenic drive. Traveling about 40 miles northeast across the Wyoming border leads to the Wyoming Centennial scenic drive. About 5 miles into Utah from the southern terminus of this route is the Logan Canyon Highway scenic drive.

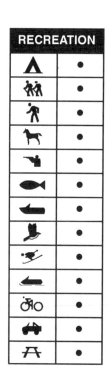

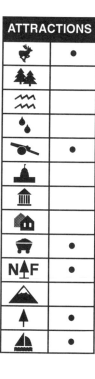

Information Sources:

Caribou National Forest, Federal Building, Suite 282, 250 S. 4th Ave., Pocatello, ID 83201 / 208-236-6700
Soda Springs Chamber of Commerce, P.O. Box 687, Soda Springs, ID 83276 / 208-547-3008
Star Valley Chamber of Commerce, P.O. Box 1097, Afton, WY 83110 / 800-426-8833

LEWIS AND CLARK

- *Route Location:* Located in east-central Idaho, southeast of Salmon near the Montana border. The southwestern access is located in the town of Tendoy off Idaho State Highway 28 and travels northeast forming a loop drive back to Tendoy.
- *Roads Traveled:* The 39 mile route follows a series of county and national forest roads that are marked with "Lewis And Clark" signage. The single-lane, gravel surfaced roads can be safely driven in an automobile. The 39 mile route has been designated a BLM Type I Back Country Byway.
- *Travel Season:* The route is normally closed from November through early June due to heavy snowpack.
- *Description:* The scenic drive travels a remote section of road through portions of the Salmon National Forest with a portion paralleling the Idaho-Montana border. This back country route offers spectacular views of the Continental Divide, the Lemhi Valley, rolling rangelands, mountain meadows, and dense forests. Lemhi Pass is the spot where Lewis and Clark crossed the Continental Divide in 1805 and unfurled the flag of the United States of America for the first time west of the Rocky Mountains. East of this spot, in Montana, is a memorial honoring the woman who served as a guide and interpreter for the expedition team. The Lewis and Clark National Historic Trail and the Continental Divide National Scenic Trail are accessed along this drive.
- *Other Nearby Routes:* About 20 miles north, the Salmon River scenic drive can be access in Salmon which also leads to the Ponderosa Pine and Sawtooth scenic drives. Approximately 25 miles east into Montana is the Big Sheep Creek scenic drive.

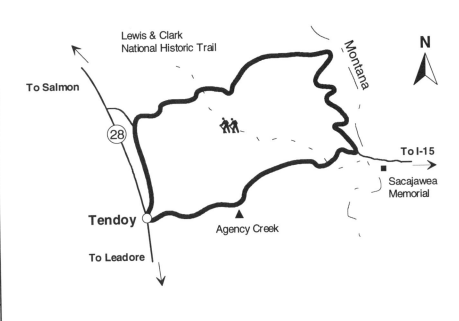

RECREATION	
⛺	•
🥾	•
🚶	
🐎	
🔫	
🐟	
🛶	
🥾	•
⛷	
🛷	•
🚵	•
🚙	
🧺	•

ATTRACTIONS	
🦌	
🌲	
〰️	
💧	
🔫	
🏛	•
🏛	
🏚	
⛏	
N↕F	
⛰	
↑	
⛵	

Information Sources:

BLM, Salmon District Office, Highway 93 South, Salmon, ID 83467 / 208-756-5400
Salmon Valley Chamber of Commerce, 200 Main St., #1, Salmon, ID 83467 / 208-756-2100

MESA FALLS

Idaho

- **Route Location:** Located in eastern Idaho, northeast of Idaho Falls near the Wyoming and Montana borders. The southern access is located in Ashton off U.S. Highway 20 and travels an open loop north back to the junction of highway 20, near Harriman State Park.
- **Roads Traveled:** The 28 mile route follows Idaho State Highway 47 and Forest Service Road 294. The route travels over narrow two-lane paved roads suitable for all vehicles, although portions of the road can be rough. The entire route has been designated a National Forest Scenic Byway.
- **Travel Season:** The entire route is generally open from mid-May through October, then portions are closed by heavy winter snows.
- **Description:** The scenic drive travels on the Targhee National Forest, winding through scenic farm lands before entering the Three Rivers Canyon and climbing to a mixed forest of lodgepole pine, Douglas-fir, and aspen. Views are offered of the west slope of the Tetons, the Mesa Falls, and the Henry's Fork of the Snake River. The Mesa Falls are the last undisturbed major waterfalls of the Columbia River system, with the Upper Mesa Falls plummeting 100 feet and the lower falls dropping 70 feet. The Three Rivers area is a popular spot for camping, fishing, inner tubing, and hiking. The rails of the Yellowstone Railway, which once operated as a passenger railroad through Idaho to Yellowstone National Park, have been removed and it is now used for hiking, bicycling, cross-country skiing, and snowmobiling.
- **Other Nearby Routes:** The Teton scenic drive is just south of Ashton.

RECREATION	
⛺	●
🚶‍♀️	●
🚶	●
🐎	
🔫	
🐟	●
🛶	●
⛷️	●
🎿	●
🛷	●
🚲	●
🚗	
🪑	●

ATTRACTIONS	
🦌	●
🌲	
〰️	
💧	●
💣	
🏛️	
🏛️	
🏠	
🛖	
N↑F	●
⛰️	●
⬆️	●
⛵	●

Information Sources:

Targhee National Forest, Ashton Ranger District, 30 S. Yellowstone Hwy., Ashton, ID 83420 / 208-652-7442
South Fremont Chamber of Commerce, 110 W. Mains St., Saint Anthony, ID 83445 / 208-624-3775
Ashton Chamber of Commerce, P.O. Box 689, Ashton, ID 83420 / 208-652-3987
West Yellowstone Chamber of Commerce, 100 Yellowstone Ave., West Yellowstone, MT 59758 / 406-646-7701

OWYHEE UPLANDS

Idaho

- *Route Location:* Located in the southwestern corner of Idaho, southwest of Mountain Home. The northeastern access is located in Grand View off Idaho State Highway 78 and travels southwest, forming an open loop drive that ends on U.S. Highway 95 near Jordan Valley, Oregon.
- *Roads Traveled:* The 101 mile route follows the Deep Creek-Mud Flat Road which averages 1½ lanes in width of gravel surfaced road with frequent opportunities for passing. There are short grades of 12% at plateau breaks, but the route can be driven safely in an automobile. The 101 mile route has been designated a BLM Type I Back Country Byway.
- *Travel Season:* The route is generally open from June through September after which heavy winter snows close the route.
- *Description:* The scenic drive travels across a remote area in Idaho with a small portion crossing into Or-

egon. This route travels through juniper and mountain mahogany woodlands, sheer-walled canyons, and mountain valleys. Camping is available anywhere on BLM administered land as well as the developed recreation areas found at either end of the route. C.J. Strike Reservoir is located near the drive's eastern terminus and offers boating, fishing, camping, picnicking, and hiking opportunities. Additional developed camping opportunities exist at the Bruneau State Park to the east of Bruneau.

- *Other Nearby Routes:* Approximately 20 miles north of Jordan Valley is the Leslie Gulch-Succor Creek scenic drive in Oregon. Less than 75 miles north to Boise is the Ponderosa Pine scenic drive. About 100 miles east to Shoshone is the Sawtooth scenic drive.

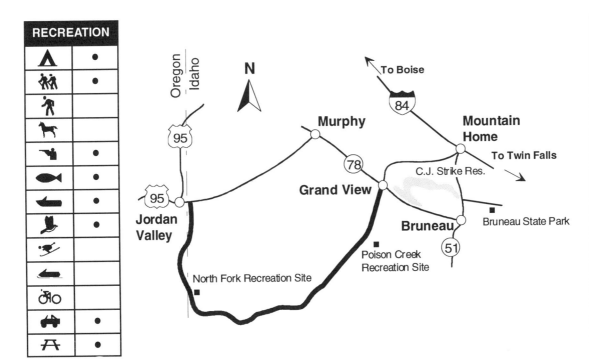

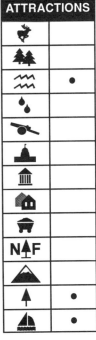

Information Sources:

BLM, Boise District Office, 3948 Development Ave., Boise, ID 83705 / 208-384-3300
Mountain Home Chamber of Commerce, 110 E. 2nd N., Mountain Home, ID 83647 / 208-587-4334
Caldwell Chamber of Commerce, 300 Frontage Rd., Caldwell, ID 83606 / 208-459-7493
Homedale Chamber of Commerce, P.O. Box 845, Homedale, ID 83628 / 208-337-4611

PONDEROSA PINE

Idaho

- *Route Location:* Located in southwestern Idaho, east of Boise. The southwestern access is located on Idaho State Highway 21 off Interstate 84 and travels northeast to the junction of Idaho State Highway 75, in the town of Stanley.
- *Roads Traveled:* The 130 mile route follows Idaho State Highway 21 which is a two-lane paved road suitable for all vehicles. Ninety-three miles from Idaho City to Stanley has been designated a National Forest Scenic Byway.
- *Travel Season:* The entire route is generally open year-round although sections may temporarily close for snow removal.
- *Description:* The scenic byway travels through the Boise and Sawtooth National Forests, along portions of the Boise River, South Fork of the Payette River, and several smaller creeks. The route passes through heavily timbered country and high mountain valleys with numerous views of the spectacular Sawtooth Mountains. Two wilderness areas offer many opportunities for horseback riding, back country camping, hiking, and backpacking. The 200,000 acre Sawtooth Wilderness is to the south of the scenic drive and the massive 2.3 million acre Frank Church-River of No Return Wilderness is to the north. Near the end of this byway is the Sawtooth National Recreation Area.
- *Other Nearby Routes:* Both the Salmon River and Sawtooth scenic drives can be accessed at the eastern terminus of this route in Stanley. The Owyhee Uplands scenic drive is approximately 70 miles south of Boise. The Leslie Gulch-Succor Creek scenic drive is about 50 miles to the west of Boise in Oregon.

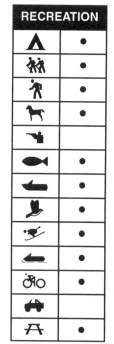

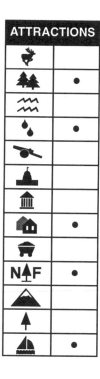

Information Sources:

Sawtooth National Forest, 2647 Kimberly Rd. E, Twin Falls, ID 83301-7976 / 208-737-3200
Boise Area Chamber of Commerce, 300 N. 6th St., Boise, ID 83701 / 208-344-5515
Stanley - Sawtooth Chamber of Commerce, P.O. Box 8, Stanley, ID 83278 / 208-774-3411

SALMON RIVER

- *Route Location:* Located in central Idaho, northeast of Boise. The southwestern access is located in the town of Stanley and travels northeast to the Idaho-Montana border.
- *Roads Traveled:* The 161 mile route follows Idaho State Highway 75 and U.S. Highway 93 which are two-lane paved roads suitable for all vehicles. Eight-three miles of this route has been designated a National Forest Scenic Byway.
- *Travel Season:* The entire route is open year-round although caution should be used during the winter months.
- *Description:* This scenic route passes through the Sawtooth, Challis, and Salmon National Forests as it travels alongside portions of the Salmon River, past the White Cloud Mountains, through forested and grassy canyons and valleys. The Sawtooth National Recreation Area is found near the southern end of this route and offers numerous opportunities for camping, picnicking, fishing, hiking, and rafting. A side trip from the scenic drive known as the Custer Motorway Adventure Road takes you to historic mining districts and ghost towns. A high-clearance vehicle is recommended to drive this 43 mile side trip. Winter sport enthusiasts enjoy downhill and cross-country skiing at the Lost Trail Ski Area, located at the northern terminus of this route.
- *Other Nearby Routes:* Both the Ponderosa Pine and Sawtooth scenic drives are accessed at the southern terminus of this route in Stanley. The Lewis And Clark scenic drive is approximately 20 miles south of Salmon. East about 70 miles into Montana is the Pioneer Mountains scenic drive.

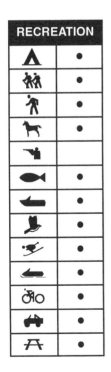

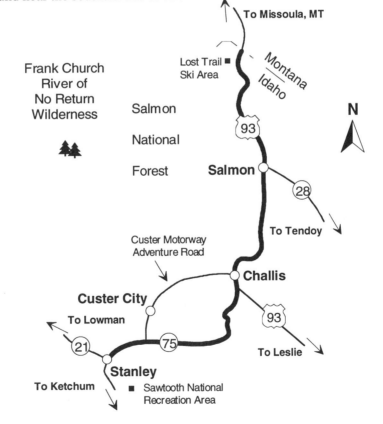

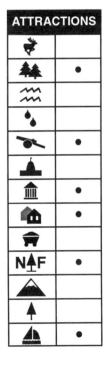

Information Sources:

Sawtooth National Forest, 2647 Kimberly Rd. E, Twin Falls, ID 83301-7976 / 208-737-3200
Stanley - Sawtooth Chamber of Commerce, P.O. Box 8, Stanley, ID 83278 / 208-774-3411
Sun Valley - Ketchum Chamber of Commerce, P.O. Box 2420, Sun Valley, ID 83353 / 800-634-3347
Hailey Chamber of Commerce, P.O. Box 100, Hailey, ID 83333 / 208-788-2700
Shoshone Chamber of Commerce, P.O. Box 575, Shoshone, ID 83352 / 208-886-2979

SAWTOOTH

Idaho

- **Route Location:** Located in south-central Idaho, north of Twin Falls. The southern access is located in Shoshone off U.S. Highway 93 and travels north to the town of Stanley.
- **Roads Traveled:** The 116 mile route follows Idaho State Highway 75 which is a two-lane paved road suitable for all vehicles. Sixty-one miles of this route from Ketchum to Stanley has been designated a National Forest Scenic Byway.
- **Travel Season:** The entire route is open year-round although caution should be used during the winter months.
- **Description:** The route travels across the Sawtooth National Forest, follows the Wood River through sagebrush covered plains, tree-line corridors, and a mountainous landscape. Wildlife seen along this scenic route includes deer, elk, black bear, bighorn sheep, and mountain goats. Located just off the drive north of Shoshone are the Shoshone Ice Caves where you will find guided tours explaining the geologic and volcanic history of the year-round ice. Magic Reservoir is a popular spot for boating water-skiing, fishing, and windsurfing. At the northern end of the drive is the Sawtooth National Recreation Area which offers many opportunities for boating, fishing, camping, picnicking, rafting, and hiking. Access to the Sawtooth Wilderness area is also provided for along the route.
- **Other Nearby Routes:** Both the Ponderosa Pine and Salmon River scenic drives are accessed at the northern terminus of this route in Stanley. Approximately 90 miles to the west of Shoshone is the Owyhee Uplands scenic drive.

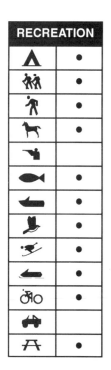

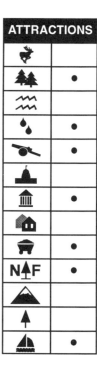

Information Sources:

Sawtooth National Forest, 2647 Kimberly Rd. E, Twin Falls, ID 83301-7976 / 208-737-3200
Sun Valley-Ketchum Chamber of Commerce, P.O. Box 2420, Sun Valley, ID 83353 / 800-634-3347
Hailey Chamber of Commerce, P.O. Box 100, Hailey, ID 83333 / 208-788-2700
Shoshone Chamber of Commerce, P.O. Box 575, Shoshone, ID 83352 / 208-886-2979

TETON

Idaho

- *Route Location:* Located in eastern Idaho, east of Idaho Falls near the Wyoming-Idaho border. The southern access is located in Swan Valley off U.S. Highway 26 and travels north to the junction of U.S. Highway 20 in the town of Ashton.
- *Roads Traveled:* The 68 mile route follows Idaho State Highways 31, 33, and 32 all of which are two-lane paved roads suitable for all vehicles. Twenty miles of this route has been designated a National Forest Scenic Byway.
- *Travel Season:* The entire route is open year-round although winter driving conditions may be hazardous.
- *Description:* Portions of this route travels alongside the Snake River and through the Targhee National Forest. The route travels through rural countryside, valleys, and mountains. Coyotes, moose, black bears, elk, and mule deer are just some of the wildlife inhabiting the wilderness surrounding the scenic drive. Primitive camping throughout the national forest is permitted as well as in the developed campground located along State Highway 31. Nearby, the Palisades Reservoir, located south of Swan Valley, offers opportunities for camping, picnicking, and fishing. Winter brings cross-country skiing, downhill skiing, and snowmobiling.
- *Other Nearby Routes:* The Mesa Falls scenic drive is also located in Ashton. Approximately 40 miles south of Swan Valley is the Bear Lake-Caribou scenic drive. About 25 miles east of Victor is the Wyoming Centennial scenic drive in Wyoming.

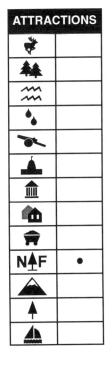

Information Sources:

Targhee National Forest, Palisades Ranger District, 3659 E. Ririe Hwy., Idaho Falls, ID 83401 / 208-624-3151
Greater Idaho Falls Chamber of Commerce, 505 Lindsay Blvd., Idaho Falls, ID 83405 / 208-523-1010
Driggs Chamber of Commerce, P.O. Box 250, Driggs, ID 83422 / 208-354-2500
South Fremont Chamber of Commerce, 110 W. Main St., Saint Anthony, ID 83445 / 208-624-3775
Ashton Chamber of Commerce, P.O. Box 689, Ashton, ID 83420 / 208-652-3987

ILLINOIS

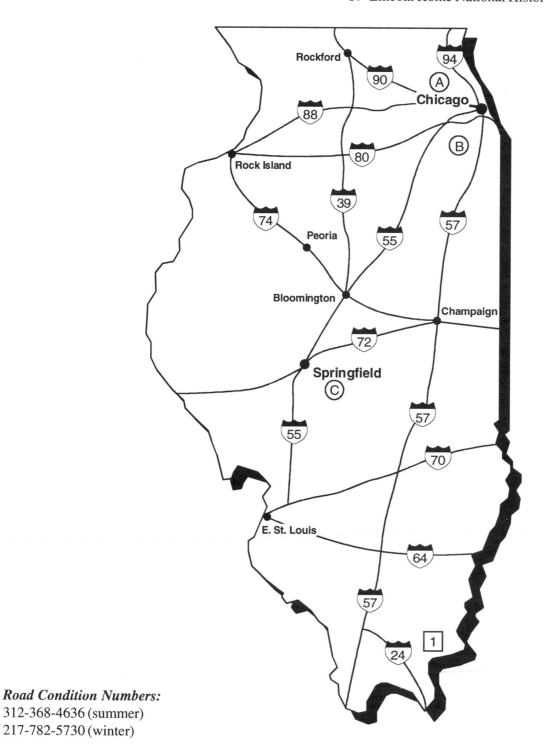

Road Condition Numbers:
312-368-4636 (summer)
217-782-5730 (winter)

SHAWNEE HILLS ON THE OHIO

Illinois

- *Route Location:* Located in the southeastern corner of Illinois, east of Carbondale. The northern access is located in Mitchellsville off Illinois State Highway 145 and travels south to the Smithland Lock & Dam, north of New Liberty and the Kentucky state line.
- *Roads Traveled:* The 70 mile route follows Illinois State Highways 34, 1, 146, and County Road 1. All of the routes are two-lane paved roads suitable for all vehicles. The entire route has been designated a National Forest Scenic Byway.
- *Travel Season:* The route is open year-round although caution should be exercised during the winter months.
- *Description:* The scenic drive travels through the heart of the Shawnee National Forest, winding through gently rolling hills and ridgetops before descending to follow the Ohio River. The Garden of the Gods Recreation Area and Wilderness features unusual rock formations and opportunities for camping, picnicking, hiking, and horseback riding. Pounds Hollow Recreational Area features a 25 acre lake set in a beautiful valley and is stocked with largemouth bass, channel catfish and sunfish. Hiking, camping, swimming, picnicking, and boating are also found in this recreation area. Access to the Rim Rock National Recreation Trail is located near this area. The River to River Trail, spanning southern Illinois from the Ohio River to the Mississippi is a popular horseback and backpacking trail accessed within this national forest. Cave In Rock State Park, located at the end of Illinois State Highway 1, highlights a cave river pirates once used to ambush river travelers.
- *Other Nearby Routes:* No other routes are located within a close distance.

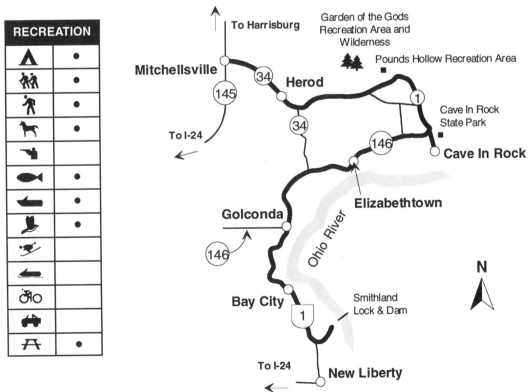

Information Sources:

Shawnee National Forest, 901 S. Commercial St., Harrisburg, IL 62946 / 618-253-7114
Harrisburg Chamber of Commerce, 325 E. Poplar, Harrisburg, IL 62946 / 618-252-4192
Paducah Area Chamber of Commerce, 417 S. 4th St., Paducah, KY 42002 / 502-443-1746

KENTUCKY

☐ *Scenic Drives*

1. Zilpo Road

○ *National Park Areas*

A. Abraham Lincoln Birthplace National Historic Site
B. Big South Fork National River and Recreation Area
C. Cumberland Gap National Historical Park
D. Mammoth Cave National Park

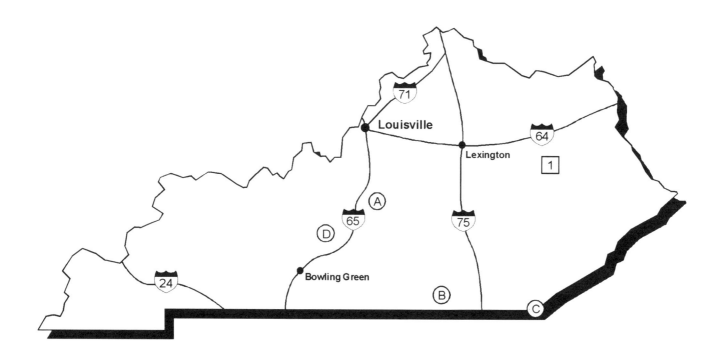

Road Condition Numbers: 502-564-4790 (construction); 502-564-4556 (conditions)

ZILPO ROAD

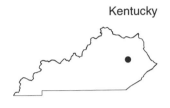

Kentucky

- *Route Location:* Located in eastern Kentucky, east of Lexington. The southwestern access is located off Forest Service Road 129, near the Clear Creek Campground and travels east to the Zilpo Recreation Area on Cave Run Lake.
- *Roads Traveled:* The 9 mile route follows Forest Service Road 918 which is a two-lane paved road suitable for all vehicles. The road dead ends in the Zilpo Recreation Area so travelers will need to retrace the route back to Kentucky State Highway 211. The route has been designated a National Forest Scenic Byway.
- *Travel Season:* The entire route is open year-round.
- *Description:* This scenic drive winds through the forested hills and ridgetops of the Pioneer Weapons Wildlife Management Area of the Daniel Boone National Forest. The Pioneer Weapons Wildlife Management Area offers 7,480 acres of wilderness inhabited by white-tailed deer and wild turkey. Several hiking trails can be accessed in this area including the Sheltowee Trace National Recreation Trail. This wildlife area is also open to hunting by pioneer-type weapons such as the bow and arrow, crossbow, and black powder firearms. The Zilpo Recreation Area is a 355 acre wooded area on the western shores of Cave Run Lake and offers campsites, a swimming beach, boat ramp, picnic areas, and hiking trails. The Red River Gorge Geological Area, located south of the scenic route, offers a unique landscape containing more than 50 major natural arches. The Clifty Wilderness area is adjacent to the geological area and offers trails for hiking and backpacking.
- *Other Nearby Routes:* There are no other routes located within a close distance of this drive.

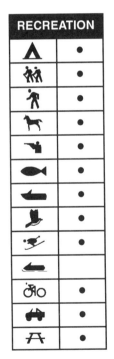

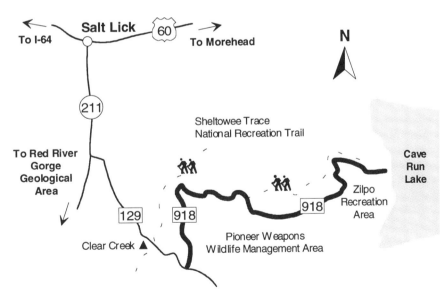

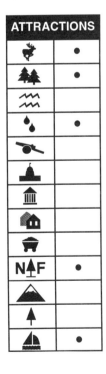

Information Sources:

Daniel Boone National Forest, 100 Vaught Rd., Winchester, KY 40391 / 606-745-3100
Daniel Boone National Forest, Morehead Ranger District, 2375 KY 801 S., Morehead, KY 40351 / 606-784-6428
Morehead - Rowan County Chamber of Commerce, 168 E. Main St., Morehead, KY 40351 / 606-784-6221

LOUISIANA

☐ *Scenic Drives*

1. Longleaf Trail

○ *National Park Areas*

A. Jean Lafitte National Historical Park and Preserve
B. Poverty Point National Monument

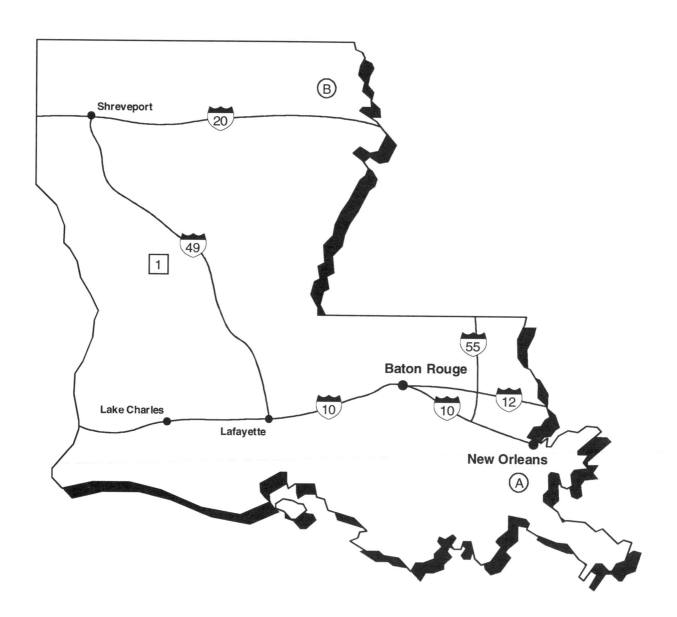

Road Condition Number: 504-379-1541

LONGLEAF TRAIL

Louisiana

- *Route Location:* Located in west-central Louisiana, northwest of Alexandria. The western access is located off Louisiana State Highway 117, south of Bellwood and travels east to the junction of Louisiana State Highway 119, south of Derry.
- *Roads Traveled:* the 17 mile route follows Forest Service Road 59 which is a two-lane paved road suitable for all vehicles. The entire 17 mile route has been designated a National Forest Scenic Byway.
- *Travel Season:* The route is open year-round.
- *Description:* This scenic drive crosses the Kisatchie Bayou and runs through the National Red Dirt Wildlife Management Preserve in the Kisatchie National Forest. This route has long been recognized as one of the most scenic drives in Louisiana as the area is exceptionally rugged for Louisiana. The Kisatchie Hills Wilderness is located along the route and is known locally as the "Little Grand Canyon" due to its steep slopes, rock outcrops, and mesas. A picnic area is located at the Longleaf Vista and is surrounding on three sides by the wilderness area. A nature trail and small visitor center is also located at the picnic area. About one mile west of this area lies access to the Caroline Dormon Hiking and Horse Trail. Wildlife inhabiting the region includes white-tailed deer, foxes, squirrels, raccoons, coyotes, and the occasional roadrunner. Several primitive campgrounds are located near the byway as are two developed campgrounds, the Dogwood and Kisatchie Bayou.
- *Other Nearby Routes:* There are no other routes within a close distance.

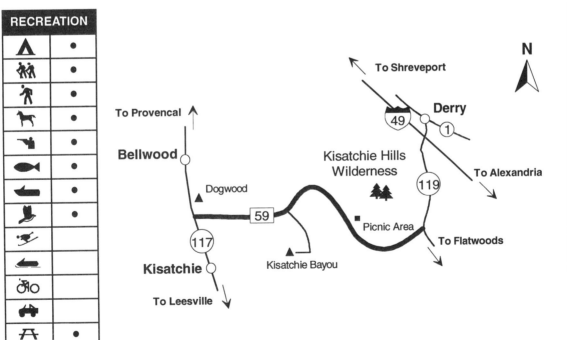

Information Sources:

Kisatchie National Forest, 2500 Shreveport Highway, Pineville, LA 71360 / 318-473-7160
Central Louisiana Chamber of Commerce, 802 Third St., Alexandria, LA 71309 / 318-442-6671
Leesville / Vernon Parish Chamber of Commerce, Hwy. 171 N., Leesville, LA 71496 / 318-238-0349
Sabine Parish Chamber of Commerce, 920 Fisher Rd., Many, LA 71449 / 318-256-3523
Natchitoches Area Chamber of Commerce, 781 Front St., Natchitoches, LA 71457 / 318-352-4411

MICHIGAN

□ *Scenic Drives*

1. Black River
2. River Road
3. Whitefish Bay

○ *National Park Areas*

A. Father Marquette National Memorial And Museum
B. Isle Royale National Park
C. Keweenaw National Historical Park
D. Pictured Rocks National Lakeshore
E. Sleeping Bear Dunes National Lakeshore

BLACK RIVER

Michigan

- *Route Location:* Located in Michigan's Upper Peninsula in the western corner, west of Wakefield. The southern access is located on Powderhorn Road off U.S. Highway 2 and travels north to the end of the road near Lake Superior.
- *Roads Traveled:* The 11 mile route follows County Road 513 which is a two-lane paved road suitable for all vehicles. It will be necessary for travelers to retrace the route back to U.S. Highway 2. The entire 11 mile route has been designated a National Forest Scenic Byway.
- *Travel Season:* The entire route is open year-round although caution should be exercised during the winter months.
- *Description:* The scenic drive travels across the Ottawa National Forest following the Black River to its end on the shore of Lake Superior. Five waterfalls located near the route's northern terminus are perhaps the main attraction to this scenic drive. Paved parking lots are available in the area of each waterfall and a trail provides access to each. The difficulty of each trail varies from easy to strenuous as there may be a series of steps and steep grades. Located at the northern end of this scenic route is the Black River Harbor, one of only two harbors within the national forest system. The harbor is a popular recreation area throughout the year, providing camping, picnicking, swimming, and access to Lake Superior.
- *Other Nearby Routes:* Approximately 45 miles southwest is the Great Divide Highway scenic drive in Wisconsin. About 75 miles southeast, also in Wisconsin, is the Heritage Drive scenic route.

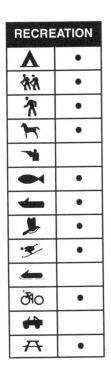

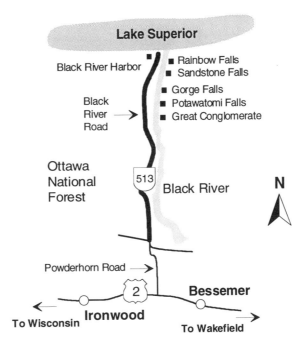

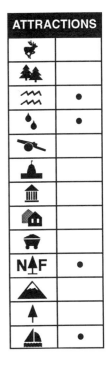

Information Sources:

Ottawa National Forest, Bessemer Ranger District, 500 North Moore St., Bessemer, MI 49911 / 906-667-0261
Bessemer Chamber of Commerce, Bessemer, MI 49911 / 906-667-0719
Ironwood Area Chamber of Commerce, 100 E. Aurora St., Ironwood, MI 49938 / 906-932-1122

RIVER ROAD

- *Route Location:* Located in northeastern Michigan, south of Alpena near Lake Huron. The eastern access is located 3 miles west of Oscoda off U.S. Highway 23 and travels west to the junction of Rollway Road about 6 miles north of Hale.
- *Roads Traveled:* The 22 mile route follows the River Road and Michigan State Highway 65 which are two-lane paved roads suitable for all vehicles. The entire 22 mile route has been designated a National Forest Scenic Byway.
- *Travel Season:* The entire route is open year-round although winter driving conditions can be hazardous.
- *Description:* This scenic drive travels through the Huron National Forest and follows a portion of an early Indian trail along the Au Sable River. There are four viewing platforms resting on the high banks above the river that offer panoramic views of the river and surrounding forest. Four dams along the river have cre-

Michigan

ated thousands of acres of tree-lined lakes that are good for canoeing and fishing for bass, walleye, northern pike, and tiger muskies. Lumbermens' Monument is a nine foot bronze statue erected in 1932 as a dedication to Michigan's logging era. A visitor center here provides information on the surrounding area and offers guided walks around the grounds. Camping and picnicking are offered in the Monument, Rollways, and Old Orchard campgrounds. Other recreational opportunities found along the scenic drive include hiking and horseback riding.

- *Other Nearby Routes:* The Whitefish Bay scenic drive is approximately 200 miles north on Interstate 75 in Michigan's Upper Peninsula.

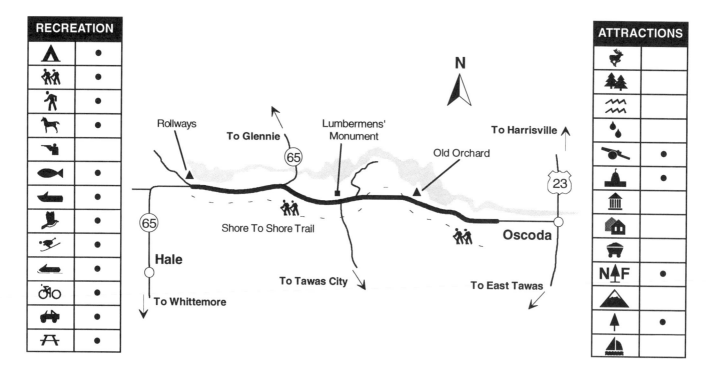

Information Sources:

Huron-Manistee National Forests, Tawas Ranger District, 326 Newman St., East Tawas, MI 48730 / 517-362-4477
Oscoda - Au Sable Chamber of Commerce, 4440 N. U.S. 23, Oscoda, MI 48750 / 800-235-4625
Hale Area Chamber of Commerce, P.O. Box 96, Hale, MI 48739 / 517-728-2603

WHITEFISH BAY

- **Route Location:** Located in Michigan's Upper Peninsula on the east, west of Sault Ste. Marie. The eastern access is located just north of Bay Mills and travels west to the junction of Michigan State Highway 123 south of Paradise.
- **Roads Traveled:** The 27 mile route follows Forest Service Roads 3150 and 42 which are two-lane paved roads suitable for all vehicles. The route has been designated a National Forest Scenic Byway.
- **Travel Season:** The entire route is open year-round although winter driving conditions may be hazardous.
- **Description:** The route travels across the Hiawatha National Forest, paralleling the southern shore of Lake Superior. Miles of undisturbed beaches, hardwood forests, and sand dunes are views offered to the traveler of this scenic drive. The panoramic views of Lake Superior and Canada at the Spectacle Lake Overlook are impressive and should not be missed. Part of the Point Iroquois lighthouse, listed on the National Register of Historic Places, has been renovated to include a museum and bookstore. Visitors are welcome to climb to the top of the 65 foot lighthouse for a panoramic view of Lake Superior. Hiking, swimming, boating, and fishing are popular activities offered at the Monocle Lake Campground, one of several campgrounds located along the route. Hiking is also offered on a portion of the North Country National Scenic Trail that crisscrosses the scenic drive.
- **Other Nearby Routes:** The next closest route is the River Road scenic drive located approximately 200 miles southeast.

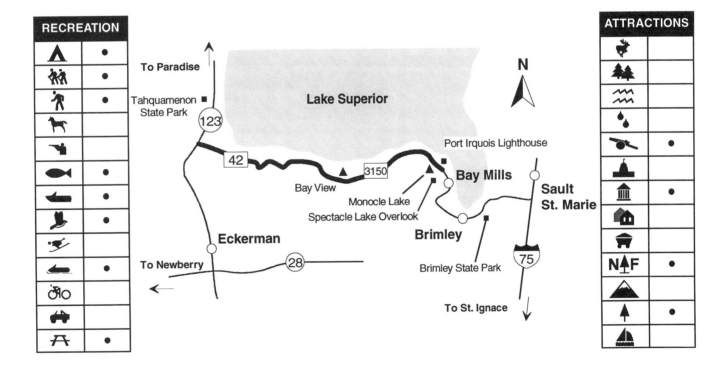

Information Sources:

Hiawatha National Forest, 2727 N. Lincoln Rd., Escanaba, MI 49829 / 906-786-4062
Sault Area Chamber of Commerce, 2581 I-75 business Spur, Sault Sainte Marie, MI 49783 / 800-647-2858
Newberry Area Chamber of Commerce, M-28 and M-123, Newberry, MI 49868 / 800-831-7292
St. Ignace Area Chamber of Commerce, 11 S. State St., Saint Ignace, MI 49781 / 800-338-6660

MINNESOTA

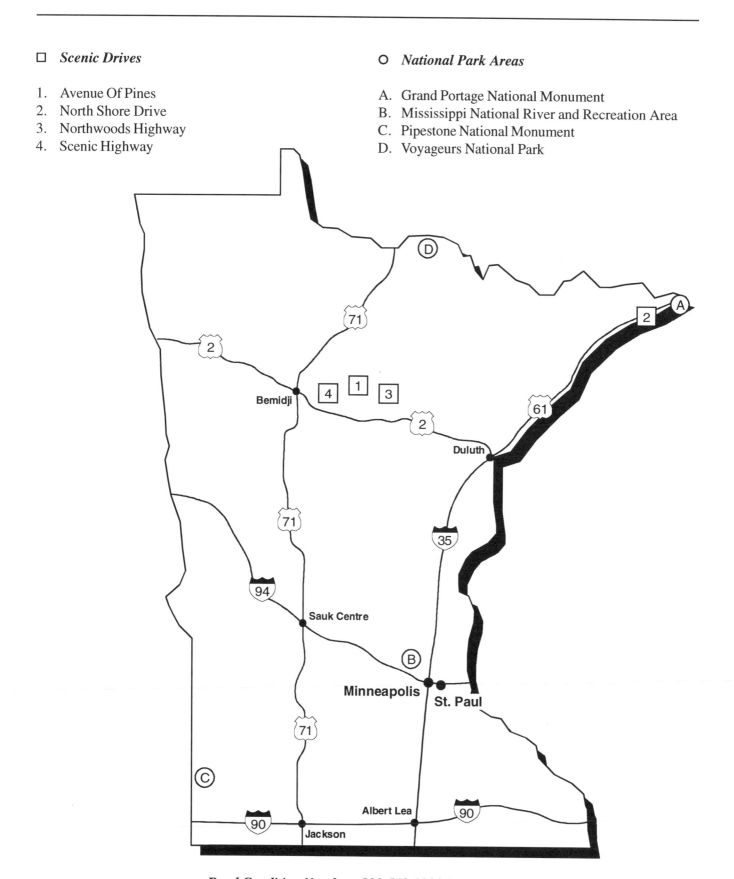

□ *Scenic Drives*

1. Avenue Of Pines
2. North Shore Drive
3. Northwoods Highway
4. Scenic Highway

O *National Park Areas*

A. Grand Portage National Monument
B. Mississippi National River and Recreation Area
C. Pipestone National Monument
D. Voyageurs National Park

Road Condition Number: 800-542-0220 (construction, summer; conditions, winter)

AVENUE OF PINES

- *Route Location:* Located in north-central Minnesota, northwest of Grand Rapids. The southern access is located in Deer River off U.S. Highway 2 and travels northwest to the junction of U.S. Highway 71 in the town of Northome.
- *Roads Traveled:* The 46 mile route follows Minnesota State Highway 46 which is a two-lane paved road suitable for all vehicles. Thirty-nine miles of this route has been designated a National Forest Scenic Byway.
- *Travel Season:* The entire route is open year-round with possible delays for winter snow removal.
- *Description:* The scenic drive winds through alleys of red pine, around many lakes and marshes as it crosses the Leech Lake Indian Reservation and the Chippewa National Forest. An excellent viewpoint for spotting bald eagles is located at the Lake Winnibigoshish Dam. Other wildlife inhabiting the national forest include osprey, black bears, gray wolves, white-tailed deer, and raccoons. A visitor information center is located near the middle of this route and offers information on the national forest. Nearby is the Cut Foot Sioux Ranger Station which was built in 1904 and was the first ranger station in the East. The Cut Foot Sioux National Recreation Trail is a popular hiking, backpacking, and cross-country skiing trail and may be accessed along the drive. Turtle Mound was built in the early 1800s and is a Sioux and Ojibwe Indian religious location and is listed as a National Historic Site.
- *Other Nearby Routes:* Approximately 15 miles to the west is the Scenic Highway scenic drive and about 30 miles to the east is the Northwoods scenic route.

Minnesota

RECREATION	
⛺	•
🧑‍🤝‍🧑	•
🚶	•
🐎	•
🛩	
🐟	•
🛶	•
🤿	•
🛷	•
🚙	•
🚴	•
🚗	
🪑	•

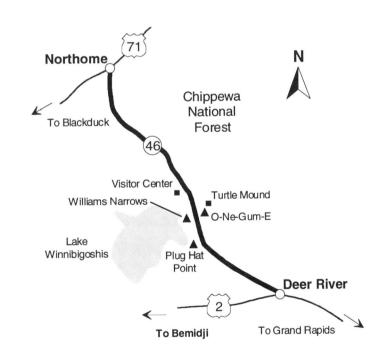

ATTRACTIONS	
🦌	
🌲	
〰	
💧	
🔭	•
⚓	
🏛	
🏠	
🛒	
NF	•
🏔	
🗼	
⛴	

Information Sources:

Chippewa National Forest, Route 3, Box 244, Cass Lake, MN 56633 / 218-335-8600
Bemidji Area Chamber of Commerce, 300 Bemidji Ave., Bemidji, MN 56601 / 218-751-3541
Grand Rapids Area Chamber of Commerce, One N.W. Third St., Grand Rapids, MN 55744 / 218-326-6619

NORTH SHORE DRIVE

Minnesota

- *Route Location:* Located in northeastern Minnesota, northeast of Duluth. The southwestern access is located in Schroeder and travels northeast to the national forest boundary, east of Red Cliff.
- *Roads Traveled:* The 58 mile route follows U.S. Highway 61 which is a two-lane paved road suitable for all vehicles. The 58 mile route has been designated a National Forest Scenic Byway.
- *Travel Season:* The entire route is open year-round although caution should be exercised during the winter months.
- *Description:* Traveling across the Superior National Forest, travelers of this scenic drive can expect to see rugged rock outcrops, hardwood forests, meandering streams, and the rugged shoreline of Lake Superior. Deer, timber wolves, moose, eagles, and falcons are among some of the wildlife inhabiting this region of Minnesota. Numerous opportunities exist along the route for camping, picnicking, hiking, backpacking, bicycling, and fishing. The winter months bring snowmobile and cross-country skiing enthusiasts to this area. Opportunities for canoeing in crystal lakes of the back country is provided by the Boundary Waters Canoe Area Wilderness, located north of the scenic drive. Many forest service roads lead to the boundary of this wilderness where access to canoeing and hiking trails may be found. The Grand Portage National Monument is located east of this route in Grand Portage. It is also here where a ferry takes you to the Isle Royale National Park.
- *Other Nearby Routes:* No other routes are located within a close distance of this route.

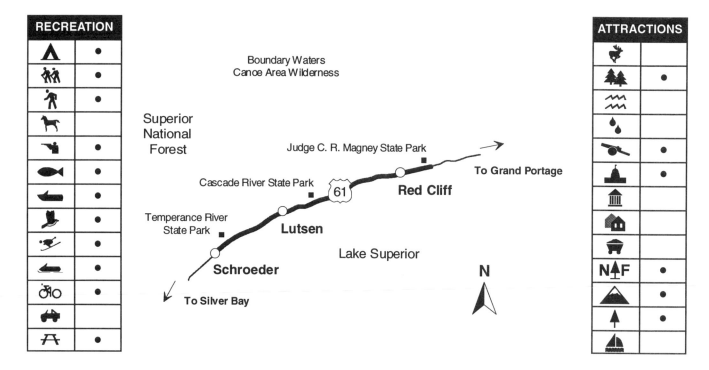

Information Sources:

Superior National Forest, 515 W. First St., Duluth, MN 55801 / 218-720-5324
Superior National Forest, Gunflint Ranger District, P.O. Box 308, Grand Marais, MN 55604 / 218-387-1750
Silver Bay Area Chamber of Commerce, P.O. Box 26, Silver Bay, MN 55614 / 218-226-4870

NORTHWOODS HIGHWAY

- *Route Location:* Located in north-central Minnesota, north of Grand Rapids. The southern access is located on the national forest boundary off U.S. Highway 2 and travels north to the national forest boundary, south of Bigfork.
- *Roads Traveled:* The 22 mile route follows Minnesota State Highway 38 which is a two-lane paved road suitable for all vehicles. The entire route has been designated a National Forest Scenic Byway.
- *Travel Season:* The route is open year-round with possible delays for winter snow removal.
- *Description:* This scenic drive travels through hardwood forests, rolling hills, and by many sparkling lakes as it crosses the Chippewa National Forest. Wildlife is abundant in the area surrounding the scenic drive and includes beavers, wolves, deer, coyotes, ospreys, and eagles. Two semiprimitive areas are located along the scenic drive, Suomi Hills and Trout Lake, that offer

opportunities for fishing, hiking, and cross-country skiing in the winter. Motorized vehicles, boats, and snowmobiles are not permitted in either area. A developed campground can be found at the North Star Lake which also offers fishing and boating opportunities. Located near this route's northern end is the Big Fork River which flows north to the Canadian border and provides for excellent canoeing and fishing.

- *Other Nearby Routes:* Approximately 30 miles to the west is the Avenue Of Pines scenic drive and an additional 15 miles west to the Scenic Highway scenic drive.

Minnesota

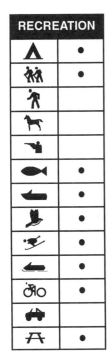

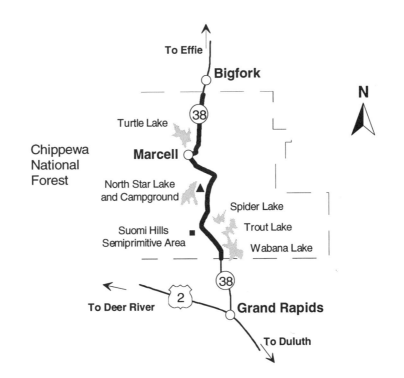

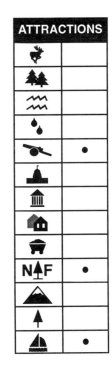

Information Sources:

Chippewa National Forest, Route 3, Box 244, Cass Lake, MN 56633 / 218-335-8600
Chippewa National Forest, Cass Lake Ranger District, Route 3 - Box 219, Cass Lake, MN 56633 / 218-335-2283
Grand Rapids Area Chamber of Commerce, One N.W. Third St., Grand Rapids, MN 55744 / 218-326-6619

SCENIC HIGHWAY

- **Route Location:** Located in north-central Minnesota, east of Bemidji. The northern access is located in Blackduck off U.S. Highway 71 and travels south to the junction of U.S. Highway 2, near Cass Lake.
- **Roads Traveled:** The 28 mile route follows County Roads 39 and 10 which are two-lane paved roads suitable for all vehicles. The entire 28 mile route has been designated a National Forest Scenic Byway.
- **Travel Season:** The route is generally open year-round with delays possible for winter snow removal.
- **Description:** The scenic drive travels across the Chippewa National Forest, through mixed stands of hardwoods, wetlands, and past numerous lakes. A variety of wildlife may be seen from the drive including white-tailed deer, black bear, timber wolves, bald eagles, and ruffed grouse. The many lakes found along this route provide opportunities for canoeing and fishing. Campgrounds and picnic areas are found at Benjamin

Minnesota

Lake, Webster Lake, North Twin Lake, Knutson Dam, Star Island, and Norway Beach. Camp Rabideau was built between August 1935 and January 1936 by the Civilian Conservation Corps. The camp was occupied for five years to complete projects inlcuding building the Forest Service Blackduck Ranger Station, two fire towers, and planting thousands of trees. Four buildings have been restored and are open to the public during the summer. The camp has been placed on the National Register of Historic Places.

- **Other Nearby Routes:** Approximately 15 miles northeast is the Avenue Of Pines scenic drive and about 45 miles east to the Northwoods scenic route.

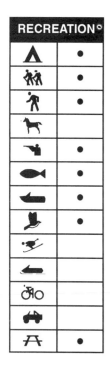

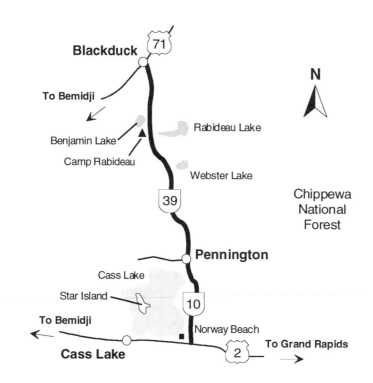

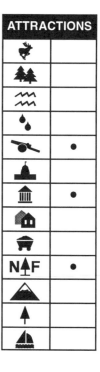

Information Sources:

Chippewa National Forest, Route 3, Box 244, Cass Lake, MN 56633 / 218-335-8600
Bemidji Area Chamber of Commerce, 300 Bemidji Ave., Bemidji, MN 56601 / 218-751-3541
Grand Rapids Area Chamber of Commerce, One N.W. Third St., Grand Rapids, MN 55744 / 218-326-6619

MISSISSIPPI

□ *Scenic Drives*

1. Natchez Trace

O *National Park Areas*

A. Brices Cross Roads National
   Battlefield Site
B. Gulf Islands National Seashore
C. Natchez Nat'l. Historical Park
D. Tupelo National Battlefield
E. Vicksburg Nat'l. Military Park

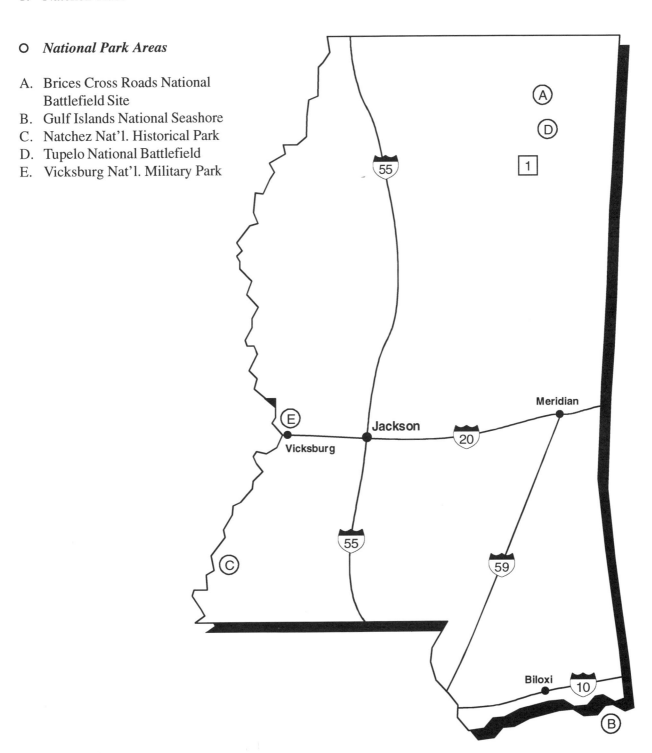

Road Condition Number: 601-987-1212

NATCHEZ TRACE

Mississippi

- *Route Location:* Located in northeastern Mississippi, south of Tupelo. The northern access is located on the Natchez Trace Parkway, just south of Troy and travels south to its end at the national forest boundary near the junction of Mississippi State Highway 8.
- *Roads Traveled:* The 17 mile route follows the Natchez Trace Parkway and the Davis Lake Road which are two-lane paved roads suitable for all vehicles. For more information on the larger Natchez Trace Parkway, see *"Other Nearby Routes."* The 17 mile route has been designated a National Forest Scenic Byway.
- *Travel Season:* The route is open year-round.
- *Description:* The scenic drive travels on the Tombigbee National Forest through pastures and rural farmland. The 200 acre Davis Lake Recreation Site is the primary recreational attraction along the route. Camping, swimming, and fishing for largemouth bass, crappie, and catfish are offered at this site. Camping and picnicking are also available in the Trace and Tombigbee State Parks, located north of the scenic drive near Tupelo. The Tupelo National Battlefield Site also lies to the north of this route. Hiking and horseback riding through the national forest is provided by the Witch Dance Horse Trail. The Owl Creek Indian Mounds, built by Native Americans and used for burial and religious ceremonies, are located near the route.
- *Other Nearby Routes:* There are no other routes within a close distance. For more information on the Natchez Trace Parkway contact: National Park Service, Natchez Trace Parkway, RR 1 / NT-143, Tupelo MS 38801. Phone: 601-842-1572

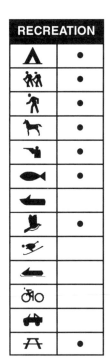

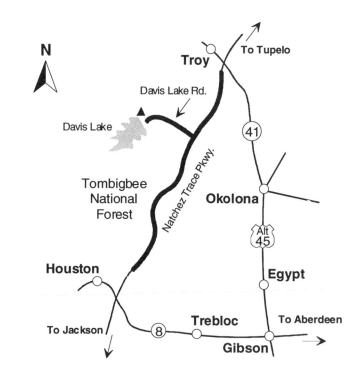

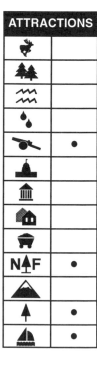

Information Sources:

National Forests In Mississippi, Tombigbee Ranger District, Rte. 1, Box 98A, Ackerman, MS 39735 / 601-285-3264
Okolona Chamber of Commerce, 219 Main St., Okolona, MS 38860 / 601-895-2600
Aberdeen - South Monroe Chamber of Commerce, P.O. Box 727, Aberdeen, MS 39730 / 601-369-6488
Chickasaw Dev. Foundation, 635 Starkville Rd., Houston, MS 38851 / 601-456-2321

MISSOURI

□ *Scenic Drives*

1. Blue Buck Knob
2. Glade Top Trail

○ *National Park Areas*

A. George Washington Carver National Monument
B. Harry S. Truman National Historic Site
C. Jefferson National Expansion Memorial
D. Ulysses S. Grant National Historic Site
E. Wilson's Creek National Battlefield

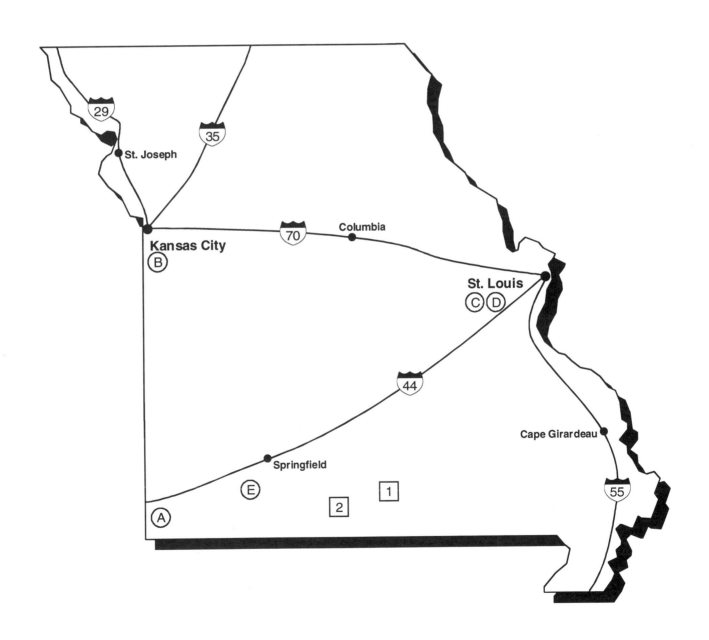

BLUE BUCK KNOB

Missouri

- *Route Location:* Located in south-central Missouri, southeast of Springfield. The northern access is located off U.S. Highway 60 south of Cabool and travels south to the junction of Missouri State Highway 14, north of Siloam Springs.
- *Roads Traveled:* The 24 mile route follows Missouri State Highways 181, 76, and "AP" which are all two-lane paved roads suitable for all vehicles. The route has been designated a National Forest Scenic Byway.
- *Travel Season:* The entire route is open year-round although caution should be exercised during the winter months.
- *Description:* Traveling across the Mark Twin National Forest, this scenic drive winds through Missouri's Ozark hill country, passing farmland, pastures, and wooded hillsides. Noblett Lake Recreation area offers a 27 acre lake offering fishing, boating, camping, and picnicking opportunities. A lakeside trail and the Ridge Runner

National Recreation Trail, which traverses the national forest into the Devil's Backbone Wilderness and North Fork Recreation Area south of the scenic drive, can be accessed here. The Carman Springs Wildlife Refuge Management Area was established in the 1930s and was instrumental in reintroducing the white-tailed deer and wild turkey into Missouri.

- *Other Nearby Routes:* Approximately 50 miles to the west is the Glade Top Trail scenic drive. About 110 miles south across the Arkansas border is the Sylamore scenic drive.

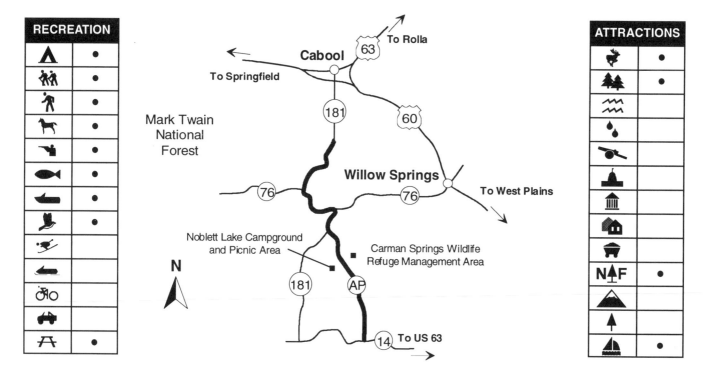

Information Sources:

Mark Twain National Forest, Ava Ranger District, P.O. Box 188, Ava, MO 65608 / 417-683-4428
Greater West Plains Area Chamber of Commerce, 220 W. Main Plaza, West Plains, MO 65775 / 417-256-4433
Willow Springs Area Chamber of Commerce, P.O. Box 5, Willow Springs, MO 65793 / 417-469-2500
Mountain Grove Area Chamber of Commerce, P.O. Box 434, Mountain Grove, MO 65711 / 417-926-4135
Cabool Area Chamber of Commerce, P.O. Box 285, Cabool, MO 65689 / 417-962-3002

GLADE TOP TRAIL

Missouri

- *Route Location:* Located in southwestern Missouri, southeast of Springfield near the Arkansas border. The northern access is located off Missouri State Highway "A" with the junction of Douglas County Road A-409. The route travels south and forks leading to the junction of Missouri State Highway 125 on the west and the junction of Missouri State Highway 95, north of Longrun, on the east.
- *Roads Traveled:* The 23 mile route follows Forest Service Roads 147 and 149 which are two-lane well maintained gravel roads suitable for most vehicles. The entire route has been designated a National Forest Scenic Byway.
- *Travel Season:* The entire route is open year-round although winter driving conditions may be hazardous.
- *Description:* This scenic drive weaves through narrow ridge tops as it crosses the Mark Twain National Forest. Wildlife commonly seen along the scenic drive includes white-tailed deer, bobwhite quail, wild turkeys, squirrels, rabbits, and a diversity of songbirds. This area also provides a home for wildlife not often encountered in the Ozarks, including the roadrunner and the endangered Bachman's Sparrow. In celebration of the brilliant fall foliage of this area, the "Flaming Fall Review" event is held. People from several states and countries gather at the Caney Picnic Area for the barbecue and music.
- *Other Nearby Routes:* The Blue Buck Knob scenic drive is approximately 50 miles to the east. About 75 miles southeast across the Arkansas border is the Sylamore scenic drive.

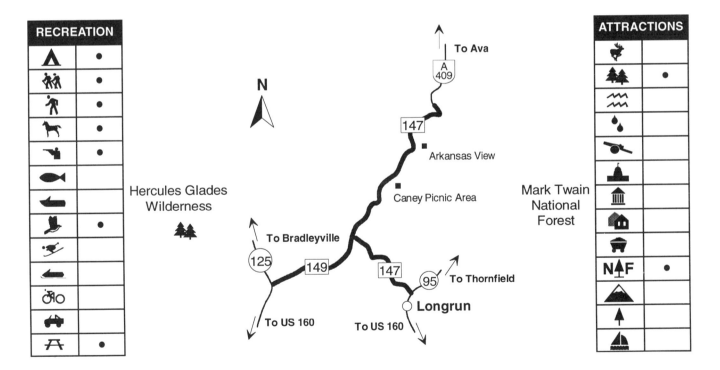

Information Sources:

Mark Twain National Forest, Ava Ranger District, P.O. Box 188, Ava, MO 65608 / 417-683-4428
Ava Area Chamber of Commerce, P.O. Box 83, Ava, MO 65608 / 417-683-4594
Theodosia Area Chamber of Commerce, P.O. Box 11, Theodosia, MO 65761 / 417-273-4444
Branson / Lakes Area Chamber of Commerce, P.O. Box 220, Branson, MO 65616 / 417-334-4136

MONTANA

□ *Scenic Drives*

1. Big Sheep Creek
2. Garnet Range
3. Kings Hill
4. Lake Koocanusa
5. Missouri Breaks
6. Pioneer Mountains
7. St. Regis - Paradise

O *National Park Areas*

A. Big Hole National Battlefield
B. Bighorn Canyon National Recreation Area
C. Glacier National Park
D. Grant - Kohrs Ranch National Historic Site
E. Little Bighorn Battlefield National Monument

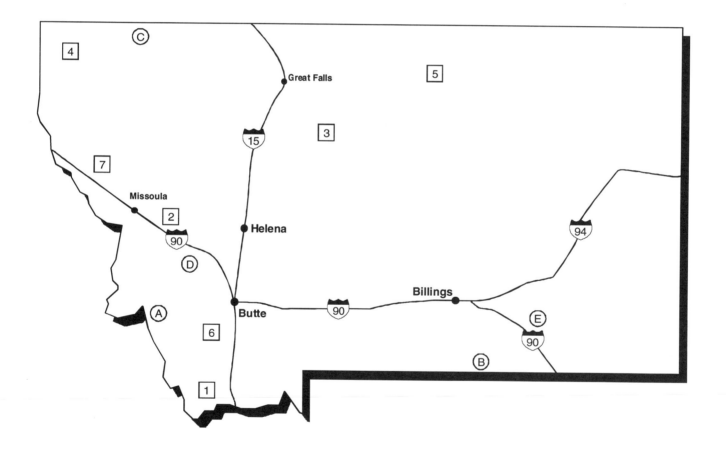

Road Condition Number: 800-332-6171 (construction)

BIG SHEEP CREEK

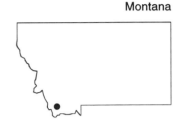

Montana

- *Route Location:* Located in the southwest corner of Montana, south of Butte near the Idaho border. The southeastern access is located off Interstate 15 in the town of Dell and travels northwest to the junction of Montana State Highway 324, east of Grant.
- *Roads Traveled:* The 50 mile route follows the Big Sheep Creek Road. The route travels over two-lane gravel road with a short stretch of one-lane dirt road. The route can safely be driven by a two-wheel drive vehicle although motor homes and vehicles pulling trailers should not attempt the entire route. The entire route has been designated a BLM Type I Back Country Byway.
- *Travel Season:* The route is generally open from May through early October and then closed by winter snows.
- *Description:* This scenic drive passes beneath the high rock cliffs of Big Sheep Canyon, offering glimpses into the clear, deep pools of the spring-fed Big Sheep Creek.

Beyond the canyon lies a vast valley completely surrounded by the Rocky Mountains. Several side roads from this scenic drive lead to the foot of the mountains, providing excellent hiking opportunities. The Continental Divide National Scenic Trail and the Lewis and Clark National Historic Trail can be accessed in the area. Camping is provided by the Clark Canyon Recreation Area as well as primitive camping anywhere on BLM administered lands.

- *Other Nearby Routes:* About 25 miles to the north is the Pioneer Mountains scenic drive. Approximately 25 miles west across the Idaho border lies the Lewis And Clark scenic drive and an additional 20 miles north to the Salmon River scenic drive.

RECREATION	
⛺	•
🥾	•
🚶	
🐎	•
🔫	•
🐟	•
🛶	•
👢	•
🎿	
🛷	
🚲	
🚙	•
🪑	•

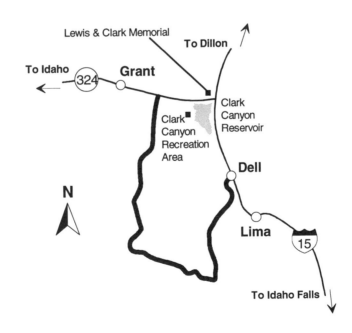

Lewis & Clark Memorial
To Dillon
To Idaho
324 Grant
Clark Canyon Reservoir
Clark Canyon Recreation Area
N
Dell
Lima
15
To Idaho Falls

ATTRACTIONS	
🦌	
🌲	
〰️	
💧	
🔭	
🏛️	•
🏛️	
🏚️	
🏪	
N↑F	•
⛰️	
↑	
⛵	•

Information Sources:

BLM, Butte District Office, 106 N. Parkmont, Butte, MT 59702-3388 / 406-494-5059
BLM, Dillon Resource Area, 1005 Selway Drive, Dillon, MT 59725 / 406-683-2337
Beaverhead Chamber of Commerce, 125 S. Montana, Dillon, MT 59725 / 406-683-5511

GARNET RANGE

- *Route Location:* Located in western Montana, east of Missoula. The northwestern access is located off Montana State Highway 200 south of Greenough and travels southeast to Reynolds City.
- *Roads Traveled:* The 12 mile route follows the Garnet Range Road which is marked and groomed as a National Winter Recreation Trail. The entire 12 mile route has been designated a BLM Type IV Back Country Byway.
- *Travel Season:* This National Winter Recreation Trail is marked and groomed by the BLM from January 1 through April 30 for snowmobile and cross-country skiing. The route is accessible by car in good weather from May through October.
- *Description:* This scenic drive climbs 2,000 feet into the evergreen forest of the Garnets and offers spectacular views of the Mission Rattlesnake, Swan, and Sapphire Mountain ranges. The main attraction of this route is

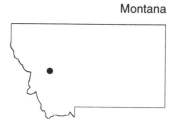

the well preserved gold mining ghost town of Garnet which once boasted a population of nearly 1,000. By 1905, many of the mines were abandoned and the town's population dropped to 200. World War I drew most of the remaining residents away and by the 1920s, Garnet was a ghost town. Two rustic cabins in Garnet are available for rent from December 1 through April 30.

- *Other Nearby Routes:* Approximately 150 miles to the east is the Kings Hill scenic drive and about 90 miles to the northwest is the St. Regis-Paradise scenic drive. The Pioneer Mountains scenic drive is about 105 miles to the south and an additional 65 miles to the west is the Salmon River scenic drive in Idaho.

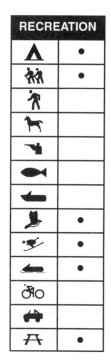

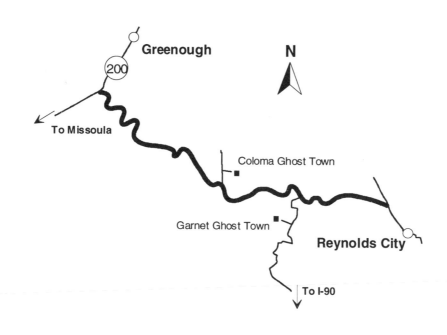

Information Sources:

BLM, Garnet Resource Area, 3255 Missoula Rd., Missoula, MT 59801-7293 / 406-329-3914
Missoula Area Chamber of Commerce, P.O. Box 7577, Missoula, MT 59807 / 406-543-6623
Powell County Chamber of Commerce, P.O. Box 776, Deer Lodge, MT 59722 / 406-846-2094
Seeley Lake Area Chamber of Commerce, P.O. Box 516, Seeley Lake, MT 59868 / 406-677-2880
Lincoln Valley Chamber of Commerce, Hwy. 200, Lincoln, MT 59639 / 406-362-4949
Philipsburg Chamber of Commerce, P.O. Box 661, Philipsburg, MT 59858 / 406-859-3388

KINGS HILL

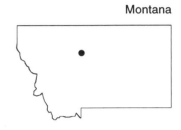
Montana

- *Route Location:* Located in central Montana, southeast of Great Falls. The northern access is located off U.S. Highway 87 south of Belt and travels south to the junction of U.S. Highway 12, north of White Sulphur Springs.
- *Roads Traveled:* The 70 mile route follows U.S. Highway 89 which is a two-lane paved road suitable for all vehicles. The entire 70 mile route has been designated a National Forest Scenic Byway.
- *Travel Season:* The entire route is open year-round although winter driving conditions may be hazardous.
- *Description:* The scenic drive travels across the Lewis and Clark National Forest through dense forests, limestone canyons, by rushing streams, and grassy parks of the Little Belt Mountain region. The route crosses Kings Hill Pass, the highest pass in Montana open year-round. Wildlife occasionally seen along the drive includes mule deer, elk, golden eagles, and red-tailed hawks. Located along this scenic drive are several developed campgrounds providing opportunities for picnicking and an overnight stay. Winter sport enthusiasts are offered many miles of groomed trails for cross-country skiing and snowmobiling while the Showdown Winter Sports Area offers downhill skiing. A side road provides access to a short hiking trail that leads to the scenic Memorial Falls. Newlan Creek Reservoir provides rainbow trout fishing activities.
- *Other Nearby Routes:* Approximately 150 miles to the northeast is the Missouri Breaks scenic drive and about 150 miles to the west is the Garnet Range scenic drive.

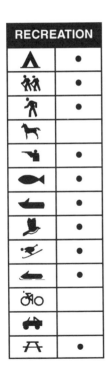

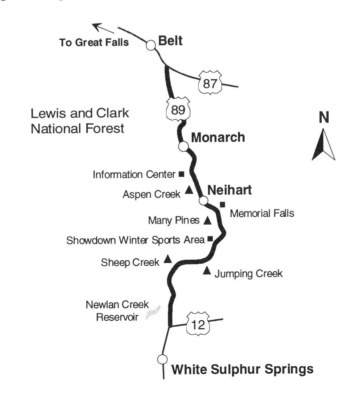

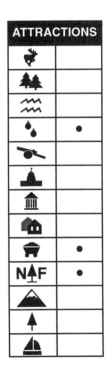

Information Sources:

Lewis And Clark National Forest, 1101 15th St. North, Great Falls, MT 59403 / 406-791-7700
Meagher County Chamber of Commerce, P.O. Box 356, White Sulphur Springs, MT 59646 / 406-547-2260
Great Falls Area Chamber of Commerce, 815 2nd St., Great Falls, MT 59404 / 406-761-4434

LAKE KOOCANUSA

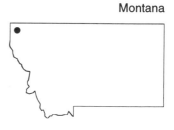

Montana

- **Route Location:** Located in the northwestern corner of Montana, northwest of Kalispell. The northeastern access is located on Montana State Highway 37 south of Rexford and travels southwest forming a loop drive back to highway 37.
- **Roads Traveled:** The 88 mile route follows Montana State Highway 37 and Forest Service Road 228 which are two-lane paved roads suitable for all vehicles. The 88 mile route has been designated a National Forest Scenic Byway.
- **Travel Season:** The entire route is generally open year-round although temporary closures are possible in the winter due to heavy snowfall.
- **Description:** Traveling across the Kootenai National Forest, this scenic drive travels through forests of ponderosa pine, lodgepole pine and Douglas-fir, offering views of steep slopes, rock outcroppings, and areas of open parks. Numerous turnouts along the route provide excellent views of the 90 mile long Lake Koocanusa and the surrounding mountains. Several developed recreation areas provide opportunities for camping, fishing, boating, swimming, and picnicking. The Koocanusa Marina offers cabins, a campground, boat ramps, store, restaurant, gas station, and picnic area. The McGillivray Recreation Site is a popular cross-country skiing area during the winter. Hiking and backpacking opportunities are plentiful with five National Recreation Trails accessed along the route. The Little North Fork Trail is a short ¼ mile hike to a waterfall.
- **Other Nearby Routes:** Approximately 115 miles south is the St. Regis-Paradise scenic drive.

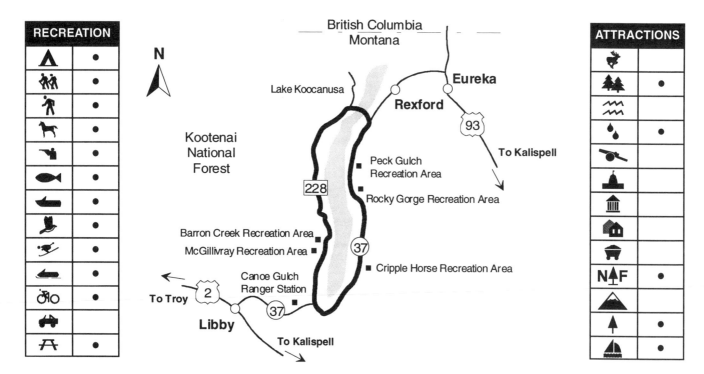

Information Sources:

Kootenai National Forest, 506 U.S. Highway 2 West, Libby, MT 59923 / 406-293-6211
Libby Area Chamber of Commerce, 905 W. 9th St., Libby, MT 59923 / 406-293-4167
Tobacco Valley Board of Commerce, P.O. Box 186, Eureka, MT 59917 / 406-296-2024

Missouri Breaks

- *Route Location:* Located in north-central Montana, northeast of Lewiston. The eastern access is located off U.S. Highway 191 in the Charles M. Russell National Wildlife Refuge and travels northwest forming a loop drive, with several spur roads, back to U.S. Highway 191.
- *Roads Traveled:* The 73 mile loop follows the Lower Two Calf and Knox Ridge Roads which are mostly two-lane gravel and dirt roads that can be negotiated by passenger cars in dry weather. Large RVs and vehicles pulling trailers should not attempt to access the route from U.S. Highway 191. Nor should they attempt the Two Calf Creek crossing or any of the spur roads off of the Lower Two Calf Road. The route has been designated a BLM Type II Back Country Byway.
- *Travel Season:* The route is generally open from May through October and then closed in the winter and spring due to snow and mud.

- *Description:* This back country route travels through a ruggedly spectacular landscape along portions of the National Wild and Scenic Missouri River.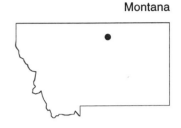

A variety of wildlife calls this rugged country home including antelope, deer, bighorn sheep, sage grouse, and prairie dogs. A small BLM campground on the river banks is located at the end of the Woodhawk Bottom Road. Camping is also available in the nearby James Kipp State Recreation Area. Hiking and backpacking opportunities are offered on the Lewis and Clark and Nez Perce National Historic Trails which run through this area.
- *Other Nearby Routes:* The Kings Hill scenic drive is approximately 150 miles to the west.

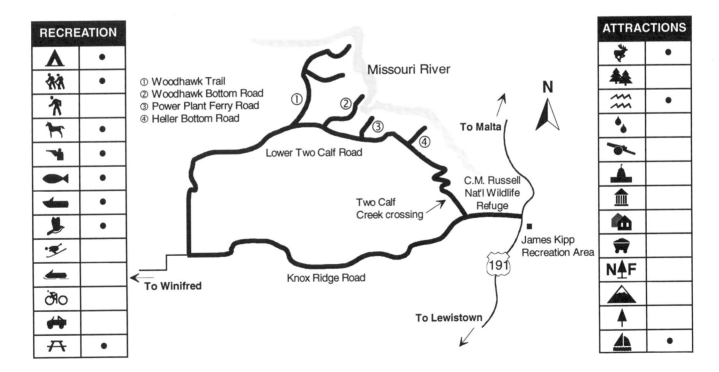

Information Sources:

BLM, Lewistown District Office, Airport Rd., P.O. Box 1160, Lewiston, MT 59457-1160 / 406-538-7461
Malta Area Chamber of Commerce, P.O. Drawer GG, Malta, MT 59538 / 406-654-1776
Lewistown Area Chamber of Commerce, 408 N.E. Main, Lewistown, MT 59457 / 406-538-5436

PIONEER MOUNTAINS

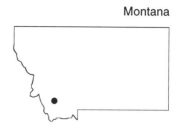

Montana

- *Route Location:* Located in southwestern Montana, southwest of Butte near the Idaho border. The northern access is located off Montana State Highway 43 in the town of Wise River and travels south to Polaris, north of Montana State Highway 278.
- *Roads Traveled:* The 27 mile route follows Forest Service Road 484. The route travels over a combination of paved and gravel surface road with segments that are not recommended for motor homes or vehicles pulling trailers. The entire route has been designated a National Forest Scenic Byway.
- *Travel Season:* The route is normally open from mid-May through mid-November and then closed by winter snows between Elkhorn Hot Springs and Sheep Creek.
- *Description:* The scenic byway crosses the Beaverhead National Forest as it travels through canyons, expansive meadows, and forests of lodgepole pine. Many trailheads for hiking, backpacking, and horseback riding are accessed along the route. Many trails lead to excellent fishing opportunities in mountain streams and lakes. Access to off-road vehicle trails are also accessed along this drive. Winter sport activities offered include downhill skiing, cross-country skiing, and snowmobiling. Several national forest campgrounds can be found along the scenic route as well as primitive camping anywhere in the forest.
- *Other Nearby Routes:* About 25 miles south is the Big Sheep Creek scenic drive and the Garnet Range scenic drive is about 105 miles to the north. About 60 miles to the west, starting at the Idaho border is the Salmon River scenic drive. Less than 50 miles southwest is the Lewis and Clark scenic drive, also in Idaho.

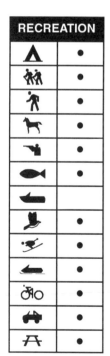

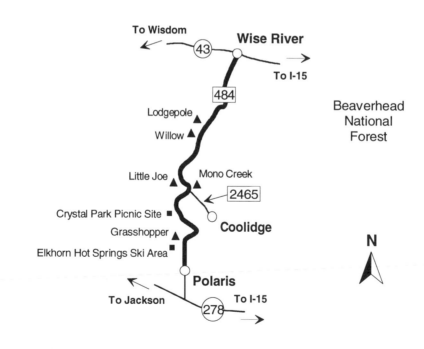

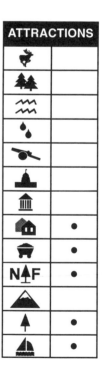

Information Sources:

Beaverhead National Forest, 610 N. Montana St., Dillon, MT 59725 / 406-683-3900
Butte - Silver Bow Chamber of Commerce, 2950 Harrison Ave., Butte, MT 59701 / 406-494-5595
Beaverhead Chamber of Commerce, 125 S. Montana, Dillon, MT 59725 / 406-683-5511

ST. REGIS - PARADISE

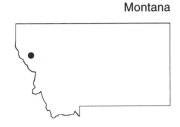

Montana

- *Route Location:* Located in western Montana, northwest of Missoula near the Idaho border. The southwestern access is located off Interstate 90 in the town of Saint Regis and travels northeast to the junction of Montana State Highway 200, south of Paradise.
- *Roads Traveled:* The 22 mile route follows Montana State Highway 135 which is a two-lane paved road suitable for all vehicles. The entire route has been designated a National Forest Scenic Byway.
- *Travel Season:* The route is open year-round although winter driving conditions may be hazardous.
- *Description:* This route was originally a meandering trail used by homesteaders in the late 1800s. As it crosses the Lolo National Forest, this scenic drive travels dense forests, grasslands, and canyons as it follows the Clark Fork River. Elk, deer, and bighorn sheep inhabit the canyon region and the heavily forested mountains surrounding the route. Bald eagles are occasionally seen, especially during the fall and winter months. Many access points to the river provide opportunities for fishing and rafting. Several trails may also be accessed along the scenic drive, offering good hiking, horseback riding, and mountain biking opportunities. Located about 25 miles east of this drive is the National Bison Range where 400 bison roam nearly 19,000 acres of natural grassland. Located further north is the largest natural freshwater lake in the western United States, the Flathead Lake.
- *Other Nearby Routes:* Approximately 115 miles to the north is the Koocanusa scenic drive and the Garnet Range scenic route is about 90 miles to the southeast.

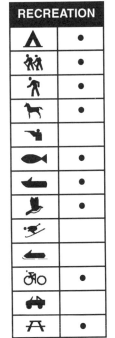

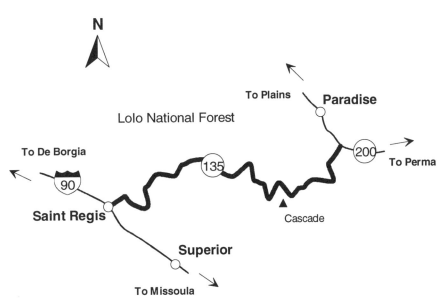

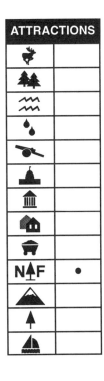

Information Sources:

Lolo National Forest, Plains Ranger District, P.O. Box 429, Plains, MT 59859 / 406-826-3821
Plains - Paradise Chamber of Commerce, P.O. Box 714, Plains, MT 59859 / 406-826-3662
Superior Area Chamber of Commerce, Box 483, Superior, MT 59872 / 406-822-4672

NEVADA

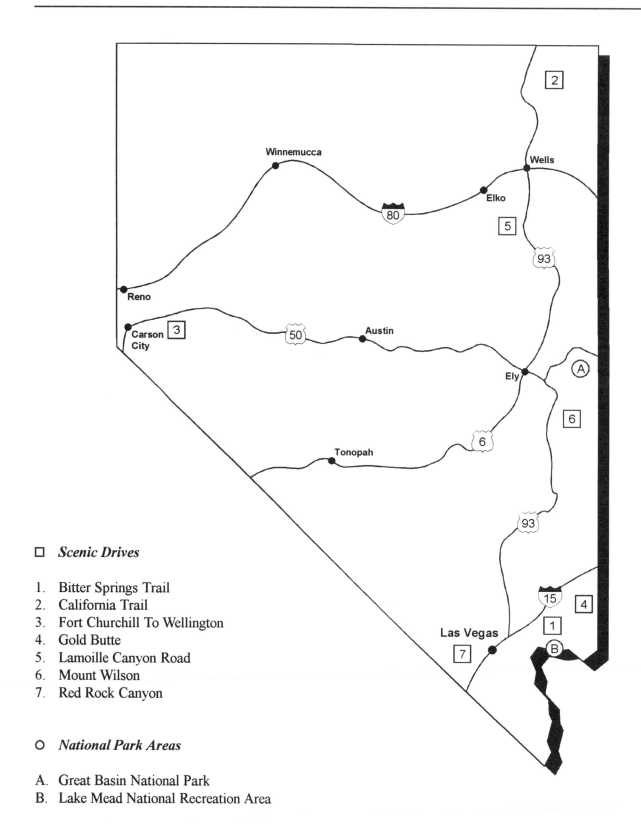

□ *Scenic Drives*

1. Bitter Springs Trail
2. California Trail
3. Fort Churchill To Wellington
4. Gold Butte
5. Lamoille Canyon Road
6. Mount Wilson
7. Red Rock Canyon

O *National Park Areas*

A. Great Basin National Park
B. Lake Mead National Recreation Area

Road Condition Numbers: 702-486-3116 (southern); 702-793-1313 (northern); 702-738-8888 (northeast)

BITTER SPRINGS TRAIL

Nevada

- *Route Location:* Located in southeastern Nevada, northeast of Las Vegas. The northern access is located at the junction of Nevada State Highway 40 and the Bitter Springs Road, off Interstate 15 and travels southeast to the junction of Nevada State Highway 169, near the Lake Mead National Recreation Area.
- *Roads Traveled:* The 28 mile route follows the Bitter Springs Road which is a single-lane dirt road that requires a two-wheel drive, high-clearance vehicle. The entire route has been designated a BLM Type II Back Country Byway.
- *Travel Season:* The entire route is open year-round.
- *Description:* The scenic drive travels through the foothills of the Muddy Mountains, past abandoned mining operations, and brightly colored sandstone hills. One of the more interesting sites encountered along the route is the Bitter Ridge, a sweeping arc that cuts for 8 miles across a rolling valley. Remnants of the American Borax mining operation can be seen along this drive. Several mine buildings still stand, along with 30 foot deep cisterns, mine tunnels, and adits (horizontal passages). Primitive camping is permitted along this drive as no developed areas exist. Valley of Fire State Park offers developed campsites with picnic tables. Lake Mead National Recreation Area is near the eastern end of this drive.

- *Other Nearby Routes:* The Gold Butte scenic drive is approximately 35 miles to the northeast and the Red Rock Canyon scenic drive is about 50 miles to the southwest. Less than 100 miles to the southwest in California is the East Mojave National Scenic Area where eight scenic drives are located.

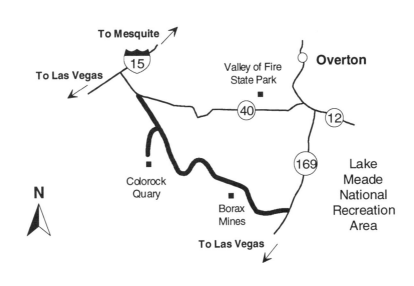

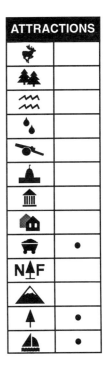

Information Sources:

BLM, Las Vegas District Office, 4765 W. Vegas Dr., Las Vegas, NV 89108-2135 / 702-647-5000
Moapa Valley Chamber of Commerce, P.O. Box 361, Overton, NV 89040 / 702-397-2193
Henderson Chamber of Commerce, 100 E. Lake Mead Dr., Henderson, NV 89015 / 702-565-8951
Boulder City Chamber of Commerce, 1497 Nevada Hwy., Boulder City, NV 89005 / 702-293-2034

CALIFORNIA TRAIL

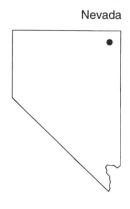

Nevada

- *Route Location:* Located in the northeastern corner of Nevada, north of Wells. The northern access is located off U.S. Highway 93 in the town of Jackpot and travels southeast forming an open loop drive back to highway 93, north of Wells.
- *Roads Traveled:* The 76 mile route follows Elko County Roads C765, C763, C761, and C762. All of the routes travel on gravel surfaced roads suitable for passenger cars except under adverse weather conditions. The 76 mile route has been designated a BLM Type I Back Country Byway.
- *Travel Season:* The route is normally open from May through October and then mud and heavy snowfall makes the road impassable.
- *Description:* This scenic drive parallels the original California Trail and offers views of sage-covered valleys, mountain ranges, and stands of juniper trees. Wagon ruts of the trail are still visible in many places including the Mammoth Ruts site. Hunting, fishing, picnicking, and primitive camping are offered along the route. Canoeing and rafting opportunities exist on the Salmon Creek with access points located north and south of Jackpot. Many side roads from this back country drive lead further into the surrounding mountains and canyons, revealing lush springs amidst the desert landscape.
- *Other Nearby Routes:* Approximately 85 miles to the southeast across the Utah border are the Silver Island Mountains and Transcontinental Railroad scenic drives. About 85 miles southwest is the Lamoille Canyon Road scenic route and approximately 75 miles north into Idaho is the Sawtooth scenic drive.

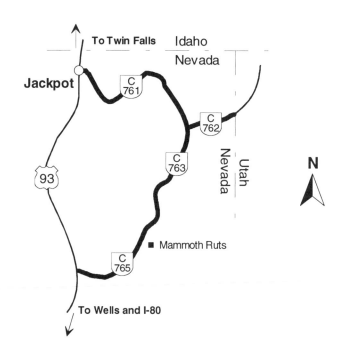

Information Sources:

BLM, Elko District Office, 3900 E. Idaho St., Elko, NV 89803-0831 / 702-753-0200
Wells Chamber of Commerce, 279 Clover Ave., Wells, NV 89835 / 702-752-3540

FORT CHURCHILL TO WELLINGTON

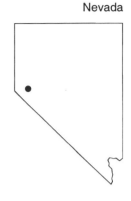

Nevada

- *Route Location:* Located in west-central Nevada, east of Carson City. The southern access is located off Nevada State Highway 208 in the town of Wellington and travels north to the junction of U.S. Highway Alt. 95, near the Fort Churchill State Historical Park.
- *Roads Traveled:* The 67 mile route follows Nevada State Highway 2B and the Como, Sunrise Pass, and Upper Colony Roads. The routes vary from relatively smooth gravel to rough unsurfaced roads. The gravel sections are mostly two-lane while the rough segment is a single-lane road with steep grades. A four-wheel drive vehicle is necessary to safely drive the entire route although a two-wheel drive, high-clearance vehicle can drive most of the route. The route has been designated a BLM Type I and Type II Back Country Byway.
- *Travel Season:* Much of the route is open year-round although the route over the Pine Nut Mountains is closed from heavy winter snows, two or three months out of the year.
- *Description:* The scenic drive follows portions of the Carson River, the Pony Express Trail, and travels into the rugged Pine Nut Mountains. Remains of the stone buildings that comprised Fort Churchill, built to protect the mail route and settlers, is found in the Fort Churchill State Historic Park. A visitor center, campground, and picnic area is located here as well. Wildlife seen along the route includes mountain lions, wild horses, and bobcats.
- *Other Nearby Routes:* Approximately 30 miles south of Carson City is the Carson Pass Highway in California. Less than 50 miles northwest are the Feather River and Yuba Donner scenic drives in California.

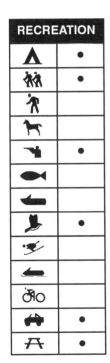

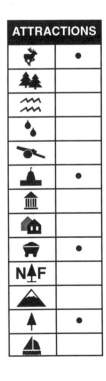

Information Sources:

BLM, Carson City District Office, 1535 Hot Springs Rd., Suite 300, Carson City, NV 89706-0638 / 702-885-6000
Mason Valley Chamber of Commerce, 227 S. Main, Yerington, NV 89447 / 702-463-3721
Virginia City Chamber of Commerce, P.O. Box 464, Virginia City, NV 89440 / 702-847-0311
Carson City Chamber of Commerce, 1900 S. Carson St., Carson City, NV 89701 / 702-882-1565
Tahoe - Douglas Chamber of Commerce, 195 Hwy. 50 - Round Hill Mall, Lake Tahoe, NV 89449 / 702-588-4591
Dayton Area Chamber of Commerce, P.O. Box 408, Dayton, NV 89403 / 702-246-7909

GOLD BUTTE

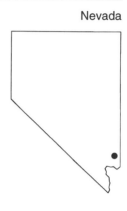

Nevada

- *Route Location:* Located in southeastern Nevada, northeast of Las Vegas near the Arizona-Nevada border. The northern access is located off Nevada State Highway 170 west of Bunkerville and travels south to Gold Butte.
- *Roads Traveled:* The 62 mile route follows the Gold Butte Road, splitting at Devil's Throat. The first 24 miles is along a narrow paved road suitable for passenger cars. The 19 mile portion heading east of Devil's Throat travels on a relatively smooth gravel road also suitable for passenger cars. The 19 mile portion heading west from Devil's Throat follows a lightly maintained dirt road that requires a high-clearance, two-wheel or four-wheel drive vehicle. The entire route has been designated a BLM Type II Back Country Byway.
- *Travel Season:* The entire route is open year-round.
- *Description:* The scenic drive follows a portion of the Virgin River, through Joshua tree forests, and offers views of the surrounding mountains. Petroglyph carvings can be seen at the colorful Whitney Pockets area and is a good spot for primitive camping. Devil's Throat is a 100 foot wide, 100 foot deep sinkhole that continues to expand, a rarity in this region. Very little remains of the abandoned mining town of Gold Butte, which was established in 1908.
- *Other Nearby Routes:* About 35 miles to the southwest is the Bitter Springs scenic drive and an additional 50 miles to the southwest lies the Red Rock Canyon scenic drive. Less than 100 miles southwest is the East Mojave National Scenic Area in California where there are eight scenic drives.

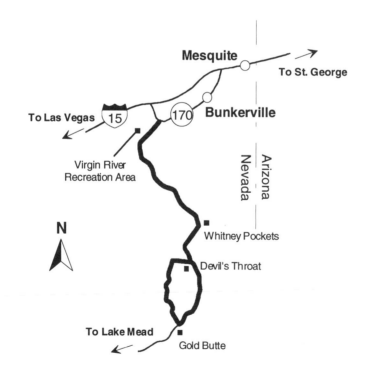

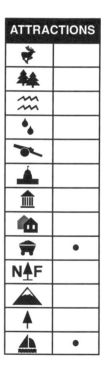

Information Sources:

BLM, Las Vegas District Office, 4765 W. Vegas Dr., Las Vegas, NV 89108-2135 / 702-647-5000
Moapa Valley Chamber of Commerce, P.O. Box 361, Overton, NV 89040 / 702-397-2193

LAMOILLE CANYON ROAD

- **Route Location:** Located in northeastern Nevada, southeast of Elko. The northern access is located off Nevada State Highway 227 west of Lamoille and travels south to the Roads End Picnic Area.
- **Roads Traveled:** The 12 mile route follows Forest Service Road 660 which is a two-lane paved road suitable for all vehicles. Travelers will need to retrace the route back to highway 227. The route has been designated a National Forest Scenic Byway.
- **Travel Season:** The route is generally open from May through October and then closed by heavy winter snows.
- **Description:** The scenic drive travels on the Humboldt National Forest through rugged canyons, past waterfalls, and a variety of native wildflowers. Several national forest campgrounds and picnic areas are located along the route. The Roads End Picnic Area provides access to the Ruby Crest National Recreation Trail which extends south for 40 miles through some very

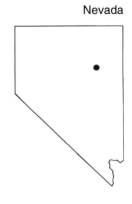

Nevada

spectacular scenery. Other trails within the forest offer opportunities for hiking, backpacking, horseback riding, and mountain biking. This route is a popular destination for snowmobilers and cross-country skiers during the winter months. Fishing is also a popular activity found in numerous lakes surrounding the drive. A small stand of Bristlecone pine, the oldest known living tree, exists in Thomas Canyon.

- **Other Nearby Routes:** The California Trail scenic drive is about 80 miles to the northeast. Approximately 115 miles to the east across the Utah border are the Silver Island Mountains and Transcontinental Railroad scenic drives.

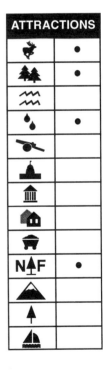

Information Sources:

Humboldt National Forest, 976 Mountain City Hwy., Elko, NV 89801 / 702-738-5171
Humboldt National Forest, Ruby Mountin Ranger District, 428 S. Humboldt, Wells, NV 89835 / 702-752-3357
Elko Chamber of Commerce, 1601 Idaho St., Elko, NV 89801 / 702-738-7135

MOUNT WILSON

- *Route Location:* Located in eastern Nevada, south of Ely near the Utah border. The northern access is located off U.S. Highway 93 at the Pony Springs rest area (milepost 147.9) and travels southeast forming an open loop drive back to U.S. Highway 93, near the town of Pioche.
- *Roads Traveled:* The 62 mile route follows County Roads 441, 440, 431, and 430, BLM Road 4045, and Nevada State Highway 322. The routes travel over a combination of paved and gravel surfaced roads that can be safely driven in a two-wheel drive, high clearance vehicle. The route has been designated a BLM Type II Back Country Byway.
- *Travel Season:* The route is generally open from May through October and then closes due to heavy winter snows. The route may also be closed after heavy rains.
- *Description:* This scenic drive takes you from the arid, brush-covered high desert into the rugged slopes of

Mount Wilson and its pines, aspen groves, and streams. Wildlife commonly seen along the route include mule deer, coyotes, hawks, and various lizards. A 65 acre lake near the Spring Valley State Park provides fishing opportunites for brown trout, rainbow trout, and Alabama striped bass. The remains of several pioneer ranches are located north of the reservoir as are old cemeteries dating back to pioneer days. Camping is available at the state park and one BLM campground.

- *Other Nearby Routes:* Approximately 160 miles to the south are the Gold Butte and Bitter Springs scenic drives. About 100 miles northeast in Ibapah, Utah is the Pony Express scenic drive.

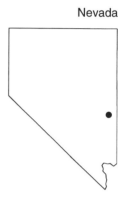

Nevada

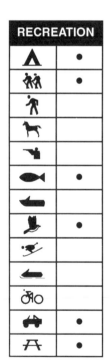

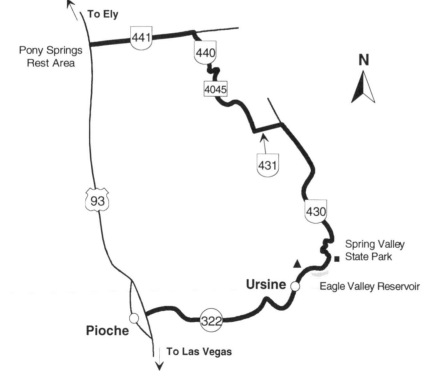

Information Sources:

Ely District Office, 702 North Industrial Way, Ely, NV 89301-9402 / 702-289-4865
Pioche Chamber of Commerce, P.O. Box 127, Pioche, NV 89043 / 702-962-5850
Caliente Chamber of Commerce, P.O. Box 553, Caliente, NV 89008 / 702-726-3129
White Pine Chamber of Commerce, 636 Aultman St., Ely, NV 89301 / 702-289-8877

RED ROCK CANYON

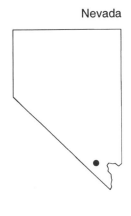

Nevada

- *Route Location:* Located in the southwest corner of Nevada, west of Las Vegas. The northern access is off Nevada State Highway 159 at the junction with Red Rock Canyon Road and travels southwest forming an open loop drive back to highway 159.
- *Roads Traveled:* The 13 mile route follows the Red Rock Canyon Road which is a one-way paved road suitable for all vehicles. The entire 13 miles have been designated a BLM Type I Back Country Byway.
- *Travel Season:* The entire route is open year-round.
- *Description:* The scenic drive travels though the desert landscape of the Red Rock Canyon National Conservation Area surrounded by towering cliffs and rugged mountains. Travelers to this route are given opportunities to see bighorn sheep, cougars, coyotes, and bobcats. Wild horses and burros can also be seen along the drive. No camping is available directly along the route, however facilities are available in the surrounding area. A developed picnic site is located at Willow Spring. This area is a favorite of nature photographers and is a good rock climbing area. At Sandstone Quarry, a trail leads you to an historic quarry dating back to the turn of the century. A visitor center is located at the beginning of this scenic drive and offers more information on the drive and the area.
- *Other Nearby Routes:* Approximately 40 miles to the northeast is the Bitter Springs scenic drive and an additional 35 miles northeast is the Gold Butte scenic route. The East Mojave National Scenic Area, in California, with eight scenic routes is about 50 miles southwest.

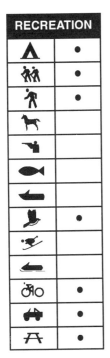

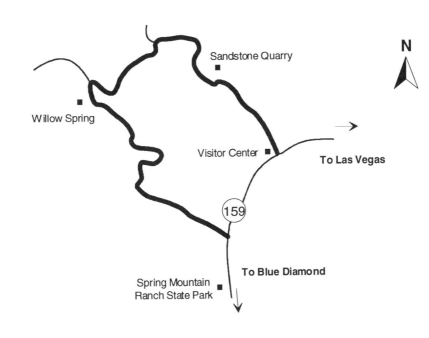

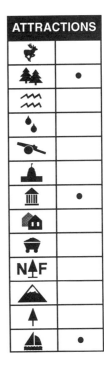

Information Sources:

BLM, Las Vegas District Office, 4765 W. Vegas Dr., Las Vegas, NV 89108-2135 / 702-647-5000
BLM, Caliente Resource Area, P.O. Box 237, Caliente, NV 89008 / 702-726-8100
Las Vegas Chamber of Commerce, 711 E. Desert Inn Rd., Las Vegas, NV 89109 / 702-735-1616

NEW HAMPSHIRE

☐ *Scenic Drives*

1. Kancamagus Highway

○ *National Park Areas*

A. Saint - Gaudens National Historic Site

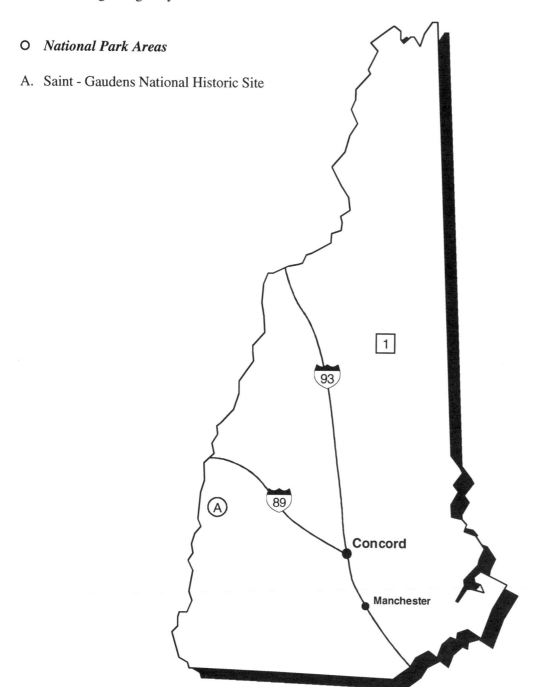

Road Condition Number: 603-485-9526

KANCAMAGUS HIGHWAY

New Hampshire

- *Route Location:* Located in central New Hampshire, southeast of Littleton. The western access is located of Interstate 93 in the town of Lincoln and travels east to the junction of New Hampshire State Highway 16, south of Conway.
- *Roads Traveled:* The 28 mile route follows New Hampshire State Highway 112 which is a two-lane paved road suitable for all vehicles. The entire route has been designated a National Forest Scenic Byway.
- *Travel Season:* The route is open year-round although winter driving conditions from November through May can be hazardous.
- *Description:* The route travels across the White Mountain National Forest and follows the Swift River. The scenic drive climbs nearly 3,000 feet offering outstanding views of white water streams and hardwood forests. Wildlife found in this part of New Hampshire includes moose, white-tailed deer, black bear, and a variety of songbirds. Several wilderness areas surrounding the drive offer hiking and backpacking opportunities, including the Appalachian National Scenic Trail. Fishing for brook and rainbow trout is a popular activity in the waters of Swift River. Camping and picnicking opportunities are plentiful in the many national forest campgrounds found along the route, several of which have short nature trails. Winter sport enthusiasts are offered skiing at the Loon Mountain Recreation Area which also has a year-round gondola ride and nature trail at the top of the mountain. Visitor centers provide maps and brochures of the route and national forest and are found at either end of the drive.
- *Other Nearby Routes:* There are no other routes nearby.

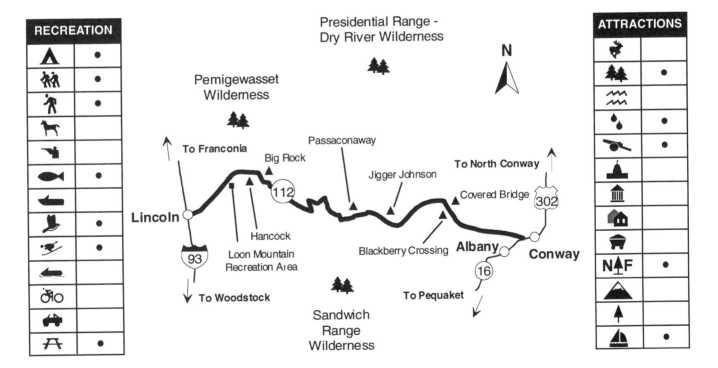

Information Sources:

White Mountain National Forest, 719 N. Main St., Laconia, NH 03247 / 603-528-8722
Conway Village Chamber of Commerce, P.O. Box 1019, Conway, NH 03818 / 603-447-2639
Lincoln - Woodstock Chamber of Commerce, P.O. Box 358, Lincoln, NH 03251 / 603-745-6621

NEW MEXICO

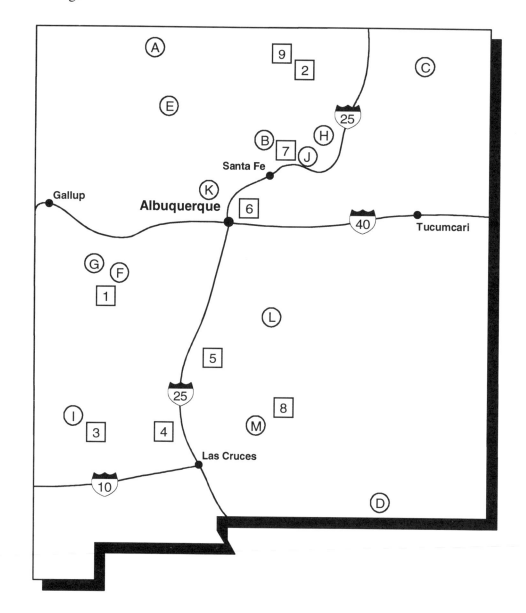

☐ *Scenic Drives*

1. Chain Of Craters
2. Enchanted Circle
3. Inner Loop - Gila Cliff Dwellings
4. Lake Valley
5. Quebradas
6. Sandia Crest Road
7. Santa Fe
8. Sunspot
9. Wild Rivers

Road Condition Numbers:
800-432-4269 (in New Mexico)
505-827-5118 (construction)
505-827-5213 (conditions)

O *National Park Areas*

A. Aztec Ruins National Monument
B. Bandelier National Monument
C. Capulin Volcano National Monument
D. Carlsbad Caverns National Park
E. Chaco Culture National Historical Park
F. El Malpais National Monument
G. El Morro National Monument
H. Fort Union National Monument
I. Gila Cliff Dwellings National Monument
J. Pecos National Historical Park
K. Petroglyph National Monument
L. Salinas Pueblo Mission National Monument
M. White Sands National Monument

CHAIN OF CRATERS

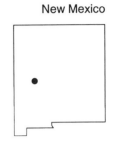

- *Route Location:* Located in west-central New Mexico, southwest of Grants. The northern access is located off New Mexico State Highway 53 with the junction of County Road 42 and travels south to the junction of New Mexico State Highway 117.
- *Roads Traveled:* The 36 mile route follows County Road 42 which is a dirt road requiring a two-wheel drive, high-clearance vehicle. A four-wheel drive vehicle is recommended during wet weather. The entire 36 mile route has been designated a BLM Type II Back Country Byway.
- *Travel Season:* The route is open year-round although the route is likely to be impassable during and after periods of inclement weather.
- *Description:* This back country scenic drive passes through a rugged volcanic landscape with views of sandstone bluffs rising above the volcanic flows. A diversity of wildlife is found in this region including coyotes, bears, mule deer, turkeys, and antelopes. No developed campgrounds exist along the route, but BLM permits primitive camping anywhere on BLM administered lands. The Continental Divide National Scenic Trail follows a portion of this route and offers hiking and backpacking. Horseback riding and mountain biking are also popular activities along this drive. Areas of interest surrounding this scenic drive include the El Malpais and El Morro National Monuments.
- *Other Nearby Routes:* A little over 100 miles to the northeast from Grants is the Sandia Crest scenic drive and an additional 60 miles northeast to the Santa Fe scenic drive. Approximately 125 miles southwest across the Arizona border are the White Mountain and Coronado Trail scenic drives.

RECREATION	
⛺	●
🚶	●
🚶	●
🐎	●
🪣	
🐟	
🛶	
👢	●
🎿	
🛷	
🚵	●
🚗	
⛴	●

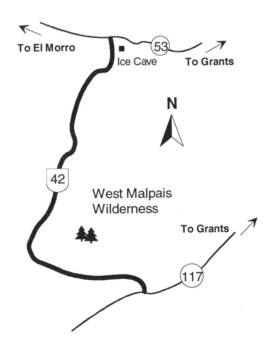

ATTRACTIONS	
🦌	
🌲	●
〰️	
💧	
🔫	
🏛	●
🏛	
🏠	
🛖	
N↟F	
⛰	
⬆	
⛴	

Information Sources:

BLM, Albuquerque District Office, 435 Montano Road NE, Albuquerque, NM 87107 / 505-761-8911
BLM, El Malpais National Conservation Area, P.O. Box 846, Grants, NM 87020 / 505-285-5406
Grants / Cibola County Chamber of Commerce, 100 Iron Ave., Grants, NM 87020 / 800-748-2142

ENCHANTED CIRCLE

New Mexico

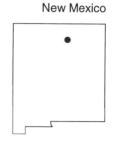

- *Route Location:* Located in north-central New Mexico, northeast of Santa Fe near the Colorado border. The northwestern access is in Questa on New Mexico State Highway 522 and travels southeast forming a loop drive back to Questa.
- *Roads Traveled:* The 84 mile route follows New Mexico State Highways 38, and 522, and U.S. Highway 64 which are two-lane paved roads suitable for all vehicles. The entire route has been designated a National Forest Scenic Byway.
- *Travel Season:* The entire route is open year-round.
- *Description:* Travels through the Carson National Forest circling Wheeler Peak, New Mexico's highest mountain. This scenic drive passes through rugged mountains, alpine valleys, vast meadows, and forests of spruce and fir. Elizabethtown, established in 1870 after gold was found, was New Mexico's first incorpo-

rated town and was a wild and wooly place with thousands of residents, 7 saloons, and 3 dance halls. All that remains today are the remains of the Mutz Hotel and the Elizabethtown Cemetery. Several opportunities exist along the route for winter activities including snowmobiling and cross-country skiing. Several developed national forest campgrounds and picnic areas are found along the route.

- *Other Nearby Routes:* The Wild Rivers scenic drive is about 5 miles to the north of Questa. Approximately 70 miles to the southwest is the Santa Fe scenic drive and an additional 60 miles southwest is the Sandia Crest scenic route. About 90 miles northeast across the Colorado border is the Highway Of Legends scenic drive.

Information Sources:

Carson National Forest, Forest Service Building, 208 Cruz Alta Rd., Taos, NM 87571 / 505-758-6200
Taos County Chamber of Commerce, 1139 Paseo del Pueblo Sur, Taos, NM 87571 / 800-732-8267
Red River Chamber of Commerce, P.O. Box 870, Red River, NM 87558 / 800-348-6444
Angel Fire Resort Chamber of Commerce, P.O. Box 547, Angel Fire, NM 87710 / 800-446-8117
Eagle Nest Chamber of Commerce, P.O. Box 322, Eagle Nest, NM 87718 / 505-377-2420
Cimarron Chamber of Commerce, P.O. Box 604, Cimarron, NM 87714 / 505-376-2614

INNER LOOP - GILA CLIFF DWELLINGS

New Mexico

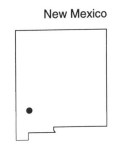

- *Route Location:* Located in southwestern New Mexico in Silver City. The southwestern access is located off U.S. Highway 180 in Silver City and travels northeast forming a loop drive back to Silver City.
- *Roads Traveled:* The 110 mile route follows New Mexico State Highways 15, 35, and 152, and U.S. Highway 180. All of the routes travel over two-lane paved roads. Vehicles over 17 feet should not attempt the portion of State Highway 15 between Pino Altos and the junction with State Highway 35 as this segment is narrow with sharp curves. The entire 110 miles have been designated a National Forest Scenic Byway.
- *Travel Season:* The entire route is open year-round.
- *Description:* The scenic drive travels across the Gila National Forest through a high desert and mountainous landscape, crossing the Continental Divide twice. Several turnouts are located along the drive and offer panoramic views of the rugged countryside. The Gila Cliff Dwellings National Monument is located at the northern end of highway 15. A moderately easy trail takes you through these cliff dwellings once inhabited by the Mogollon Indians. Several hiking trails into the Gila Wilderness may also be found here. Camping and picnicking is provided by several developed national forest campgrounds scattered along the scenic drive. Near the Mesa Campground is Lake Roberts, a 72 acre lake that offers boating and fishing opportunities and access to hiking and backpacking trails.
- *Other Nearby Routes:* Approximately 35 miles to the east is the Lake Valley scenic drive and an additional 85 miles north on Interstate 25 is the Quebradas scenic route. About 120 miles northwest are the White Mountain and Coronado Trail scenic drives in Arizona.

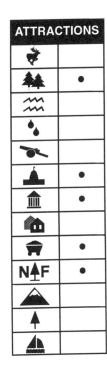

Information Sources:

Gila National Forest, 3005 E. Camino Del Bosque, Silver City, NM 88053 / 505-388-8201
Silver City - Grant County Chamber of Commerce, 1103 N. Hudson St., Silver City, NM 88062 / 800-548-9378
Truth or Consequences / Sierra County Chamber of Commerce, 201 S. Foch St., T or C, NM 87901 / 800-831-9487

LAKE VALLEY

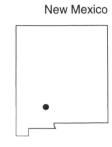

New Mexico

- **Route Location:** Located in southwestern New Mexico, northwest of Las Cruces. The southern access is located off New Mexico State Highway 26 in the town of Nutt and travels northeast to the junction of Interstate 25, south of Caballo.
- **Roads Traveled:** The 44 mile route follows New Mexico State Highways 27 and 152 which are narrow paved roads suitable for all vehicles. The entire 44 mile route has been designated a BLM Type I Back Country Byway.
- **Travel Season:** The entire route is open year-round.
- **Description:** The back country scenic drive travels through historic mining towns offering views of the Black Range Mountains, Caballo Mountains, and the Uvas Mountains. Although there are no established hiking and backpacking trails accessed along the route, the surrounding hills invite careful exploration of abandoned rock cabins and mining camps. Primitive camping is allowed anywhere on BLM administered lands and developed campgrounds can be found east of this route in the Caballo Lake and Elephant Butte State Parks. The lakes in these state parks also provides opportunities for year-round boating and fishing. The present town site of Lake Valley was established in 1878 after the original site was flooded. The original site was located 3 miles to the north and a few remains of the town and mining operations may be seen.
- **Other Nearby Routes:** The Inner Loop - Gila Cliff Dwellings scenic drive is about 35 miles to the west and approximately 85 miles to the north is the Quebradas scenic drive. The White Mountain and Coronado Trail scenic drives are about 155 miles northwest in Arizona.

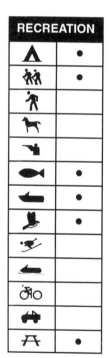

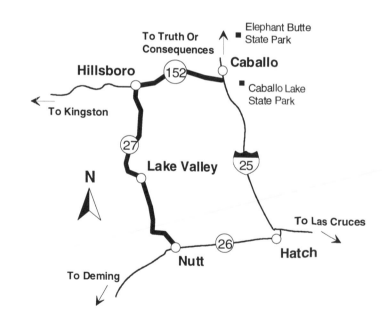

Information Sources:

Las Cruces District Office, 1800 Marquess St., Las Cruces, NM 88005-1420 / 505-525-8228
Hatch Valley Chamber of Commerce, 224 Elm St., Hatch, NM 87937 / 505-267-5050
Truth or Consequences / Sierra County Chamber of Commerce, 201 S. Foch St., T or C, NM 87901 / 800-831-9487

QUEBRADAS

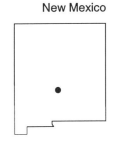

- *Route Location:* Located in central New Mexico, north of Socorro. The northern access is located off Interstate 25 east of Escondida and travels southeast to the junction of County Road A129, north of U.S. Highway 380.
- *Roads Traveled:* The 24 mile route follows the Quebradas Road which is a dirt road requiring a two-wheel drive, high-clearance vehicle. A four-wheel drive vehicle is recommended during wet weather. The 24 mile route has been designated a BLM Type II Back Country Byway.
- *Travel Season:* The route is normally open year-round but heavy rains can make the dry wash crossing impassable.
- *Description:* Situated between two National Wildlife Refuges, this back country route travels along multicolored cliffs, unusual rock formations, and badlands with glimpses of the Rio Grande and surrounding rugged mountains. Wildlife inhabiting this region of New Mexico includes mule deer, coyotes, bobcats, gray foxes, and jack rabbits. The endangered whooping crane is also seen occasionally. Two wilderness study areas located along the route provide great opportunities for hiking, backpacking, and primitive camping. No developed campgrounds are available along this drive, but the nearby Cibola National Forest, west of the route, does have camping facilities.
- *Other Nearby Routes:* Approximately 90 miles to the north is the Sandia Crest scenic drive and about 80 miles to the south is the Lake Valley scenic drive which is also close to the Inner Loop - Gila Cliff Dwellings. About 135 miles southeast is the Sunspot scenic route.

RECREATION	
⛺	•
🥾	•
🚶	
🐎	
🔫	•
🐟	
🛶	
⛷	•
🎿	
🛷	
🚵	
🚙	
⛱	•

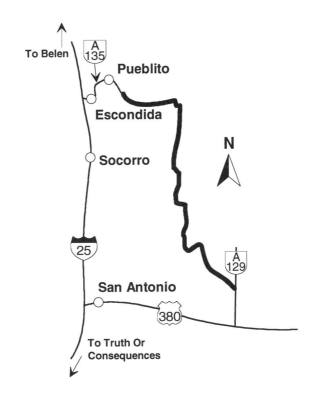

ATTRACTIONS	
🦌	•
🌲	•
〰	
💧	
🔫	
⛲	
🏛	
🏠	
🛖	
N↑F	
🏔	
↑	
⛵	

Information Sources:

BLM, Las Cruces District Office, 1800 Marquess St., Las Cruces, NM 88005-1420 / 505-525-8228
BLM, Socorro Resource Area, 198 Neel Ave. NW, Socorro, NM 87801-1219 / 505-835-0412
Socorro County Chamber of Commerce, 103 Francisco de Avondo, Socorro, NM 87801 / 505-835-0424

SANDIA CREST ROAD

- *Route Location:* Located in central New Mexico, northeast of Albuquerque. The eastern access is located off New Mexico State Highway 14 in the town of Sandia Park and travels northwest, ending at the Sandia Mountain Wilderness area.
- *Roads Traveled:* The 11 mile route follows Forest Service Road 536 which is a two-lane paved road suitable for all vehicles although there are some sharp curves. Travelers will need to retrace the route back to either highway 165 or 14. The entire 11 mile route has been designated a National Forest Scenic Byway.
- *Travel Season:* The entire route is open year-round. Winter driving conditions may exist at the higher elevations and chains or snow tires are sometimes required.
- *Description:* The scenic drive climbs nearly 4,000 feet as it travels through the high desert and thick forests of the Cibola National Forest. No developed camp-grounds are located along the route, however camping can be found in the Coronado State Park which is west of the drive on State Highway 44 a few miles west of Interstate 25. Several picnic areas are provided and offer nature trails or access to hiking trails. Winter activities are found at the Capulin Snow Play Area and the Sandia Peak Ski Area, which also runs the ski lift during the summer.
- *Other Nearby Routes:* About 60 miles northeast from Albuquerque is the Santa Fe scenic drive and an additional 70 miles northeast is the Enchanted Circle scenic route which is also close to the Wild River scenic drive. Approximately 90 miles to the south is the Quebradas route and less than 100 miles to the west is the Chain Of Craters scenic drive.

New Mexico

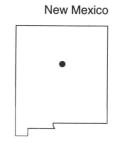

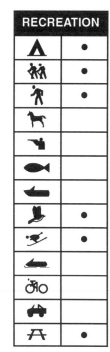

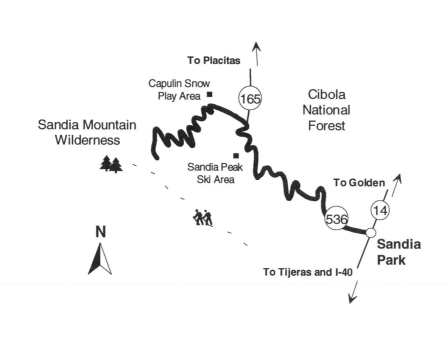

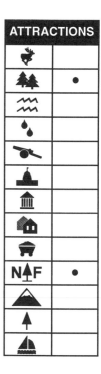

Information Sources:

Cibola National Forest, 2113 Osuna Rd. NE, Suite A, Albuquerque, NM 87113-1001 / 505-275-5207
Cibola National Forest, Sandia Ranger District, 11776 Highway 337, Tijeras, NM 87059 / 505-281-3304
Greater Albuquerque Chamber of Commerce, 401 Second St., N.W., Albuquerque, NM 87125 / 505-764-3700

SANTA FE

- *Route Location:* Located in north-central New Mexico in Santa Fe. The southern access is located in downtown Santa Fe at the corner of Palace and Washington Streets and travels northeast to the roads end at the Santa Fe Ski Area.
- *Roads Traveled:* The 15 mile route follows New Mexico State Highway 475 which is a narrow two-lane paved road with sharp curves and steep grades. Caution should be used by all drivers. Travelers will need to retrace the route back to Santa Fe. The route has been designated a National Forest Scenic Byway.
- *Travel Season:* The entire route is open year-round although winter driving conditions can be hazardous and temporary delays are possible for snow removal.
- *Description:* This route travels across the Santa Fe National Forest through rolling foothills into the dense forest of the Sangre de Cristo Mountains. Several developed campgrounds and picnic areas can be found

along the route. Hyde Memorial State Park also provides year-round camping opportunities. A small ice skating pond and tubing hill are provided in the state park while the Santa Fe Ski Area provides excellent downhill and cross-country skiing. A trail is also found here that leads into the Pecos Wilderness and is used for hiking and backpacking during the summer and cross-country skiing in winter. The Palace of the Governor in Santa Fe was built in 1610 by the Spanish government and is the oldest continuously occupied public building in the United States.

- *Other Nearby Routes:* Approximately 70 miles northeast is the Enchanted Circle scenic drive which is also near the Wild Rivers scenic route. About 60 miles to the southwest is the Sandia Crest scenic drive.

New Mexico

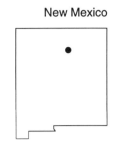

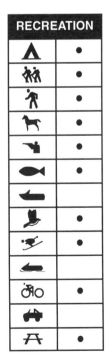

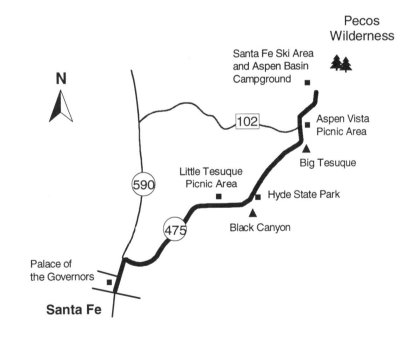

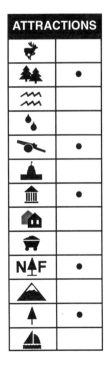

Information Sources:

Santa Fe National Forest, 1220 St. Francis Dr., Santa Fe, NM 87504 / 505-988-6940
Santa Fe National Forest, Espanola Ranger District, P.O. Drawer R, Espanola, NM 87532 / 505-753-7331
Santa Fe County Chamber of Commerce, P.O. Box 1928, Santa Fe, NM 87504 / 505-983-7317

SUNSPOT

- *Route Location:* Located in south-central New Mexico, east of Alamogordo. The northern access is located off U.S. Highway 82 south of Cloudcroft and travels south to the Sunspot Solar Observatory.
- *Roads Traveled:* The 14 mile route follows New Mexico State Highway 6563 which is a two-lane paved road suitable for all vehicles. The entire route has been designated a National Forest Scenic Byway.
- *Travel Season:* The route is open year-round.
- *Description:* Traversing the Lincoln National Forest, this scenic drive travels along the front rim of the Sacramento Mountains through a mixed forest of Douglas-fir, white fir, Southwestern white pine, ponderosa pine, and aspen. Mule deer, black bears, elk, and the occasional eagle and spotted owl can be seen from this drive. Turnouts along the route provide spectacular views of the Tularosa Basin and the shifting sand dunes of the nearby White Sands National Monument. On a clear day you can see the space port for the landing of the space shuttle. Camping and picnicking opportunities are found in the several national forest campgrounds located along or near the drive. Hiking and backpacking is found on the Rim National Recreation Trail which parallels the scenic drive for 13 miles. Winter activities include cross-country skiing and snowmobiling. Two facilities are open to the public at the Sunspot Solar Observatory, the Vacuum Tower Telescope and the John W. Evans Solar Facility.
- *Other Nearby Routes:* Approximately 120 miles to the east is the Lake Valley scenic drive and an additional 50 miles east is the Inner Loop - Gila Cliff Dwelling scenic drive. About 120 miles northwest is the Quebradas scenic route.

New Mexico

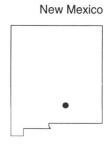

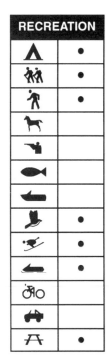

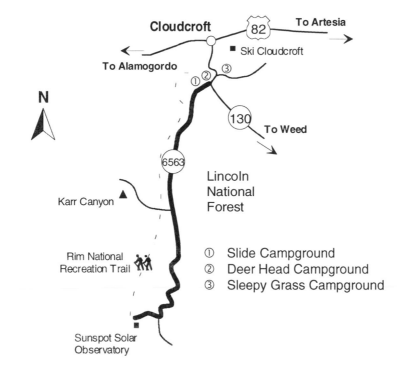

RECREATION	
⛺	•
🥾	•
🚶	•
🐎	
🎣	
🐟	
🛶	
💧	•
🎿	•
🚤	•
🚲	
🚗	
⛱	•

Cloudcroft (82) To Artesia →

■ Ski Cloudcroft

To Alamogordo ← ③
① ②

(130) To Weed →

N

(6563)

Karr Canyon ▲

Lincoln
National
Forest

Rim National
Recreation Trail

① Slide Campground
② Deer Head Campground
③ Sleepy Grass Campground

■ Sunspot Solar
Observatory

ATTRACTIONS	
🦌	
🌲	
♨	
💧	
🔭	
🏛	•
🏛	
🏠	
🛒	
N🇫F	•
🔺	
⛰	•
⛵	

Information Sources:

Lincoln National Forest, 11th & New York, Alamogoroo, NM 88310 / 505-437-6030
Alamogordo Chamber of Commerce, 1301 White Sands Blvd., Alamogordo, NM 88310 / 505-437-6120
Cloudcroft Chamber of Commerce, P.O. Box 125, Cloudcroft, NM 88317 / 505-682-2733

WILD RIVERS

- *Route Location:* Located in north-central New Mexico, north of Taos near the Colorado border. The northern access is located off New Mexico State Highway 522 west of Cerro and travels south through the Wild Rivers Recreation Area.
- *Roads Traveled:* The 13 mile route follows the Wild Rivers Road which is a two-lane paved road suitable for all vehicles. The entire 13 mile route has been designated a BLM Type I Back Country Byway.
- *Travel Season:* The route is generally open year-round, however, the road is not maintained during the winter and heavy snows may restrict access.
- *Description:* As it winds through sagebrush and grass plains with scattered stands of juniper and pinion woodlands, views of the rugged Rio Grande and Red River Gorges are offered. Scenic overlooks along the drive provide views of the canyon and the Rio Grande Wild and Scenic River below. Access to several trails that

descend into the gorge, where riverside camping is available, are provided. Several campgrounds are also located along the rim of the gorge and offer breathtaking views. A visitor center is located near the routes southern end and is staffed during summer months. A guided hike by a park ranger takes place every Saturday and Sunday afternoons, while a campfire program is offered on Saturday evenings.
- *Other Nearby Routes:* The Enchanted Circle scenic drive is about 5 miles to the south and an additional 80 miles southwest to the Santa Fe scenic route. About 140 miles southwest is the Sandia Crest scenic drive and approximately 90 miles northeast is the Highway Of Legends scenic drive in Colorado.

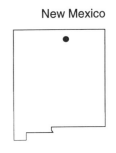
New Mexico

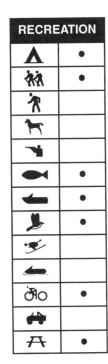

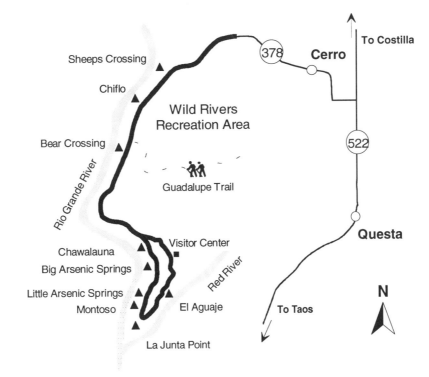

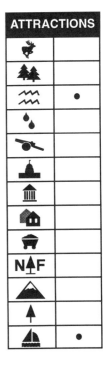

Information Sources:

BLM, Albuquerque District Office, 435 Montano Road NE, Albuquerque, NM 87107 / 505-761-8911
BLM, Taos Resource Area, 224 Cruz Alta Rd., Taos, NM 87571 / 505-758-8851
Taos County Chamber of Commerce, 1139 Paseo del Pueblo Sur, Taos, NM 87571 / 800-732-8267

NEW YORK

□ *Scenic Drives*

Road Condition Numbers: 800-843-7623 (NY only)
800-247-7204 (Canada and N.E. states)

1. Seaway Trail

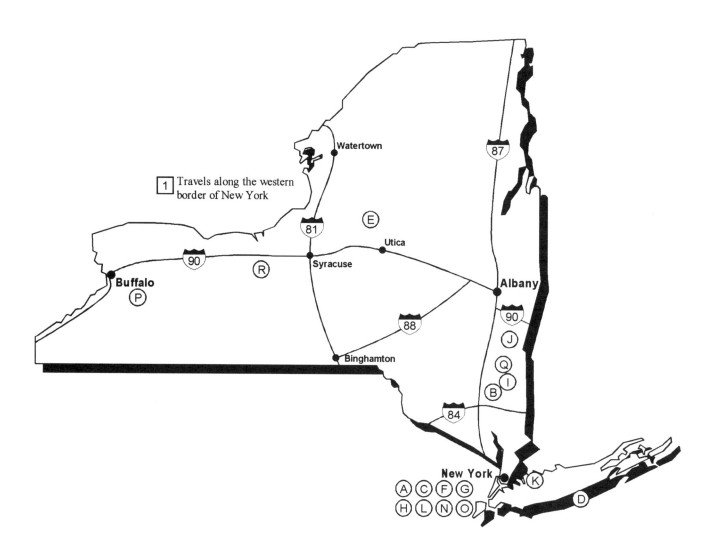

1 Travels along the western border of New York

○ *National Park Areas*

A. Castle Clinton National Monument	J. Martin Van Buren National Historic Site
B. Eleanor Roosevelt National Historic Site	K. Sagamore Hill National Historic Site
C. Federal Hall National Memorial	L. Saint Paul's Church National Historic Site
D. Fire Island National Seashore	M. Saratoga National Historical Park
E. Fort Stanwix National Monument	N. Statue of Liberty National Monument
F. Gateway National Recreation Area	O. Theodore Roosevelt Birthplace Nat'l. Historic Site
G. General Grant National Memorial	P. Theodore Roosevelt Inaugural Nat'l. Historic Site
H. Hamilton Grange National Memorial	Q. Vanderbilt Mansion National Historic Site
I. Home of Franklin D. Roosevelt Nat'l. Historic Site	R. Women's Rights National Historical Park

SEAWAY TRAIL

- *Route Location:* This route is located in northern New York and travels almost the entire length of the state following along the border with Canada. The western terminus is located in Ripley, near the Pennsylvania border and the eastern terminus is in Rooseveltown, which is northeast of Massena.
- *Roads Traveled:* The 454 mile route follows a series of routes that are all two-lane paved roads suitable for all vehicles. For a detailed listing of the routes followed, refer to page 135. The entire route has been designated a New York State Scenic Byway.

- *Travel Season:* The route is open year-round although winter driving conditions may be hazardous.
- *Description:* The Seaway Trail is the open road and nautical connection to New York State's Great Lakes, Niagara River, and St. Lawrence River coastlines.

For motorists, green-and-white Seaway Trail-blazer signs mark the 454 mile scenic byway, the longest National Recreation Trail in the United States. Boaters can navigate by fol-

RECREATION	
⛺ (camping)	•
🚶 (hiking)	•
🏃 (walking)	•
🐎 (horse)	•
🦆 (hunting)	•
🐟 (fishing)	•
🛶 (boating)	•
🎿 (skiing)	•
⛷ (downhill)	•
🛷 (snowmobile)	•
🚲 (biking)	•
🚐 (RV)	
🪑 (picnic)	•

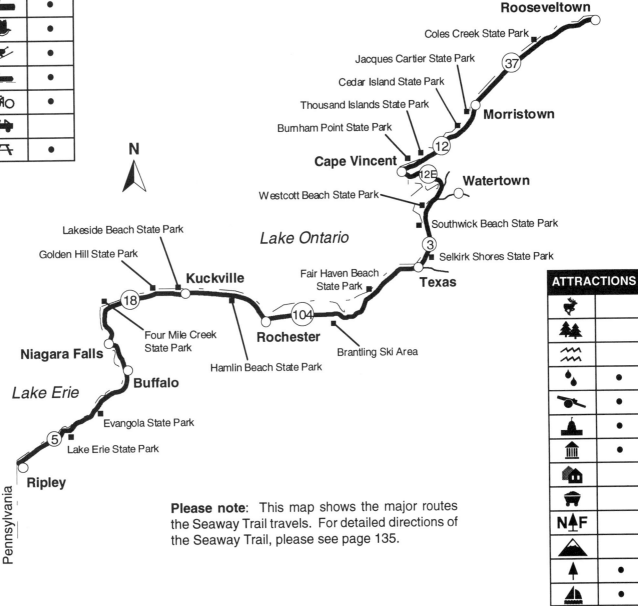

N

ATTRACTIONS	
🦌	
🌲	
〰	
💧	•
🔭	•
🏛	•
🏛	•
🏠	
🚋	
N↑F	
⛰	
↑	•
⛵	•

Please note: This map shows the major routes the Seaway Trail travels. For detailed directions of the Seaway Trail, please see page 135.

SEAWAY TRAIL (CONT.)

lowing the Nautical Seaway Trail Chartbook and Waterfront Guide. Six eastern Seaway Trail Bicycling loops take two-wheeled travelers to a fish hatchery, battlefield, lighthouse, Black Creek, Black Lake, and the scenic Raquette and Grass River areas.

Multi-modal travelers of many interests will find a diverse assortment of attractions on the trail. Learn to sail, visit a World War II LT-5 Tug. Travel by trolley into Buffalo's architectural past, see natural landscapes built by the movement of rocks and ice 500 million years ago in Niagara Falls. Watch a reenactment of the War of 1812. Bicycle to an historic lighthouse or hike through habitats for bird and beast. Study basket-making or massage. Taste apples, wine, 1000 Islands dressing and how hot do you want your Buffalo wings? Take part in a murder mystery set in a museum. Sleep and dine in historic bed and breakfasts, view more than 1000 Islands from a hot air balloon or airplane, and from a riverside campsite watch international oceanliners.

Unique learning vacation experiences await travelers who wish to "enroll" in the unique new Seaway Trail "Roads" Scholars Diploma Program. Participating sites, accommodations and restaurants are offering special discounts to registered "students" of all ages. Those completing "degrees" in Scenic Byway Education will become eligible for four weekends and one week's vacation on the Seaway Trail.

"Roads" Scholars may choose to stroll through 11 acres of beautiful plants at the Buffalo & Erie County Botanical Gardens; see sea life at the Aquarium of Niagara Falls or enjoy hands-on artistic endeavors at Artpark, the only New York State Park devoted to the arts, in Lewiston. Pause for a tasty treat at Brown's Berry Patch, Waterport,

rest a night in an historic bed and breakfast before climbing to the lantern room atop the Old Sodus Lighthouse; learn fascinating facts at the Susan B. Anthony House in Rochester. Step back to 16th century Elizabethan England at the Sterling Renaissance Festival; take a class in boat building or refinishing at the Antique Boat Museum in Clayton; meet native Northern New York wildlife at the Thompson Park Zoo, Watertown; or watch the world's oceanliners rise and fall at the Eisenhower Locks in Massena. These are just some of the marvelous opportunities awaiting Seaway Trail "Roads" Scholars. Families, singles, seniors are all encouraged to enroll by writing Seaway Trail, Inc., 109 Barracks Drive, Sackets Harbor, NY 13685 or call 1-800-SEAWAY-T.

Four seasons of food, festivals and fun await year-round vacationers on the Seaway Trail. Nature's colorful transition begins in September and is generally over by Halloween. Fall foliage tours can be taken by car, boat, floatplane, and train. Farmer's markets and roadside stands offer autumn's harvest of fruits and vegetables or pick-your-own apples. "Shocktober" in Buffalo is celebrated with costume contests, an annual murder mystery, and "BOO!ks" at the Buffalo & Erie County Public Library.

Winter snows often dress the trail in scenic white as Niagara Falls' Festival of Lights illuminates the majestic waterflow. Trailwide you'll find a chance to cut-your-own Christmas tree, ride in a sleigh, rev up your snowmobile, point your skis downhill or cross-country, and watch dog sled races. In February, enjoy a frosty hot air balloon ride at the 1000 Islands Winter Balloon Festival in Clayton. Farther north, the Odgensburg "River Shiver" reenacts its War of 1812 battle history.

continued

Information Sources:

Seaway Trail, Inc., Madison Barracks, 109 Barracks Drive, Sackets Harbor, NY 13685 / 800-SEAWAY-T
Chautauqua County Vacationlands Assoc., 4 N. Erie St., Mayville, NY 14757 / 1-800-242-ILNY
Greater Buffalo Convention and Visitors Bureau, 107 Delaware Ave., Buffalo, NY 14202 / 1-800-BUFFALO
Niagara County Tourism and Sportfishing, 139 Niagara St., Lockport, NY 14094 / 1-800-338-7890
Orleans County Tourism Office, 14016 Route 31 W., Wlbion, NY 14411 / 716-589-7004
Greater Rochester Visitors Association, 126 Andrews St., Rochester, NY 14604 / 716-546-3070
Wayne County Public Information Office, 9 Pearl St., Lyons, NY 14489 / 1-800-527-6510
Fair Haven Area Chamber of Commerce, Box 317, Fair Haven, NY 13064 / 315-947-6037
County of Oswego Dept. of Tourism and Promotion, 46 E. Bridge St., Oswego, NY 13126 / 1-800-248-4FUN
1000 Islands/Jefferson County, Box 400, Alexandria Bay, NY 13607 / 1-800-8-ISLAND
St. Lawrence County Chamber of Commerce, Drawer A, Canton, NY 13617 / 315-386-4000

SEAWAY TRAIL (CONT.)

As spring approaches, sugar-on-snow gives way to April showers and Lilac flowers in May at Rochester's Lilac Festival. The kids will find treasure at the S'easter Egg Hunt at the Aquarium in Niagara Falls while everyone becomes Irish at Watertown's Irish Festival.

Fishermen test their skills year-round against world-class salmon, trout, bass, walleye, and an assortment of panfish. Register for the Lake Ontario International Fishing Classic, and the Empire State/Lake Ontario Spring Trout & Salmon, Walleye and Summer Derbies, the Niagara County Fall Classic, and a number of ice fishing tournaments trailwide.

Summer sunshine enhances visits to nature centers, architectural walking tours past Victorian, Greek Revival, cobblestone and Federal-style farmhouses and homes, a Shaker farmstead, two restored military forts, and an historic War of 1812 battlefield and through Chautauqua vineyards, apple orchards, and the 1000 Islands. Arrive early for America's oldest and largest outdoor production - the Hill Cumorah Pageant takes place each July in Palmyra and don't miss Oswego's July Harborfest celebration. Pirates invade Alexandria Bay in August, but Heart Island and Boldt Castle will prevail so you can visit this replica of a Rhineland castle.

To request a free Journey Magazine & Directory to New York State's Seaway Trail and information on Seaway Trail guidebooks on architecture, bicycling, geology, historic lighthouses, the War of 1812, and the Nautical Seaway Trail or register for the Seaway Trail "Roads" Scholars program, write the Seaway Trail, Inc. at the address found in the *Information Sources*.

- *Other Nearby Routes:* Approximately 30 miles south of the western terminus is the Grand Army Of The Republic Highway in Pennsylvania which travels the entire length of the state.

Following The Seaway Trail

Beginning at the Pennsylvania - New York state line near the town of Ripley, the Seaway Trail follows state route 5 in a northeasterly direction toward the village of Silver Creek to a point where route 5 merges with U.S. Highway 20. The trail continues along routes 5 and 20 to the community of Irving, where the trail leaves routes 5 and 20 and follows the Old Lake Shore Road, running roughly along the Lake Erie shoreline, to the community of Wanakah. At Wanakah, the trail picks up state route 5 and continues northeasterly and then northerly to the city of Lackawanna and proceeds across the Skyway to the Delaware Avenue exit. The trail then follows Delaware Avenue to Niagara Square in the city of Buffalo and then around Niagara Square to Niagara Street and along Niagara Street to the River Road, state route 265. The trail continues along the River Road, route 265 through the cities of Tonawanda and North Tonawanda to Buffalo Avenue. Following Buffalo Avenue, the trail then turns onto the westbound lanes of the Robert Moses State Parkway until it reaches the Quay Street exit in the city of Niagara Falls. The trail then leaves the Robert Moses State Parkway and follows Quay Street until it reaches Rainbow Boulevard. The trail then continues northerly along Rainbow Boulevard, being state route 384, until it intersects with Niagara Street. The trail then turns westerly onto Niagara Street and continues until it reaches the Rainbow Bridge. From the Rainbow Bridge in the city of Niagara Falls, the trail follows state route 104E to the community of Lewiston, where the trail intersects with route 18F. The trail continues along route 18F until it merges into state route 18. Following route 18, the trail passes the villages of Roosevelt Beach, Olcott, Ashwood and Kuckville. Once inside Lakeside Beach State Park, the trail leaves route 18 and follows Lake Ontario State Parkway. In the town of Irondequoit, Lake Ontario State Parkway joins with Stutson Street. The trail then follows Stutson Street, turns right onto Saint Paul Boulevard, then left onto Lake Shore Boulevard. The trail continues east on Lake Shore Boulevard to Culver Road. The trail then turns right onto Culver Road, then left onto Empire Boulevard, state route 104, then left onto Bay Road and then right onto Lake Road. The trail follows Lake Road through the community of Pultneyville and continues to the village of Sodus Point. At Sodus Point, the trail bears south on state route 14 to Alton, where it intersects Ridge Road. Following Ridge Road, the trail passes through the villages of Resort and Wolcott. Once outside of Wolcott, the trail picks up Old Ridge Road until it reaches the village of Red Creek. There it joins state route 104A. The trail continues north on route 104A through the village of Fair Haven, Sterling and Southwest Oswego to the city of Oswego, then north on state route 104 through the community of Scriba to state route 104B. Proceeding north through the community of Texas, the trail follows route 104B to the intersection with state route 3. There it joins route 3 north through Port Ontario, and roughly parallel to the Lake Ontario shoreline. At Baggs Corners, the trail follows state route 180 north through the village of Dexter to the intersection of state route 12E at Limerick. The trail then follows route 12E west through the village of Chaumont to the village of Cape Vincent, and north along the St. Lawrence River to Clayton where it connects with state route 12 north. The trail follows route 12 past the village of Alexandria Bay, Chippewa Bay and Oak Point. Near Morristown, the trail joins state route 37 north to the city of Ogdensburg. The trail follows state route 124 onto the state arterial, then north on State street (state routes 68/87), and then east on Washington street. The trail turns onto North Rossell street, then left on Ford street. The trail turns left onto Proctor Avenue, then turns right onto state route 812 and south to state route 37. After passing through the village of Waddington, the trail continues on 37 through the town of Louisville, connecting by a left turn onto state route 131. The trail turns right at the intersection of Tunnel Road, still on route 131. At the junction with county route 42, the trail continues straight over the Grasse River Bridge to the junction with state route 37 north. The trail turns left onto route 37 north to the trail's northern terminus at the Rooseveltown International Bridge to Canada.

NORTH CAROLINA

□ *Scenic Drives*

1. Forest Heritage

○ *National Parks*

A. Cape Hatteras National Seashore
B. Cape Lookout National Seashore
C. Carl Sandburg Home National Historic Site
D. Fort Raleigh National Historic Site
E. Great Smoky Mountains National Park
F. Guilford Courthouse National Military Park
G. Moores Creek National Battlefield
H. Wright Brothers National Memorial

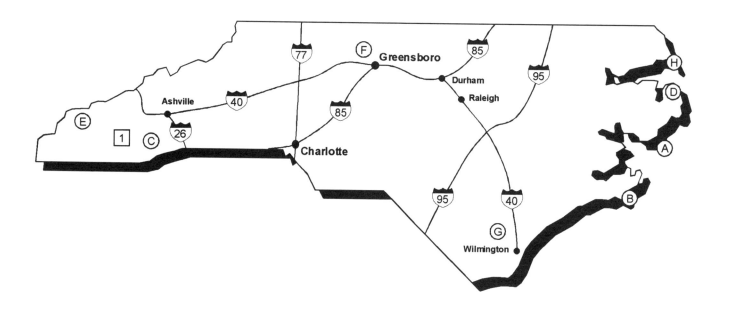

FOREST HERITAGE

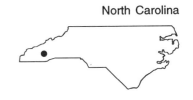

North Carolina

- *Route Location:* Located in western North Carolina, southwest of Asheville. The southern access is located in the town of Roseman and travels northeast forming a loop drive back to Roseman.
- *Roads Traveled:* The 79 mile route follows North Carolina State Highway 215 and U.S. Highways 276 and 64 which are all two-lane paved roads suitable for all vehicles. The 79 mile loop drive has been designated a National Forest Scenic Byway.
- *Travel Season:* The route is open year-round although occasional snow and ice may require the use of chains.
- *Description:* This scenic drive crosses the Pisgah National Forest through hardwood forests along meandering streams, and past cascading waterfalls. Wildlife in this region includes black bears, deer, wild turkeys, and gray foxes. Looking Glass Falls plummets 60 feet in an unbroken rush of white water 30 feet wide into the deep pool below. Nearby is the Sliding Rock, a 60 foot smooth rock natural waterslide. Looking Glass Rock is a granite monolith that glistens like a mirror, or looking glass, when water freezes on its surface. It can be accessed by a 3 mile trail beginning on Forest Service Road 475. Two wilderness areas provide additional hiking and backpacking opportunities.

- *Other Nearby Routes:* About 35 miles southwest in South Carolina is the Oscar Wigington scenic drive and approximately 90 miles to the southwest is the Ocoee scenic drive in Tennessee. The Russell-Brasstown scenic drive is about 80 miles southwest in Georgia. The Blue Ridge Parkway begins near this route and travels through North Carolina and Virginia. For more information contact the National Park Service at the address listed below.

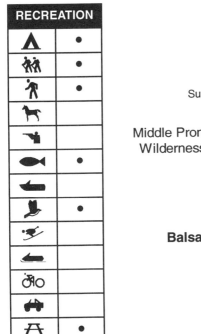

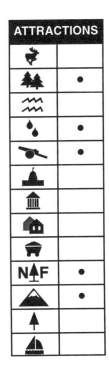

Information Sources:

Pisgah National Forest, Pisgah Ranger District, 1001 Pisgah Hwy., Pisgah Forest, NC 28768 / 704-877-3350
Brevard - Transylvania Chamber of Commerce, 35 W. Main St., Brevard, NC 28712 / 800-648-4523
Greater Haywood Cnty. Chamber of Commerce, 1124 Sulphur Springs Rd., Waynesville, NC 28786 / 704-456-3021
Asheville Area Chamber of Commerce, 151 Haywood St., Asheville, NC 28802 / 704-258-3858
Greater Hendersonville Chamber of Commerce, 330 N. King St., Hendersonville, NC 28792 / 704-692-1413
National Park Service, Blue Ridge Parkway, 200 BB&T Building, One Pack Square, Asheville, NC 28801

OHIO

☐ *Scenic Drives*

Road Condition Number: 614-466-7170

1. Covered Bridge

○ *National Park Areas*

A. Cuyahoga Valley National Recreation Area
B. David Berger National Memorial
C. Dayton Aviation National Historical Park
D. Hopewell Culture National Historical Park
E. James A. Garfield National Historic Site
F. Perry's Victory and International Peace Memorial
G. William Howard Taft National Historic Site

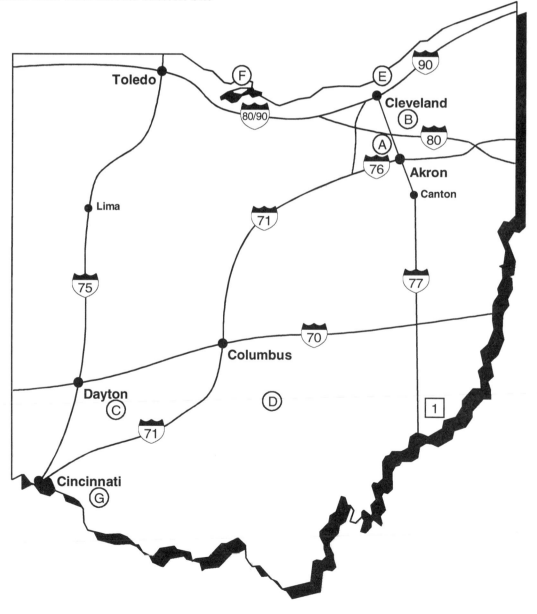

COVERED BRIDGE

- *Route Location:* Located in southeastern Ohio, east of Marietta near the West Virginia border. The southwestern access is located off Interstate 77 east of Marietta on the national forest boundary and travels northeast to the junction of Ohio State Highway 78 in the town of Woodsfield.
- *Roads Traveled:* The 44 mile route follows Ohio State Highway 26 which is a narrow two-lane paved road suitable for most vehicles. The 44 mile route has been designated a National Forest Scenic Byway.
- *Travel Season:* The entire route is open year-round.
- *Description:* This scenic drive winds through the scenic hills and valleys of southeastern Ohio as it travels across the Wayne National Forest. Wildlife inhabiting this region of Ohio includes white-tailed deer, turkeys, beavers, red foxes, raccoons, and minks. The Little Muskingum River follows alongside much of the route and provides fishing and canoeing opportunities. Several covered bridges are seen along this scenic drive with recreation areas nearby that provide camping and picnicking opportunities. Many of the recreation areas also provide access points to the river for launching a canoe. Hiking and horseback riding opportunities are offered on the Wayne National Forest as is backpacking, but it is recommended that a detailed forest map be obtained to insure a safe hike, and reduce the chances of straying onto private lands.
- *Other Nearby Routes:* No other scenic drives are located within a close distance.

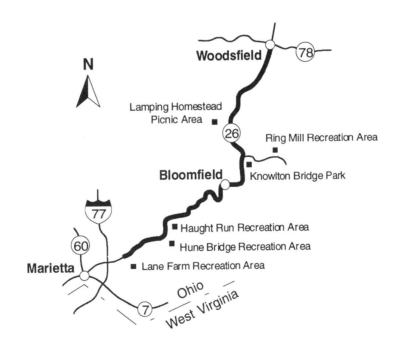

Information Sources:

Wayne - Hoosier National Forests, Marietta Field Office, Route 1, Box 132, Marietta, OH 45750 / 614-373-9055
Marietta Area Chamber of Commerce, 316 third St., Marietta, OH 45750 / 614-373-5176
Monroe County Chamber of Commerce, 112 E. Court St., Woodsfield, OH 43793 / 614-472-5499

OKLAHOMA

☐ *Scenic Drives*

1. Talimena

○ *National Park Areas*

A. Chickasaw National Recreation Area

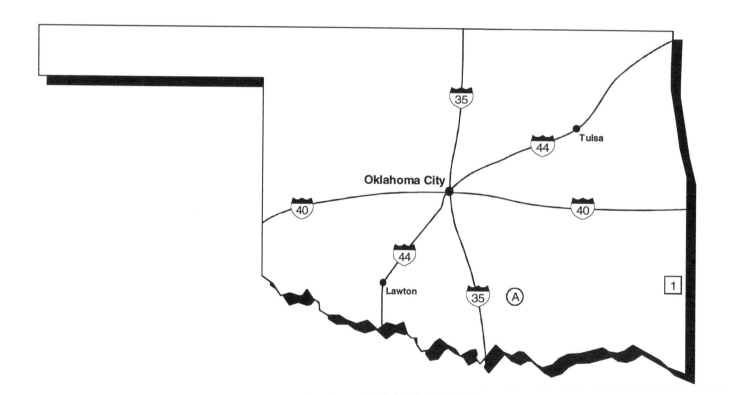

Road Condition Number: 405-425-2385

TALIMENA

* *Route Location:* Located in southeastern Oklahoma and southwestern Arkansas, south of fort smith, Arkansas. The western access is located off U.S. Highway 271 north of Talihina and travels east to the junctions of U.S. Highway 71 in Mena, Arkansas.
* *Roads Traveled:* The 54 mile route follows Oklahoma State Highway 1 and Arkansas State Highway 88. The routes are two-lane paved roads with some steep grades and sharp curves, but are suitable for all vehicles. The entire route has been designate a National Forest Scenic Byway.
* *Travel Season:* The route is generally open year-round although heavy winter snows can occasionally close the route for snow removal.
* *Description:* The scenic drive rides the crest of the forested Rich and Ouachita Mountains, one of America's oldest land masses, as it crosses the Ouachita National Forest. Several turnouts are located along the route providing panoramic views of the surrounding wilderness. A 90 acre lake at the Cedar Lake Recreation Area provides good sailing, canoeing, and fishing opportunities. Hiking, backpacking, and horseback riding are popular activities found along this scenic drive including the Ouachita National Recreation Trail. The Robert S. Kerr Memorial Arboretum and Nature Center is located midway along the drive and offers exhibits and three interpretive nature trails. Camping and picnicking opportunities are plentiful along and nearby the scenic drive.
* *Other Nearby Routes:* Approximately 100 miles to the northeast are the Mount Evans and southern section of the Arkansas Highway 7 scenic drive.

Oklahoma

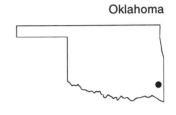

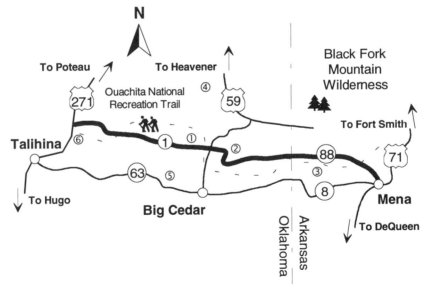

RECREATION	
⛺ (tent)	•
🥾 (hiking)	•
🚶 (walking)	•
🐎 (horseback)	•
🎣 (boat ramp)	•
🐟 (fishing)	•
🛶 (canoe)	•
🚤 (water ski)	•
🤿 (swimming)	
🚣 (boat)	
🚵 (biking)	•
🚗 (vehicle)	•
🏕️ (picnic)	•

① Winding Stair Campground
② Robert S. Kerr Arboretum
③ Queen Wilhelmina State Park
④ Cedar Lake Recreation Area
⑤ Billy Creek Campground
⑥ Talimena State Park

ATTRACTIONS	
🦌	
🌲	•
〽️	
💧	
🔫	•
🏛️	•
🏛️	
🏠	
🛒	
N↕F	•
🏔️	
⛰️	•
⛵	•

Information Sources:

Ouachita National Forest, 100 Reserve St., Hot Springs, AR 71902 / 501-321-5202
Talihina Chamber of Commerce, P.O. Box 548, Talihina, OK 74571 / 918-563-4338
Heavener Chamber of Commerce, 600 W. First St., Heavener, OK 74937 / 918-653-4303
Mena / Polk County Chamber of Commerce, 524 Sherwood Ave., Mena, AR 71953 / 501-394-2912

OREGON

☐ *Scenic Drives*

1. Blue Mountain
2. Cascade Lakes Highway
3. Christmas Valley
4. Cow Creek
5. Diamond Loop
6. Elkhorn Drive
7. Galice - Hellgate
8. Grave Creek To Marial
9. Hells Canyon
10. Lakeview To Steens
11. Leslie Gulch - Succor Creek

12. Lower Crooked River
13. Lower Deschutes River
14. McKenzie - Santiam Pass Loop
15. Nestucca River
16. Robert Aufderheide Memorial Drive
17. Rogue - Coquille
18. Rogue Umpqua
19. Snake River / Mormon Basin
20. South Fork Alsea River
21. South Fork John Day River
22. Steens Mountain

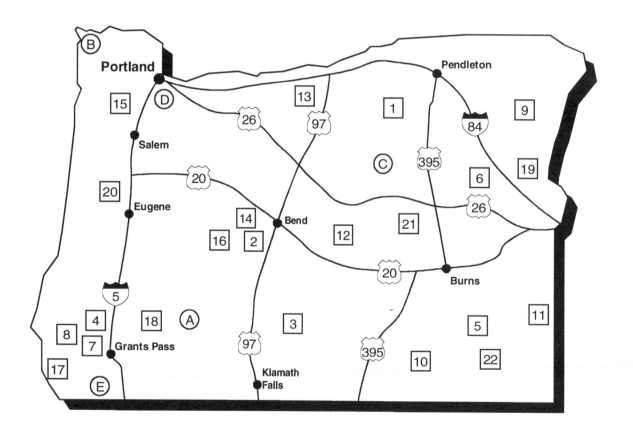

○ *National Park Areas*

A. Crater Lake National Park
B. Fort Clatsop National Memorial
C. John Day Fossil Beds National Monument
D. McLoughlin House National Historic Site
E. Oregon Caves National Monument

Road Condition Numbers:
503-889-3999 (construction)
800-976-7277 (In OR only)

BLUE MOUNTAIN

Oregon

- **Route Location:** Located in northeastern Oregon, west of Hermiston. The northern access is located off Interstate 84 east of Arlington and travels southeast to the junction of Forest Service Road 73, north of Granite.
- **Roads Traveled:** The 130 mile route follows Oregon State Highway 74 and Forest Service Roads 53 and 52 which are two-lane paved roads suitable for all vehicles. The entire 130 mile route has been designated a National Forest Scenic Byway
- **Travel Season:** The entire route is generally open from about June through mid-November and then the portions crossing the national forest are usually closed due to winter snows.
- **Description:** A portion of this scenic drive crosses the Umatilla National Forest and offers a variety of scenery along with historical sites and many recreational opportunities. Several sites found along this route are of national or state significance and include a crossing

of the Oregon Trail, located about 16 miles south of Interstate 84, the Wild and Scenic John Day River, and the North Fork John Day Wilderness. Penland Lake provides opportunities for camping, picnicking, boating, swimming, and fishing. At the ghost town of Hardman, about 20 miles southwest of Heppner, the town's buildings remain, along with a renovated dance hall, as it was at the beginning of the century.

- **Other Nearby Routes:** The southeastern terminus of this route connects with the Elkhorn Drive scenic route which is also next to the Snake River/Mormon Basin and Hells Canyon scenic drives. Approximately 60 miles to the south is the South Fork John Day River scenic drive. About 80 miles southwest of the northern terminus is the Lower Deschutes River scenic route.

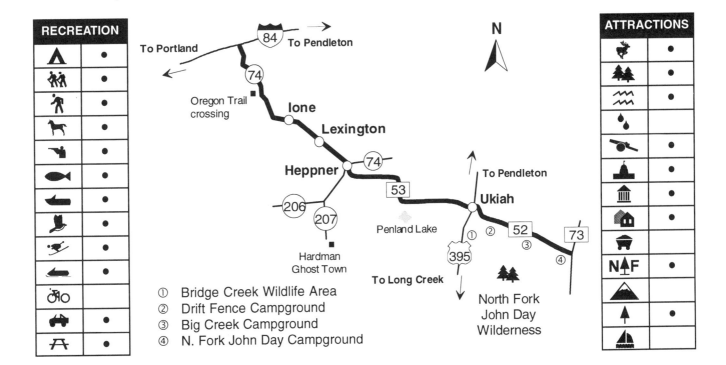

RECREATION	
⛺ (tent)	•
🥾 (hiking)	•
🚶 (walking)	•
🐎 (horse)	•
(boat launch)	•
🐟 (fish)	•
🛶 (boating)	•
(water ski)	•
⛷ (skiing)	•
🛷 (snowmobile)	•
🚵 (biking)	•
🚙 (4-wheel)	•
⛱ (picnic)	•

To Portland — 84 — To Pendleton

74

Oregon Trail crossing

Ione

Lexington

74

Heppner

206

207

Hardman Ghost Town

53

Penland Lake

To Pendleton

Ukiah

52

73

① ②

③

④

395

To Long Creek

North Fork John Day Wilderness

N

① Bridge Creek Wildlife Area
② Drift Fence Campground
③ Big Creek Campground
④ N. Fork John Day Campground

ATTRACTIONS	
🦌 (deer)	•
🌲 (forest)	•
⛰ (mountains)	•
💧 (water)	
(cannon)	•
🏛 (capitol)	•
🏛 (museum)	
🏠 (house)	•
🛖 (cabin)	
N⋏F	•
🏔 (mountain)	
⛺ (trail)	•
⛴ (ferry)	

Information Sources:

Umatilla National Forest, 2717 SW Hailey Ave., Pendleton, OR 97801 / 503-278-3716
Arlington Chamber of Commerce, P.O. Box 2000, Arlington, OR 97812 / 503-454-2643
Heppner Chamber of Commerce, P.O. Box 1232, Heppner, OR 97836 / 503-676-5536
Baker County Chamber of Commerce, 490 Campbell St., Baker City, OR 97814 / 503-523-5855

CASCADE LAKES HIGHWAY

Oregon

- *Route Location:* Located in central Oregon starting in Bend. The northeastern access starts in Bend and travels southwest to the junction of State Highway 58.
- *Roads Traveled:* The 79 mile route follows County Road 46 which is a two-lane paved road suitable for all vehicles. The entire 79 mile route has been designated a National Forest Scenic Byway.
- *Travel Season:* The route from Bend to the Mt. Bachelor Ski and Summer Resort is open year-round. The remaining portion is closed by heavy winter snows.
- *Description:* Travels through the Deschutes National Forest with magnificent views of snow-covered peaks of the Cascade Mountain Range. Surrounded by mountains, lakes, and forests, this scenic drive provides a wide array of recreational opportunities. A variety of wildlife inhabits this region of Oregon including mule deer, black bears, bald eagles, and many species of hawks. Many trails accessed from the scenic drive lead

into the 200,000 acre Three Sisters Wilderness area. Several hiking, snowmobiling, mountain biking, and cross-country skiing trails are also found along this route. The numerous lakes and reservoirs found along the drive offer opportunities for camping, picnicking, boating, and fishing. The Mt. Bachelor ski area operates the ski lift during the summer which provides a spectacular 360 degree view of the Cascade Mountains

- *Other Nearby Routes:* Approximately 35 miles east is the Lower Crooked River scenic drive and about 45 miles to the southeast is the Christmas Valley scenic route. To the northwest about 30 miles is the McKenzie-Santiam Pass Loop scenic drive. About 40 miles northwest from the southern terminus is the Robert Aufderheide Memorial Drive.

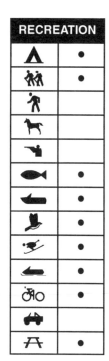

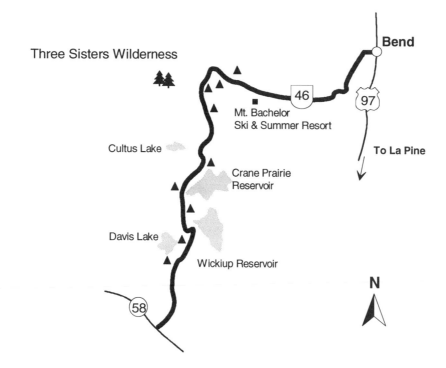

Information Sources:

Deschutes National Forest, 1645 Hwy. 20 East, Bend, OR 97701 / 503-388-8574
Bend Chamber of Commerce, 63085 N. Hwy. 97, Bend, OR 97701 / 503-382-3221
Sunriver Area Chamber of Commerce, P.O. Box 3246, Sunriver, OR 97707 / 503-593-8149

CHRISTMAS VALLEY

- **Route Location:** Located in south-central Oregon, southeast of Bend. The northwestern access is located off Oregon State Highway 31 west of Fort Rock and travels southeast, forming an open loop drive back to highway 31 east of Silver Lake.
- **Roads Traveled:** The 102 mile route follows Lake County Roads 5-10, 5-12, 5-12B, 5-14, 5-14C, 5-14D, 5-14E, and 5-14F, and BLM Road 6109C. The route travels over a combination of paved and unsurfaced roads suitable to passenger cars except for BLM Road 6109C which requires a high-clearance vehicle. The route has been designated a BLM Type I and Type II Back Country Byway.
- **Travel Season:** Much of the route is open year-round although some sections will close in the winter from heavy snowfall. Portions of the route may also become impassable due to flooding and extremely muddy conditions from March through May.

- **Description:** The route travels through the high desert landscapes and unique features which surround Christmas Valley. The Lost Forest is an isolated pine forest growing in the desert while the adjacent 15,000 acre Fossil Lake Sand Dunes rise 60 feet above the desert floor. Crack In The Ground is a two mile long fracture in a lava flow that reaches depths of 50 feet in some places and is 10 to 15 feet wide. Camping, picnicking, hunting, and fishing opportunities are offered along or near the route.
- **Other Nearby Routes:** About 85 miles southeast is the Lakeview To Steens scenic drive which is also near the Steens Mountain and Diamond Loop scenic drives. Approximately 60 miles northwest in Bend is the Cascade Lakes Highway and an additional 30 miles northwest lies the McKenzie-Santiam Pass Loop scenic drive.

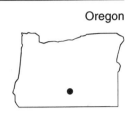

Oregon

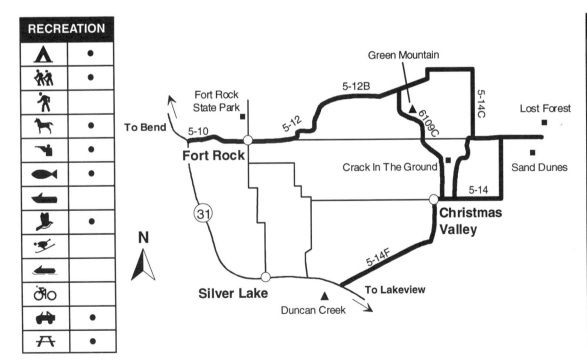

Information Sources:

BLM, Lakeview District Office, 1000 Ninth St. S, Lakeview, OR 97630 / 503-947-6110
Lake County Chamber of Commerce, 513 Center St., Lakeview, OR 97630 / 503-947-6040
Bend Chamber of Commerce, 63085 N. Hwy. 97, Bend, OR 97701 / 503-382-3221

COW CREEK

Oregon

- *Route Location:* Located in southwestern Oregon, south of Roseburg. The southern access is located off Interstate 5 east of Glendale and travels northwest forming an open loop drive to the town of Riddle, just west of Interstate 5.
- *Roads Traveled:* The 45 mile route follows the Cow Creek Road which is a two-lane paved road suitable for all vehicles. The entire 45 mile route has been designated a BLM Type I Back Country Byway.
- *Travel Season:* The entire route is open year-round.
- *Description:* This back country scenic drive follows alongside Cow Creek for most of the route, offering views of the creek, large rock bluffs, mixed conifer forests, and large areas of serpentine soils with its unique Jeffrey Pine forests. The railroad passes through the canyon providing views of railroad bridges, tunnels, and retaining walls from the historic O&C railroad line. Cow Creek has been and continues to be a popular mining area. Gold mining occurs along the route and the BLM maintains the Cow Creek Recreation Gold Panning site located near the midpoint of the drive. Nickel mining operations take place in this area as well and Nickel Mountain, with its nickel mine, can be viewed from the road. No developed campgrounds are provided along this route, however, camping and picnicking facilities can be found along the other nearby scenic drives.
- *Other Nearby Routes:* About 20 miles to the north is the Rogue Umpqua scenic drive and approximately 10 miles to the west is the Grave Creek To Marial scenic route that also connects with the Galice-Hellgate scenic drive. About 65 miles to the southwest is the northern terminus for the State Of Jefferson scenic drive that travels into California.

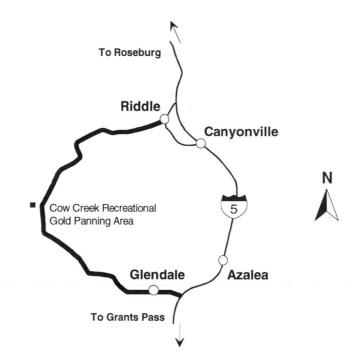

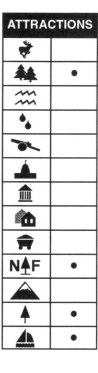

Information Sources:

BLM, Medford District Office, 3040 Biddle Rd., Medford, OR 97504 / 503-770-2200
Canyonville Chamber of Commerce, 250 N.W. Main, Canyonville, OR 97417 / 503-839-4258
Grants Pass / Josephine County, 1501 N.E. 6th St., Grants Pass, OR 97526 / 800-547-5927
Roseburg Area Chamber of Commerce, 410 S.E. Spruce St., Roseburg, OR 97470 / 503-672-2648

DIAMOND LOOP

Oregon

- *Route Location:* Located in southeastern Oregon, southeast of Burns. The northern access is located off Oregon State Highway 78 in the town of Princeton and travels southwest to the town of Frenchglen.
- *Roads Traveled:* The 64 mile route follows a series of county and state secondary roads which are a combination of paved and gravel surfaced roads. The route can safely be traveled by passenger cars although vehicles towing a trailer or larger RVs should check with BLM about current road conditions. All of the 64 miles have been designated a BLM Type I Back Country Byway.
- *Travel Season:* The entire route is open year-round although the graveled sections can be difficult during and after inclement weather.
- *Description:* This scenic drive travels through a patchwork of high desert terrains, from mountain vistas and sage-covered hills to red rimrock canyons and grassy marshes and valleys. Numerous species of wildlife can be seen including wild horses, mule deer, pronghorn antelope, hawks, and eagles. For viewing wild horses, the best place is the established Kiger Mustang Viewing Area located approximately 14 miles east of Diamond. The road to this viewing area requires the use of a high-clearance vehicle and is passable only in dry weather. The unusual design of the Round Barn, built in the late 1870s, is perfectly suited for its purpose which was to break horses during the long, cold winters of eastern Oregon.
- *Other Nearby Routes:* This route connects with the Steens Mountain scenic drive which also connects with the Lakeview To Steens scenic route. Approximately 120 miles to the east, near the Oregon-Idaho border, is the Leslie Gulch-Succor Creek scenic drive.

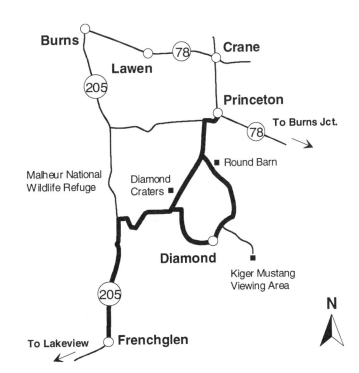

Information Sources:

BLM, Burns District Office, HC74-12533 Hwy. 20 West, Hines, OR 97738 / 503-573-5241
Harney County Chamber of Commerce, 18 W. "D" St., Burns, OR 97720 / 503-573-2636

ELKHORN DRIVE

Oregon

- *Route Location:* Located in northeast Oregon starting in Baker. The southeastern access starts in Baker and travels northwest forming a loop drive back to Baker.
- *Roads Traveled:* The 106 mile route follows Oregon State Highway 7, County Road 24, Forest Service Road 73, county Road 1146, and U.S. Highway 30. All of the routes travel over two-lane paved roads suitable for all vehicles. The entire 106 mile route has been designated a National Forest Scenic Byway.
- *Travel Season:* Most of the route is open year-round except the highway between Granite and Anthony Lake which is usually closed because of snow cover from about mid-November through mid-June.
- *Description:* This scenic drive travels across the Wallowa-Whitman National Forest through the Elkhorn Mountains providing outstanding scenery with an abundance of history, geology, and natural resources. Scenic overlooks along the drive offer spectacular views of the surrounding wilderness. Wildlife that may be seen along the scenic drive includes elk, mule deer, bald eagles, sandhill cranes, and hawks. Numerous developed national forest campgrounds and picnic areas can be found along the route. Hiking, backpacking, and horseback riding activities are offered in the North Fork John Day Wilderness. Winter sport enthusiasts can enjoy snowmobiling, downhill skiing, and cross-country skiing.
- *Other Nearby Routes:* The Blue Mountain scenic drive can be accessed from the western portion of this route. The Hells Canyon and Snake River/Mormon Basin scenic drives are also next to this drive. Approximately 80 miles to the southwest is the South Fork John Day River scenic drive.

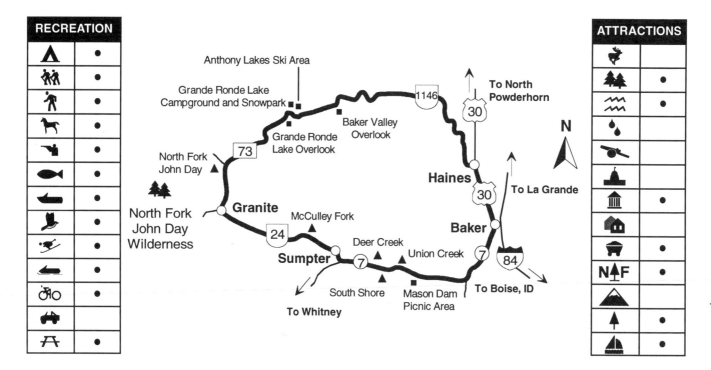

Information Sources:

Wallowa - Whitman National Forest, Baker Ranger District, 3165 10th St., Baker, OR 97814 / 503-523-4476
Umatilla National Forest, 2717 SW Hailey Ave., Pendleton, OR 97801 / 503-278-3716
Baker County Chamber of Commerce, 490 Campbell St., Baker, OR 97814 / 503-523-5855

GALICE - HELLGATE

Oregon

- *Route Location:* Located in the southwestern corner of Oregon, northwest of Grants Pass. The eastern access is located off Interstate 5 east of Merlin and travels west before the route splits in Galice. Continuing west leads to the national forest boundary. Heading north from Galice, the route officially ends at Grave Creek.
- *Roads Traveled:* The 39 mile route follows the Merlin-Galice, Hellgate, and Galice Access roads and Forest Service Road 23. The route travels mostly over two-lane paved roads with a short stretch of one-lane road. The route is suitable for all vehicles although caution should be exercised on the one-lane segment. The route has been designated a BLM Type I Back Country Byway.
- *Travel Season:* The route is generally open year-round except the portions that travel through the Siskiyou National Forest which closes due to heavy snowfall.

- *Description:* The route follows alongside the Rogue National Wild and Scenic River which is recognized for its outstanding scenery and challenging rapids. Traveling high into the Siskiyou Mountains, spectacular views of the rugged river canyon are offered. Several access points to the river are provided for white water rafting and fishing opportunities. Recreational opportunities include hiking, backpacking, and camping. Maps, brochures, and river permits are available at the visitor center.
- *Other Nearby Routes:* The Grave Creek To Marial scenic drive is accessed from the northern terminus and the Rogue-Coquille scenic drive is about 15 miles west of the western terminus. About 20 miles to the north is the Cow Creek scenic drive and 20 miles to the southeast is the Rogue Umpqua scenic route.

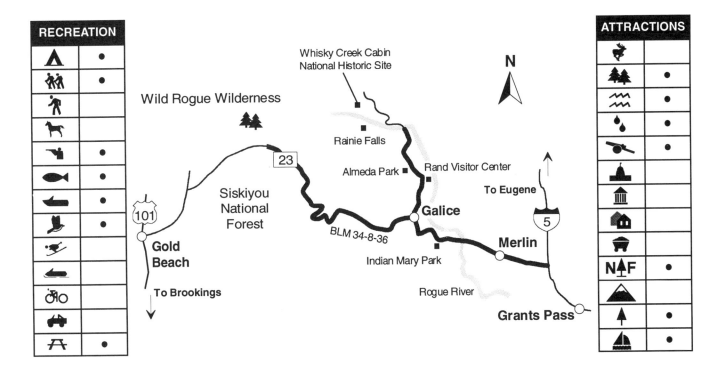

Information Sources:

BLM, Medford District Office, 3040 Biddle Rd., Medford, OR 97504 / 503-770-2200
Grants Pass/Josephine County Chamber of Commerce, 1501 N.E. 6th St., Grants Pass, OR 97526 / 800-547-5927
Gold Beach Chamber of Commerce, 1225 S. Ellensburg Ave., #3, Gold Beach, OR 97444 / 800-525-2334
Myrtle Point Chamber of Commerce, P.O. Box 265, Myrtle Point, OR 97458 / 503-572-2626

GRAVE CREEK TO MARIAL

Oregon

- *Route Location:* Located in the southwestern corner of Oregon, northwest of Grants Pass. This scenic drive is accessed from the northern terminus of the Galice-Hellgate scenic route and travels west to Marial, near the Rogue River Ranch National Historic Site.
- *Roads Traveled:* The 33 mile route follows the Mt. Reuben, Kelsey Mule, and Marial Roads. The route travels over a combination of one-lane paved and gravel surfaced roads that are suitable for passenger cars. The route has been designated a BLM Type I Back Country Byway.
- *Travel Season:* The route is closed in the winter due to heavy snowfall.
- *Description:* The scenic drive climbs out of the Rogue River canyon through a forested landscape before descending to the Rogue River and the settlement of Marial. Two viewpoints found along the route overlook the Rogue River and the thundering Rainie Falls.

Wildlife inhabiting the rugged canyon and mountains include elk, bears, deer, and wild turkeys. Many hiking trails, including the Rogue River National Recreation Trail and Mule Creek Canyon Trail into the Wild Rogue Wilderness, can be accessed from the route. The Rogue River Ranch, located near the scenic drive's end, has been converted to a museum and is staffed every day from May through October. Camping, fishing, and rafting are popular activities found along this drive.

- *Other Nearby Routes:* The Galice-Hellgate scenic route that this drive was accessed from also leads to the Rogue-Coquille scenic drive about 15 miles west. About 10 miles east in Glendale is the Cow Creek scenic drive. Located approximately 20 miles to the east is the Rogue-Umpqua scenic drive.

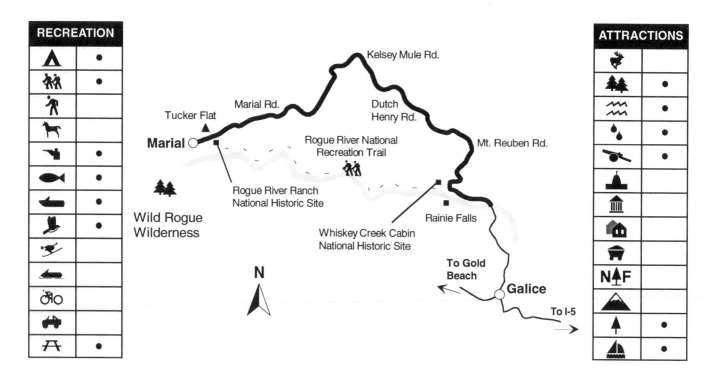

Information Sources:

BLM, Medford District Office, 3040 Biddle Rd., Medford, OR 97504 / 503-770-2200
Grants Pass/Josephine County Chamber of Commerce, 1501 N.E. 6th St., Grants Pass, OR 97526 / 800-547-5927
Gold Beach Chamber of Commerce, 1225 S. Ellensburg Ave., #3, Gold Beach, OR 97444 / 800-525-2334

HELLS CANYON

- *Route Location:* Located in northeastern Oregon, the southwestern access starts in Baker and travels northeast forming an open loop drive to the town of La Grande on Interstate 84.
- *Roads Traveled:* The main loop of the 314 mile route follows Oregon State Highways 86 and 82 and Forest Service Road 39 which are two-lane paved roads suitable for all vehicles. The spur roads follow State Highway 350 and Forest Service Roads 454, 3965, 3955, and 4240 which vary from two-lane paved to gravel surfaced roads. The spur roads are suitable for automobile travel but vehicles pulling trailers or larger RVs may have difficulty turning around. The route has been designated a National Forest Scenic Byway.
- *Travel Season:* Most of the route is open year-round although winter driving conditions can be hazardous and portions will temporarily close in the winter.
- *Description:* The scenic drive crosses portions of the Wallowa-Whitman National Forest as it travels through the Wallowa Mountains passing narrow, ponderosa pine covered canyons and across alpine meadows. Views of the Hells Canyon of the Snake River, the deepest river-carved gorge in North America, are provided along some of the spur roads. Other spur roads lead you well into the steep-sided canyon and to the beginning of the wild and scenic portion of the Snake River. Many recreational opportunities are offered along this route.
- *Other Nearby Routes:* Both the Elkhorn Drive and Snake River/Mormon Basin scenic drives are next to the southern portion of this route. The Blue Mountain scenic drive can also be accessed from the Elkhorn Drive. About 100 miles south is the Leslie Gulch-Succor Creek scenic drive.

Oregon

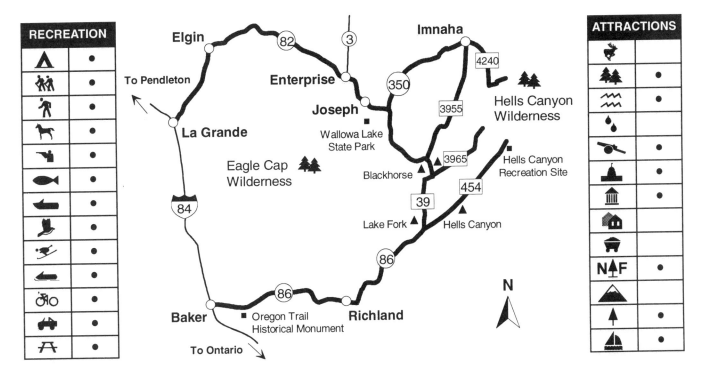

Information Sources:

Wallow - Whitman National Forest, 1550 Dewey Ave., Baker City, OR 97814 / 503-523-6391
Baker County Chamber of Commerce, 490 Campbell St., Baker City, OR 97814 / 503-523-5855
La Grande - Union County Chamber of Commerce, 2111 Adams Ave., La Grande, OR 97850 / 800-848-9969
Wallowa County Chamber of Commerce, 107 S.W. 1st St., Enterprise, OR 97846 / 503-426-4622
Joseph Chamber of Commerce, P.O. Box 13, Joseph, OR 97848 / 503-432-1015

LAKEVIEW TO STEENS

Oregon

- *Route Location:* Located in southeastern Oregon, northeast of Lakeview. The southwestern access is located off U.S. Highway 395 north of Lakeview and travels northeast to the junction of Oregon State Highway 205, near Frenchglen.
- *Roads Traveled:* The 90 mile route follows County Roads 3-13 and 3-12 which travel over a combination of paved and gravel surfaced roads. The route is suitable for most vehicles although the gravel segment can be rough. Vehicles pulling trailers are not recommended on the gravel portion. The route has been designated a BLM Type I and Type II Back County Byway.
- *Travel Season:* The entire route is generally open year-round although temporary closure is possible after heavy rains or in the winter for snow removal.
- *Description:* The scenic drive crosses a portion of the Fremont National Forest through the northern portion of the Warner Mountains and a broad expanse of high desert country. The national forest provides access to developed campgrounds, a hang gliding launch site, fishing in lakes and streams, and many miles of hiking trails. Travelers of this route pass through the Hart Mountain National Wildlife Refuge which offers views of the Warner Wetlands and the opportunity to see mule deer, bighorn sheep, golden eagles, sage grouse, and burrowing owls. Opportunities for camping, hiking, hunting, and fishing can be found here.
- *Other Nearby Routes:* The northeastern terminus of this route leads into the Steens Mountain scenic drive which also leads to the Diamond Loop scenic route. About 85 miles northwest of Lakeview is the Christmas Valley scenic drive and approximately 30 miles south into California is the Barrel Springs scenic drive.

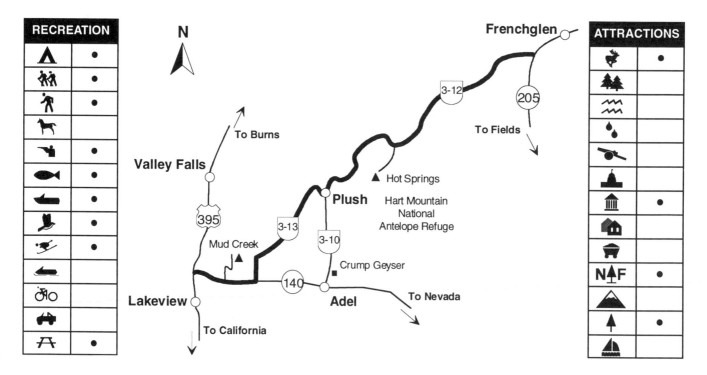

Information Sources:

BLM, Lakeview District Office, 1000 Ninth St. S, Lakeview, OR 97630 / 503-947-6110
Lake County Chamber of Commerce, 513 Center St., Lakeview, OR 97630 / 503-947-6040
Harney County Chamber of Commerce, 18 W. "D" St., Burns, OR 97720 / 503-573-2636

LESLIE GULCH - SUCCOR CREEK

Oregon

- *Route Location:* Located in eastern Oregon, south of Ontario near the Idaho border. The northern access is off Oregon State Highway 201 west of Homedale, Idaho and travels south to the junction of U.S. Highway 95, north of Jordan Valley.
- *Roads Traveled:* The 52 mile route follows a combination of county and BLM roads that travel over graded dirt and gravel surfaced roads. A high-clearance, two-wheel drive vehicle is recommended to travel the entire route. Larger RVs and vehicles pulling trailers are strongly discouraged from traveling this route. The entire route has been designated a BLM Type I and Type II Back Country Byway.
- *Travel Season:* The route is generally open from mid-April through October and then closed by winter snows. Heavy summer thunderstorms can also make the route temporarily impassable.
- *Description:* This back country route travels through some of the most spectacular and rugged country in eastern Oregon with views of unique geologic formations and narrow gorges bound by towering cliffs and ragged spires. Recreational opportunities are provided by two state parks, a BLM recreation site, and Lake Owyhee. Wildlife seen in this area includes antelope, mule deer, coyotes, and collared lizards.
- *Other Nearby Routes:* Approximately 70 miles to the north is the Snake River/Mormon Basin scenic drive which also leads to the Elkhorn Drive and Hells Canyon scenic routes. About 110 miles southwest is the Diamond Loop scenic drive which connects with the Steens Mountain and Lakeview To Steens scenic drives. About 45 miles to the east in Idaho is the Ponderosa Pine scenic drive.

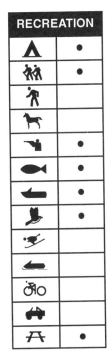

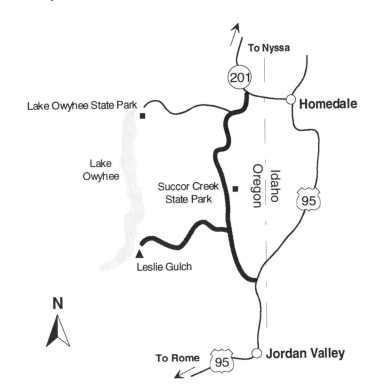

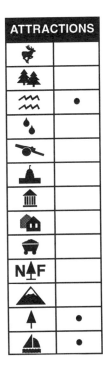

Information Sources:

BLM, Vale District Office, 100 Oregon St., Vale, OR 97918 / 503-473-3144
Nyssa Chamber of Commerce, 212 Main, Nyssa, OR 97913 / 503-372-3091
Ontario Chamber of Commerce, 88 S.W. 3rd Ave., Ontario, OR 97914 / 503-889-8012
Homedale Chamber of Commerce, P.O. Box 845, Homedale, ID 83628 / 208-337-4611

LOWER CROOKED RIVER

- *Route Location:* Located in central Oregon, east of Redmond. The northern access is located off U.S. Highway 26 in Prineville and travels south to the junction of U.S. Highway 20, west of Brothers.
- *Roads Traveled:* The 43 mile route follows Oregon State Highway 27 which is a combination of two-lane paved and gravel surfaced road. The entire route is suitable for all vehicles. The 43 mile route has been designated a BLM Type I Back Country Byway.
- *Travel Season:* The route is usually open year-round although the gravel portion can become muddy after heavy rains and snow.
- *Description:* Travels alongside a portion of the Wild and Scenic Crooked River through a steep-walled canyon before opening up to the vast expanse of Oregon's High Desert. Deer, coyotes, and hawks can be seen along the river while antelope, mule deer, and sagegrouse are found in the high desert region. Bald

Oregon

eagles winter in the area and black bear have been seen on occasion. Several primitive BLM camp sites are located within the canyon in addition to the Chimney Rock Recreation Site. Other nearby camping and picnicking opportunities are found at the Ochoco Lake and Prineville Reservoir State Parks. Fishing for native rainbow trout is best in late spring and early summer when river flows are high.

- *Other Nearby Routes:* About 40 miles to the west is the McKenzie-Santiam Pass Loop scenic drive and an additional 30 miles southeast to the Cascade Lakes Highway scenic route. Approximately 80 miles to the east is the South Fork John Day River scenic drive and about 70 miles north is the Lower Deschutes River scenic drive.

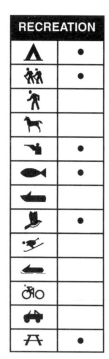

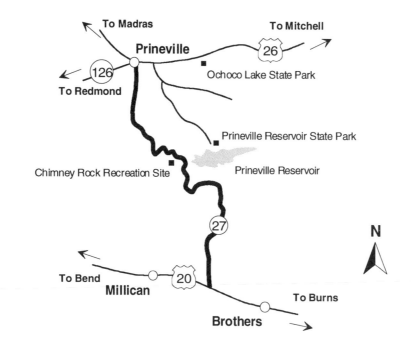

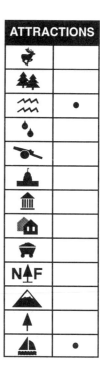

Information Sources:

BLM, Prineville District Office, 185 E. 4th St., Prineville, OR 97754 / 503-447-4115
Prineville - Crook County Chamber of Commerce, 390 N. Fairview, Prineville, OR 97754 / 503-447-6304
Bend Chamber of Commerce, 63085 N. Hwy. 97, Bend, OR 97701 / 503-382-3221

LOWER DESCHUTES RIVER

- *Route Location:* Located in north-central Oregon, south of The Dalles. The route can be accessed from U.S. Highway 197 in Maupin or off Oregon State Highway 216 between Tygh Valley and Grass Valley. The route travels north and south from either of the access points as it follows the eastern bank of the Deschutes River.
- *Roads Traveled:* The 36 mile route follows an old railroad grade which is a combination of paved and gravel surfaced road. The route can safely be driven in a passenger car although vehicles pulling trailers are not recommended on the 8 mile segment upriver from Maupin. The 36 mile route has been designated a BLM Type I Back Country Byway.
- *Travel Season:* The entire route is open year-round.
- *Description:* This scenic drive follows alongside the Wild and Scenic Deschutes River through a canyon carved into the Columbia River Basalt formation. This

Oregon

segment of the river is nationally known for its outstanding trout, steelhead, and salmon fishing. Sherar's Falls is still used today by Native American dipnet fishermen for catching steelhead and salmon. The river also offers a challenging float trip for rafters. Two BLM recreation sites are north of Maupin and provide camping and picnicking facilities. The fenced remains of a prehistoric pithouse village can be seen at the Macks Canyon Recreation Site.

- *Other Nearby Routes:* About 70 miles to the south is the Lower Crooked River scenic drive and an additional 40 miles west is the McKenzie-Santiam Pass Loop and Cascade Lakes Highway scenic drives. Approximately 95 miles northeast is the Blue Mountain scenic drive.

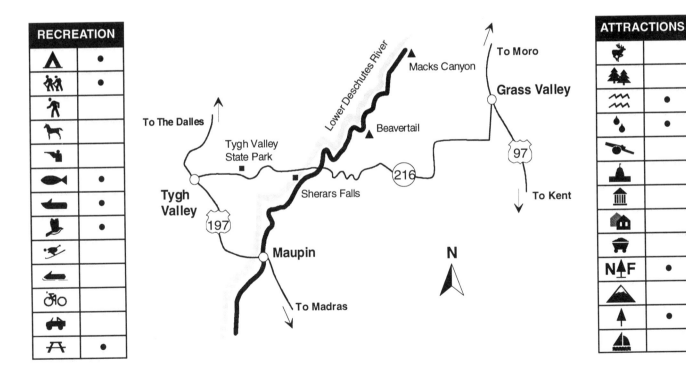

Information Sources:

BLM, Prineville District Office, 185 E. 4th St., Prineville, OR 97754 / 503-447-4115
The Dalles Area Chamber of Commerce, 404 W. 2nd St., The Dalles, OR 97058 / 503-296-2231
Madras - Jefferson County Chamber of Commerce, 197 S.E. 5th St., Madras, OR 97741 / 503-475-2350

McKenzie - Santiam Pass Loop

Oregon

- *Route Location:* Located in west-central Oregon, west of Redmond. The eastern access is located in the town of Sisters and travels northwest forming a loop drive back to Sisters.
- *Roads Traveled:* The 82 mile route follows Oregon State Highways 126 and 242, and U.S. Highway 20. All of the routes are two-lane paved roads suitable for all vehicles. Motor homes over 22 feet long and vehicles pulling trailers are not recommended on Oregon State Highway 242. The entire route has been designated a National Forest Scenic Byway.
- *Travel Season:* Much of the route is open year-round, however, most of Oregon Route 242 is closed by heavy winter snows from November through early July.
- *Description:* Travels through a variety of scenic beauty from arid high desert to open ranch country as it crosses the Willamette and Deschutes National Forests. Located at the top of McKenzie Pass is the Dee Wright Observatory offering views of Mt. Hood, Belknap Crater, and the Collier Glacier which is one of fourteen glaciers in the Sisters region and the largest in Oregon. The Pacific Crest National Scenic Trail also crosses the route in this area. Other trails accessed along the route provide opportunities for hiking, backpacking, horseback riding, cross-country skiing, and snowmobiling. Portions of this route follow the McKenzie River which is popular for rafting and fishing. Several lakes and reservoirs also provide excellent fishing and boating opportunities.
- *Other Nearby Routes:* The Robert Aufderheide Memorial Drive is 10 miles to the west and the Cascade Lakes Highway scenic drive is about 20 miles to the southeast. Approximately 30 miles to the east is the Lower Crooked River scenic drive.

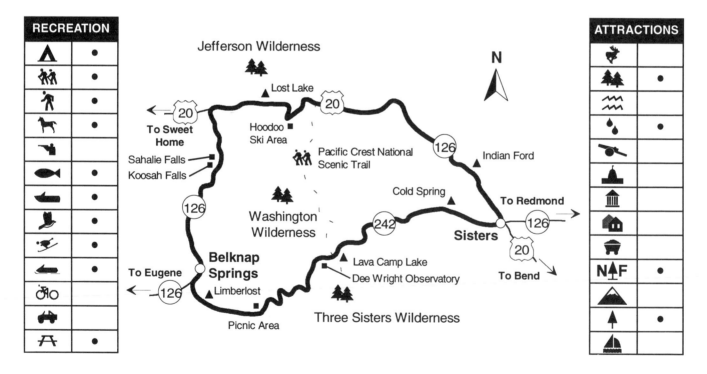

Information Sources:

Willamette National Forest, 211 E. Seventh Ave., Eugene, OR 97440 / 503-465-6521
Sisters Area Chamber of Commerce, 151 N. Spruce St., Sisters, OR 97759 / 503-549-0251
Sweet Home Chamber of Commerce, 1575 Main St., Sweet Home, OR 97386 / 503-367-6186
Eugene Area Chamber of Commerce, 1401 Willamette St., Eugene, OR 97440 / 503-484-1314

NESTUCCA RIVER

Oregon

- *Route Location:* Located in northwestern Oregon, southwest of Portland. The eastern access is located in Carlton off Oregon State Highway 47 and travels west to the junction of U.S. Highway 101 in the town of Beaver.
- *Roads Traveled:* The 45 mile route follows Meadow Lake County Road, BLM Nestucca Access Road, and Blaine Road. The routes travel over mostly two-lane paved roads with a 3 mile stretch of gravel road. All of the routes are suitable for all vehicles. Eleven miles of this route has been designated a BLM Type I Back Country Byway.
- *Travel Season:* The entire route is generally open year-round although heavy winter snows can make the route temporarily impassable.
- *Description:* The scenic drive travels through Oregon's coastal forest with portions following the Nestucca River through a wooded canyon. Elk and deer are commonly seen in the area. The river offers excellent opportunities for catching Coho salmon, Chinook salmon, steelhead, and trout. Four BLM recreation sites provide access to the river, camping, and picnicking facilities. Portions of this route travel through the Siuslaw National Forest which provides access to developed camping and picnicking areas.
- *Other Nearby Routes:* Approximately 65 miles south is the South Fork Alsea River scenic drive.

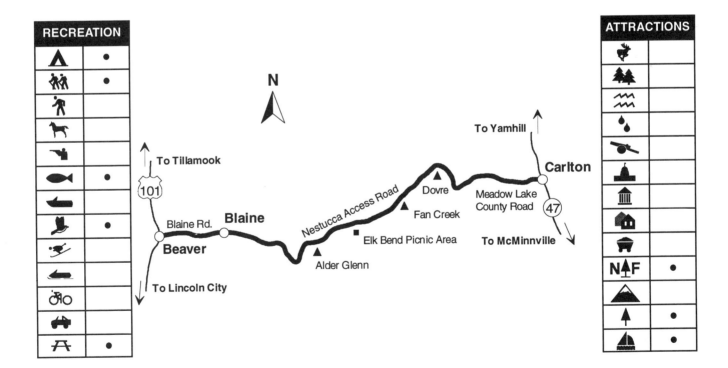

Information Sources:

BLM, Salem District Office, 1717 Fabry Rd., S.E., Salem, OR 97306 / 503-399-5646
Tillamook Chamber of Commerce, 3705 Hwy. 101 N., Tillamook, OR 97141 / 503-842-7525
McMinnville Chamber of Commerce, 417 N. Adams St., McMinnville, OR 97128 / 503-472-6196
Newberg Area Chamber of Commerce, 115 N. Washington St., Newberg, OR 97132 / 503-538-2014
Lincoln City Chamber of Commerce, 801 S.W. Hwy. 101, #3, Lincoln City, OR 97367 / 503-994-3070

ROBERT AUFDERHEIDE MEMORIAL DRIVE

- *Route Location:* Located in west-central Oregon, east of Eugene. The southern access is located off Oregon State Highway 58 north of Oakridge and travels northeast to the junction of Oregon State Highway 126, east of Blue River.
- *Roads Traveled:* The 70 mile route follows Forest Service Road 19 which is a two-lane paved road suitable for all vehicles. Travelers can pick up an audio cassette tape tour, free of charge, from the Ranger Stations at either Blue River or Oakridge and return it at the other end of the drive. The 70 mile route has been designated a National Forest Scenic Byway.
- *Travel Season:* The route is generally open from about early April through October and then closed by heavy winter snows.
- *Description:* The scenic drive winds through the lush undergrowth of the majestic Willamette National Forest and follows the meandering South Fork of the

Oregon

McKenzie and North Fork of the Middle Fork of the Willamette River. A special attraction found along this route is the Westfir Covered Bridge which is Oregon's longest, spanning 180 feet. Wildlife inhabiting this area includes blacktail deer, mountain lions, elk, black bears, and bald and golden eagles. A nature trail located in the Delta Campground leads you through towering old growth trees, some being 200 to 500 years old. Several other hiking trails lead into the Waldo Lake Wilderness area.
- *Other Nearby Routes:* The McKenzie-Santiam Pass Loop scenic drive is about 10 miles to the east. Approximately 40 miles to the southeast is the Cascade Lakes Highway scenic route. About 75 miles to the northwest is the South Fork Alsea River scenic drive.

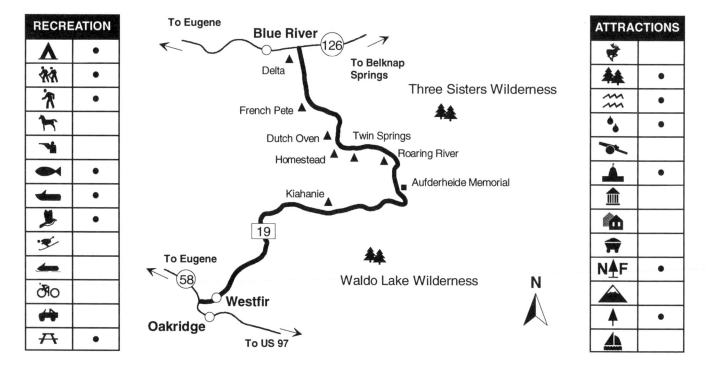

Information Sources:

Willamette National Forest, 211 E. Seventh Ave., Eugene, OR 97440 / 503-465-6521
Oakridge - Westfir Chamber of Commerce, P.O. Box 217, Oakridge, OR 97463 / 503-782-4146
Eugene Area Chamber of Commerce, 1401 Willamette St., Eugene, OR 97440 / 503-484-1314
Sisters Area Chamber of Commerce, 151 N. Spruce St., Sisters, OR 97759 / 503-549-0251

ROGUE - COQUILLE

- *Route Location:* Located in southwestern Oregon, south of Myrtle Point. The northern access is located off Oregon State Highway 42 south of Myrtle Point and travels southwest to the junction of U.S. Highway 101 in the town of Gold Beach.
- *Roads Traveled:* The 83 mile route follows Oregon State Highway 242 and Forest Service Road 33 which are two-lane paved roads suitable for all vehicles. The 83 mile route has been designated a National Forest Scenic Byway.
- *Travel Season:* The entire route is open year-round.
- *Description:* This scenic route crosses the Siskiyou National Forest and follows a portion of the Rogue Wild and Scenic River to Agness where it begins to follow the Coquille River. The drive travels through a narrow canyon rimmed with high cliffs and waterfalls before opening up into a green pastoral valley. Wildlife is abundant along the scenic route and includes deer, bob-

cats, mountain lions, bald eagles, and river otters. Both scenic rivers provide numerous opportunities for rafting and salmon and steelhead fishing. A short 5 minute walk will take you to the base of the spectacular Elk Creek Falls that plummet from the creek 120 feet above. The Wild Rogue Wilderness can be accessed from hiking trails located along the route. Several opportunities for camping and picnicking are provided by the many national forest campgrounds found along the drive.

Oregon

- *Other Nearby Routes:* The Galice-Hellgate scenic drive is about 15 miles east which also leads to the Grave Creek To Marial scenic drive. Approximately 50 miles south is the Smith River scenic route in California. About 60 miles northeast of Myrtle Point is the Rogue-Umpqua scenic drive.

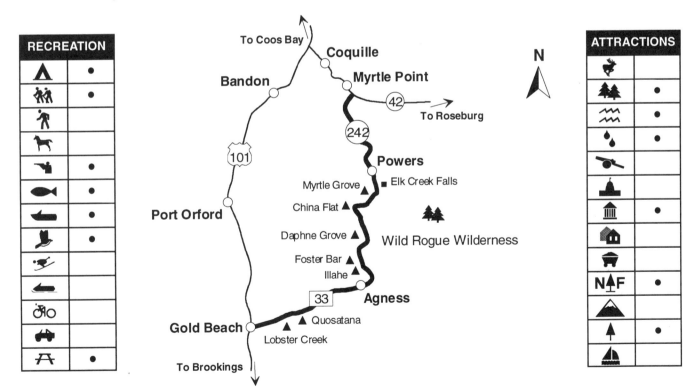

Information Sources:

Siskiyou National Forest, 200 NE Greenfield Rd., Grants Pass, OR 97526 / 503-471-6500
Gold Beach Chamber of Commerce, 1225 S. Ellensburg Ave., #3, Gold Beach, OR 97444 / 800-525-2334
Myrtle Point Chamber of Commerce, P.O. Box 265, Myrtle Point, OR 97458 / 503-572-2626

ROGUE UMPQUA

Oregon

- *Route Location:* Located in southwestern Oregon, south of Eugene. The northwestern access is located off Interstate 5 in the town of Roseburg and travels southeast forming an open loop drive back to Interstate 5 in Gold Hill.
- *Roads Traveled:* The 172 mile route follows Oregon State Highways 138, 230, 62, and 234. All the routes travel over two-lane paved roads suitable for all vehicles. The entire 172 mile route has been designated a National Forest Scenic Byway.
- *Travel Season:* The route is open year-round although winter driving conditions may be hazardous.
- *Description:* This scenic drive travels on the Umpqua and Rogue River National Forests offering views of the Cascade mountains, lakes, waterfalls, and the Upper Rogue and the North Umpqua Wild and Scenic Rivers. Numerous opportunities for hiking, backpacking, and horseback riding is found in four wilderness areas and several trails accessed from the route, including the Pacific Crest National Scenic Trail. Camping, picnicking, rafting, and fishing activities are found at the many recreation areas, state parks, and campgrounds found along or near the drive. Crater Lake National Park is just to the east of this scenic drive off State Highway 230. Winter sport activities available include cross-country skiing, downhill skiing, and snowmobiling. Historical structures are also found along the route.
- *Other Nearby Routes:* The Cow Creek scenic drive is about 20 miles south of Roseburg and about 20 miles west from Gold Hill is the Galice-Hellgate scenic drive which also leads to the Grave Creek To Marial scenic route. Approximately 55 miles southwest is the State Of Jefferson scenic drive in California.

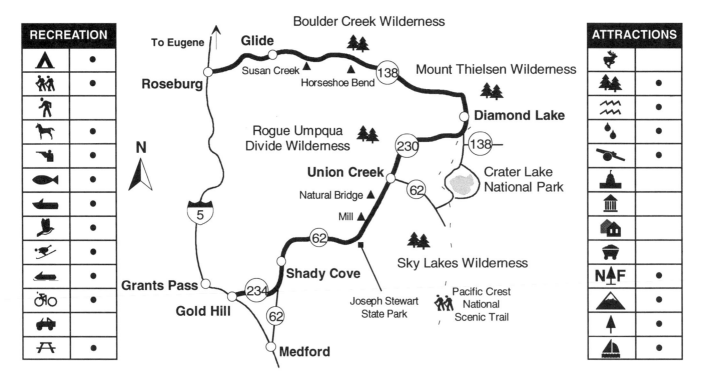

Information Sources:

Rogue River National Forest, 333 West 8th St., Medford, OR 97501 / 503-776-3684
Roseburg Area Chamber of Commerce, 410 S.E. Spruce St., Roseburg, OR 97470 / 503-672-2648
Grants Pass/Josephine County Chamber of Commerce, 1501 N.E. 6th St., Grants Pass, OR 97526 / 800-547-5927
Rogue River Area Chamber of Commerce, 111 E. Main St., Rogue River, OR 97537 / 503-582-0242
Chamber of Medford/Jackson County, 101 W. 8th, Medford, OR 97501-7293 / 503-779-4847

SNAKE RIVER / MORMON BASIN

Oregon

- *Route Location:* Located in eastern Oregon. The northwestern access starts in Baker and travels southeast forming a loop drive back to Baker.
- *Roads Traveled:* The 150 mile route follows Oregon State Highway 86 and a series of BLM and county roads marked with "Snake River / Mormon Basin" signage. The routes travel over a combination of paved, gravel, and dirt roads, most of which require a two-wheel drive, high-clearance vehicle. Due to narrow segments, RVs are not recommended on the route. The BLM has designated 130 miles of this route as a Type I and Type II Back Country Byway.
- *Travel Season:* The entire route is open year-round although winter driving conditions may be hazardous. The route may be impassable at certain times during the winter and for short periods following severe thunderstorms.
- *Description:* This back country route travels through winding picturesque river canyons, aspen lined meadows, rolling hills covered with wildflowers, and heavily timbered mountains. Red-tailed hawks, quail, deer, elk, cougars, pronghorn antelope and black bears are just some of the wildlife inhabiting this region of Oregon. The Snake River flows alongside a portion of this route and offers rafting and fishing opportunities. Camping is provided by the BLM maintained Spring Recreation Site and the Farewell Bend State Park.
- *Other Nearby Routes:* Both the Hells Canyon and Elkhorn Drive scenic routes can be accessed from this route. The Blue Mountains scenic drive can be accessed from the Elkhorn Drive. Approximately 70 miles to the south is the Leslie Gulch-Succor Creek scenic drive.

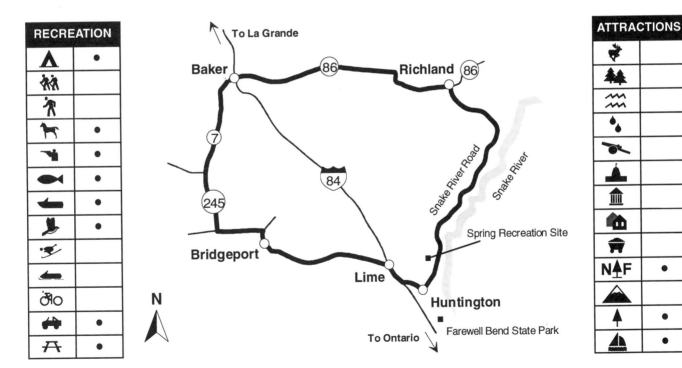

Information Sources:

BLM, Vale District Office, 100 Oregon St., Vale, OR 97918 / 503-473-3144
Baker County Chamber of Commerce, 490 Campbell St., Baker, OR 97814 / 503-523-5855
Ontario Chamber of Commerce, 88 S.W. 3rd Ave., Ontario, OR 97914 / 503-889-8012

SOUTH FORK ALSEA RIVER

- *Route Location:* Located in western Oregon, northwest of Eugene. The eastern access is located west of Oregon State Highway 99W in the town of Alpine and travels west to the junction of Oregon State Highway 34 in the town of Alsea.
- *Roads Traveled:* The 17 mile route follows the Alpine Road, BLM south Fork Access Road, and County Road 48200. The routes travel over a combination of paved and gravel surfaced roads suitable for all vehicles. Eleven miles of this route has been designated a BLM Type I Back Country Byway.
- *Travel Season:* The entire route is open year-round.
- *Description:* The scenic drive traverses the Oregon Coast Range through a Douglas-fir forest, some reaching 200 feet high and over 400 years old, along portions of the South Fork Alsea River. Fishing for Coho salmon, Chinook salmon, steelhead, and trout is a popular activity along this route. The Alsea Falls Recreation site provides camping and picnicking facilities as well as a hiking trail that leads to the pool at the waterfall's base. The Hubert McGee Memorial Park also provides camping and picnicking areas with one 85 foot long picnic table carved from a single log. Deer are commonly seen, especially in the evening, along the road. Other wildlife found in the area includes black bears, bobcats, and raccoons.

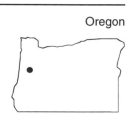

Oregon

- *Other Nearby Routes:* Approximately 65 miles north is the Nestucca River scenic drive and a little over 100 miles south are the Rogue Umpqua, Cow Creek, Galice-Hellgate, and Grave Creek To Marial scenic drives. Less than 100 miles east are the McKenzie-Santiam Pass Loop, Robert Aufderheide Memorial Drive, and Cascade Lakes Highway scenic drives.

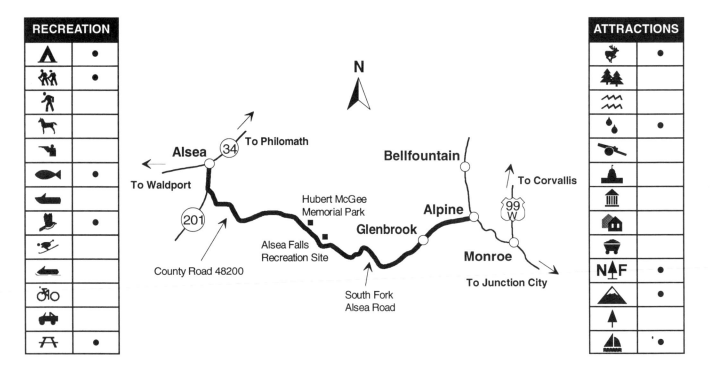

Information Sources:

BLM, Salem District Office, 1717 Fabry Rd., S.E., Salem, OR 97306 / 503-399-5646
Yachats Area Chamber of Commerce, P.O. Box 728, Yachats, OR 97498 / 503-547-3530
Junction City-Harrisburg Area C of C, 565 Greenwood St., Junction City, OR 97448 / 503-998-6154
Corvallis Area Chamber of Commerce, 420 N.W. 2nd St., Corvallis, OR 97330 / 503-757-1505
Newport Chamber of Commerce, 555 S.W. Coast Hwy., Newport, OR 97365 / 503-265-8801

SOUTH FORK JOHN DAY RIVER

Oregon

- **Route Location:** Located in central Oregon, west of John Day. The northern access is located off U.S. Highway 26 in the town of Dayville and travels south to the junction of Forest Service Road 47, south of Izee.
- **Roads Traveled:** The 50 mile route travels over a combination of narrow two-lane paved roads to sing-lane gravel and dirt surfaced roads. The route is usually suitable for passenger cars, depending on the weather. The 50 mile route has been designated a BLM Type I Back Country Byway.
- **Travel Season:** The route is normally open year-round except for the single-lane sections which may become impassable in the winter and early spring due to snow and mud.
- **Description:** This scenic drive follows alongside the Wild and Scenic South Fork of the John Day River through a scenic canyon with spectacular cliff formations, old growth ponderosa pine, and a variety of willow and hardwood vegetation. Excellent views of the surrounding mountain ranges are offered at various locations. Camping is available at one BLM primitive campground as well as developed campgrounds in the nearby Ochoco National Forest. About 10 miles south of Dayville, the Murderer's Creek Wild Horse Management Area lies east of the scenic drive and is home to about 100 wild horses on 150,000 acres.
- **Other Nearby Routes:** Less than 100 miles to the east are the Blue Mountain, Elkhorn Drive, Snake River/ Mormon Basin, and Hells Canyon scenic drives. About 90 miles to the west is the Lower Crooked River scenic drive and an additional 40 miles west is the McKenzie-Santiam Pass Loop, Cascade Lakes Highway, and Robert Aufderheide Memorial Drive scenic routes.

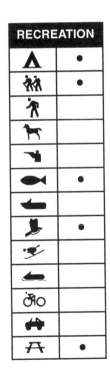

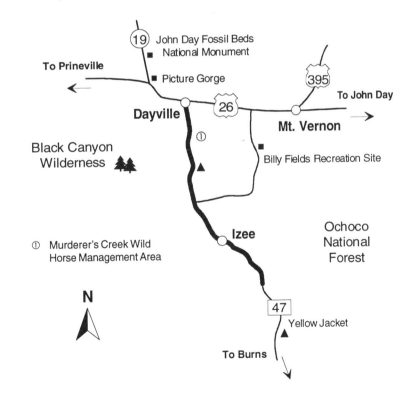

Information Sources:

BLM, Prineville District Office, 185 E. 4th St., Prineville, OR 97754 / 503-447-4115
Grant County Chamber of Commerce, 281 W. Main St., John Day, OR 97845 / 800-769-5664
Harney County Chamber of Commerce, 18 W. "D" St., Burns, OR 97720 / 503-573-2636

STEENS MOUNTAIN

Oregon

- *Route Location:* Located in southeastern Oregon, south of Burns. The northern access is located on Oregon State Highway 205 in the town of Frenchglen and travels southeast forming a loop drive back to Frenchglen.
- *Roads Traveled:* The 66 mile route follows the North Loop and South Loop Roads and Oregon State Highway 205. The roads travel over an extremely rough surface which requires a two-wheel drive, high-clearance vehicle. Passenger cars, RVs, and vehicles pulling trailers are not recommended on this route. The 66 mile loop drive has been designated a BLM Type II Back Country Byway.
- *Travel Season:* The entire route is generally open from mid-July through October. Five gates are located at various elevations to control access during wet or snowy conditions. The lower gates are usually opened by May 1 while the upper gates open around mid-July.
- *Description:* This scenic drive traverses the scenic Steens Mountain, a 30 mile long fault-block mountain in the high desert region of southeastern Oregon. The route climbs the western slope of the mountain to the summit which is the highest point in Oregon that can be reached by a two-wheel drive vehicle. Camping and picnicking facilities are located at three BLM recreation sites adjacent to the North Loop Road. Free roaming wild horses can be viewed from the Kiger Gorge Overlook. Bighorn sheep, elk, mule deer, and pronghorn antelope can also be seen at various locations along this route. The historic Frenchglen hotel offers overnight accommodations. For reservations, call 503-493-2825.
- *Other Nearby Routes:* Both the Diamond Loop and Lakeview To Steens scenic drives connect with this back country route.

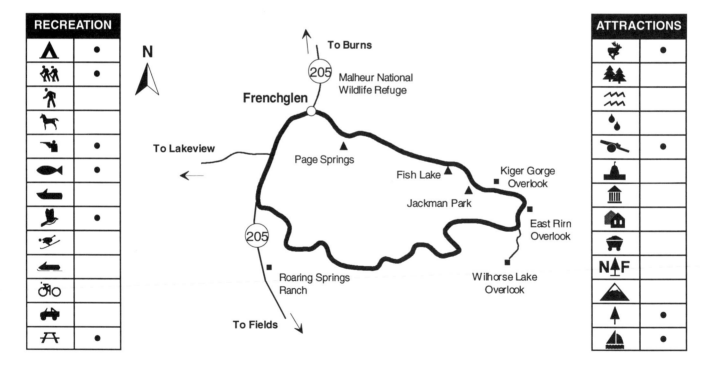

Information Sources:

BLM, Burns District Office, HC74-12533 Hwy. 20 West, Hines, OR 97738 / 503-573-5241
Lake County Chamber of Commerce, 513 Center St., Lakeview, OR 97630 / 503-947-6040
Harney County Chamber of Commerce, 18 W. "D" St., Burns, OR 97720 / 503-573-2636

PENNSYLVANIA

☐ *Scenic Drives*

Road Condition Number: 717-939-9551 ext. 5550

1. Grand Army Of The Republic Highway
2. Longhouse

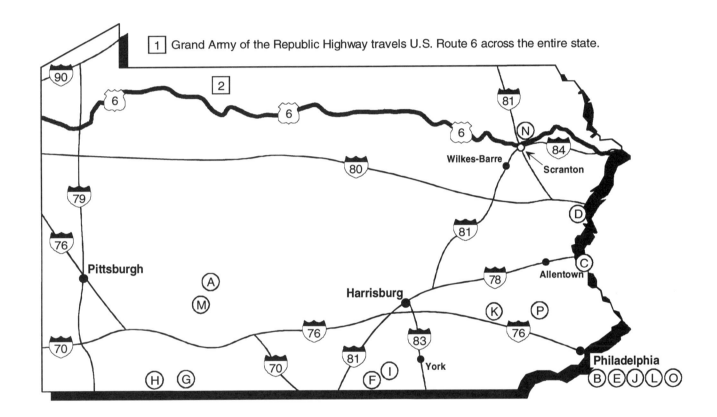

1 Grand Army of the Republic Highway travels U.S. Route 6 across the entire state.

○ *National Park Areas*

A. Allegheny Portage Railroad National Historic Site
B. Benjamin Franklin National Memorial
C. Delaware And Lehigh Navigation Canal National Heritage Corridor
D. Delaware Water Gap National Recreation Area
E. Edgar Allan Poe National Historic Site
F. Eisenhower National Historic Site
G. Fort Necessity National Battlefield
H. Friendship Hill National Historic Site

I. Gettysburg National Military Park
J. Gloria Dei (Old Swedes) Church National Historic Site
K. Hopewell Furnace National Historic Site
L. Independence National Historical Park
M. Johnstown Flood National Memorial
N. Steamtown National Historic Site
O. Thaddeus Kosciuszko National Memorial
P. Valley Forge National Historical Park

GRAND ARMY OF THE REPUBLIC HIGHWAY

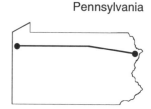

Pennsylvania

RECREATION	
⛺ (camping)	•
🥾 (hiking)	•
🚶 (walking)	
🐴 (horseback)	•
🦆 (hunting)	•
🐟 (fishing)	•
🛶 (boating)	•
👢 (climbing)	•
🎿 (skiing)	•
🛷 (sledding)	•
🚵 (biking)	
🚙 (off-road)	
🏕 (picnic)	•

- *Route Location:* This scenic drive is located in northern Pennsylvania and travels from the Ohio-Pennsylvania border, east across the state to the New Jersey border. The western access is located in the town of Pennline and the route ends near the town of Matamoras.
- *Roads Traveled:* The 410 mile route follows U.S. Highway 6 which is a two-lane paved road suitable for all vehicles.
- *Travel Season:* The entire route is open year-round although winter driving conditions can be hazardous.
- *Description:* US Route 6 travels through 14 states on its transcontinental journey from the Atlantic Ocean to the Pacific Ocean. No other highway in America captures the legacy of our rich national heritage. From Massachusetts near the site of the Pilgrims' landing in 1620 to the original western terminus in Long Beach, California near the bluff overlooking the bay where Juan Rodriquez Cabrillo first saw this shore in 1542.

It was in 1937 that U.S. Route 6 became the longest transcontinental highway in the United States, spanning 3,652 miles. However, designation of U.S. Route 6 as the Grand Army of the Re-

ATTRACTIONS	
🦌	
🌲	
〰	
💧	
🔭	•
🏛	•
🏛	•
🏠	
🎡	
N▲F	•
⛰	
🏕	•
⛵	•

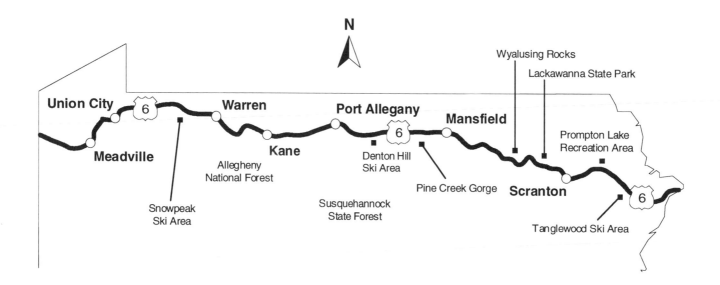

Union City — Meadville — 6 — Snowpeak Ski Area — Warren — Kane — Allegheny National Forest — Port Allegany — 6 — Denton Hill Ski Area — Susquehannock State Forest — Mansfield — Pine Creek Gorge — Wyalusing Rocks — Lackawanna State Park — Scranton — 6 — Tanglewood Ski Area — Prompton Lake Recreation Area — 6

GRAND ARMY OF THE REPUBLIC HIGHWAY (CONT.)

public Highway would come many years after it had been assigned its "US 6" numerical designation.

The Sons of Union Veterans of the Civil War conceived the idea in 1937 to declare U.S. Route 6 as a memorial route. On February 12, 1937, the Governor of the Commonwealth of Massachusetts signed a bill naming Route 6 as the Grand Army of the Republic Highway. This began a national effort to petition all 14 states that US Route 6 traverses to pass enabling legislation for naming Route 6. In 1948, Governor James Duff of Pennsylvania named the Pennsylvania segment.

It was not until May, 1953 that the entire route was completely named and marked as the Grand Army of the Republic Highway. Today, the Grand Army of the Republic Highway is a tribute of peace from the Northern States to the Veterans of 1861 to 1865.

The Grand Army of the Republic Highway is America's transcontinental route with a sense of grandeur and determination marching from "coast to coast". The Pennsylvania segment best represents the essence of the whole.

The greater part of U.S. Highway 6 through Pennsylvania consists of various early Indian trails. Once known as the "Forbidden Path," "Wyoming or Great Warrior's Path," "General Sullivan's Trail," "Venango Trail," "Pine Creek Trail," and "Lackawanna Trail". These segments of U.S. Route 6 were long denied to the white man by the Indians of the Seneca Nation, to whose territory it provided a southern gateway. Today U.S. Route 6 lays on top of segments of the early Indian trails.

Pennsylvania's portion of U.S. Highway 6 was chosen as Pennsylvania's best touring road by Harley-Davidson in 1987 and as one of the top scenic routes in the US by Car and Driver magazine in 1985.

- **Other Nearby Routes:** From the western portion of this route, the Seaway Trail is within 50 to 100 miles north in New York. The Longhouse scenic drive may also be accessed 10 miles east of Warren.

Information Sources:

Grand Army Of The Republic Highway Association, R.D. 1, Box 91A, Kane, PA 16735 / 800-344-2742
Meadville - West Crawford County Chamber of Commerce, 211 Chestnut St., Meadville, PA 16335 / 814-337-8030
Union City Chamber of Commerce, 33 N. Main St., Union City, PA 16438 / 814-438-7293
Corry Area Chamber of Commerce, 112 N. Center St., Corry, PA 16407 / 814-665-9925
Warren County Chamber of Commerce, 315 Second Ave., Room 409, Warren, PA 16365 / 814-723-3050
Kane Chamber of Commerce, 14 Greeves St., Kane, PA 16735 / 814-837-6565
Port Allegany Chamber of Commerce, P.O. Box 434, Port Allegany, PA 16743 / 814-642-2181
Coudersport Chamber of Commerce, Box 261, Coudersport, PA 16915 / 814-274-8165
Wellsboro Area Chamber of Commerce, 114 Main St., Wellsboro, PA 16901 / 717-724-1926
Mansfield Area Chamber of Commerce, 14 S. Main St., Mansfield, PA 16933 / 717-662-3442
Towanda Area Chamber of Commerce, P.O. Box 146, Towanda, PA 18848 / 717-268-2732
Greater Scranton Chamber of Commerce, 222 Mulberry St., Scranton, PA 18501 / 717-342-7711
Carbondale Area Chamber of Commerce, One N. Main St., Carbondale, PA 18407-2356 / 717-282-1690
Wayne County Chamber of Commerce, 742 Main St., Honesdale, PA 18431 / 717-253-1960
Pike County Chamber of Commerce, 305 Broad St., Mildord, PA 18337 / 717-296-8700

LONGHOUSE

- **Route Location:** Located in northwestern Pennsylvania, southwest of Bradford. The northeastern access is located off Pennsylvania State Highway 59 with the junction of State Highway 321 and travels southwest forming a loop drive back to the starting point.
- **Roads Traveled:** The 29 mile route follows Pennsylvania State Highways 59 and 321, and Forest Service Road 262. All of the routes are two-lane paved roads suitable for all vehicles. The 29 mile route has been designated a National Forest Scenic Byway.
- **Travel Season:** Most of the route is open year-round with the exception of Forest Service Road 262 which is closed from about mid-December through March due to winter snow.
- **Description:** The scenic drive travels around the Kinzua arm of the Allegheny Reservoir on the Allegheny National Forest through hardwood forests. Several scenic turnouts are provided along the route offering panoramic views of the surrounding wilderness. Hiking opportunities are provided by several trails accessed from the drive, including the North Country National Scenic Trail. Several campgrounds are located along the route, many being near the shores of the reservoir and having swimming beaches. Water-skiing, boating, and fishing are popular activities on the lake. Winter brings cross-country and snowmobiling enthusiasts to the area. Wildlife found in this region of Pennsylvania includes white-tailed deer, black bears, eagles, and hawks.
- **Other Nearby Routes:** The Grand Army Of The Republic Highway, which travels the entire length of the state, can be accessed in Warren. About 50 miles north across the New York border is the Seaway Trail.

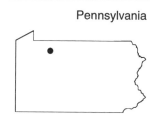

Pennsylvania

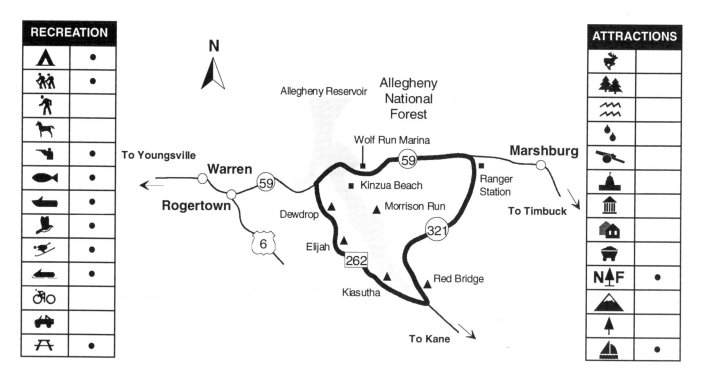

Information Sources:

Allegheny National Forest, Bradford Ranger District, Star Rt. 1, Box 88, Bradford, PA 16701 / 814-362-4613
Warren County Chamber of Commerce, 315 Second Ave., Room 409, Warren, PA 16365 / 814-723-3050
Kane Chamber of Commerce, 14 Greeves St., Kane, PA 16735 / 814-837-6565
Bradford Area Chamber of Commerce, 10 Main St., Seneca Bldg., Bradford, PA 16701 / 814-368-7115

SOUTH CAROLINA

☐ *Scenic Drives*

1. Oscar Wigington

○ *National Park Areas*

A. Charles Pinckney National Historic Site
B. Congaree Swamp National Monument
C. Cowpens National Battlefield
D. Fort Sumter National Monument
E. Historic Camden
F. Kings Mountain National Military Park
G. Ninety Six National Historic Site

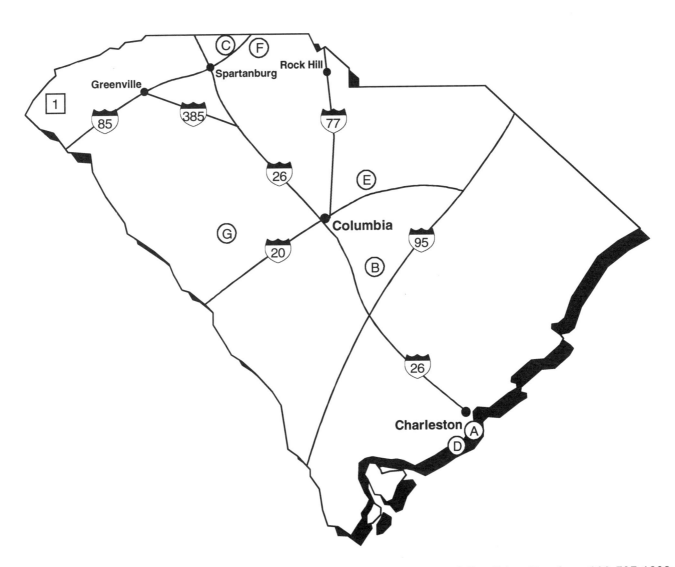

OSCAR WIGINGTON

- *Route Location:* Located in the northwestern corner of South Carolina, west of Greenville. The southern access is located off South Carolina State Highway 28 southeast of Mountain Rest and travels north to the North Carolina border.
- *Roads Traveled:* The 20 mile route follows South Carolina State Highways 107 and 413 which are two-lane paved roads suitable for all vehicles. Fourteen miles of this route has been designated a National Forest Scenic Byway.
- *Travel Season:* The route is generally open year-round with temporary closure possible in January and February due to icy conditions.
- *Description:* The scenic drive travels through the mountainous region of South Carolina through hardwood forests and by rushing streams with many waterfalls. Several scenic viewing points offer panoramic vistas of the surrounding wilderness. Several developed camping and picnicking facilities are found along this scenic drive. The Foothills National Recreation Trail is a 43 mile hiking trail crossing the upper part of South Carolina and can be accessed from this route. Fishing for brown and rainbow trout and rafting opportunities are found in the Chattooga National Wild and Scenic River, accessed by Forest Service Road 708. Hiking trails along the banks of the river are found here as well as the Ellicott Rock Wilderness.
- *Other Nearby Routes:* The Forest Heritage scenic drive is about 35 miles northeast in North Carolina. About 50 miles to the west in Georgia is the Russell-Brasstown scenic drive.

South Carolina

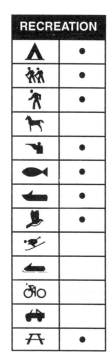

RECREATION	
⛺	•
🚶	•
🧍	•
🐎	
🦆	•
🐟	•
🛶	•
🚤	•
🎿	
⛄	
🚲	
🚙	
⛱	•

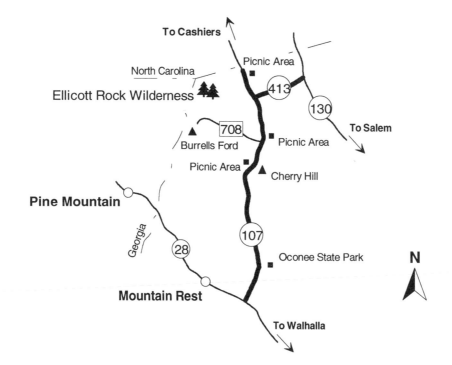

ATTRACTIONS	
🦌	
🌲	•
〰	•
💧	•
💥	•
🏛	
🏛	
🏠	
🛒	
N⛰F	•
⛰	
🏕	•
⛴	

Information Sources:

Francis Marion & Sumter National Forests, 1835 Assembly St., Room 333, Columbia, SC 29201 / 803-765-5222
Walhalla Chamber of Commerce, 220 E. Main St., Walhalla, SC 29691 / 803-638-2727
Cashiers Area Chamber of Commerce, Hwy. 107 S., Cashiers, NC 28717 / 704-743-5191
Greater Seneca Chamber of Commerce, P.O. Box 855, Seneca, SC 29679 / 803-882-2097

SOUTH DAKOTA

□ *Scenic Drives*

1. Fort Meade
2. Peter Norbeck
3. Spearfish Canyon Highway

○ *National Park Areas*

A. Badlands National Park
B. Jewel Cave National Monument
C. Mount Rushmore National Memorial
D. Wind Cave National Park

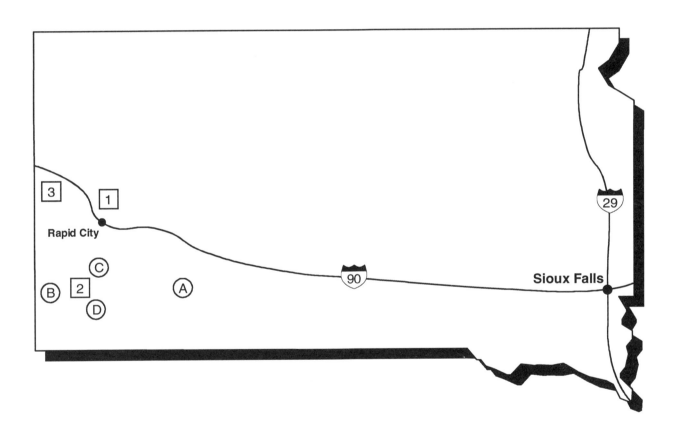

Road Condition Number: 605-773-3536

FORT MEAD

- **Route Location:** Located in west-central South Dakota, east of Sturgis. The northern access is located off South Dakota State Highway 34 east of Sturgis and travels south to the junction of Interstate 90, north of Tilford.
- **Roads Traveled:** The 5 mile route follows the Fort Meade Road which is a two-lane gravel surfaced road suitable for all types of vehicles. The 5 mile route has been designated a BLM Type I Back Country Byway.
- **Travel Season:** The entire route is open year-round.
- **Description:** The scenic drive travels through ponderosa pine covered hills of the northeastern flank of the Black Hills and some of the most historic country in the area. Fort Meade was established in 1878 by the Seventh Cavalry. Many of the old buildings surrounding the parade ground still remain intact and are listed on the National Register of Historic Places. A museum here contains exhibits and many historic artifacts.

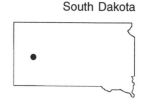

South Dakota

Located just south of Fort Meade is the cemetery where 119 of the 200 burials date back prior to 1900. In addition to history, a variety of recreational opportunities can be found along or near this route. The Centennial trail is accessed from this drive and offers hiking, backpacking, and horseback riding. A BLM recreation site is located near the southern terminus of this drive with camping and picnicking facilities. Several miles north is the Fort Meade Reservoir that offers fishing. White-tailed deer, mule deer, turkeys, and numerous songbirds are commonly seen along the route.

- **Other Nearby Routes:** The Spearfish Canyon Highway scenic drive is about 20 miles to the west and approximately 60 miles to the south is the Peter Norbeck scenic route.

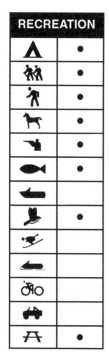

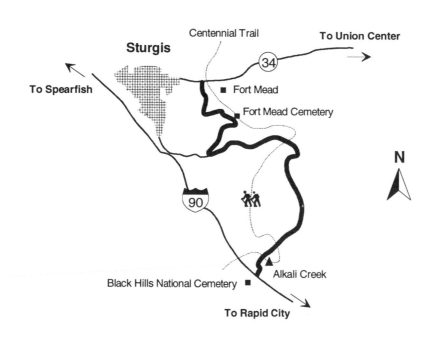

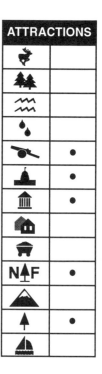

Information Sources:

BLM, South Dakota Resource Area, 310 Roundup St., Belle Fourche, SD 57717-1698 / 605-892-2526
Sturgis Area Chamber of Commerce, 606 Anna St., Sturgis, SD 57785 / 605-347-2556
Rapid City Area Chamber of Commerce, 444 Mt. Rushmore Rd., N., Rapid City, SD 57709 / 605-343-1744
Deadwood / Lead Area Chamber of Commerce, 460 Main St., Deadwood, SD 57732 / 605-578-1876

PETER NORBECK

- **Route Location:** Located in southwestern South Dakota, southwest of Rapid City. The southwestern access is located off U.S. Highway 16 east of Custer and travels northeast over a series of connecting roads forming a loop drive back to the starting point.
- **Roads Traveled:** The 70 mile route follows South Dakota State Highways 89, 244, and 87, and U.S. Highway 16A. All of the routes are two-lane paved roads suitable for most vehicles. Vehicles pulling trailers and RVers may want to inquire before attempting to travel highways 16A and 87. These routes have many curves and narrow tunnels along with short radius pigtailed bridges. The entire route has been designated a National Forest Scenic Byway.
- **Travel Season:** Most of the route is open year-round with the exception of highway 87 and sections of 16A which are closed from December through March due to heavy winter snows.

- **Description:** The scenic drive travels through the heart of the Black Hills as it crosses the Black Hills National Forest and the 73,000 acre Custer State Park. An abundance of wildlife can be seen from the route including bighorn sheep, antelope, wild burros, and the American bison. The Black Elk Wilderness provides an extensive trail system offering hiking, backpacking, and horseback riding opportunities. The famous Mount Rushmore National Memorial lies at the northern end of the drive. Opportunities for cross-country skiing and snowmobiling are available in winter, with fishing, camping, and mountain biking offered during summer.
- **Other Nearby Routes:** Approximately 60 miles to the north are the Spearfish Canyon Highway and Fort Meade scenic drives.

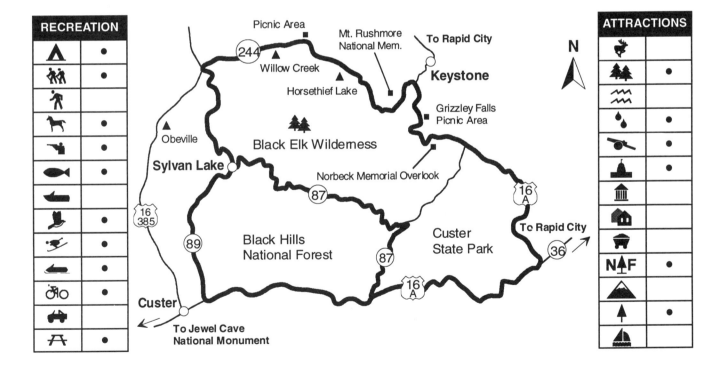

Information Sources:

Black Hills National Forest, Route 2, Box 200, Custer, SD 57730 / 605-673-2251
Custer County Chamber of Commerce, 447 Crook St., Custer, SD 57730 / 800-992-9818
Rapid City Area Chamber of Commerce, 444 Mt. Rushmore Rd. N, Rapid City, SD 57709 / 605-343-1744
Hot Springs Area Chamber of Commerce, 801 S. 6th St., Hot Springs, SD 57747 / 800-325-6991

SPEARFISH CANYON HIGHWAY

- *Route Location:* Located in west-central South Dakota in Spearfish, near the Wyoming border. The northern access is located off Interstate 90 in the town of Spearfish and travels south to the junction of U.S. Highway 85 in Cheyenne Crossing.
- *Roads Traveled:* The 20 mile route follows U.S. Highway 14A which is a two-lane paved road suitable for all vehicles. The entire route has been designated a National Forest Scenic Byway.
- *Travel Season:* The route is open year-round.
- *Description:* Traveling across the Black Hills National Forest, this scenic drive takes you into the Black Hills through a narrow canyon alongside Spearfish Creek. The surrounding forest is filled with spruce, pine, aspen, birch, and oak trees. White-tailed deer, mule deer, bald eagles, and a variety of hawks inhabit this region of South Dakota. Excellent fishing for brown, brook, and rainbow trout is offered in the Spearfish and Little Spearfish Creeks. Several side roads leading from the canyon to the plateaus above provide for enjoyable and challenging trips for off-road vehicle users and mountain bikers. Several developed picnic areas and campgrounds are found along or near the drive, with some campgrounds providing access to hiking and backpacking trails. The winter months bring cross-country skiing and snowmobiling enthusiasts to the area. Abandoned mining operations and towns can be seen from the drive as can two cascading waterfalls, the Bridal Veil Falls and Roughlock Falls. A Forest Service office in Spearfish provides maps and brochures.
- *Other Nearby Routes:* The Fort Meade scenic drive is about 20 miles east and approximately 60 miles southeast is the Peter Norbeck scenic route.

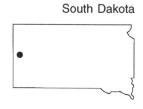

South Dakota

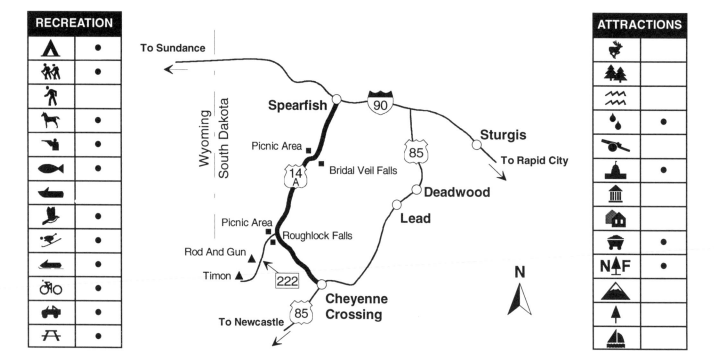

Information Sources:

Black Hills National Forest, Spearfish Ranger District, 2014 N. Main St., Spearfish, SD 57783 / 605-642-4622
Spearfish Area Chamber of Commerce, 115 E. Hudson, Spearfish, SD 57783 / 800-626-8013
Deadwood / Lead Area Chamber of Commerce, 460 Main St., Deadwood, SD 57732 / 605-578-1876

TENNESSEE

☐ *Scenic Drives*

1. Ocoee

○ *National Park Areas*

A. Andrew Johnson National Historic Site
B. Big South Fork National River and Recreation Area
C. Cumberland Gap National Historical Park
D. Fort Donelson National Battlefield
E. Great Smoky Mountains National Park
F. Shiloh National Military Park
G. Stones River National Battlefield

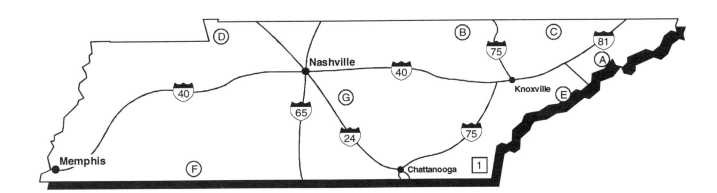

OCOEE

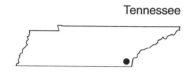

- *Route Location:* Located in the southeastern corner of Tennessee, southeast of Cleveland. The western access is located off U.S. Highway 411 in Ocoee and travels east to the junction of Tennessee State Highway 68 in Ducktown.
- *Roads Traveled:* The 29 mile route follows U.S. Highway 64 and Forest Service Road 77 which are two-lane paved roads suitable for all vehicles. Twenty-six miles of this route has been designated a National Forest Scenic Byway.
- *Travel Season:* The entire route is open year-round although winter driving conditions can be hazardous.
- *Description:* The scenic drive winds through a spectacular portion of the Cherokee National Forest, running alongside panoramas of steep forested hillsides, rock outcrops, and the Ocoee River. During the summer months, this river attracts throngs of white water users and viewers. The nearly 2,000 acre Lake Ocoee offers opportunities for boating, swimming, and fishing. Several trails can be accessed for this scenic drive providing hiking, bicycling, and wildlife viewing opportunities. Forest Service Road 77 provides a scenic side trip from the main route and offers spectacular panoramic views stretching as far as 40 miles. Located along this route is the Chilhowee Recreation Area with camping and picnicking facilities in addition to a small lake for fishing and swimming.
- *Other Nearby Routes:* The Forest Heritage scenic drive is about 90 miles to the northeast in North Carolina. Approximately 40 miles southwest is the Russell-Brasstown scenic drive in Georgia and about 50 miles to the east is the Oscar Wigington scenic route in South Carolina.

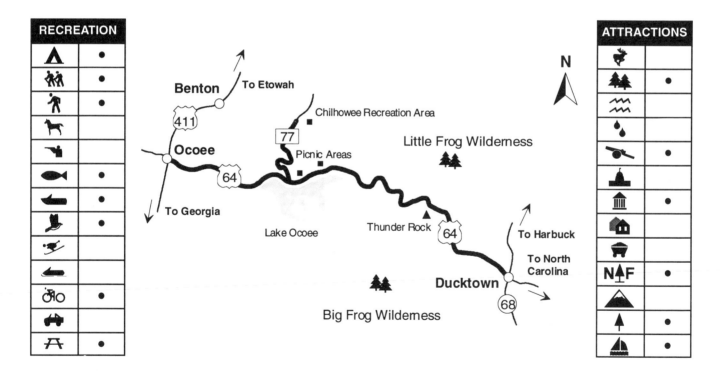

Information Sources:

Cherokee National Forest, 2800 N. Ocoee St. NW, Cleveland, TN 37320 / 615-476-9700
Cherokee N.F., Ocoee Ranger District, Hwy 64E, Rt. 1 - Box 348D, Benton, TN 37307 / 615-338-5201
Cleveland / Bradley Chamber of Commerce, 2145 Keith St., Cleveland, TN 37320 / 615-472-6587

Denali Highway, Alaska - by James Thomson. Courtesy Bureau of Land Management.

Beartooth Highway Scenic Byway, Wyoming.
Courtesy National Forest Service.

Kancamagus Scenic Byway, New Hampshire - by Matthew Morgan.
Courtesy National Forest Service.

Beartooth Highway Scenic Byway, Wyoming.
Courtesy National Forest Service

Denali Highway, Alaska - by James Thomson.
Courtesy Bureau of Land Management.

Blue Buck Knob Scenic Byway, Missouri.
Courtesy National Forest Service.

Ponderosa Pine Scenic Byway, Idaho.
Courtesy Idaho Department of Parks and Recreation.

River Road Scenic Byway, Michigan.
Courtesy National Forest Service.

Mesa Falls Scenic Byway, Idaho. Courtesy National Forest Service.

Fishlake Scenic Byway, Utah.
Courtesy National Forest Service.

Quebradas Back Country Byway, New Mexico.
Courtesy Bureau of Land Management

Lassen Scenic Byway, California. Courtesy National Forest Service.

Denali Highway, Alaska - by James Thomson.
Courtesy Bureau of Land Management.

Kings Canyon Scenic Byway, California.
Courtesy National Forest Service.

Lassen Scenic Byway, California. Courtesy National Forest Service.

Sawtooth Scenic Byway, Idaho.
Courtesy Idaho Department of Parks and Recreation.

Nine-Mile Canyon Back Country Byway, Utah - by
Kelly Rigby. Courtesy Bureau of Land Management.

Mountain Loop Scenic Byway, Washington - by Fred Harnisch.
Courtesy Mt. Baker - Snoqualmie National Forest Service.

Salmon River Scenic Byway, Idaho.
Courtesy Idaho Department of Parks and Recreation.

Garnet Back Country Byway, Montana. Courtesy Bureau of Land Management.

Missouri Breaks Back Country Byway, Montana. Courtesy Bureau of Land Management.

Kings Canyon Scenic Byway, California. Courtesy National Forest Service.

Hells Canyon Scenic Byway, Oregon.
Courtesy National Forest Service.

Lower Rio Grand Drive, Texas - by Mario
Sanchez. Courtesy Texas Historical Commission.

Beartooth Highway Scenic Byway, Wyoming. Courtesy National Forest Service.

Covered Bridge Scenic Byway, Ohio.
Courtesy National Forest Service.

San Juan Skyway Scenic Byway, Colorado - by Richard Ostergaard. Courtesy San Juan National Forest.

San Juan Skyway Scenic Byway, Colorado - by Richard Ostergaard.
Courtesy San Juan National Forest.

White Pass Scenic Byway, Washington - by Henry Maekawa.
Courtesy National Forest Service.

TEXAS

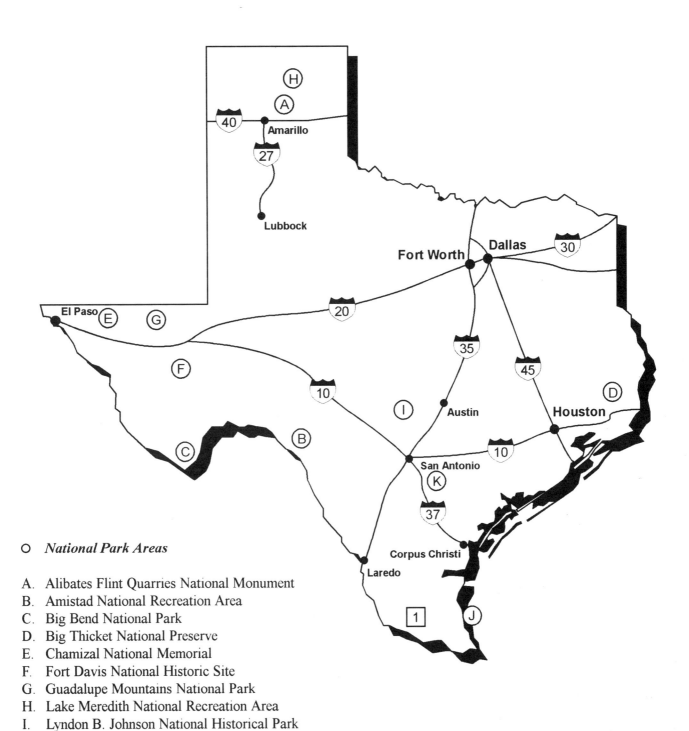

Road Condition Number: 512-463-8588

LOWER RIO GRANDE HERITAGE CORRIDOR

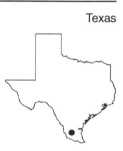

- **Route Location:** This scenic drive is located in southern Texas, starting north of Laredo and travels southeast to South Padre Island. The route follows the USA - Mexico border along the Rio Grande River to the Gulf of Mexico.
- **Roads Traveled:** The 200 mile route follows U.S. Highways 83 and 281, and Texas State Highway 48. All of the routes are two-lane paved roads suitable for all vehicles.
- **Travel Season:** The entire route is open year-round.
- **Description:** This route explores the history, architecture and historical designations found along the Lower Rio Grande Heritage

Corridor. The route links the 18th and 19th century river communities, on both sides of the border. Historic themes of the early colonial settlements and ranches, river trade on the Rio Grande steamboats, the Mexican-American War, the U.S. Civil War, and the development of the Valley's agricultural industry are represented in historical landmarks, sites, and structures along the entire drive.

Following is a brief description of some of the historic sites found along the corridor. In all, 196 sites in the United States and 35 sites in Mexico have been identified.

RECREATION	
▲	•
🚶🚶	
🚶	
🐴	
🪝	
🐟	•
🚣	•
🤿	•
🎿	
🚤	
🚲	
🚙	
🏕	•

ATTRACTIONS	
🦌	
🌲	
〰〰	
💧	
🔫	•
🏛	•
🏦	•
🏠	•
🚃	
N↑F	
🏔	
↑	•
⛵	•

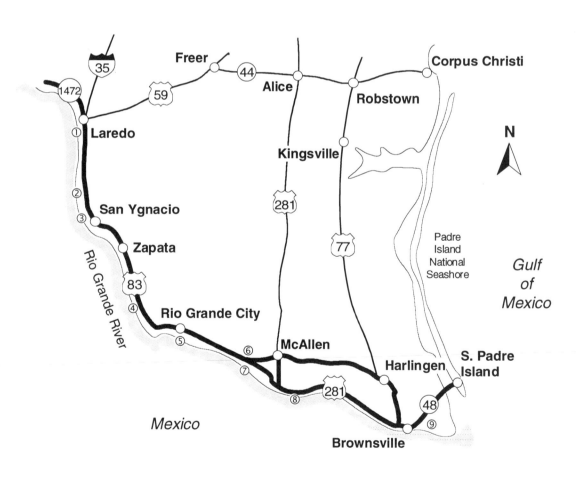

① St. Augustine's Church Historic Landmark
② Dolores Nuevo Historic Landmark
③ Corralitos Ranch
④ Falcon State Recreation Area
⑤ Juan Gonzales Home

⑥ La Lomita Historic District
⑦ Bentsen-Rio Grande Valley State Park
⑧ San Juan Plantation Historical Landmark
⑨ Old Brulay Plantation

LOWER RIO GRANDE HERITAGE CORRIDOR (CONT.)

1) The St. Augustine's Church, built in 1778 was the first church constructed in Laredo. The church is a Texas Historic Landmark.

2) Dolores Nuevo - Texas Historic Landmark. The ruins of seven stone houses and a cemetery from an 1860 community is located on this site.

3) Corralitos Ranch. This is the site of a large Hispanic ranch from around 1870 consisting of two sandstone houses and associated artifacts. The ranch is listed in the National Register of Historic Places.

4) Juan Gonzales Home - Texas Historic Landmark. The site of a one-story residence built around 1853. The building served as the town's first hotel.

5) La Lomita Historic District. The area includes a stuccoed stone chapel and several original buildings on 122 acres that served as a rural mission until around 1960. The site is a Texas Historic Landmark and is listed in the National Register of Historic Places.

6) San Juan Plantation - Texas Historic Landmark. A foreman's house built around 1904 is the only structure that remains from this 45,000-acre sugar plantation.

7) Old Brulay Plantation. The site features brick tenant houses, a sugar refinery, barns, and a residence owned by a French immigrant who introduced irrigation to the Lower Rio Grande Valley. The site is listed in the National Register of Historic Places.

8) Brazos Santiago Depot. This military depot was established during the Mexican-American War in 1846 to supply Fort Brown. The complex was destroyed during a storm in 1867. The site is listed in the National Register of Historic Places.

The Texas Historical Commission recently published *A Shared Experience: The History, Architecture and Historic Designations of the Lower Rio Grande Heritage Corridor.* The publication provides more detailed descriptions of the 231 historic sites and designations located along the corridor. A map showing the location of sites is provided with the book.

For more information on the book contact the Texas Historical Commission at the address listed below.

• *Other Nearby Routes:* There are no other scenic drives within a close distance.

Information Sources:

Texas Historical Commission, P.O. Box 12276, Austin, TX 78711-2276 / 512-463-6100
Laredo - Webb County Chamber of Commerce, 2310 San Bernardo Ave., Laredo, TX 78042 / 512-722-9895
Zapata Chamber of Commerce, P.O. Box 1028, Zapata, TX 78076 / 800-292-LAKE
McAllen Chamber of Commerce, 10 N. Broadway, McAllen, TX 78505 / 210-682-2871
Donna Chamber of Commerce, 210 N. D. Salinas Blvd., Donna, TX 78537 / 210-464-3272
Mercedes Chamber of Commerce, 400 S. Ohio, Mercedes, TX 78570 / 210-565-2221
Harlingen Area Chamber of Commerce, 311 E. Tyler, Harlingen, TX 78550 / 210-423-5440
San Benito Area Chamber of Commerce, 210 E. Heywood, San Benito, TX 78586 / 210-399-5321
Port Isabel Chamber of Commerce, 213 Yturria, Port Isabel, TX 78578 / 800-527-6102
South Padre Island Chamber of Commerce, 2600 Padre Blvd., #X, South Padre Island, TX 78597 / 210-761-2739
Brownsville Chamber of Commerce, 1600 E. Elizabeth St., Brownsville, TX 78522 / 210-542-4341
Rio Grande Valley Chamber of Commerce, FM 1015 & Expressway 83, Weslaco, TX 78599 / 210-968-3141
Hidalgo Chamber of Commerce, 611 E. Coma, Hidalgo, TX 78557 / 210-843-2302

UTAH

□ *Scenic Drives*

1. Beaver Canyon
2. Big Cottonwood Canyon
3. Boulder Mountain Highway
4. Brian Head - Panguitch Lake
5. Bull Creek Pass
6. Cedar Breaks
7. Eccles Canyon
8. Fishlake
9. Flaming Gorge - Uinta's
10. Huntington Canyon
11. Little Cottonwood Canyon
12. Logan Canyon Highway
13. Markaguant
14. Mirror Lake
15. Nebo Loop
16. Nine Mile Canyon
17. Ogden River
18. Pony Express
19. Silver Island Mountains
20. Smithsonian Butte
21. Transcontinental Railroad

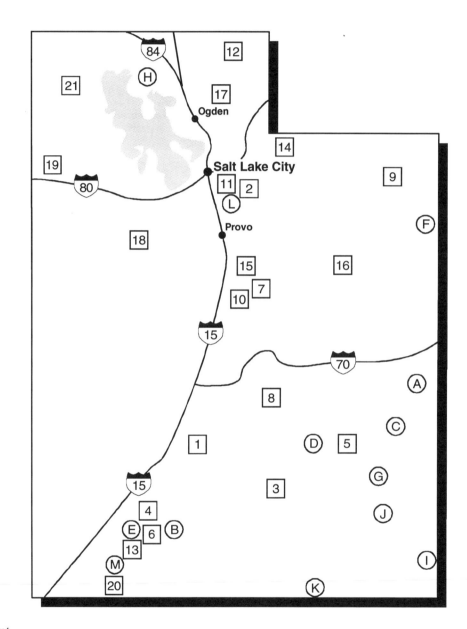

O *National Park Areas*

A. Arches National Park
B. Bryce Canyon National Park
C. Canyonlands National Park
D. Capitol Reef National Park
E. Cedar Breaks National Monument
F. Dinosaur National Monument
G. Glen Canyon National Recreation Area
H. Golden Spike National Historic Site
I. Hovenweep National Monument
J. Natural Bridges National Monument
K. Rainbow Bridge National Monument
L. Timpanogos Cave National Monument
M. Zion National Park

Road Condition Number: 801-964-6000

BEAVER CANYON

Utah

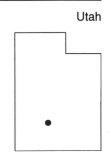

- *Route Location:* Located in southwestern Utah, northeast of Cedar City. The western access is located off Interstate 15 in the town of Beaver and travels east to the junction of U.S. Highway 89, in the town of Junction.
- *Roads Traveled:* The 32 mile route follows Utah State Highway 153 which is a two-lane paved road, to the Elk Meadows Ski Area, suitable for all vehicles. The route from Elk Meadows Ski Area heading east travels over an unsurfaced dry-weather-only road. Seventeen miles of this route, from Beaver to the ski area, has been designated a National Forest Scenic Byway.
- *Travel Season:* Most of the route is open year-round except the portion from Elk Meadows Ski Area east to the junction of highway 89, which closes during the winter months and may also become impassable after heavy rains.
- *Description:* The scenic drive travels through a beautiful canyon alongside the rushing Beaver River. Several scenic overlooks are provided along the route. Mule deer, elks, hawks, falcons, and eagles are just some of the wildlife seen from this scenic drive. Camping and picnicking opportunities are provided by several developed national forest campgrounds located along or near the drive. Fishing for rainbow and brook trout is a popular activity found in a the lakes and reservoirs. Horseback riding, mountain biking, cross-country skiing, downhill skiing, and snowmobiling are additional opportunities found along the drive.
- *Other Nearby Routes:* Approximately 50 miles south are the Markaguant, Cedar Breaks, and Brian Head-Panguitch Lake scenic drives. About 70 miles to the northeast is the Fishlake scenic drive.

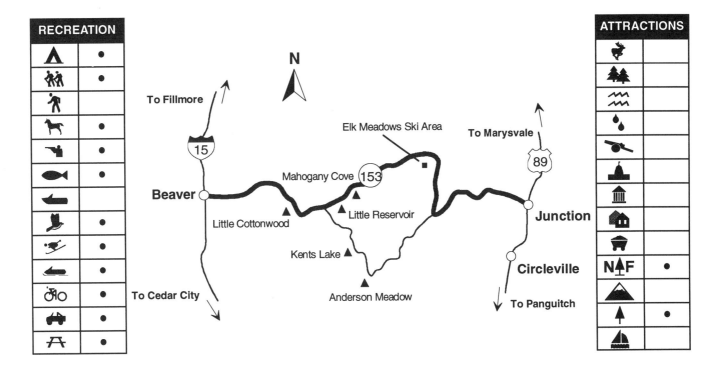

Information Sources:

Fishlake National Forest, Beaver Ranger District, 190 N. 100 E., Beaver, UT 84713 / 801-438-2436
Beaver Valley Chamber of Commerce, P.O. Box 760, Beaver, UT 84713 / 801-438-2975
Panguitch Chamber of Commerce, P.O. Box 400, Panguitch, UT 84759 / 801-676-2311
Richfield Area Chamber of Commerce, 15 East 100 North, Richfield, UT 84701 / 801-896-4241

BIG COTTONWOOD CANYON

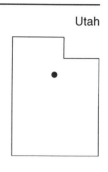

Utah

- *Route Location:* Located in north-central Utah, south of Salt Lake City. The western access is located off Interstate 215 east of Cottonwood and travels southeast to the town of Brighton.
- *Roads Traveled:* The 15 mile route follows Utah State Highway 190 which is a two-lane paved road suitable for all vehicles. The 15 mile route has been designated a National Forest Scenic Byway.
- *Travel Season:* The entire route is generally open year-round although delays or closure is possible during the winter due to avalanche danger. Snow tires or chains may be required November 1 through May 1.
- *Description:* The scenic drive crosses the Wasatch-Cache National Forest and travels through a beautiful canyon following alongside the Big Cottonwood Creek and takes you high up into the forested mountains. Several picnic areas are available on the route that offer nice places to enjoy a lunch or watch the many rock climbers scale the sheer-walled canyon. Opportunities exist for spotting mule deer, elk, moose, golden eagles, and hawks all along the drive. Winter sport enthusiasts are offered downhill skiing, cross-country skiing, and snowmobiling opportunities. Many trails can be found along the route that lead you deep into the rugged and spectacular wilderness areas.
- *Other Nearby Routes:* Located just to the south is the Little Cottonwood Canyon scenic drive. About 15 miles south is the Pony Express scenic route and an additional 30 miles south is the Nebo Loop scenic drive. Approximately 60 to 70 miles southeast are the Huntington Canyon, Eccles Canyon, and Nine Mile Canyon scenic drives. The Ogden River scenic route is located about 40 miles to the north.

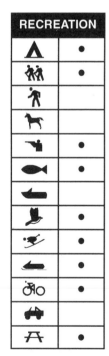

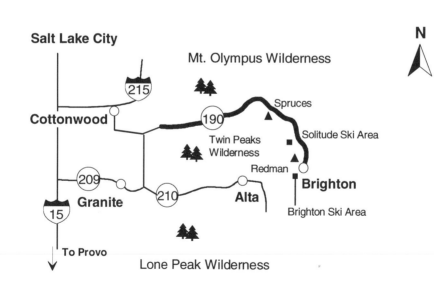

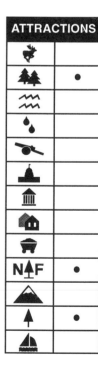

Information Sources:

Wasatch - Cache National Forest, 8236 Federal Building, 125 S. State, Salt Lake City, UT 84138 / 801-524-5030
Park City Chamber of Commerce, P.O. Box 1630, Park City, UT 84060 / 801-649-6100
Sandy Area Chamber of Commerce, 8807 S. 700 E., Sandy, UT 84070 / 801-566-0344
Murray Area Chamber of Commerce, 111 E. 5600 S., #104, Murray, UT 84107 / 801-263-2632

BOULDER MOUNTAIN HIGHWAY

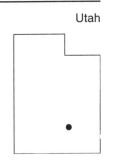

Utah

- *Route Location:* Located in south-central Utah, west of Hanksville. The northern access is located off Utah State Highway 24 in the town of Grover and travels south to Boulder.
- *Roads Traveled:* The 30 mile route follows Utah State Highway 12 which travels over a two-lane paved road suitable for all vehicles. The entire 30 mile route has been designated a National Forest Scenic Byway.
- *Travel Season:* The route is generally open year-round except for temporary closure for snow removal after major winter snows.
- *Description:* This scenic drive travels across the Dixie National Forest through agricultural fields, grassy pastures and then climbs into areas of aspen trees and meadows ablaze with colorful wildflowers. Several scenic turnouts and overlooks provide opportunities for photographing the surrounding landscape. The Anasazi Indian Village State Park offers a museum with exhib-

its of the ancient Indian village. Side roads from this route provide hiking and mountain biking opportunities that lead to the Capitol Reef National Park. Please note that motorized vehicles cannot access the national park from these roads. Fishing opportunities are provided by the Oak Creek Reservoir and Deer Creek Lake among other lakes found near the drive. Camping and picnicking opportunities are offered at several developed campgrounds.

- *Other Nearby Routes:* The Fishlake scenic drive is about 20 miles to the northwest while the Bull Creek Pass scenic route lies approximately 60 miles to the east. Less than 100 miles to the southwest are the Markaguant, Cedar Breaks, and Brian Head-Panguitch Lake scenic drives.

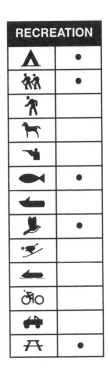

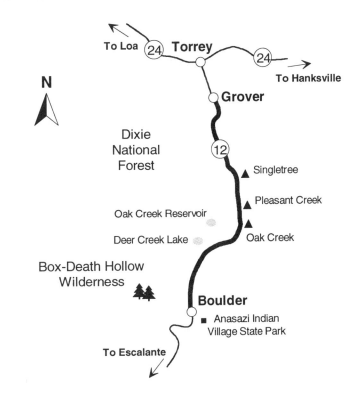

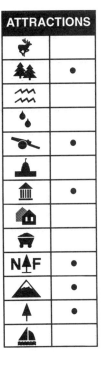

Information Sources:

Dixie National Forest, 82 North 100 East, Cedar City, UT 84721-0580 / 801-865-3700
Dixie National Forest, Escalante Ranger District, 270 W. Main, Escalante, UT 84726 / 801-826-4221
Dixie National Forest, Teasdale Ranger District, 138 E. Main, Teasdale, UT 84773 / 801-425-3702

BRIAN HEAD - PANGUITCH LAKE

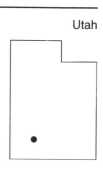

Utah

- **Route Location:** Located in southwestern Utah, east of Cedar City. The western access is located off Interstate 15 in the town of Parowan and travels southeast to Panguitch on U.S. Highway 89.
- **Roads Traveled:** The 55 mile route follows Utah State Highway 143 which is a two-lane paved road suitable for all vehicles. The entire 55 mile route has been designated a National Forest Scenic Byway.
- **Travel Season:** The route is generally open year-round although winter driving conditions can be hazardous.
- **Description:** The scenic drive travels through the Dixie National Forest as it crosses the forested hills of the Markaguant Plateau. The Cedar Breaks National Monument, a large natural amphitheater ½ mile deep and 3 miles wide, is skirted as you travel along this drive. The Brian Head Ski Resort offers excellent downhill skiing during the winter months and good mountain biking trails during the summer. Fishing for rain-bow and brown trout is a popular activity offered at Panguitch Lake. The lake sits in a sagebrush basin with colorful aspens and pine trees covering the surrounding hills. Hiking and backpacking trails are found along this scenic drive that lead deep into the forest offering excellent wildlife viewing opportunities.
- **Other Nearby Routes:** The Cedar Breaks scenic drive, which connects with the Markaguant scenic drive, can be accessed from this route. About 35 miles north is the Beaver Canyon scenic drive and 70 miles south lies the Smithsonian Butte scenic route. Approximately 100 miles to the west is the Boulder Mountain Highway and a little over 100 miles to the west is the Mount Wilson scenic route in Nevada.

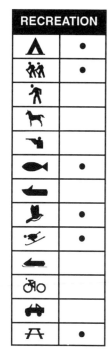

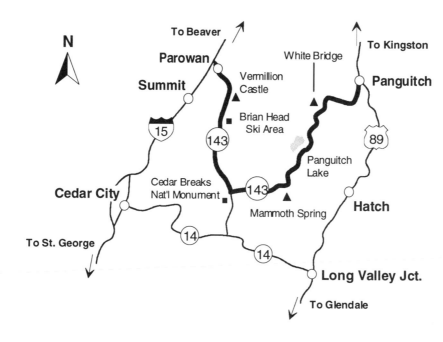

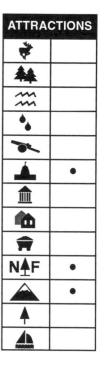

Information Sources:

Dixie National Forest, 82 North 100 East, Cedar City, UT 84721-0580 / 801-865-3700
Cedar City Area Chamber of Commerce, 286 N. Main St., Cedar City, UT 84720 / 801-586-4484
Panguitch Chamber of Commerce, P.O. Box 400, Panguitch, UT 84759 / 801-676-2311

BULL CREEK PASS

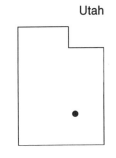

Utah

- *Route Location:* Located in south-central Utah, south of Hanksville. The northeastern access is located off Utah State Highway 95 twenty-one miles south of Hanksville and travels southwest, forming an open loop drive ending with the junction of Utah State Highway 276.
- *Roads Traveled:* The 68 mile route travels through remote country along the Bull Creek Pass Road which is a one-lane dirt surfaced road. There are numerous rough sections, steep grades, and blind curves. A four-wheel drive vehicle is strongly recommended for traveling this route. The entire route has been designated a BLM Type III Back Country Byway.
- *Travel Season:* The route is generally open from July through October and then the higher elevations are closed by winter snows. The lower elevations are normally open year-round although heavy thunderstorms during the summer can wash out sections of the road.

- *Description:* The scenic drive travels from the desert up into and through the Henry Mountains which was the last mountain range to be explored and named in the lower 48 states. As you travel this remote back country route, you will pass badlands and buttes, canyons and cliffs, and meander through forested slopes of spruce and ponderosa pine. A variety of wildlife is seen along the route including one of the few free-roaming herds of buffalo in the U.S. An old log cabin and the foundation of a second home can be seen at the Trachyte Ranch. Remnants of Eagle City can also be seen decaying amidst the aspen trees.
- *Other Nearby Routes:* About 60 miles west is the Boulder Mountain Highway scenic route and an additional 30 miles northwest is the Fishlake scenic drive.

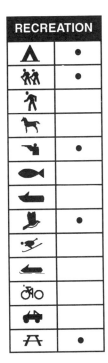

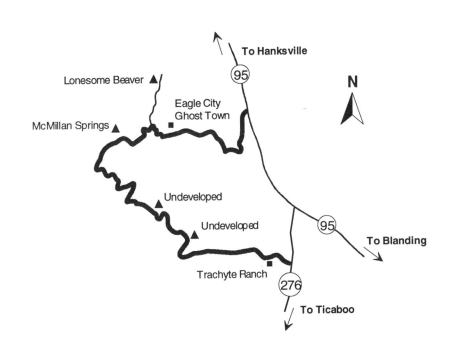

Information Sources:

BLM, Richfield District Office, 150 E. 900 N., Richfield, UT 84701 / 801-896-8221
BLM, Henry Mountain Resource Area, P.O. Box 99, Hanksville, UT 84734 / 801-542-3461

CEDAR BREAKS

Utah

- **Route Location:** Located in southwestern Utah, east of Cedar City. The southern access is located off Utah State Highway 14 with the junction of Utah State Highway 148 and travels north to the junction of State Highway 143.
- **Roads Traveled:** The 6 mile route follows State Highway 148 which is a two-lane paved road suitable for all vehicles. The route has been designated a National Forest Scenic Byway.
- **Travel Season:** The route is generally open from June through mid-October and then closed by winter snows.
- **Description:** This scenic drive travels across the Dixie National Forest before entering the Cedar Breaks National Monument. The route climbs from sagebrush meadows and hills, through ponderosa pines and aspen before reaching the forested high elevation plateau. Wildlife inhabiting this region of Utah includes mule deer, black bears, coyotes, mountain lions, foxes, bob-cats, golden eagles, and red-tailed hawks. Trails can be accessed from the route that lead into the Ashdown Gorge Wilderness Area. At the northern end of this short drive is the Cedar Breaks National Monument, a large natural amphitheater ½ mile deep and 3 miles wide. The amphitheater glows with brilliant hues of orange, coral, rose, and white, especially when viewed in the morning or evening. A small stand of ancient Bristlecone pines grow along the rim.

- **Other Nearby Routes:** Both the Markaguant and Brian Head-Panguitch Lake scenic routes can be accessed from this drive. About 70 miles to the north is the Beaver Canyon scenic route and about 75 miles to the south is the Smithsonian Butte scenic drive. Less than 100 miles northeast is the Boulder Mountain Highway.

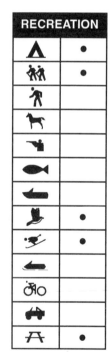

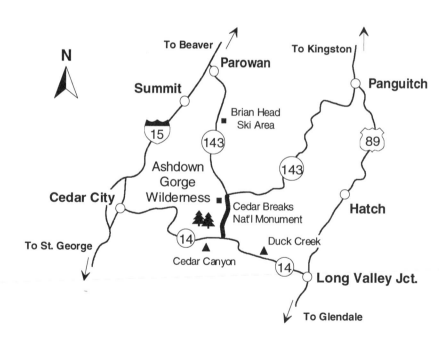

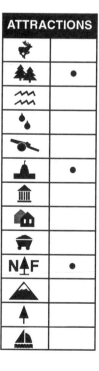

Information Sources:

Dixie National Forest, 82 North 100 East, Cedar City, UT 84721-0580 / 801-865-3700
Cedar City Area Chamber of Commerce, 286 N. Main St., Cedar City, UT 84720 / 801-586-4484
Panguitch Chamber of Commerce, P.O. Box 400, Panguitch, UT 84759 / 801-676-2311

ECCLES CANYON

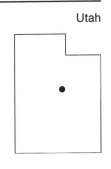

- *Route Location:* Located in central Utah, northwest of Price. The eastern access is located in Scofield off Utah State Highway 96 and travels southwest to the junction of Utah State Highway 31, east of Fairview.
- *Roads Traveled:* The 16 mile route follows Utah State Highway 264 which is a two-lane paved road suitable for all vehicles. The 16 mile route has been designated a National Forest Scenic Byway.
- *Travel Season:* The entire route is generally open year-round although winter driving conditions can be hazardous. Snow tire or chains may be required between October 1 and April 30.
- *Description:* The scenic drive travels through the Manti-La Sal National Forest as it crosses the Skyline Drive on top of the 10,000 foot Wasatch Plateau. The Skyline Mine is a major working coal mine that produces millions of tons of coal per year. Recreational opportunities are primarily found at the Scofield Res-

ervoir State Park, which lies north of the eastern terminus of this route on Utah State Highway 96. Found here are opportunities for boating, fishing, camping, and picnicking. During the winter, ice fishing, cross-country skiing, and snowmobiling trails are groomed by the state park. About 1 mile east of the Flat Canyon Campground is a boat ramp on Electric Lake, providing access to this reservoir for boating and fishing.

- *Other Nearby Routes:* The Huntington Canyon scenic route connects with the southwestern terminus of this route. About 30 miles to the southeast is the Nine Mile Canyon scenic drive. Approximately 50 miles to the northwest is the Nebo Loop scenic drive and an additional 20 miles north is the Pony Express scenic route.

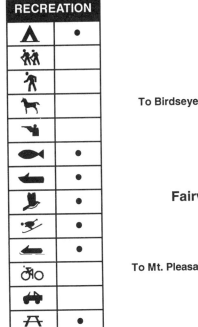

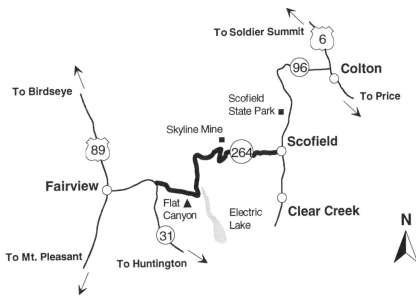

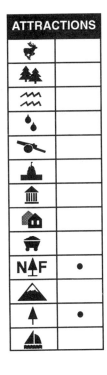

Information Sources:

Manti - La Sal National Forest, 599 W. Price River Dr., Price, UT 84501 / 801-637-2817
Carbon County Chamber of Commerce, P.O. Box 764, Price, UT 84501 / 801-637-2788
Mount Pleasant Chamber of Commerce, 115 W. Main St., City Hall, Mount Pleasant, UT 84647 / 801-462-2456
Emery County Chamber of Commerce, 190 E. Main, Castle Dale, UT 84513 / 801-381-2547

FISHLAKE

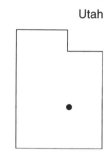

Utah

- **Route Location:** Located in south-central Utah, southwest of Price. The southwestern access begins at the junction of Utah State Highways 24 and 25, and travels northeast to the junction of Forest Service Road 036, north of Utah State Highway 72.
- **Roads Traveled:** The 16 mile route follows Utah State Highway 25 which is a two-lane paved road suitable for all vehicles. Thirteen miles of this route have been designated a National Forest Scenic Byway.
- **Travel Season:** The entire route is open year-round although winter driving conditions may be hazardous.
- **Description:** The scenic drive, crossing the Fish Lake National Forest, meanders through stands of quaking aspen, Engelmann spruce and White fir to the cool, emerald waters of Fish Lake which extends 5½ miles in length, 1½ miles in width, and reaches depths over 120 feet. This natural high mountain lake offers excellent trout fishing, hiking or mountain biking on the Lakeshore National Recreation Trail, or staying overnight in any of the national forest campgrounds surrounding the lake. All-terrain vehicle enthusiasts are provided access to the Piute ATV trail near the routes northeastern terminus. Wildlife inhabiting this region of Utah includes moose, elk, mule deer, golden eagles, night herons, and hawks.
- **Other Nearby Routes:** Approximately 80 to 100 miles northeast are the Huntington Canyon, Eccles Canyon, and Nine Mile Canyon scenic drives. About 30 miles southeast is the Boulder Mountain Highway and 70 miles to the southwest is the Beaver Canyon scenic drive. About 110 miles to the south are the Cedar Breaks, Brian Head-Panguitch Lake, and Markaguant scenic drives.

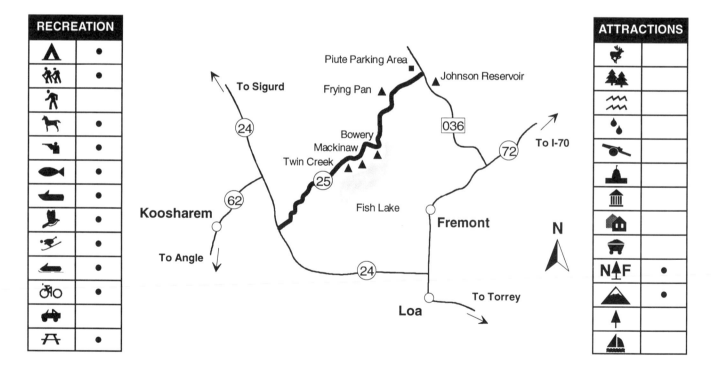

Information Sources:

Fishlake National Forest, 115 E. 900 N., Richfield, UT 84701 / 801-896-9233
Fishlake National Forest, Loa Ranger District, 150 S. Main St., Loa, UT 84747 / 801-836-2800
Richfield Area Chamber of Commerce, 15 East 100 North, Richfield, UT 84701 / 801-896-4241

FLAMING GORGE - UINTA'S

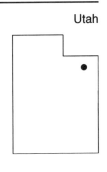
Utah

- *Route Location:* Located in eastern Utah, starting in Vernal. The southern access is located off U.S. Highway 40 in Vernal and travels north to Utah State Highway 43 in Manila, near the Wyoming border.
- *Roads Traveled:* The 67 mile route follows U.S. Highway 191 and Utah State Highway 44. Both routes are tow-lane paved roads suitable for all vehicles. The 67 mile route has been designated a National Forest Scenic Byway.
- *Travel Season:* The entire route is open year-round although winter driving conditions can be hazardous, especially at higher elevations.
- *Description:* The scenic drive crosses the Ashley National Forest, climbs from Vernal through sculptured layers of sandstone and steep slopes of juniper, pinion, and aspen before entering the Flaming Gorge National Recreation Area's forests and meadows. Bighorn sheep, deer, elk, and moose can be seen from various places along this scenic drive. Several marked trails can be found in the area and along the route, providing opportunities for hiking, mountain biking, horseback riding, cross-country skiing, and snowmobiling. Camping is provided by the many developed national forest campgrounds found along the scenic drive. The 210,000 acre Flaming Gorge National Recreation Area provides opportunities for fishing, boating, swimming, and water-skiing. The Flaming Gorge Dam Visitor Center offers guided tours of the dam.
- *Other Nearby Routes:* The Nine Mile Canyon scenic drive is about 45 miles southwest and approximately 110 miles to the southeast is the Flat Tops Trail scenic route in Colorado. About 135 miles to the west is the Mirror Lake scenic drive.

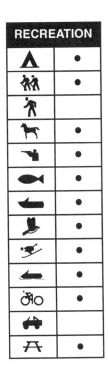

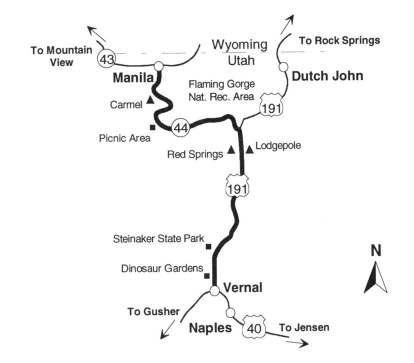

Information Sources:

Ashley National Forest, 355 N. Vernal Ave., Vernal, UT 84078 / 801-789-1181
Vernal Area Chamber of Commerce, 134 W. Main, Vernal, UT 84078 / 801-789-1352
Flaming Gorge Area Chamber of Commerce, P.O. Box 122, Manila, UT 84046 / 801-784-3483

HUNTINGTON CANYON

- *Route Location:* Located in central Utah, west of Price. The southeastern access is located off Utah State Highway 10 in the town of Huntington and travels northwest to Fairview on U.S. Highway 89.
- *Roads Traveled:* The 48 mile route follows Utah State Highway 31 which is a two-lane paved road suitable for all vehicles. The entire 48 mile route has been designated a National Forest Scenic Byway.
- *Travel Season:* The entire route is generally open year-round although winter driving conditions may be hazardous. Snow tires or chains may be required between October 1 and April 30.
- *Description:* The scenic drive travels through the Manti-La Sal National Forest up Huntington Canyon and across the Wasatch Plateau. Scenic turnouts are provided along the drive that provide opportunities for photographing the surrounding wilderness. Portions of the route travel alongside Huntington Creek which offers excellent fly fishing opportunities for rainbow, cutthroat, and brown trout. Huntington Lake State Park also provides fishing opportunities during the summer and snowmobiling and cross-country skiing trails in the winter. Wildlife inhabiting this region of Utah includes elk, black bears, mountain lions, deer, golden eagles, and red-tailed hawks.

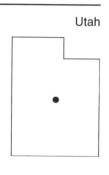

Utah

- *Other Nearby Routes:* The Eccles Canyon scenic drive can be accessed from this route. About 25 miles northeast is the Nine Mile Canyon scenic drive. Approximately 40 miles to the west is the Nebo Loop scenic route and an additional 40 miles north is the Pony Express scenic drive. To the south, approximately 70 miles, is the Fishlake scenic drive and an additional 30 miles to the south is the Boulder Mountain Highway.

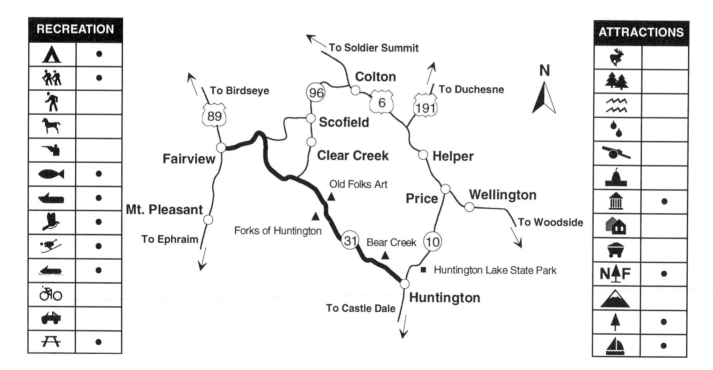

Information Sources:

Manti - La Sal National Forest, 599 W. Price River Dr., Price, UT 84501 / 801-637-2817
Mount Pleasant Chamber of Commerce, 115 W. Main St., City Hall, Mount Pleasant, UT 84647 / 801-462-2456
Carbon County Chamber of Commerce, P.O. Box 764, Price, UT 84501 / 801-637-2788
Emery County Chamber of Commerce, 190 E. Main, Castle Dale, UT 84513 / 801-381-2547

LITTLE COTTONWOOD CANYON

Utah

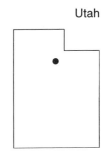

- *Route Location:* Located in north-central Utah, south of Salt Lake City. The western access is located off Interstate 15, near the town of Granite and travels east ending three miles south of Alta.
- *Roads Traveled:* The 12 mile route follows Utah State Highway 210 which is a narrow two-lane paved road to Alta. The last three miles, south from Alta, travel over a gravel surfaced road. The route is suitable for all vehicles. Travelers will need to retrace the route back out. The entire 12 mile route has been designated a National Forest Scenic Byway.
- *Travel Season:* Most of the route is open year-round with the exception of the last three miles past Alta which is closed from November through May due to winter snows.
- *Description:* The scenic drive travels through a sheer-walled canyon up into the high mountains of the Wasatch Cache-National Forest. Numerous scenic turnouts along the route provide scenic vistas of the two wilderness areas that surround this scenic drive. The wilderness areas provide opportunities for hiking during warmer months and cross-country skiing during winter. Many other recreational opportunities are offered along this route including camping, picnicking, mountain biking, hunting, and fishing.
- *Other Nearby Routes:* Located just north of this route is the Big Cottonwood Canyon scenic drive. About 15 miles south is the Pony Express scenic route and an additional 30 miles south is the Nebo Loop scenic drive. Approximately 60 to 70 miles southeast are the Huntington Canyon, Eccles Canyon, and Nine Mile Canyon scenic drives. Located to the north about 40 miles is the Ogden River scenic route.

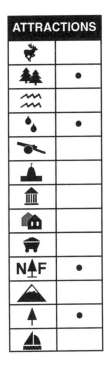

Information Sources:

Wasatch - Cache National Forest, 8236 Federal Building, 125 S. State, Salt Lake City, UT 84138 / 801-524-5030
Sandy Area Chamber of Commerce, 8807 S. 700 E., Sandy, UT 84070 / 801-566-0344
American Fork Chamber of Commerce, 31 N. Church St., American Fork, UT 84003 / 801-756-5110

LOGAN CANYON HIGHWAY

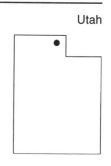

Utah

- *Route Location:* Located in the northeastern corner of Utah, north of Ogden near the Idaho border. The southwestern access is located off U.S. Highway 91 in the town of Logan and travels northeast to the junction of Utah State Highway 30 in Garden City.
- *Roads Traveled:* The 39 mile route follows U.S. Highway 89 which is a two-lane paved road suitable for all vehicles. The entire 39 mile route has been designated a National Forest Scenic Byway.
- *Travel Season:* The entire route is open year-round although winter driving conditions may be hazardous, especially at the higher elevations.
- *Description:* The scenic drive travels across the Wasatch-Cache National Forest through the Logan Canyon and over a small pass offering unusual rock formations, limestone cliffs, spectacular overlooks, and rugged rock falls. Found in the lower canyon's nearly vertical walls and rock formations are numerous fossils. Sweeping views of the turquoise waters of Bear Lake can be seen from the 7,800 foot Bear Lake Summit. A variety of wildlife inhabits the wilderness surrounding the scenic drive and includes mule deer, elk, beavers, muskrats, and a wide variety of birds. Several hiking trails are accessed from along the route, many leading into the Mt. Naomi Wilderness. Other recreational opportunities found along this drive include camping, fishing, hunting, and skiing.
- *Other Nearby Routes:* The Ogden River scenic drive is about 40 miles to the south and 55 miles to the west is the Transcontinental Railroad scenic drive which provides access to the Silver Island Mountains scenic route. Approximately 5 miles to the north is the Bear Lake-Caribou scenic drive in Idaho.

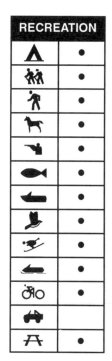

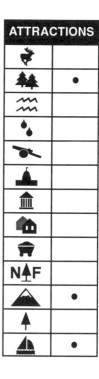

Information Sources:

Wasatch - Cache National Forest, 8236 Federal Building, 125 S. State, Salt Lake City, UT 84138 / 801-524-5030
Cache Chamber of Commerce, 160 N. Main, Logan, UT 84321 / 801-752-2161
Bear Lake Chamber of Commerce, P.O. Box 55, Garden City, UT 84028 / 801-946-2901
Brigham City Area Chamber of Commerce, P.O. Box 458, Brigham City, UT 84302 / 801-723-3931

MARKAGUANT

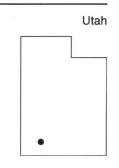

Utah

- *Route Location:* Located in southwestern Utah. The western access starts in Cedar City and travels east to the junction of U.S. Highway 89 in the town of Long Valley Junction.
- *Roads Traveled:* The 40 mile route follows Utah State Highway 14 which is a two-lane paved road suitable for all vehicles. The entire route has been designated a National Forest Scenic Byway.
- *Travel Season:* The route is generally open year-round although winter driving conditions may be hazardous.
- *Description:* This scenic drive traverses the forests and lakes of the Markaguant Plateau offering spectacular views of the surrounding wilderness. The route climbs through the Cedar Canyon and travels across the Dixie National Forest. Just to the north of this scenic drive is the 7,000 acre Ashdown Gorge Wilderness where you will find many miles of strenuous hiking trails. Fishing and canoeing opportunities, in addition to camping, can be found at the popular Navajo Lake, a short drive south on Forest Service Road 053. Located at the canyon summit is the Zion Overlook which provides a panoramic view of the distant towers and buttes found in the Zion National Park.
- *Other Nearby Routes:* The Cedar Breaks scenic drive, which also intersects with the Brian Head-Panguitch Lake scenic drive, can be accessed from the midpoint of this route. To the south about 50 miles is the Smithsonian Butte scenic route. Approximately 50 miles to the north is the Beaver Canyon scenic drive and less than 100 miles to the northwest is the Mount Wilson scenic drive in Nevada. About 110 miles to the northeast is the Boulder Mountain Highway scenic drive.

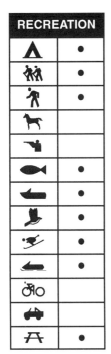

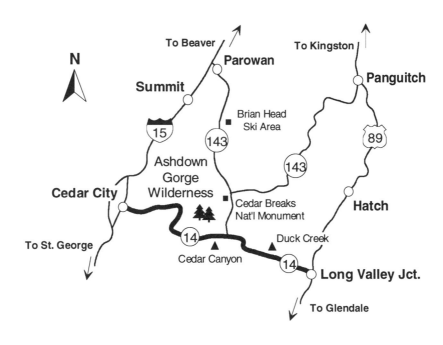

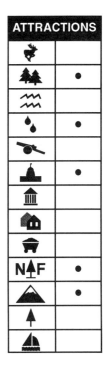

Information Sources:

Dixie National Forest, 82 North 100 East, Cedar City, UT 84721-0580 / 801-865-3700
Cedar City Area Chamber of Commerce, 286 N. Main St., Cedar City, UT 84720 / 801-586-4484
Panguitch Chamber of Commerce, P.O. Box 400, Panguitch, UT 84759 / 801-676-2311

MIRROR LAKE

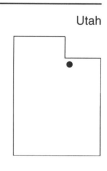

Utah

- *Route Location:* Located in north-central Utah, east of Salt Lake City. The southwestern access is located off U.S. Highway 189 in the town of Kamas and travels northeast to the Wyoming border.
- *Roads Traveled:* The 65 mile route follows Utah State Highway 150 which is a two-lane paved road suitable for all vehicles. The 65 mile route has been designated a National Forest Scenic Byway.
- *Travel Season:* The route is generally open from late May through mid-October then closed by winter snows. A portion of the route becomes a snowmobile trail during the winter months.
- *Description:* As it crosses the Wasatch-Cache National Forest, this scenic drive winds through heavily forested mountains accented by vast meadows and rugged peaks and cliffs. A variety of wildlife inhabits the surrounding wilderness including mountain goats, bobcats, coyotes, elk, and mule deer. Several trails along the route

provide opportunities for hiking, mountain biking, and horseback riding in warmer weather while offering cross-country skiing and snowmobiling during the winter. The High Uintas Wilderness offers back country hiking, backpacking, and horseback riding opportunities. For those less interested in roughing it, many developed campgrounds line the roadway.
- *Other Nearby Routes:* Less than 75 miles to the northwest is the Ogden River scenic drive and an additional 40 miles north to the Logan Canyon Highway. About 30 miles to the west are the Big Cottonwood Canyon and Little Cottonwood Canyon scenic routes. Less than 100 miles southeast lies the Nine Mile Canyon scenic drive and about 70 miles to the southwest is the Pony Express scenic route.

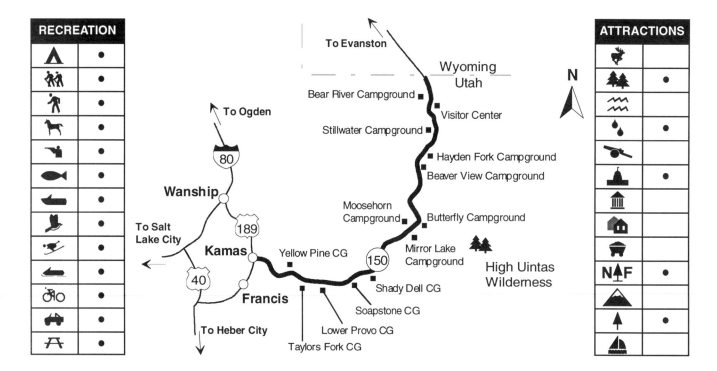

Information Sources:

Wasatch - Cache National Forest, 8236 Federal Building, 125 S. State, Salt Lake City, UT 84138 / 801-524-5030
Evanston Chamber of Commerce, 36 10th St., Evanston, WY 82931-0365 / 307-789-2757
Heber Valley Chamber of Commerce, 475 N. Main St., Heber City, UT 84032 / 801-654-3666

NEBO LOOP

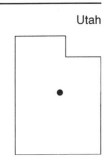

Utah

- *Route Location:* Located in central Utah, south of Provo. The northern access is located off U.S. Highway 6 south of Payson and travels south to the junction of Utah State Highway 132, east of Nephi.
- *Roads Traveled:* The 38 mile route follows Forest Service Road 015 which is a two-lane paved road suitable for all vehicles. The 38 mile route has been designated a National Forest Scenic Byway.
- *Travel Season:* The route is generally open from late May through November and then closed by heavy winter snows.
- *Description:* Traveling across the Uinta National Forest, this scenic drive climbs breathtaking mountain passes, past babbling mountain streams and unusual rock formations. Scenic overlooks found at various locations along the route provide opportunities for the professional and amateur photographer to capture on film the surrounding wilderness. The Payson Lakes Recreation Area offers hiking on paved trails, picnic areas, camping, and excellent fishing. Moose can often be seen grazing around the lakes in this area. Other wildlife inhabiting this area includes black bears, bighorn sheep, coyotes, beavers, and mule deer. Hiking, backpacking, and horseback riding opportunities are available throughout the national forest including many trails accessed from this route leading into the rugged Mount Nebo Wilderness.
- *Other Nearby Routes:* Approximately 30 miles to the north is the Pony Express scenic drive and an additional 15 miles north will lead to the Big Cottonwood Canyon scenic route. Approximately 50 to 75 miles to the east are the Huntington Canyon, Eccles Canyon, and Nine Mile Canyon scenic drives.

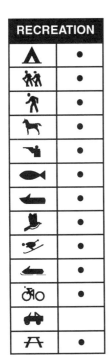

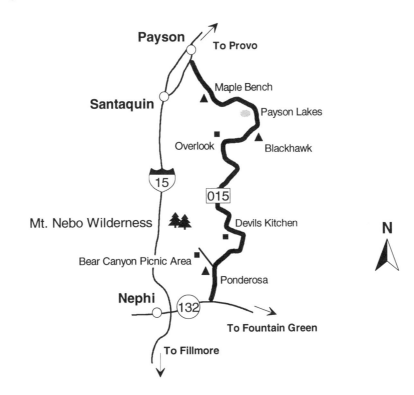

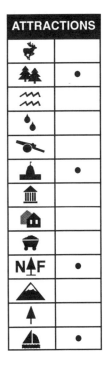

Information Sources:

Uinta National Forest, 88 West 100 North, Provo, UT 84601 / 801-377-5780
Nephi Area Chamber of Commerce, P.O. Box 71, Nephi, UT 84648 / 801-623-2411
Payson Area Chamber of Commerce, P.O. Box 21, Payson, UT 84651 / 801-465-2634
Spanish Fork Area Chamber of Commerce, 40 S. Main, Spanish Fork, UT 84660 / 801-798-8352

NINE MILE CANYON

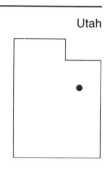

Utah

- **Route Location:** Located in east-central Utah, east of Price. The southern access is located off U.S. Highway 6 just east of Wellington and travels northeast to the junction of U.S. Highway 40, west of Myton.
- **Roads Traveled:** The 78 mile route follows the Nine Mile Canyon Road which is a two-lane graded gravel road suitable for most vehicles. Large RVs or vehicles pulling trailers are not recommended on this route due to occasional steep grades and sharp turns. The 78 mile route has been designated a BLM Type I Back Country Byway.
- **Travel Season:** The route is generally open year-round although several dry wash crossings can become impassable after heavy rains in the summer or winter snow storms.
- **Description:** The back country drive travels through a spectacular sandstone canyon and atop high plateaus. This area is nationally significant for its concentration of Fremont Indian Culture archaeological sites which include many rock art panels. The area also offers views of many historic cabins dating back to the 1880s. Wildlife is diverse and plentiful, especially along streams and canyon bottoms. Deer and elk are commonly seen in the fields alongside the road. Jeep roads in side canyons lead to the rim of the West Tavaputs Plateau and offer excellent mountain biking opportunities. Primitive camping is available anywhere on BLM administered lands.
- **Other Nearby Routes:** Approximately 30 miles to the west are the Huntington Canyon and Eccles Canyon scenic drives. About 35 miles to the northeast is the Flaming Gorge-Uintas scenic route and about 90 miles northwest is the Mirror Lake scenic drive.

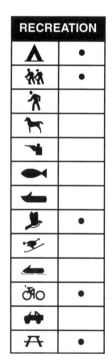

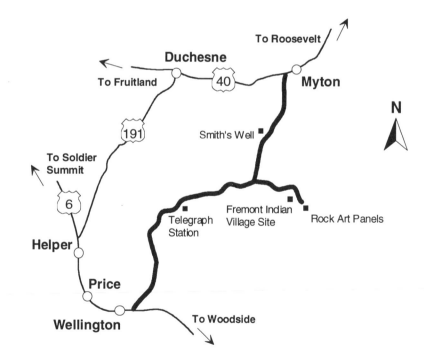

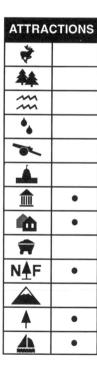

Information Sources:

BLM, Moab District Office, 82 E. Dogwood, Moab, UT 84532 / 801-259-6111
Carbon County Chamber of Commerce, P.O. Box 764, Price, UT 84501 / 801-637-2788
Duchesne County Area Chamber of Commerce, 48 South 200 East, Roosevelt, UT 84066 / 801-722-4598

OGDEN RIVER

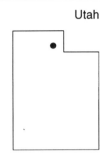

Utah

- *Route Location:* Located in northeastern Utah, north of Salt Lake City. The western access is located off Interstate 15 in Ogden and travels east to the junction of Utah State Highway 16 in the town of Woodruff.
- *Roads Traveled:* The 60 mile route follows Utah State Highway 39 which is a two-lane paved road suitable for all vehicles. Thirty-three miles of this route has been designated a National Forest Scenic Byway.
- *Travel Season:* The route is generally open from late April through mid-December then closed by winter snows. The route across the national forest becomes a snowmobile trail during the winter months.
- *Description:* The scenic drive crosses the Wasatch-Cache National Forest and travels through a narrow canyon, past the Pineview Reservoir, and high up into the mountain meadows. Autumn colors are quite spectacular as aspens turn gold in preparation for winter. Pineview Reservoir lies in a valley surrounded by mountains and is a very popular recreational spot for camping, picnicking, boating, fishing, swimming, and wind surfing. Recreational activities are not limited to the reservoir as several campgrounds, picnic areas and opportunities for fishing, cross-country skiing, hiking, horseback riding, and bicycling are offered along the entire length of this scenic drive.
- *Other Nearby Routes:* Approximately 20 miles to the north is the Logan Canyon Highway scenic route and about 70 miles northwest is the Transcontinental Railroad scenic drive. About 40 miles to the south are the Big Cottonwood Canyon and Little Cottonwood Canyon scenic drives and an additional 15 miles south to the Pony Express scenic route. Less than 75 miles to the southeast is the Mirror Lake scenic drive.

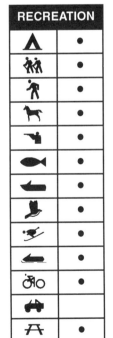

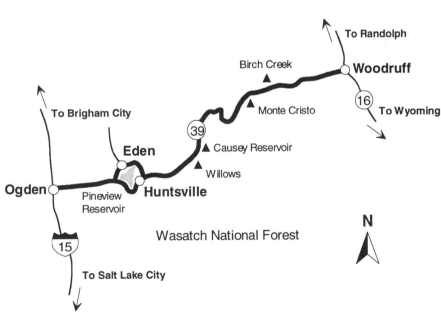

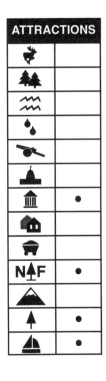

Information Sources:

Wasatch - Cache National Forest, 8236 Federal Building, 125 S. State, Salt Lake City, UT 84138 / 801-524-5030
The Chamber - Ogden/Weber, 2404 Washington Blvd., #1100, Ogden, UT 84401 / 801-621-8300
Evanston Chamber of Commerce, 36 10th St., Evanston, WY 82931-0365 / 307-789-2757

PONY EXPRESS

Utah

* **Route Location:** Located in central Utah, northwest of Provo. The eastern access is located off Interstate 15 in Lehi and travels west to the Nevada border, west of Ibapah.
* **Roads Traveled:** The 160 mile route follows Utah State Highway 73 and the Pony Express Trail Road. Highway 73 is a two-lane paved road suitable for all vehicles. The remainder of the route travels over sand and gravel surfaced roads. A two-wheel drive, high clearance vehicle is recommended on this segment. RVers and vehicles pulling trailers should inquire with the BLM about your vehicle and the current road conditions. The BLM has designated 133 miles of this route, from Fairfield to Ibapah, a Type II Back Country Byway.
* **Travel Season:** The route is generally open year-round although heavy thunderstorms can cause flash floods and wash out sections of the road.

* **Description:** By traveling this route through Utah's western desert rangeland, you trace the historic Pony Express Trail. The BLM has identified and marked several historical sites of the Pony Express Trail along this route. The Simpson Springs Station, located midway along the drive, has a restored structure closely resembling the original building located here in 1860. A BLM campground is also found here.
* **Other Nearby Routes:** About 10 miles north are the Little Cottonwood Canyon and Big Cottonwood Canyon scenic drives. Approximately 30 miles south is the Nebo Loop scenic route and an additional 30 to 50 miles southeast are the Eccles Canyon, Huntington Canyon, and Nine Mile Canyon scenic drives. Northeast about 50 miles is the Mirror Lake scenic route.

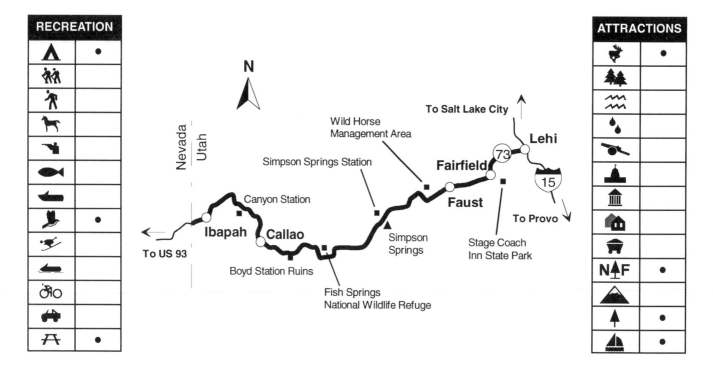

Information Sources:

BLM, Richfield District Office, 150 E. 900 N., Richfield, UT 84701 / 801-896-8221
Lehi Chamber of Commerce, P.O. Box 154, Lehi, UT 84043 / 801-768-8665
Tooele County Chamber of Commerce, 50 E. 1st N., Tooele, UT 84074 / 801-882-0690
American Fork Chamber of Commerce, 31 N. Church St., American Fork, UT 84003 / 801-756-5110
White Pine Chamber of Commerce, 636 Aultman St., Ely, NV 89301 / 702-289-8877

SILVER ISLAND MOUNTAINS

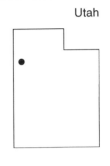

- *Route Location:* Located in northwestern Utah, west of Salt Lake City near the Nevada border. The southern access is located off Interstate 80 (exit #4), east of Wendover and travels northeast forming a loop drive back to the original starting point.
- *Roads Traveled:* The 54 mile route follows the Silver Island Mountains Road which is a graded gravel road requiring a two-wheel drive, high-clearance vehicle. RVers and vehicles pulling trailers should inquire with the BLM about any vehicle limitations and the current road conditions. The 54 mile route has been designated a BLM Type II Back Country Byway.
- *Travel Season:* The entire route is generally open year-round although severe thunderstorms can make the road muddy and impassable in sections.
- *Description:* This route travels around the rugged Silver Island Mountains, perhaps one of the most isolated mountain ranges in Utah. Silver-white mud and salt frame this beautiful mountain range in a 320 degree arch of desert solitude. Often views will appear distorted, with distances running together or becoming disguised in the heat. The Donner-Reed Party, one of many explorers and wagon trains crossing the mountain range, attempted this route only to abandon their wagons in the soft mud east of here. Part of their route can be seen on the north end. No developed campgrounds exist along the route, however, car camping is permitted within 100 feet of existing roads.
- *Other Nearby Routes:* The Transcontinental Railroad scenic drive is located approximately 50 miles north. About 50 miles to the south is the Pony Express scenic drive. Less than 70 miles west is the California Trail scenic route in Nevada.

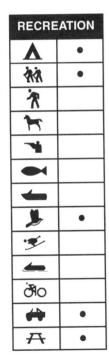

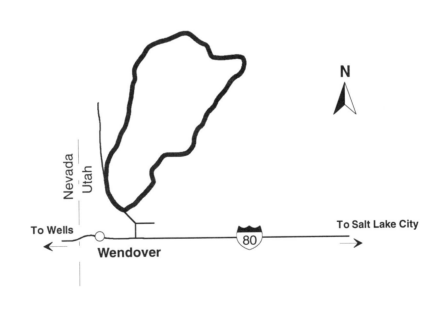

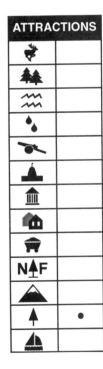

Information Sources:

BLM, Salt Lake District Office, 2370 S. 2300 W., Salt Lake City, UT 84119 / 801-977-4300
Tooele County Chamber of Commerce, 50 E. 1st N., Tooele, UT 84074 / 801-882-0690

SMITHSONIAN BUTTE

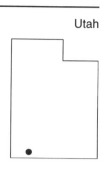

Utah

- **Route Location:** Located in the southwestern corner of Utah, east of St. George. The northern access is located off Utah State Highway 9 in the town of Rockville and travels south to the junction of Utah State Highway 59.
- **Roads Traveled:** The 9 mile route follows the Smithsonian Butte County Road which is a graded unsurfaced road but is suitable for most vehicles. Due to sharp curves and a half-mile section of steep grade, large RVs and travel trailers are not recommended. The 9 mile route has been designated a BLM Type I Back Country Byway.
- **Travel Season:** The route is normally open year-round except for the section located on the north facing slope of Smithsonian Butte which can remain snow-covered during the winter. The route should not be attempted after heavy snow or rains.
- **Description:** This back country route crosses the Virgin River on the Old Rockville Bridge and then follows alongside the river offering spectacular views of the nearby Zion National Park. A short 2 mile spur road leads to one of the most picturesque and well preserved ghost towns in Utah. Grafton was settled in 1862 and abandoned in the early 1900s. All that remains today are some historic homes, a school, and a cemetery. Camping and picnicking facilities can be found in the nearby Zion National Park, as no developed campgrounds are found along this route.
- **Other Nearby Routes:** Approximately 50 miles to the north are the Cedar Breaks, Markaguant, and Brian Head-Panguitch Lake scenic drives. About 70 miles southeast across the Arizona border is the Kaibab Plateau-North Rim Parkway.

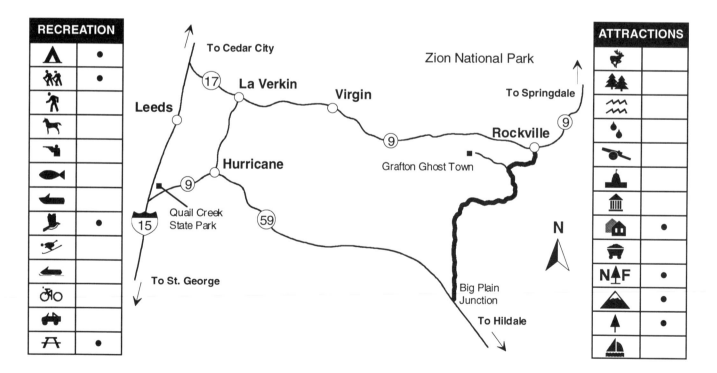

Information Sources:

BLM, Cedar City District Office, 176 E. D.L. Sargent Dr., Cedar City, UT 84720 / 801-586-2401
Hurricane Valley Chamber of Commerce, P.O. Box 101, Hurricane, UT 84737 / 801-635-4194
Rockville Board of Trade, 144 East 250 South, Rockville, UT 84763 / 801-772-3472

TRANSCONTINENTAL RAILROAD

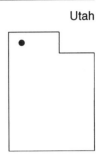

Utah

- *Route Location:* Located in northwestern Utah, west of Brigham City. The eastern access is located west of the Golden Spike National Historic Site off Utah State Highway 83 and travels southwest to the town of Lucin.
- *Roads Traveled:* The 90 mile route follows the Transcontinental Railroad Road which is a narrow gravel and dirt surfaced road. The route requires a two-wheel drive, high-clearance vehicle no more than 30 feet in length. The 90 mile route has been designated a BLM Type II Back Country Byway.
- *Travel Season:* The entire route is generally open year-round although hazardous driving conditions may exist after heavy rains when portions may become impassable.
- *Description:* The scenic drive follows the last 90 miles of grade laid by the Central Pacific Railroad before their rails met the Union Pacific's at Promontory Summit. The landscape seen along the route today looks much the same as it did in 1869. Many original trestles and culverts can be seen along the route as well as remnants of two railroad communities and several workers' camps. The Bureau of Land Management has identified 30 interpretive sites along the route. The Golden Spike National Historic Site offers information, exhibits, and working replica steam locomotives.
- *Other Nearby Routes:* The Silver Island Mountains scenic drive is located about 50 miles south of the western terminus of this route. About 100 miles south is the Pony Express scenic drive. From the eastern terminus of this route the Logan Canyon and Ogden River scenic drives are about 70 miles east. To the west about 50 miles is the California Trail scenic drive in Nevada.

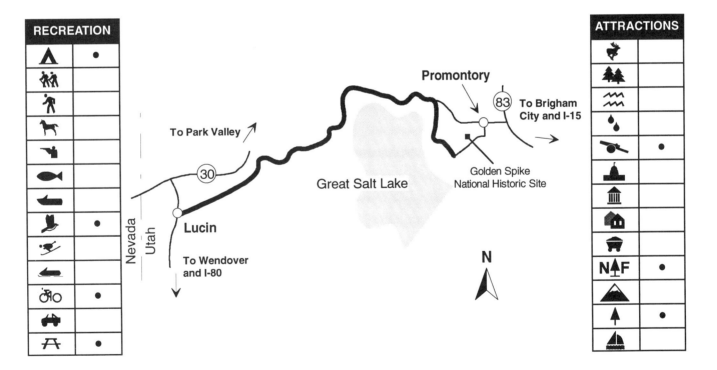

Information Sources:

BLM, Salt Lake District Office, 2370 S. 2300 W., Salt Lake City, UT 84119 / 801-977-4300
Brigham City Area Chamber of Commerce, P.O. Box 458, Brigham City, UT 84302 / 801-723-3931
Tooele County Chamber of Commerce, 50 E. 1st N., Tooele, UT 84074 / 801-882-0690

VIRGINIA

☐ *Scenic Drives*

1. Big Walker Mountain
2. Highlands Scenic Tour
3. Mount Rogers

Road Condition Numbers: 804-786-3181
800-367-ROAD (In VA only)

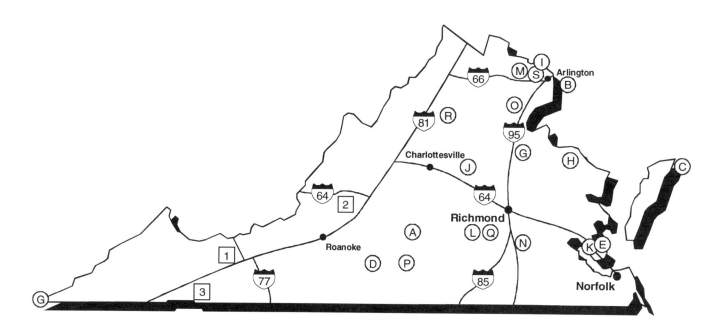

O *National Park Areas*

A. Appomattox Court House National Historical Park
B. Arlington House, The Robert E. Lee Memorial
C. Assateague Island National Seashore
D. Booker T. Washington National Monument
E. Colonial National Historical Park
F. Cumberland Gap National Historical Park
G. Fredericksburg and Spotsylvania County Battle-fields Memorial National Military Park
H. George Washington Birthplace National Monument
I. Great Falls Park

J. Green Springs Historic District
K. Jamestown National Historic Site
L. Maggie L. Walker National Historic Site
M. Manassas National Battlefield Park
N. Petersburg National Battlefield
O. Prince William Forest Park
P. Red Hill Patrick Henry National Memorial
Q. Richmond National Battlefield Park
R. Shenandoah National Park
S. Wolf Trap Farm Park for the Performing Arts

BIG WALKER MOUNTAIN

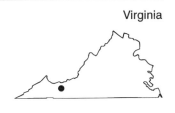

Virginia

- *Route Location:* Located in southwestern Virginia, north of Wytheville. The northeastern access is located off Interstate 77 in the town of Bland and travels southwest forming an open loop drive back to Interstate 77, north of Wytheville.
- *Roads Traveled:* The 16 mile route follows U.S. Highway 52 and Virginia State Highway 717 which are two-lane paved roads suitable for all vehicles. The 16 mile route has been designated a National Forest Scenic Byway.
- *Travel Season:* The entire route is open year-round.
- *Description:* The scenic drive crosses the Jefferson National Forest through some of Virginia's most scenic land, showcasing the natural beauty and history of the area. State Highway 717 follows alongside the meandering East Fork of Stony Fork Creek. The creek is stocked periodically and offers fishing opportunities for trout and sunfish. The Stony Fork Campground is nestled alongside the creek and offers a peaceful setting for fishing, watching wildlife, or walking on the nature trail. Further north of the campground is the Big Walker Lookout, a 100 foot tower that provides a spectacular view of several states. The Big Bend Picnic Area is located about 4 miles off U.S. Highway 52 on Forest Service Road 206. The picnic area is set among orchard grass under a canopy of oaks at an elevation of 4,000 feet. This site offers scenic vistas of the ridge and valley landscape to the south. In addition to camping and picnicking opportunities, the Appalachian National Scenic Trail can be accessed from the drive.
- *Other Nearby Routes:* About 50 miles to the southwest is the Mount Rogers scenic drive.

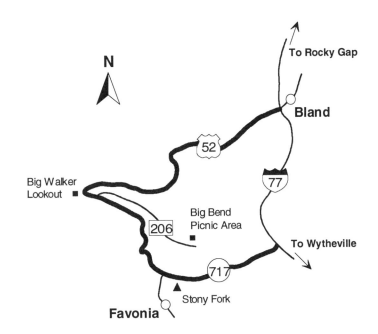

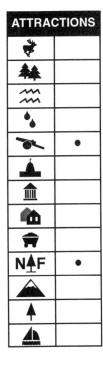

Information Sources:

Jefferson National Forest, 5162 Valleypointe Parkway, Roanoke, VA 24019-3050 / 703-982-6270
Jefferson National Forest, Wythe Ranger District, 1625 W. Lee Hwy., Wytheville, VA 24382 / 703-228-5551
Wytheville - Wythe - Bland Chamber of Commerce, 150 Monroe St., Wytheville, VA 24382 / 703-228-3211

HIGHLANDS SCENIC TOUR

- *Route Location:* Located in west-central Virginia, northwest of Buena Vista. The southwestern access is located in the town of Longdale Furnace south of Interstate 64 and travels northeast forming a loop drive back to Longdale Furnace.
- *Roads Traveled:* The 20 mile route follows Virginia State Highways 770 and 850, and Forest Service Road 447. The routes travel over a combination of paved and gravel surfaced roads. The routes are suitable for all vehicles with the exception of State Highway 770 which is narrow with steep hairpin turns and is not recommended for vehicles pulling trailers. The entire 20 mile route has been designated a National Forest Scenic Byway.
- *Travel Season:* State Route 850 is open year-round while State Route 770 and Forest Service Road 447 are not maintained during the winter months and are typically impassable from December to early March.

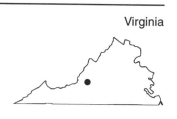

Virginia

- *Description:* The scenic drive travels across the George Washington National Forest through narrow forested valleys alongside meandering streams offering scenic views of Shenandoah Valley and the Blue Ridge Mountains. The 6,450 acre Rich Hole Wilderness can be accessed from highway 850. A short hiking trail here takes you through the wilderness and ends back out on the highway. There are several developed overlooks and wayside areas that offer short nature trails and picnicking facilities. Located just south of the scenic drive is the Longdale Recreation Area which has a small lake with swimming beach, picnic sites, and a nature trail.
- *Other Nearby Routes:* About 65 miles northwest is the Highland Scenic Highway in West Virginia.

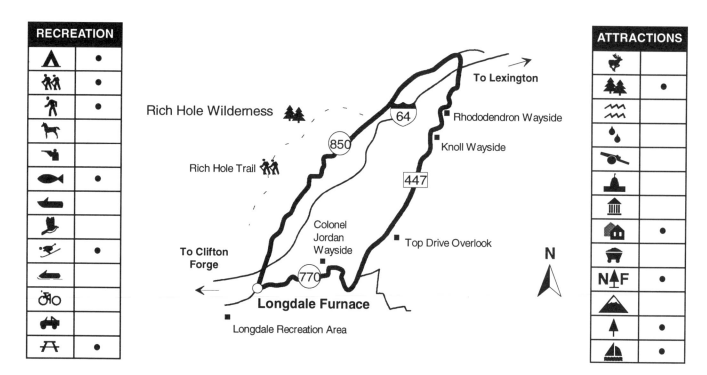

Information Sources:

George Washington National Forest, Harrison Plaza, 101 N. Main St., Harrisonburg, VA 22801 / 703-433-2491
Lexington - Rockbridge County Chamber of Commerce, 312 S. Main St., Lexington, VA 24450 / 703-463-5375
Alleghany Highlands Chamber of Commerce, 403 E. Ridgeway St., Clifton Forge, VA 24422 / 703-862-4969

MOUNT ROGERS

- *Route Location:* Located in southwestern Virginia, east of Bristol. The western access is located off Virginia State Highway 91 in the town of Damascus and travels east to the junction of Virginia State Highway 16 in Troutdale. The southern segment starts just west of Konnarock and travels southeast to Volney, also on Virginia State Highway 16.
- *Roads Traveled:* The 56 mile route follows U.S. Highway 58 and Virginia State Highway 603 which are two-lane paved roads. Because of sharp curves and winding road, U.S. Highway 58 is not recommended for vehicles longer than 35 feet. The entire route has been designated a National Forest Scenic Byway.
- *Travel Season:* The entire route is open year-round.
- *Description:* The scenic drive winds through hardwood forested areas and rural countryside as it crosses the Jefferson National Forest and the Mount Rogers National Recreation Area. Views of Mount Rogers,

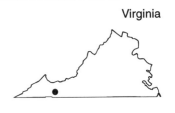

Virginia

the highest point in Virginia, are provided at various spots along the scenic drive. There are many trails that can be accessed from this route which provide opportunities for hiking, mountain biking, horseback riding, and cross-country skiing. Some of the trails lead to the top of Mount Rogers or into either of the two wilderness areas found along the route. The Appalachian National Scenic Trail can also be accessed from the drive as it crosses the route three times. The Beartree Recreation Area provides camping and picnic facilities in addition to a large fishing and swimming lake.
- *Other Nearby Routes:* Approximately 50 miles northeast is the Big Walker Mountain scenic drive.

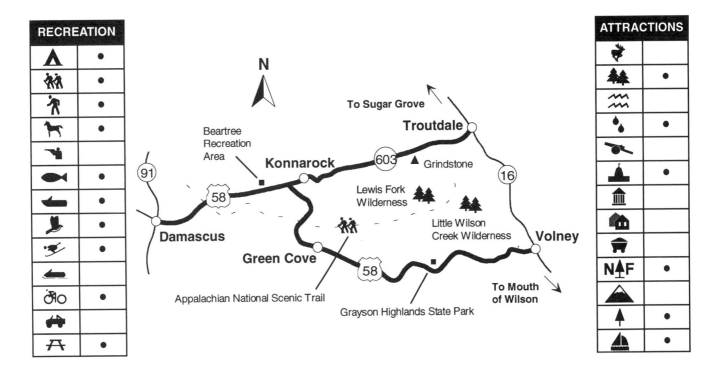

Information Sources:

Jefferson National Forest, Mt. Rogers Ranger District, Route 1, Box 303, Marion, VA 24354 / 703-783-5196
Washington County Chamber of Commerce, 179 E. Main St., Abingdon, VA 24210 / 703-628-8141
Chamber of Commerce of Smyth County, 124 W. Main St., Marion, VA 24354 / 703-783-3161
Alleghany County Chamber of Commerce, 348 S. Main St., Sparta, NC 28675 / 919-372-5473

WASHINGTON

□ *Scenic Drives*

Road Condition Number: 206-434-ROAD (Mountain passes)

1. Mount Baker Highway
2. Mountain Loop Highway
3. Sherman Pass
4. Stevens Pass
5. White Pass

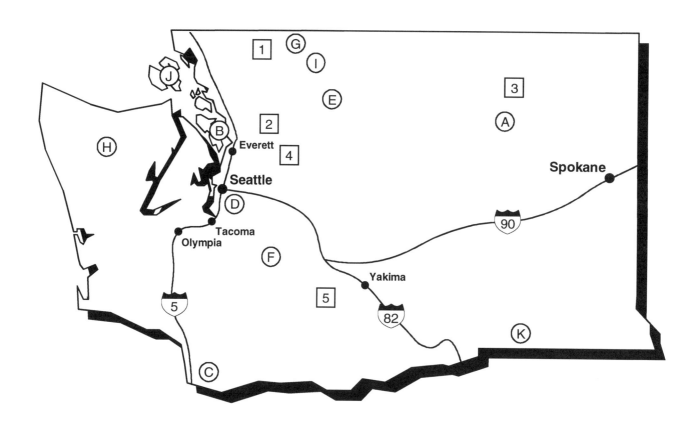

O *National Park Areas*

A. Coulee Dam National Recreation Area
B. Ebey's Landing National Historical Reserve
C. Fort Vancouver National Historic Site
D. Klondike Gold Rush National Historical Park
E. Lake Chelan National Recreation Area
F. Mount Rainier National Park
G. North Cascades National Park
H. Olympic National Park
I. Ross Lake National Recreation Area
J. San Juan Island National Historical Park
K. Whitman Mission National Historic Site

MOUNT BAKER HIGHWAY

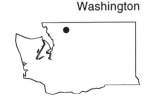

Washington

- *Route Location:* Located in northwestern Washington, northeast of Bellingham. The western access is located on Washington State Highway 542 in the town of Glacier and travels southeast to the roads end at the Heather Meadows Recreation Area
- *Roads Traveled:* The 24 mile route follows Washington State Highway 542 which is a two-lane paved road suitable for all vehicles. Travelers will need to retrace the route back. The 24 mile route has been designated a National Forest Scenic Byway.
- *Travel Season:* Most of the route is open year-round except the last 3 miles to the Heather Meadows Recreation Area which is subject to closure from about November to mid-July, depending on the weather conditions.
- *Description:* The scenic drive crosses the Mt. Baker-Snoqualmie National Forest through the narrow valley floor of the Nooksack River as it climbs from the dense rain forest to the rugged timberline of the North Cascades. The spectacular views offered at the end of this route are of the Mt. Baker Wilderness, North Cascades National Park, and Canada. Several trails can be accessed from the drive, many leading into the surrounding wilderness area and to the North Cascades National Park. Winter sport enthusiasts will find opportunities for downhill and cross-country skiing at the Mt. Baker Ski Area. The Heather Meadows Recreation Area provides access to the wilderness area and national park in addition to picnicking facilities and self guided interpretive trails.
- *Other Nearby Routes:* About 100 miles south is the Mountain Loop Highway scenic drive and an additional 40 miles south to the Stevens Pass scenic route.

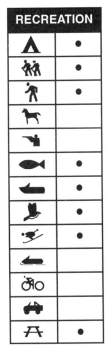

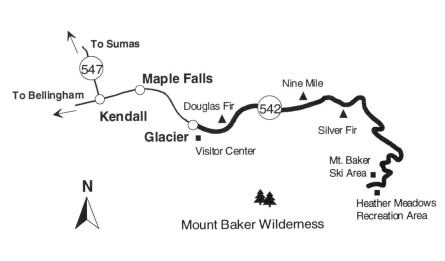

Information Sources:

Mt. Baker-Snoqualmie National Forest, 21905 64th Ave. W., Mount Lake Terrace, WA 98043-2278 / 206-744-3200
Mt. Baker Foothills Chamber of Commerce, P.O. Box 866, Maple Falls, WA 98266 / 206-599-1205
Bellingham / Whatcom Chamber of Commerce, 1801 Roeder Ave., Bellingham, WA 98227 / 206-734-1330
Sedro - Woolley Chamber of Commerce, 116 Woodworth St., Sedro-Woolley, WA 98284 / 206-855-1841

MOUNTAIN LOOP HIGHWAY

- **Route Location:** Located in northwestern Washington, northeast of Everett. The western access is located on Washington State Highway 92 in the town of Granite Falls and travels northeast to the junction of State Highway 530 in Darrington.
- **Roads Traveled:** The 55 mile route follows Washington State Highway 92 and Forest Service Road 20. The route travels over a combination of two-lane paved and gravel surfaced roads that are suitable for all vehicles. The 55 mile route has been designated a National Forest Scenic Byway.
- **Travel Season:** Most of the route is open year-round although the middle section can be closed by winter snows from about mid-December through May.
- **Description:** The scenic drive travels through the heart of the Mt. Baker-Snoqualmie National Forest following alongside several rivers and through the dense forest of the Cascade Mountains. The route surrounds

Washington

the Boulder River Wilderness which offers back country hiking and backpacking opportunities. Trails also provide access into the Henry M. Jackson Wilderness. A closed county road at Barlow Pass is now used as a hiking and mountain biking trail that leads to the old mining site at Monte Cristo. Numerous opportunities for camping and picnicking are available at the developed national forest campgrounds found along or near the route. The middle portion of this drive is usually closed in winter and becomes a cross-country and snowmobiling trail. The rivers found in the area offer good fishing and white water rafting.

- **Other Nearby Routes:** Approximately 100 miles north is the Mount Baker Highway scenic drive and about 25 miles to the southeast is the Stevens Pass scenic route.

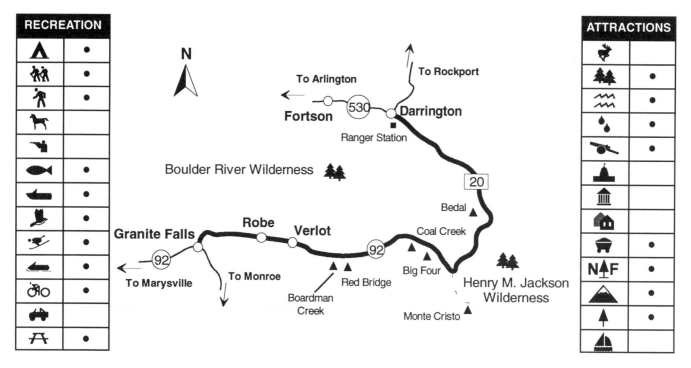

Information Sources:

Mt. Baker - Snoqualmie National Forest, 21905 64th Ave. W., Mount Lake Terrace, WA 98043 / 206-744-3200
Darrington Chamber of Commerce, P.O. Box 351, Darrington, WA 98241 / 206-436-1177
Greater Lake Stevens Chamber of Commerce, 515 State Route 9 - #106, Lake Stevens, WA 98258 / 206-334-0433
Arlington Chamber of Commerce, P.O. Box 102, Arlington, WA 98223 / 206-435-3708
Everett Area Chamber of Commerce, 1710 W. Marine View Dr., Everett, WA 98206 / 206-252-5181
Snohomish Chamber of Commerce, 116 Ave. B, Snohomish, WA 98291 / 206-568-2526

SHERMAN PASS

Washington

- *Route Location:* Located in northeastern Washington, west of Colville. The eastern access is located in Kettle Falls and travels west to the town of Republic.
- *Roads Traveled:* The 40 mile route follows Washington State Highway 20 which is a two-lane paved road suitable for all vehicles. Thirty-five miles of this route have been designated a National Forest Scenic Byway.
- *Travel Season:* The entire route is generally open year-round although winter driving conditions may be hazardous and delays are possible for snow removal.
- *Description:* The scenic drive travels on the Colville National Forest through the heavily forested mountains and crosses over the highest mountain pass in Washington. This route once served as a migratory trail for the Native Americans and later became a wagon route for miners. Today the scenic drive is part of an interstate bicycle route and offers many recreational and scenic opportunities. Access is provided to the Kettle Crest National Recreation Trail offering opportunities to hike, backpack, or horseback ride through the national forest. Other trails can be found that provide mountain biking opportunities in the summer and cross-country skiing and snowmobiling in the winter. Also found along the route are several developed national forest campgrounds and picnic areas. The Coulee Dam National Recreation Area is located to the south of this scenic drive and provides opportunities for fishing and boating in addition to having developed camping and picnicking facilities.
- *Other Nearby Routes:* The Mount Baker Highway and Mountain Loop Highway scenic drives are the closest routes and are about 200 miles to the west.

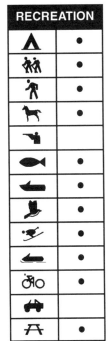

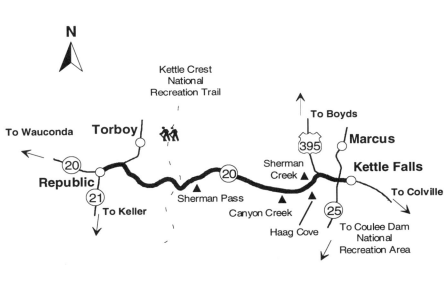

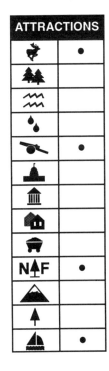

Information Sources:

Colville National Forest, 765 S. Main St., Colville, WA 99114 / 509-684-3711
Republic Area Chamber of Commerce, P.O. Box 502, Republic, WA 99166 / 509-775-3222
Kettle Falls Area Chamber of Commerce, 265 W. 3rd St., Kettle Falls, WA 99141 / 509-738-2300
Colville Chamber of Commerce, 309 S. Main, Colville, WA 99114 / 509-684-5973

STEVENS PASS

- *Route Location:* Located in west-central Washington, northwest of Wenatchee. The eastern access is located on U.S. Highway 2 in the town of Leavenworth and travels west to the town of Gold Bar.
- *Roads Traveled:* The 69 mile route follows U.S. Highway 2 which is a two-lane paved road suitable for all vehicles. The 69 mile route has been designated a National Forest Scenic Byway.
- *Travel Season:* The entire route is open year-round although winter driving conditions my be hazardous, especially at the higher elevations.
- *Description:* The scenic drive crosses the Mt. Baker-Snoqualmie and Wenatchee National Forests as it travels through the densely forested Cascade Mountains following alongside portions of the Skykomish River and Nason Creek. The Stevens Pass Historic District is listed on the National Register of Historic Places. The remains of tunnels, snowsheds, switchbacks, con-

struction towns and camps are clustered together here, near the summit. The scenic drive travels between two wilderness areas, the Henry M. Jackson Wilderness to the north, and the Alpine Lakes Wilderness to the south. Both areas offer opportunities for back country hiking, backpacking, and cross-country skiing. The Pacific Crest National Scenic Trail crosses the route at Stevens Pass and provides excellent hiking through the national forests. Other recreational activities found along the route include camping, picnicking, fishing, and downhill skiing.

Washington

- *Other Nearby Routes:* Approximately 25 miles northwest is the Mountain Loop Highway scenic drive and about 100 miles south from the eastern terminus is the White Pass scenic drive.

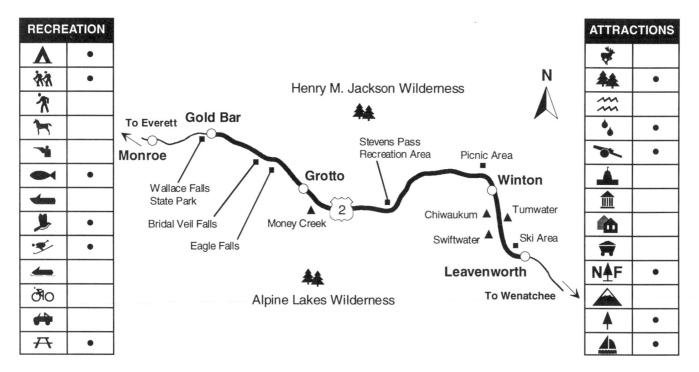

Information Sources:

Mt. Baker-Snoqualmie National Forest, 21905 64th Ave. W., Mount Lake Terrace, WA 98043-2278 / 206-744-3200
Monroe Chamber of Commerce, 211 E. Main St., Monroe, WA 98272 / 206-794-5488
Sultan Chamber of Commerce, P.O. Box 46, Sultan, WA 98294 / 206-793-2211
Leavenworth Chamber of Commerce, 894 Hwy. 2, Leavenworth, WA 98826 / 509-548-5807
Wenatchee Area Chamber of Commerce, 2 S. Chelan, Wenatchee, WA 98807 / 509-662-2116
Snohomish Chamber of Commerce, 116 Ave. B, Snohomish, WA 98291 / 206-568-2526

WHITE PASS

- *Route Location:* Located in south-central Washington, northwest of Yakima. The eastern access is located at the junction of Washington State Highway 410 and U.S. Highway 12, north of Naches. The route travels west to the town of Packwood.
- *Roads Traveled:* The 58 mile route follows U.S. Highway 12 which is a two-lane paved road suitable for all vehicles. Fifty-five miles of this route has been designated a National Forest Scenic Byway.
- *Travel Season:* The route is open year-round although winter driving conditions can be hazardous, especially at the higher elevations.
- *Description:* The scenic drive travels across the Gifford Pinchot and Wenatchee National Forests as it winds through alpine meadows, old-growth forests, and past pristine lakes and waterfalls. Wildlife inhabiting the wilderness surrounding the route includes bighorn sheep, elk, mule deer, eagles, and hawks. Fishing, boat-

Washington

ing, camping, and picnicking opportunities are offered in the Rimrock Lake area. The Tieton Dam, at the east end of Rimrock Lake, is on the National Register of Historic Places as the largest earth-filled dam of its time. The Mt. Rainier National Park can be accessed from this drive and is home to the tallest peak in the Cascade Range. Winter snows bring downhill skiers, cross-country skiers and snowmobilers to this area. Hiking and backpacking enthusiasts are offered back country trails through the Goat Rocks Wilderness area. The Pacific Crest Trail can also be accessed from the route.

- *Other Nearby Routes:* Approximately 100 miles to the north is the Stevens Pass scenic drive and about 125 to 150 miles south are the Blue Mountain and Lower Deschutes River scenic drives in Oregon.

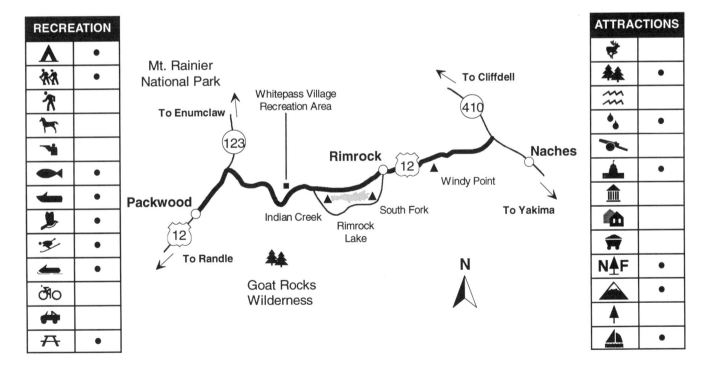

Information Sources:

Wenatchee National Forest, 301 Yakima St., Wenatchee, WA 98807 / 509-662-4367
Morton Chamber of Commerce, P.O. Box 10, Morton, WA 98356 / 206-496-6086
Packwood Improvement Club, Packwood, WA 98361 / 206-494-7126
Greater Yakima Chamber of Commerce, 10 N. Ninth St., Yakima, WA 98907-1490 / 509-248-2021

WEST VIRGINIA

□ *Scenic Drives*

1. Highland Scenic Highway

○ *National Park Areas*

A. Gauley River National Recreation Area
B. Harpers Ferry National Historical Park

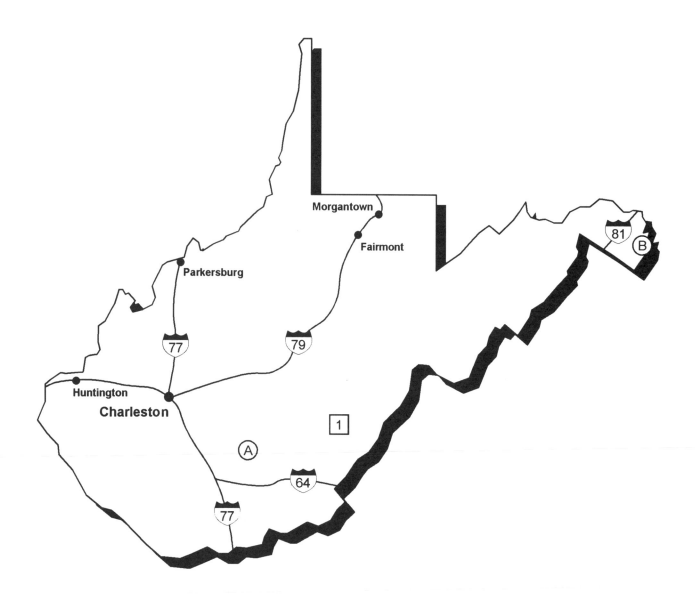

HIGHLAND SCENIC HIGHWAY

West Virginia

- *Route Location:* Located in eastern West Virginia, north of White Sulpher Springs. The eastern access is located at the junction of U.S. Highway 219 and West Virginia State Highway 150, north of Edray. The route travels southeast to the town of Richwood.
- *Roads Traveled:* The 43 mile route follows West Virginia State Highways 150 and 39/55 which are two-lane paved roads suitable for all vehicles. The route has been designated a National Forest Scenic Byway.
- *Travel Season:* State Route 39 is open year-round but State Route 150 is not maintained for winter travel and is usually closed from early December to March.
- *Description:* The scenic drive traverses the mountainous terrain of the Allegheny Highlands and Plateau as it crosses the Monongahela National Forest. Several scenic overlooks are found along the route that provide spectacular views of the Allegheny Highlands. The 750 acre Cranberry Glades Botanical Area contains four high elevation bogs which are acidic wetlands typically found in Canada and the northern United States. A ½ mile long barrier-free boardwalk with interpretive signing provides access to two of the bogs.

Several hiking and backpacking trails can be accessed from the scenic drive that take you into the Cranberry Wilderness area. Three waterfalls cascading over rock layers of sandstone and shale are offered in the Falls of Hills Creek Scenic Area. A ¾ mile trail provides access to the falls, including a paved, barrier-free trail to the first falls. Many camping and picnicking opportunities are to be found along the route as well.
- *Other Nearby Routes:* The Highlands Scenic Tour route is approximately 65 miles southeast in Virginia.

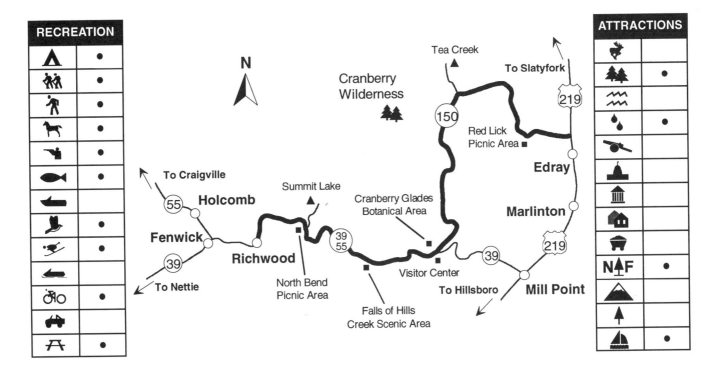

Information Sources:

Monongahela National Forest, Gauley Ranger District, P.O. Box 110, Richwood, WV 26261 / 304-846-2695
Pocahontas County Tourism Commission, P.O. Box 275, Marlinton, WV 24954 / 800-336-7009
Richwood Area Chamber of Commerce, 50 Oakford Ave., Richwood WV 26261 / 304-846-6790
Marlinton Chamber of Commerce, 1010 3rd Ave., Marlinton, WV 24954 / 304-799-4048

WISCONSIN

☐ *Scenic Drives*

1. Great Divide Highway
2. Heritage Drive

○ *National Park Areas*

A. Apostle Islands National Lakeshore
B. Ice Age National Scientific Reserve

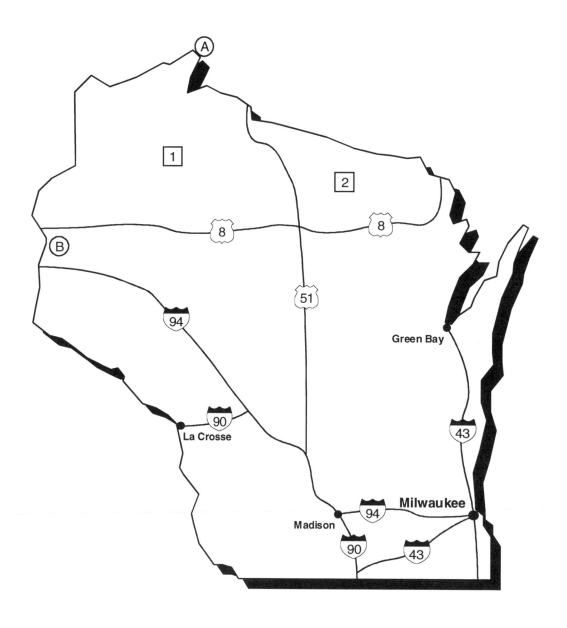

Road Condition Number: 800-762-3947 (Construction, summer; conditions, winter)

GREAT DIVIDE HIGHWAY

Wisconsin

- *Route Location:* Located in northwestern Wisconsin, south of Ashland. The eastern access is located at the junction of Wisconsin State Highways 13 and 77, north of Glidden and travels west to the Chequamegon National Forest boundary.
- *Roads Traveled:* The 29 mile route follows Wisconsin State Highway 77 which is a two-lane paved road suitable for all vehicles. The entire 29 mile route has been designated a National Forest Scenic Byway.
- *Travel Season:* The entire route is open year-round although caution should be exercised during the winter months.
- *Description:* As it crosses the Chequamegon National Forest, this scenic drive travels through forests of northern hardwoods, pines, and meadowlands, passing by several lakes, rivers, and streams. Black bear, timber wolves, and white-tailed deer inhabit the forested areas along the drive, while beavers, loons, and bald eagles can be found in the lakes, swamps, and bogs. The many lakes and rivers in this area provide excellent opportunities to fish for walleye, musky, largemouth bass, and panfish. Several trails are found along the route and within the national forest that offer opportunities for hiking and mountain biking during summer months while offering snowmobiling and cross-country skiing in winter. Day Lake is a popular recreational area offering a developed campground, swimming beach, picnic area, and boat launching facilities in addition to some of the best musky fishing found in northern Wisconsin.
- *Other Nearby Routes:* Approximately 100 miles to the east is the Heritage Drive scenic route and about 45 miles northeast is the Black River Road in Michigan.

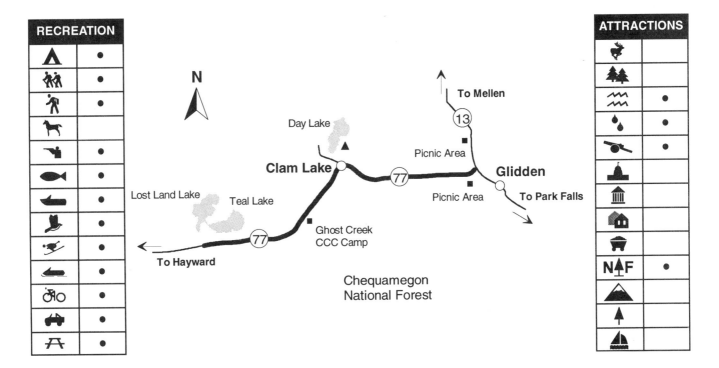

Information Sources:

Chequamegon National Forest, 1170 S. Fourth Ave., Park Falls, WI 54552 / 715-762-2461
Hayward Chamber of Commerce, P.O. Box 726, Hayward, WI 54843 / 800-826-3474
Park Falls Area Chamber of Commerce, 400 4th Ave. S., Park Falls, WI 54552 / 715-762-2703
Mellen Area Chamber of Commerce, 125 E. Bennett St., Mellen, WI 54546 / 715-274-2330

HERITAGE DRIVE

- **Route Location:** Located in northeastern Wisconsin, northeast of Rhinelander. The southwestern access is located off U.S. Highway 45 in the town of Three Lakes and travels northeast to the junction of Wisconsin State Highway 70, east of Eagle river.
- **Roads Traveled:** The 21 mile route follows Wisconsin State Highway 32 and Forest Service Roads 2178 (Military Road) and 2181 (Butternut Lake Road). The routes are narrow, two-lane paved roads suitable for all vehicles. Fifteen miles of this route has been designated a National Forest Scenic Byway.
- **Travel Season:** The entire route is open year-round although winter driving conditions may be hazardous.
- **Description:** The scenic drive crosses the Nicolet National Forest as it winds through forests of old-growth pine and northern hardwoods. Many lakes are found along the route offering excellent opportunities to fish for walleye, northern pike, bass, and musky. A side

Wisconsin

trip east on Forest Service Road 2182 takes you through the 20,000 acre Headwaters Wilderness providing opportunities for exploring bogs and black spruce swamps. A variety of wildlife inhabits this area including beavers, great blue herons, white-tailed deer, and timber wolves. The Franklin Lake Recreation Area is one of the more popular camping and recreation areas. The campground located here with its historic structures has been placed on the National Register of Historic Places. The Franklin Lake Nature Trail is also found here.

- **Other Nearby Routes:** About 100 miles to the west is the Great Divide Highway scenic route and approximately 75 miles northwest is the Black River road scenic drive in Michigan.

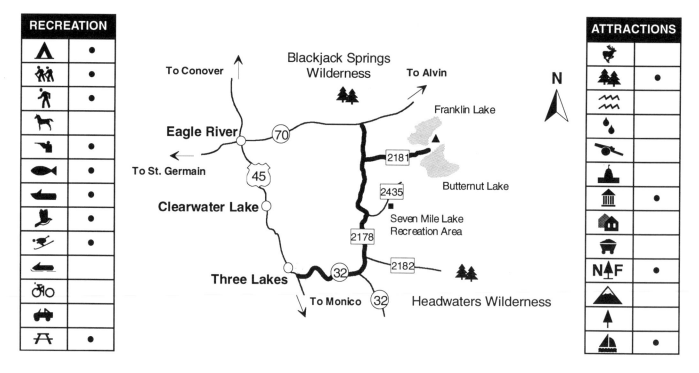

Information Sources:

Nicolet National Forest, Eagle River Ranger District, 4364 Wall St., Eagle River, WI 54521 / 715-479-2827
Vilas County Chamber of Commerce, P.O. Box 369, Eagle River, WI 54521 / 715-479-3649
Three Lakes Chamber of Commerce, P.O. Box 276, Three Lakes, WI 54562 / 715-546-3344

WYOMING

□ *Scenic Drives*

1. Beartooth Highway
2. Bighorn
3. Cloud Peak Skyway
4. Medicine Wheel Passage
5. North Fork Highway
6. Red Gulch / Alkali
7. Seminoe To Alcova
8. Snowy Range Highway
9. South Bighorn / Red Wall
10. Wyoming Centennial

○ *National Park Areas*

A. Bighorn Canyon National Recreation Area
B. Devils Tower National Monument
C. Fort Laramie National Historic Site
D. Fossil Butte National Monument
E. Grand Teton National Park
F. Yellowstone National Park

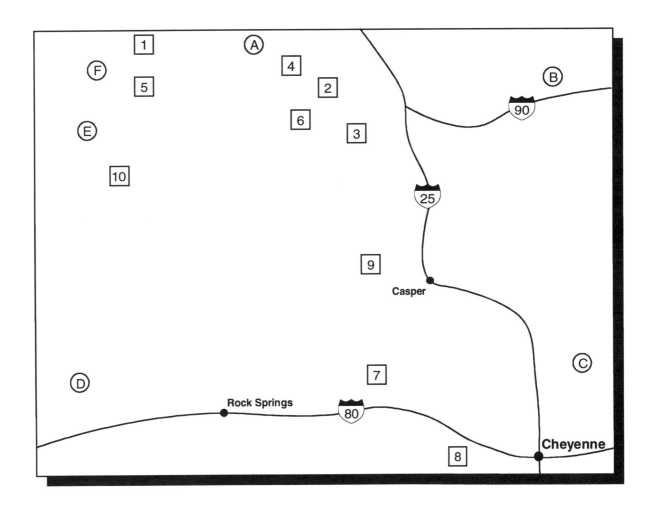

Road Condition Number: 307-635-9966

BEARTOOTH HIGHWAY

- **Route Location:** Located in northwestern Wyoming and southern Montana, north of Cody, Wyoming. The northeastern access is located in Red Lodge, Montana and travels southwest to the entrance of Yellowstone National Park.
- **Roads Traveled:** The 69 mile route follows U.S. Highway 212 which is a two-lane paved road suitable for all vehicles. The entire 69 mile route has been designated a National Forest Scenic Byway.
- **Travel Season:** The entire route is generally open from about late May through mid-October and then sections are closed by winter snows. The closed sections become popular trails for snowmobilers.
- **Description:** The scenic drive travels through the Gallatin, Shoshone, and Custer National Forests as it crosses the spectacular Beartooth Mountains. This route generally follows the "Sheridan Trail" which was laid out in 1882, and is the highest elevation motor cross-

ing in both Wyoming and Montana. Wildlife inhabiting the wilderness surrounding the scenic drive includes elk, mule deer, moose, grizzly bears, mountain goats, golden eagles, prairie falcons, and hawks. Many hiking trails can be accessed from the road, offering short hikes or day long hikes into the forests or wilderness areas. Winter activities offered include snowmobiling and cross-country skiing.

- **Other Nearby Routes:** The North Fork Highway scenic drive is about 90 miles south via a trip through Yellowstone National Park. Less than 100 miles east are the Medicine Wheel Passage, Bighorn, and Red Gulch/Alkali scenic drives. Approximately 120 miles west through Yellowstone and into Idaho is the Mesa Falls scenic route.

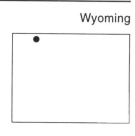

Wyoming

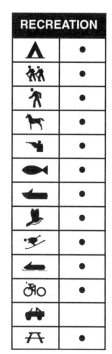

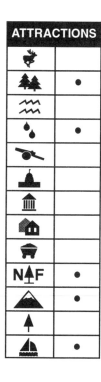

Information Sources:

Shoshone National Forest, Clarks Fork Ranger District, 1002 Road 11, Powell, WY 82435 / 307-754-7207
Custer National Forest, Beartooth Ranger District, Route 2 - Box 3420, Red Lodge, MT 59068 / 406-446-2103
Red Lodge Area Chamber of Commerce, 601 N. Broadway, Red Lodge, MT 59068 / 406-446-1718
Gardiner Chamber of Commerce, P.O. Box 81, Gardiner, MT 59030 / 406-848-7971

BIGHORN

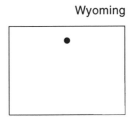

Wyoming

- *Route Location:* Located in north-central Wyoming, west of Sheridan. The northeastern access is located on U.S. Highway 14 in Dayton and travels southwest to the town of Shell.
- *Roads Traveled:* The 44 mile route follows U.S. Highway 14 which is a two-lane paved road suitable for all vehicles. Forty miles of this route has been designated a National Forest Scenic Byway.
- *Travel Season:* The route is generally open year-round although occasional temporary closures are possible for snow removal.
- *Description:* The scenic drive traverses the Bighorn National Forest as it climbs steep switchbacks into the Bighorn Mountains, passes through grassy parks, and then descends into the rugged Shells Canyon. Scenic overlooks along the route provide views of Buffalo Tongue Mountain and the Fallen City rock slide area. Sibley Lake Campground provides camping among lodgepole pines, picnicking, and fishing for rainbow trout. Several miles of cross-country ski trails can be found in this area. Shell Falls is a good resting spot for a picnic or to view the falls and the valley below. Walkways have been installed for a closer view of the falls. The Antelope Butte ski area provides opportunities for winter sport enthusiasts.
- *Other Nearby Routes:* The Medicine Wheel Passage scenic drive connects with this route and about 15 miles from the southwestern terminus is the Red Gulch/Alkali scenic drive. Approximately 40 miles south of Sheridan is the Cloud Peak Skyway scenic route. Less than 100 miles to the west are the Beartooth Highway and North Fork Highway scenic drives.

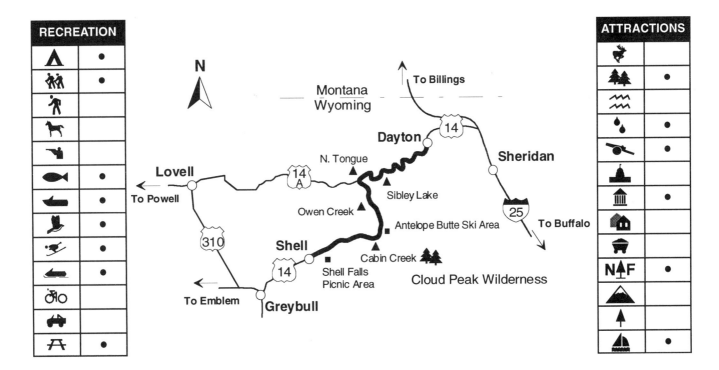

Information Sources:

Bighorn National Forest, 1969 S. Sheridan Ave., Sheridan, WY 82801 / 307-672-0751
Greybull Chamber of Commerce, 333 Greybull Ave., Greybull, WY 82426 / 307-765-2100
Sheridan County Chamber of Commerce, E. 5th St. & I-90, Sheridan, WY 82801 / 307-672-2485

CLOUD PEAK SKYWAY

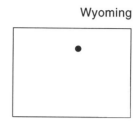

Wyoming

- **Route Location:** Located in north-central Wyoming, south of Sheridan. The northeastern access is located in Buffalo and travels southwest to the junction of Wyoming State Highways 434 and 31 in the town of Tensleep.
- **Roads Traveled:** The 67 mile route follows U.S. Highway 16 which is a two-lane paved road suitable for all vehicles. Forty-three miles of this route (across the national forest) has been designated a National Forest Scenic Byway.
- **Travel Season:** The entire route is open year-round although temporary closures and delays are possible for winter snow removal.
- **Description:** The scenic drive crosses the Bighorn National Forest as it climbs into the Big Horn Mountains, crossing Powder River Pass, and then descending into open rangelands and the Tensleep Canyon. At 9,677 feet, Powder River Pass is the scenic route's high-

est point and offers breathtaking views of the Cloud Peak Wilderness, Big Horn Basin, Powder River Basin, and many 13,000 foot peaks. The Meadowlark Recreation Area is centered around Meadowlark Lake and offers boating, fishing, camping, and picnicking opportunities in the summer, while winter activities include snowmobiling and cross-country skiing. Numerous other developed campgrounds are found along the drive.

- **Other Nearby Routes:** The South Big Horn/Red Wall scenic drive is about 130 miles to the south. About 50 miles to the north is the Bighorn scenic drive which connects with the Medicine Wheel Passage scenic drive. The Red Gulch/Alkali scenic route is approximately 25 miles northwest from the western terminus.

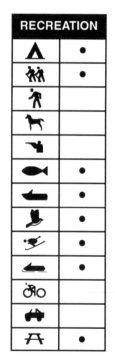

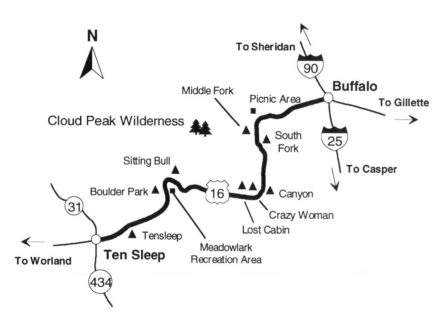

Information Sources:

Bighorn National Forest, 1969 S. Sheridan Ave., Sheridan, WY 82801 / 307-672-0751
Worland Area Chamber of Commerce, 120 N. 10th St., Worland, WY 82401 / 307-347-3226
Buffalo Chamber of Commerce, 55 N. Main St., Buffalo, WY 82834 / 307-684-5544

MEDICINE WHEEL PASSAGE

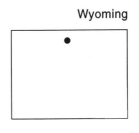

Wyoming

- *Route Location:* Located in north-central Wyoming, east of Lovell. The western access is located on U.S. Highway 14A east of Lovell starting on the Bighorn National Forest and travels east to the junction of U.S. Highway 14.
- *Roads Traveled:* The 27 mile route follows U.S. Highway 14A which is a two-lane paved road suitable for all vehicles. The 27 mile route has been designated a National Forest Scenic Byway.
- *Travel Season:* The route is normally open from about May through mid-November and then closed by winter snows.
- *Description:* The scenic drive crosses the Bighorn National Forest as it follows a very winding road through the rugged Big Horn Mountains. Wildlife is abundant through this area and the watchful eye may spot elk, moose, mule deer, or hawks soaring up above. A side trip on the narrow Forest Service Road 12 will take you to the Medicine Wheel Historic Site. The Medicine Wheel was built by Indians but its exact origin is not known. It is used today by Native Americans for religious ceremonies. The views of the Big Horn Mountains here are spectacular. Camping and picnicking facilities can be found at developed national forest campgrounds along and near this route. Following highway 14A further west will lead to the Bighorn Canyon National Recreation Area.

- *Other Nearby Routes:* The eastern terminus of this route connects with the Bighorn scenic drive which is also about 15 miles east of the Red Gulch/Alkali scenic drive. Less than 100 miles west are the Beartooth Highway and North Fork Highway scenic drives. About 50 miles south is the Cloud Peak Skyway scenic route.

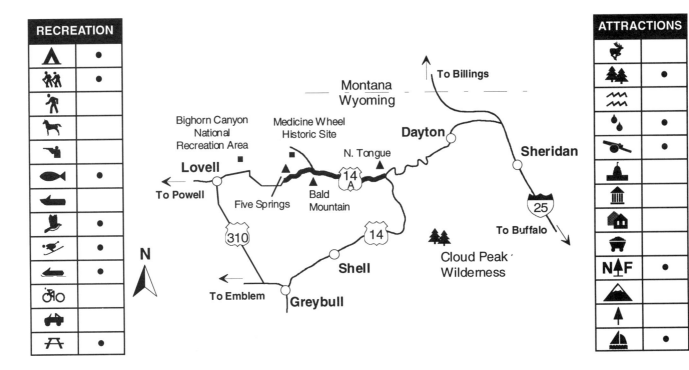

Information Sources:

Bighorn National Forest, 1969 S. Sheridan Ave., Sheridan, WY 82801 / 307-672-0751
Lovell Area Chamber of Commerce, 287 E. Main, Lovell, WY 82431 / 307-548-7552
Sheridan County Chamber of Commerce, E. 5th St. & I-90, Sheridan, WY 82801 / 307-672-2485

NORTH FORK HIGHWAY

- *Route Location:* Located in the northwestern corner of Wyoming, southwest of Powell. The eastern access is located on U.S. Highway 20 in the town of Wapiti and travels west to the entrance of Yellowstone National Park.
- *Roads Traveled:* The 30 mile route follows U.S. Highway 20 which is a two-lane paved road suitable for all vehicles. Twenty-eight miles of this route has been designated a National Forest Scenic Byway.
- *Travel Season:* The entire route is open year-round although the road continuing into Yellowstone National Park is closed from about mid-November through March but is open to snowmobilers and cross-country skiers.
- *Description:* This scenic drive travels through a beautiful canyon as it follows alongside the North Fork of the Shoshone River, crossing the heart of the Shoshone National Forest. Black bears, mule deer, moose, elk, bighorn sheep, and the highest concentration of grizzly bears in the lower 48 states call this region of Wyoming home. There are two wilderness areas surrounding this scenic drive that offer back country experiences for hiking, wildlife viewing or exploring. Several trailheads are located along the drive that provide foot access into these rugged mountain wilderness areas.
- *Other Nearby Routes:* Approximately 90 miles north via a trip through Yellowstone is the Beartooth Highway scenic drive. About 100 miles to the south is the Wyoming Centennial scenic route. Less than 100 miles to the east are the Medicine Wheel Passage, Bighorn, and Red Gulch/Alkali scenic drives. Traveling west about 120 miles is the Mesa Falls scenic route in Idaho.

Wyoming

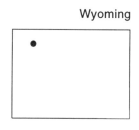

Information Sources:

Shoshone National Forest, 225 W. Yellowstone Ave., Cody, WY 82414 / 307-527-6241
Shoshone National Forest, Wapita Ranger District, 203A Yellowstone Ave., Cody, WY 82414 / 307-527-6921
Cody Country Chamber of Commerce, 836 Sheridan Ave., Cody, WY 82414 / 307-587-2297

RED GULCH / ALKALI

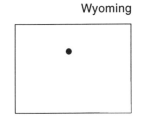

Wyoming

- *Route Location:* Located in north-central Wyoming, east of Greybull. The southern access is located off Wyoming State Highway 31 in Hyattville and travels northwest to the junction of U.S. Highway 14.
- *Roads Traveled:* The 32 mile route follows the Red Gulch/Alkali Road which is a combination of gravel and dirt surfaced road. The route requires a two-wheel drive, high clearance vehicle to safely travel. The 32 mile route has been designated a BLM Type II Back Country Byway.
- *Travel Season:* The route is generally open from about May through October except during and after periods of rain which makes the road very muddy and impassable.
- *Description:* This scenic drive travels over a remote stretch of road offering views of the rugged Big Horn Mountains and the red hills of the Chugwater formation. This back country route travels countryside that

was once inhabited by the Paleo-Indian mammoth hunters. Native American petroglyphs may be seen at the nearby Medicine Lodge State Archaeological Site, just a short drive east of this route. Also seen along the route are "sheepherder monuments", piles of rocks built by sheepherders during the late 1800s and early 1900s as a way to pass the long hours spent tending their sheep. Camping and picnicking facilities are found in the nearby Bighorn National Forest.

- *Other Nearby Routes:* About 10 miles to the east is the southern terminus of the Bighorn scenic drive which also intersects with the Medicine Wheel Passage scenic route. Approximately 25 miles to the southeast is the Cloud Peak Skyway scenic drive and 80 miles to the west is the North Fork Highway scenic route.

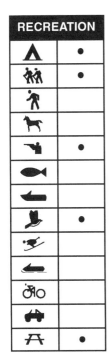

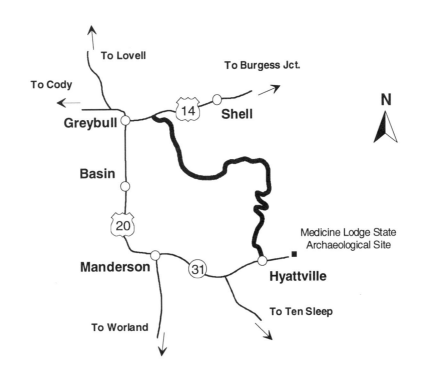

Information Sources:

BLM, Worland District Office, 101 S. 23rd, Worland, WY 82401-0119 / 307-347-9871
Greybull Chamber of Commerce, 333 Greybull Ave., Greybull, WY 82426 / 307-765-2100
Worland Area Chamber of Commerce, 120 N. 10th St., Worland, WY 82401 / 307-347-3226

Seminoe To Alcova

- **Route Location:** Located in central Wyoming, south-west of Casper. The northern access is located off Wyoming State Highway 220 in the town of Alcova and travels southwest to Sinclair on Interstate 80.
- **Roads Traveled:** The 64 mile route follows County Roads 351, 407, and 408. The route's gravel surfaced roads vary from two-lane to single-lane which are suitable for most vehicles. Motor homes and vehicles pulling trailers are not recommended on the short segment from Seminoe State Park to Miracle Mile. The 64 mile route has been designated a BLM Type I Back Country Byway.
- **Travel Season:** The route is generally open from about May to early December and then closed by winter snows.
- **Description:** This back country drive offers some spectacular wildlife viewing opportunities. Antelope, mule deer, and elk can be seen grazing along the road. With the aid of binoculars, pelicans, ducks, geese, bald eagles, a variety of hawks, and golden eagles can be seen. Magnificent views of the Seminoe, Bennett, and Pedro Mountains are also offered from the scenic drive. Excellent fishing opportunities are found at the Seminoe Reservoir and at the area known as the Miracle Mile, a stretch of the North Platte River renowned as a blue-ribbon trout stream. Developed camping and picnicking facilities are found at the Seminoe State Park and the Alcova Lake Recreation Area.
- **Other Nearby Routes:** The Snowy Range Highway scenic drive is about 60 miles southeast and the South Big Horn/Red Wall scenic route is approximately 60 miles to the north.

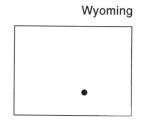

Wyoming

Information Sources:

BLM, Rawlins District Office, 1300 N. 3rd St., Rawlins, WY 82301-0670 / 307-324-7171
Rawlins - Carbon County Chamber of Commerce, 519 W. Cedar, Rawlins, WY 82301 / 800-228-3547
Casper Area Chamber of Commerce, 500 N. Center St., Casper, WY 82602 / 307-234-5311

SNOWY RANGE HIGHWAY

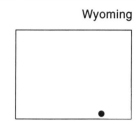

Wyoming

- *Route Location:* Located in southern Wyoming, west of Laramie. The eastern access is located on the Medicine Bow National Forest, west of Centennial and travels west to the forest boundary, near Ryan Park.
- *Roads Traveled:* The 29 mile route follows Wyoming State Highway 130 which is a two-lane paved road suitable for all vehicles. The entire 29 mile route has been designated a National Forest Scenic Byway.
- *Travel Season:* The route is generally open from late May through early November and then closed by winter snows.
- *Description:* The scenic drive crosses the Medicine Bow National Forest as it climbs into the Snowy Range Mountains following alongside many small lakes and meandering streams and creeks. The view from the top of Snowy Range Pass offers a wide vista of the surrounding mountain ranges. Summer travelers are rewarded with a dazzling display of wildflowers while the aspen leaves of autumn sprinkle the mountain side with gold. Several hiking trails can be found along or near the scenic drive that wander among the lakes and open parks or take you to the top of high mountain peaks. Fishing opportunities are excellent in the many trout streams or mountain lakes. Numerous camping and picnicking opportunities also exist along the drive. During the winter months, this area attracts cross-country and snowmobiling enthusiasts. A downhill skiing area is located about 5 miles west of Centennial. A visitor center is located just west of Centennial and provides maps and brochures on the scenic drive and the national forest.
- *Other Nearby Routes:* Approximately 60 miles to the northwest is the Seminoe To Alcova scenic drive.

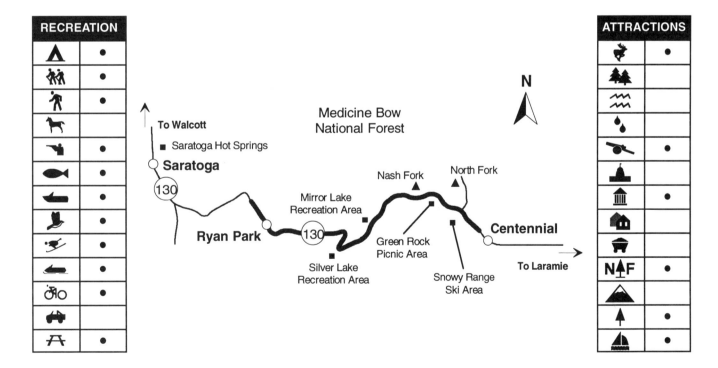

Information Sources:

Medicine Bow National Forest, 605 Skyline Dr., Laramie, WY 82070-6535 / 307-745-8971
Laramie Area Chamber of Commerce, 800 S. Third St., Laramie, WY 82070 / 307-745-7339
Saratoga - Platte Valley Chamber of Commerce, 114 S. First St., Saratoga, WY 82331 / 307-326-8855

SOUTH BIGHORN / RED WALL

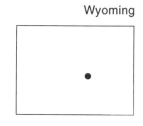
Wyoming

- *Route Location:* Located in central Wyoming, northwest of Casper. The southeastern access is located at the junction of U.S. Highway 20 and Natrona County Road 125, near Bucknum. The route travels northwest forming an open loop drive back to highway 20 in Waltman.
- *Roads Traveled:* The 101 mile route follows Natrona County Roads 125, 110, 109, and 104 which are a combination of gravel and dirt surfaced roads. Although the roads are well maintained, a two-wheel drive, high-clearance vehicle is recommended. The 101 mile route has been designated a BLM Type II Back Country Byway.
- *Travel Season:* The entire route is generally open from about May through November and then closed by winter snows. The route may also become impassable after heavy rains.
- *Description:* As you climb the east slope of the Big Horns, you travel from the predominately sagebrush lowlands to lush, open pastures along the summit. This route retraces the path originally taken by early livestock pioneers who used it to trail cattle and sheep to the higher mountain pastures. As you descend from the summit, this back country road parallels the famous Red Wall where Butch Cassidy and his "Hole-in-the-Wall" gang once temporarily hid out. Opportunities for camping and picnicking are provided by two BLM maintained campgrounds.
- *Other Nearby Routes:* Approximately 50 miles to the south is the Seminoe To Alcova scenic drive. About 110 miles north of Casper is the Cloud Peak Skyway scenic drive and an additional 50 miles north to the Bighorn and Medicine Wheel Passage scenic routes.

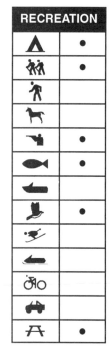

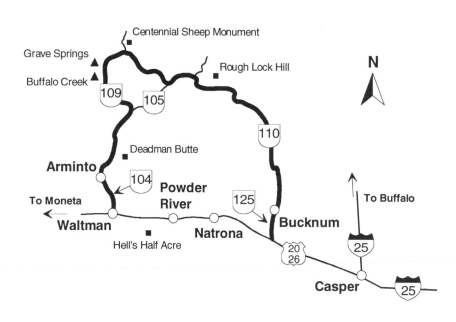

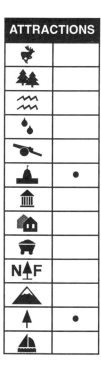

Information Sources:

BLM, Casper District Office, 1701 East E St., Casper, WY 82601-2167 / 307-261-7600
BLM, Platt River Resource Area, 815 Connie St., Mills, WY 82644-2420 / 307-261-7500
Casper Area Chamber of Commerce, 500 N. Center St., Casper, WY 82602 / 307-234-5311

WYOMING CENTENNIAL

- *Route Location:* Located in west-central Wyoming, northwest of Lander. The southeastern access is located on U.S. Highway 191 in Pinedale and travels northwest forming an open loop drive to Dubois.
- *Roads Traveled:* The 161 mile route follows U.S. Highways 191 and 287 which are two-lane paved roads suitable for all vehicles. The entire 161 mile route has been designated a National Forest Scenic Byway.
- *Travel Season:* The route is open year-round although winter driving conditions may be hazardous with delays possible for snow removal.
- *Description:* Crossing the Shoshone and Bridger-Teton National Forests, the scenic drive travels through the spectacular mountains of northwestern Wyoming, alongside rushing rivers and streams, and across vast mountain meadows. This scenic drive also provides access to the Grand Teton National Park and Yellowstone National Park. Scenic overlooks provide

Wyoming

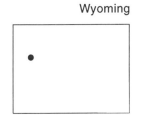

many opportunities for photographing the beautiful landscape or enjoying a picnic lunch. Several wilderness areas surrounding the scenic drive offer opportunities for hiking and exploring the mountainous back country. Thousands of elk can be seen during the winter at the National Elk Refuge. Snowmobiling and skiing activities are also offered during winter months. Summertime brings fishermen, mountain bikers, and river floaters to the scenic drive. Several campgrounds can also be found along the drive.

- *Other Nearby Routes:* Approximately 100 miles to the north is the North Fork Highway scenic route. About 25 miles west of Jackson is the Teton scenic drive in Idaho and 50 miles southwest of Jackson is the Bear Lake-Caribou scenic route, also in Idaho.

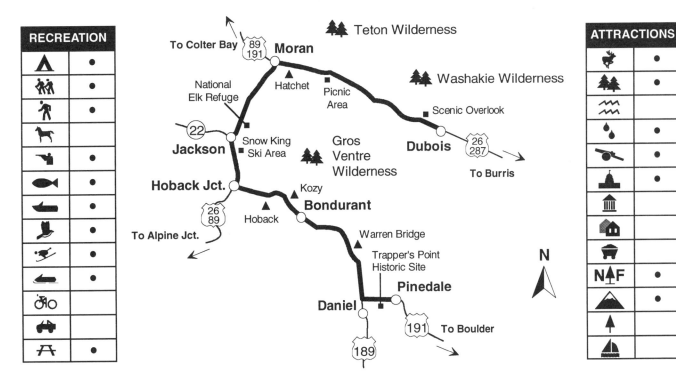

Information Sources:

Bridger - Teton National Forest, 340 North Cache, Jackson, WY 83001 / 307-739-5500
Dubois Chamber of Commerce, 616 W. Ramshorn, Dubois, WY 82513 / 307-455-2556
Jackson Hole Chamber of Commerce, 532 N. Cache St., Jackson, WY 83001 / 307-733-3316
Pinedale Area Chamber of Commerce, 35 S. Tyler, Pinedale, WY 82941 / 307-367-2242

ALPHABETICAL LIST OF SCENIC DRIVES

Route Name	State	Page

Route Name	State	Page

Route Name	State	Page

ROAD TRAVELER'S RESOURCE GUIDE

USING THE RESOURCE GUIDE

This resource guide provides information on outdoor recreation and travel related services, products, newsletters, magazines, directories, clubs and associations. It has been provided to let you know of the many organizations and publications available that can help you receive more enjoyment from your travels and outdoor recreational interests.

Although every effort was made to provide current information and prices, things do change with time. It is recommended that before you send any money you first contact the companies to verify prices and/or availability.

Many of the organizations will be happy to send you additional information or a sample issue of their publication, usually for free or at a nominal charge to cover postage. It should also be noted that many of the magazines are available on newsstands and usually you will find a special offer to subscribe at an introductory price.

In the event a phone number has been disconnected or changed, you can call the long distance operator by dialing 1 plus the area code, followed by 555-1212 and ask the operator for the new number. To see if a company offers an 800 number, you simply dial 1-800-555-1212 and tell the operator the company name.

You will notice that each listing starts off with a set of three numbers. This will allow you to quickly cross reference the listings. After some of the subject headings you will find *"for other related information see..."* followed by the additional listing numbers you can refer to for related information.

TOURIST ATTRACTIONS

•001• The *National Directory Of Free Tourist Attractions* locates over 900 free attractions across the country. The sites include restored villages, ships, exhibitions of folk and fine art, plus scenic wonders. Listings include a brief description, visiting days and hours, and telephone numbers. Pilot Books, 103 Cooper Street, Babylon NY 11702. Phone: 516-422-2225. Price: $4.95 plus $1.00 S&H.

•002• The *Guide To Free Attractions* list more than 6,000 free American attractions alphabetically by state. The 640 page guide covers attractions like ghost towns, historical sites, fish hatcheries, gold mines, caves, zoos, museums, exhibits, plant tours, waterfalls, covered bridges, and much more. Cottage Publications Inc., 24396 Pleasant View Dr., Elkhart IN 46517. Phone: 219-293-7553. Price: $14.95 plus $2.95 S&H.

•003• *The Amusement Park Guide: Fun For The Whole Family At Over 250 Amusement Parks From Coast To Coast* is the only comprehensive guide to amusement parks in the U.S. and Canada. From roller coasters to water rides, big-name parks to the lesser-known, the guide covers them all. The 320 page book provides park name and location, description, operating hours, top rides, admission policy, and nearby attractions. You will also find 25 tips for making your next trip to an amusement park more fun. The Globe Pequot Press, 6 Business Park Road, Old Saybrook CT 06475. Phone: 800-243-0495 or 800-962-0973 in Connecticut. Price: $12.95 plus $3.00 S&H. Aalso available in bookstores.

•004• The *Directory Of Theme & Amusement Parks* provides a state by state listing and brief description of more than 550 fun places. Admission fees generally include rides, shows and special attractions. Many of the parks have a pay one price policy which entitles you to unlimited use of the park's rides and attractions. Pilot Books, 103 Cooper Street, Babylon NY 11702. Phone: 516-422-2225. Price: $5.95 plus $1.00 S&H.

•005• *Fairs and Festivals in the Northeast and Southeast* provides information on more than 900 festivals in 26 states and the District of Columbia. The 140 page guide list dates, locations, and descriptions. AES Publications, Arts Extension Service, Division of Continuing Education, University of Massachusetts, Amherst MA 01003. Phone: 413-545-2360. Price: $12.00 plus $3.75 S&H.

•006• *Watch It Made in the U.S.A.: A Visitor's Guide to the Companies that Make Your Favorite Things* is a 272 page guide to 250 factory tours across the country that make your favorite products. These are fun and interesting tours for the whole family and they are either free or very inexpensive. Many of the tours also feature samples. Each tour listed provides a complete description, directions, hours, costs, freebies, age and group requirements, disabled access, gift shops, nearby attractions, and much more. John Muir Publications, P.O. Box 613, Santa Fe NM 87504. Phone: 505-982-4078. Price: $16.95 plus S&H.

•007• The *Guide To Over 500 Aircraft Museums* provides an alphabetical listing, by state, of 566 aircraft museums across the country. Each entry provides name, address, phone, hours, price of admission, and the aircrafts on display. It also lists 228 cities that have an aircraft on display and 43 restaurants that have an aircraft inside or outside the building. Michael A. Blaugher, 124 East Foster Parkway, Ft. Wayne IN 46806-1730. Phone: 219-744-1020. Price: $7.00 postpaid.

•008• The *North American Indian Landmarks: A Traveler's Guide* takes traveler's on a guided tour throughout the U.S. and Canada to the Native North American landmarks that best represent the pageant of this group's rich and varied history. Many of the important landmarks are only a short detour away from most interstate highways. Arranged by region the 409 page book provides practical information on how to reach the site, hours and seasons, admission fees, and special exhibits and programs. The book also has maps pinpointing locations, photos, and a glossary defining frequently used terms. Visible Ink Press, P.O. Box 33477, Detroit MI 48232-5477. Phone: 800-776-6265. Price: $17.95 postpaid.

•009• *Indian American: A Traveler's Companion* informs traveler's how and where to find more than 300 Indian tribes in the United States and what ceremonies, arts and crafts, and historical sites are available. John Muir Publications, P.O. Box 613, Santa Fe NM 87504. Phone: 505-982-4078. Price: $18.95 plus S&H.

•010• The *Historic Black Landmarks: A Traveler's Guide* takes the reader on a cross-country tour to those landmarks uniquely related to African-American history and culture. The 408 page book is filled with the achievement and tragedy, art and action, and insight and blindness that characterize black history in America. Visible Ink Press, P.O. Box 33477, Detroit MI 48232-5477. Phone: 800-776-6265. Price $17.95 postpaid.

•011• *Great American Ships* is a 312 page guide to the 225 ships across the country that are part of our national maritime heritage. Arranged by region, the book tells how to find these landmarks and provides key historical and maritime information, including each vessel's current use. Attention Order Dept., The Preservation Press, 1785 Massachusetts Avenue NW, Washington DC 20036. Phone: 800-766-6847. Price: $19.95 plus $4.00 S&H.

•012• *Great American Lighthouses* is a traveler's guide to more than 300 of the nation's most significant lighthouses and lightships. The 350 page guide includes 445 b&w photographs and an introductory look at the evolution of lighthouse technology. Attention Order Dept., The Preservation Press, 1785 Massachusetts Avenue NW, Washington DC 20036. Phone: 800-766-6847. Price: $16.95 plus $4.00 S&H.

•013• *Great American Bridges and Dams* describes 330 feats of engineering genius including bridges from the Brooklyn to the Golden Gate and landmark dams such as the Hoover, Grand Coulee, Norris, and Shasta. The 360 page guide includes 555 b&w photographs and presents an overview of bridge and dam history. Attention Order Dept., The Preservation Press, 1785 Massachusetts Avenue NW, Washington DC 20036. Phone: 800-766-6847. Price: $15.95 plus $4.00 S&H.

•014• The *Caves & Caverns Directory* is a free brochure listing 85 caves across the country. The cave name, address, and phone number is provided so interested travelers can call or write for their free folders, travel directions and informational material. The brochure also provides a map of the U.S. showing locations of the caves. Price: Free. *Gurnee Guide To American Caves* contains all the information that might be useful for the traveler who is planning a cave visit. Over 150 photographs illustrate this guide to the 200 caves open for visitors in the 50 States and Puerto Rico. Included in the listings are mailing address, phone number, driving directions, seasons and times the caves are open, kind of tours offered, and what facilities are available on the premises as well as nearby. Price: $9.95 (softcover) and $11.95 (hardcover) postpaid. The brochure and book are available from: National Caves Association, 4138 Dark Hollow Road, McMinnville TN 37110. Phone: 615-668-3925.

•015• *Guide to Prehistoric Ruins of the Southwest* guides the visitor or armchair adventurer to the archaeological treasures of New Mexico, Arizona, Utah, and Colorado. Over 200 sites are described in detail emphasizing appreciation and protection of these cultural resources. Pruett Publishing Company, 2928 Pearl Street, Boulder CO 80301. Phone: 800-247-8224. Price: $12.95 plus S&H.

•016• RedBrick Press offers several publications about Americas Microbreweries and Brewpubs. *Star Spangled Beer: A Guide To America's New Microbreweries And Brewpubs* details the classic history of the North American microbrewing revolution. The 155 page book includes a history of beer, famous dates in brewing, beer styles, and a directory of the first American and Canadian microbreweries. Price: $13.95 plus S&H. *Brewery Adventures In The Wild West: The First Travel Guide To Western Microbreweries* features 143 microbreweries and brewpubs in 13 Western States and 2 Provinces. The 204 page book includes the history of Western microbrewing, survey, labels, pictures and descriptions of 549 beers. Price: $14.95 plus S&H. *Brewery Adventures In The Big East* includes a history and directory of 100 craft and regional breweries from Maine to Florida. The 168 page book includes chapters on the colonial tradition in American brewing and eastern regional breweries that survived prohibition. Price: $12.95 plus S&H. All three titles are available from: RedBrick Press P.O. Box 2184, Reston VA 22090. Phone: 703-476-6420.

•017• *Where The Animals Are: A Guide To The Best Zoos, Aquariums, And Wildlife Sanctuaries In North America* offers families a comprehensive and fun-to-use resource guide. Discusses where and what you can find at over 250 of the best zoos, aquariums, and other domestic and exotic wildlife attractions. Each entry in the 301 page book includes information on hours and seasons of operation, featured species and speciality animals, special exhibits, events, and entertainment, plus much more. The Globe Pequot Press, 6 Business Park Road, Old Saybrook CT 06475. Phone: 800-243-0495 or 800-962-0973 in Connecticut. Price: $12.95 plus $3.00 S&H. Also available in bookstores.

•018• The *Motorcycle Heritage Museum* depicts the many domestic and international influences that have affected motorcycling in America from the late 19th century to the present. On display are the beautiful designs and remarkable technologies that have often placed motorcycles on the leading edge of the transportation industry. Motorcycle Heritage Museum, P.O. Box 6114, Westerville OH 43081-6114. Phone: 614-882-2782. Price: Free information.

•019• *The 100 Best Small Art Towns in America* is the perfect guide for the traveler looking for off-the-beaten path cultural gems. Town descriptions in the 256 page book includes information on population, geography, climate, recreational opportunities, arts organizations, and festivals, as well as interviews with the local artists. John Muir Publications, P.O. Box 613, Santa Fe NM 87504. Phone: 505-982-4078. Price: $12.95 plus S&H.

•020• *Great Hot Springs Of The West* reveals the location of more than 1,700 mineral springs from remote wilderness settings to accessible luxury spas with maps, photographs and directions. The 208 page book also includes information about water temperatures, mineral contents, accessibility, healing and recreational facilities. Capra Press, P.O. Box 2068, Santa Barbara CA 93120. Phone: 805-966-4590. Price: $16.95 plus $2.00 S&H.

•021• *Events USA* is a monthly publication for those planning to attend events such as music festivals, state fairs, and other happenings around the U.S. Provides cost estimates for food and lodging at each event. Events USA, 386 Park Avenue South, New York NY 10016. Phone: 212-684-2222. Price: $12.00 per year.

•022• The *Travel Holiday* magazine is published 10 times per year for the travel enthusiast who likes to visit tourist attractions. Provides listings for off-beat locations as well as well-known tourist attractions in the United States and foreign locations. Features articles on food and beverages, safety tips, recreational vehicles, tours and special packages information. Travel Holiday, P.O. Box 5192, Harlan IA 51593-2692. Phone: 800-937-9241. Price: $13.97 per year.

FAMILY VACATIONS

For other related information see listings #: 080, 130, 136, 137, 138, 229, 252, and 268.

•023• *Super Family Vacations* describes 115 vacation suggestions including ski resorts, cruises, historic places, nature spots, and many other suitable family vacations. Each entry provides information on accommodations, activities for adults and children, dining, nearby places of interest, and suggestions for obtaining additional information. Harper Collins Publishers, 1000 Keystone Industrial Park, Scranton PA 18512-4621. Phone: 800-242-7737. Price: $14.00 for the current edition and $15.00 for the new edition available in February 1995.

•024• The *International Family Recreation Association* (IFRA) addresses the concerns relating to family recreation. Supports recommendations and legislation advantageous to recreation, leisure, and travel. Reviews and evaluates products. Conducts rallies, caravans, tours, cruises, and tournaments. Members receive the IFRA newsletter *Recreation Advisor* featuring the latest recreation news events, recreational travel, club and association events and many other activities offered by IFRA. Members also receive the IFRA discount merchandise catalog providing discounts up to 50% on quality merchandise. IFRA, P.O. Box 6279, Pensacola FL 32503-0279. Phone: 904-477-7992. Dues: $15.00 per year.

•025• The *Family Travel Times* newsletter is devoted to helping you make your family vacation experiences easier and more enjoyable by helping you plan fun and successful family vacations. Each issue has three regular features: *What's Happening Where* is a newsy round-up of the latest travel opportunities for families. *Children's Programs* keeps you up-to-date on resort activities designed for kids. *The Bookshelf* reviews guidebooks for parents, plus books for you to read to and with your kids to help enhance the vacation experience. Subscribers receive 10 issues per year, discounts on their other publications, and the invitation to call their office for Free individual consultation in planning your trips. TWYCH, Travel With Your Children, 45 West 18th Street, 7th Floor Tower, New York NY 10011. Phone: 212-206-0688. Price: $55.00 per year.

•026• The *North American Family Campers Association* is for families interested in camping. The association works to improve camping conditions and promote good camping manners while fostering a fellowship among family campers. Sponsors camping shows, competitions, and workshops for the public. All members receive the monthly newsletter *Campfire Chatter* which informs members about camping areas, equipment, and techniques. North American Family Campers Association, 16 Evergreen Terrace, North Reading MA 01864. Phone: 508-664-4294. Dues: $15.00 first year and $12.00 for renewals. Free information packet also available.

•027• The *Endless Vacation* magazine is for families who are frequent vacation travelers. The bimonthly issues serve as a planning guide with the focus on ideas for a variety of domestic and international vacation opportunities. Each issue includes travel tips, guide to regional dining, shopping and recommendations for unusual places to visit. Endless Vacations, 3502 Woodview Trace, Indianapolis IN 46268-1104. Phone: 317-871-9504. Price: $65.00 per year.

•028• The *Family Travel Log* provides information on fun vacation spots, theme festivals, camping recipes and more for the family vacation. Each issue also offers memories of past trips and humorous stories the whole family will enjoy. Family Travel Log, P.O. Box 406, Kewanee IL 61443-0406. Phone: 309-852-3474. Price: Call for current price.

VOLUNTEER VACATIONS

For other related information see listing #: 360.

•029• The *Volunteer Vacations* program offered by the American Hiking Society (AHS) sends teams of volunteers into the backcountry, where they spend a ten-day "vacation" on projects ranging from trail maintenance to bridge building. Most work sites are in remote, primitive areas and volunteers should be experienced hikers, 18 years of age and up, who are comfortable in these settings and physically able to backpack in and work hard. American Hiking Society, P.O. Box 20160, Washington DC 20041-2160. Phone: 703-255-9304. Price: Free information.

•030• The *Helping Out In The Outdoors* lists over 2,000 volunteer work and internships available on America's public lands. The 128 page directory published by the American Hiking Society (AHS) offers thousands of fascinating opportunities like campground hosts, trail crews, graphic artist, geologist, carpenter, computer and data entry, diver, gardener, librarian, river patrol, writer and much more. You can sign up solo, with a friend, family member or club. AHS Helping Out, P.O. Box 20160, Washington DC 20041-2160. Phone: 703-255-9304. Price: $7.00 postpaid.

•031• The *Passport in Time Clearinghouse* is a new program where forest visitors volunteer to work with forest service archaeologists and historians on heritage projects such as digs and restorations. Passport in Time Clearinghouse, CEHP Inc., P.O. Box 18364, Washington DC 20036. Price: Write for a free list of current projects.

MATURE TRAVELER'S

For other related information see listing #: 065.

•032• The *American Association of Retired Persons* (AARP) is the nation's leading organization (over 33 million members) for people age 50 and older. AARP membership has many benefits including the monthly newspaper *AARP Bulletin* and the bimonthly magazine *Modern Maturity*. Plus publications on all kinds of consumer, economic, employment, and health issues. AARP offers several benefits for travelers including the *AARP Travel Experience from American Express* which offers fully escorted tours, discounted cruises, and special programs across the nation. The *AARP Motoring Plan from Amoco* offers low rates, emergency road and towing services, maps and trip planning service, hospital emergency room bond, check-cashing, and other benefits. The *Purchase Privilege Program* provides discounts and special rates for members at more than 9,000 fine hotels, motels, and resorts nationwide including 28 major lodging chains and auto rental discounts through Avis, Hertz, National, and Thrifty. You also receive discounts on city sightseeing tours with Grey Line. Some of the other many benefits include savings on prescriptions, free publications, AARP investment program, access to affordable health care coverage, special discounts on auto and homeowner insurance, low-cost/low-fee AARP Visa card, and much more. AARP also maintains the largest library in the country devoted to information on aging which is available to everyone. American Association of Retired Persons, 601 E Street, NW, Washington DC 20049. Phone: 202-434-2277. Price: $8.00 per year which includes the monthly newspaper *AARP Bulletin* and the bimonthly magazine *Modern Maturity*.

•033• *The Mature Traveler: Travel Bonanzas for 49ers - Plus* is a monthly newsletter with news of current discounts and trips for 49ers+, reports on senior-friendly places and senior-specific travel tips. Coverage includes both domestic and international travel. Other special reports available include *Lodging Deals For 49ers+* which describes age-based discounts available at more than 10,000 motels and hotels in North America, *Airline Deals For 49ers+*, *Supersaver Deals For 49ers+*, *Senior-Friendly Las Vegas*, and *Ski Deals For 49ers+*. The Mature Traveler, P.O. Box 50820, Reno NV 89513. Price: Newsletter $29.50 per year or $2.00 for sample issue. The special reports are $5.00 each or free to subscribers.

•034• *Golden Companions* is a national network of active people over the age of 45 who are looking for others with whom to share their favorite leisuretime activities. Members include people who are looking for a travel companion, golf partner, friend for a concert and dinner, a walking/hiking buddy, and many other fun ventures. Benefits of membership include the bimonthly newsletter *Golden Gateways* that includes new member listings, club announcements, useful information, and articles covering a broad range of subjects. Discounts on various services and products are also passed along to members through the newsletter. Golden Companions, P.O. Box 754, Pullman WA 99163. Phone: 208-858-2183. Price: $85.00 per year, or $2.00 for a sample copy of newsletter.

•035• *The Senior Citizen's Guide To Budget Travel In The United States And Canada* shows you how to discover low cost transportation, accommodations, restaurants, tours, and more. Lists the outstanding attractions to visit in all 50 states and Canada and where to get free information. Pilot Books, 103 Cooper Street, Babylon NW 11702. Phone: 516-422-2225. Price: $5.95 plus $1.00 S&H.

•036• The *AARP Bulletin* covers news and items of interest to older Americans with a special emphasis on legislative action. The AARP Bulletin is published monthly by the American Association of Retired Persons, see listing #032 for more details.

•037• *A Better Tomorrow* is a Christian magazine for senior citizens ages fifty and over. The quarterly issues cover health, nutrition and fitness, family relationships, retirement, finances, and advice from trusted experts to help you look forward to the future. A Better Tomorrow, Thomas Nelson Inc., 5301 Wisconsin Avenue NW - Suite 620, Washington DC 20015. Phone: 202-364-8000. Price: $19.80 per year.

•038• The *American Senior* is published quarterly and covers government programs and benefits affecting seniors and their lifestyles. Also features articles on medical breakthroughs. American Senior, Publishing & Business Consultants, 951 South Oxford - #109, Los Angeles CA 90006. Phone: 213-732-3477. Price: $26.99 per year.

•039• *Fifty Plus* is for seniors over 50 in the United States and Canada. The monthly magazine covers legislation, health care, travel ideas and more geared toward the active and affluent individual. Fifty Plus, News and Observer Publishing Co., P.O. Box 8309, Myrtle Beach SC 29578. Phone: 803-236-3602. Price: $12.00 per year.

•040• *Fifty Something Magazine* is published bimonthly for the 50 and over age group. Each issue covers fitness, travel, entertainment, and other topics of interest to seniors. Fifty Something Magazine, Media Trends Publications, 8250 Tyler Blvd., Mentor OH 44060-4219. Phone: 216-974-9594. Price: $12.00 per year.

•041• *Mature Outlook* is for active men and women over 50 years of age. The bimonthly magazine focuses on health, fitness, and nutrition, travel and personal relationships and many other areas of interest to active seniors. Mature Outlook, Meredith Corp., 1912 Grand Ave., Des Moines IA 50309-3379. Phone: 515-284-2007. Price: $9.95 per year.

•042• The *Mature Years* quarterly publication is designed to help persons in and nearing their retirement years with articles on preparation problems and the joys of retirement. Also features articles on travel, health and fitness, hobbies, poetry, and Bible study. Mature Years, United Methodist Publishing House, 201 Eighth Avenue South, Nashville TN 37202. Phone: 615-749-6292. Price: $10.00 per year.

•043• *Modern Maturity* caters to the varied lifestyles and interest of senior citizens. The bimonthly publication edited by the American Association of Retired Persons covers career and financial planning, travel, current affairs, hobbies, health, nostalgia, inspiration, entertainment and the arts. See listing #032 for more details.

•044• *New Choices* is published monthly for active men and women over the age of 50. Regular articles cover health, money and investments, travel, people, real estate and housing, taxes, entertainment, politics, and retirement. New Choices For Retirement Living, Retirement Living Publishing Co., 28 West 23rd Street, New York NY 10010-5204. Phone: 212-366-8800. Price: $16.00 per year.

•045• *Retirement Life* is published monthly for retired federal employees and their families. Provides an overview of current activities and legislation of interest to members as well as updated medical and travel information, coming events, hobbies, and other member-related activities and information. Retirement

Life, National Association of Retired Federal Employees, 1533 New Hampshire Avenue NW, Washington DC 20036-1279. Phone: 202-234-0832. Price: $24.00 per year.

•046• The *Senior Citizen News* is published 11 times a year with articles on the political, social, and cultural arenas that directly affect senior citizens and their lifestyles. Senior Citizen News, National Council of Senior Citizens, 1331 F Street NW, Washington DC 20004. Phone: 202-347-8800. Price: $12.00 per year.

•047• *Senior Highlights* magazine, published monthly, covers fitness, health, finance, vacation spots, arts and entertainment, money matters, and more for active adults over 50 years of age. Senior Highlights Inc., 26081 Merit Circle #101, Laguna Hills CA 92653. Phone: 714-367-0776. Price: $18.00 per year.

•048• *Travel 50 & Beyond* is the first travel magazine for the 50 and over age group. The quarterly publication covers vacation alternatives and practical vacation information geared to finding the best value for the dollar. Travel 50 & Beyond, Vacation Publications Inc., 1502 Augusta Drive - #415, Houston TX 77057. Phone: 713-974-6903. Price: $10.00 per year.

•049• *Where To Retire* is a quarterly publication designed to be used as a guide in helping you find the ideal setting for the new retirement lifestyle. Articles include both consumer stories as well as destination options with details. Where To Retire, Vacation Publications Inc., 1502 Augusta Drive - #415, Houston TX 77057. Phone: 713-974-6903. Price: $15.80 per year.

PHYSICALLY CHALLENGED

•050• The *Travelin' Talk Directory* lists all the resources a traveler with a disability should ever need to plan their trips and find help should any emergencies arise. The 550 page guide provides information on all known locations for vans with wheelchair lifts for rent, accessible taxi and shuttle systems, travel and tour agencies who specialize in travel for the disabled, resources for accessible lodging information, plus much more. Travelin' Talk also publishes a quarterly newsletter providing timely information. For more information and a sample copy of the newsletter send a business size, self-addressed, stamped envelope. Travelin' Talk, P.O. Box 3534, Clarksville TN 37043-3534. Phone: 615-552-6670. Price: $35.00 postpaid.

•051• *Travel For The Disabled* is a 192 page book full of how-to and where-to get free travel information and access guides for the traveler with disabilities. Includes hundreds of hard-to-find travel resources including 500 access guides and accessible places in the U.S., Canada and worldwide and most are free. Also available on 3 audio cassettes. Twin Peaks Press, P.O. Box 129, Vancouver WA 98666-0129. Phone: 800-637-2256 Price: $19.95 plus S&H for the book or tapes.

•052• *Directory Of Travel Agencies For The Disabled* lists more than 370 travel agencies and tour operators that specialize in travel for deaf, blind, developmentally and physically limited persons. Also available on 2 audio cassettes. Twin Peaks Press, P.O. Box 129, Vancouver WA 98666-0129. Phone: 800-637-2256. Price: $19.95 plus S&H for the book or tapes.

•053• *Wheelchair Vagabond* is for those who like to travel by automobile, RV or van. It includes choosing the right vehicle, what to take and where to put it, planning your trip, where to stop, gourmet cooking, camping equipment, and hundreds of hints. Twin Peaks Press, P.O. Box 129, Vancouver WA 98666-0129. Phone: 800-637-2256. Price: $14.95 plus S&H.

•054• *Directory Of Accessible Van Rentals* provides a list of van rental companies throughout the United States that rent lift-equipped vans. Twin Peaks Press, P.O. Box 129, Vancouver WA 98666-0129. Phone: 800-637-2256. Price: $9.95 plus S&H.

•055• *The Disability Bookshop Catalog* lists more than 350 books about computers, travel, arts/crafts, education, exercise, self-help, resource directories, and much more. Twin Peaks Press, P.O. Box 129, Vancouver WA 98666-0129. Phone: 800-637-2256. Price: $3.00 plus S&H.

•056• The *Illustrated Directory of Handicapped Products* features hard to find products for the physically challenged. The 300 page directory includes products like exercise equipment, wheelchairs, eating and drinking aids, respiratory products, adapted vehicles, and much more. Doyle Publishing, 2101 Rexford Road #172, Charlotte NC 28211. Phone: 704-364-0719. Price: $30.00 plus S&H.

•057• The *National Library Service for the Blind and Physically Handicapped* provides the free loan of recorded and braille books and magazines, music scores in braille and large print, and specially designed playback equipment to residents of the United States and U.S. citizens living abroad who are unable to read or use standard print materials because of visual or physical impairment. For more information on the program request their *Facts* brochure which explains the program in more detail and includes an order form to receive the free material. Of special interest for traveler's is their reference circular entitled *Information for Handicapped Travelers* which provides information about books on travel, travel agencies, travel information centers, and transportation services. National Library Service for the Blind and Physically Handicapped, Library of Congress, Washington DC 20542. Phone: 202-707-0712. Price: Free.

•058• *Disabled Outdoors Magazine* is a quarterly publication that covers all types of outdoor recreation and travel for people of all ages with disabilities. Provides information on adaptive products, accessible facilities across the U.S. and Canada, and services providers. They also act as a clearinghouse for accessible information. If you are looking for a product or information on an accessible area, you can call and they will try to locate the information for you. Disabled Outdoors Magazine, 2052 West 23rd Street, Chicago IL 60608. Phone: 708-358-4160. Price: $10.00 per year.

•059• The *Over the Rainbow* is a quarterly newsletter offering educational exchanges and travel referral services for the physically challenged. Provides information on the organization's programs and publications, news of tours, services, and recreational programs for the disabled. Also available on audio cassette. Mobility International USA, P.O. Box 10767, Eugene OR 97440-0551. Phone: 503-343-1284. Price: $10.00 per year.

•060• *Accessible Journeys* is a tour agency operated by healthcare professionals specializing in recreational programs exclusively for special need travelers. They design accessible vacations, escort groups on accessible vacations, and arrange travel companions for travelers who need assistance away from home. A convenient way to learn about upcoming travel opportunities is to subscribe to their newsletter *Travel Notes* which provides information on their accessible pursuits. You will receive the newsletter four times a year along with periodic travel announcements. Accessible Journeys, 35 West Sellers Avenue, Ridley Park PA 19078. Phone: 800-846-4537. Price: $15.00 per year for the newsletter or you can write for additional information on the services provided by the company.

•061• The *Handicapped Travel Club* sponsors one national convention and several mini-rallies a year for travelers with special needs. Members also receive a monthly newsletter with current information on club news and activities. Handicapped Travel Club Inc., Rt. 1 - Box 233, Centralia MO 65240. Phone: 314-682-3898. Price: $5.00 per year.

•062• *New Mobility* is a bimonthly publication for mobility impaired individuals and their families. Features articles on sports, recreation, travel, and family. New Mobility, P.O. Box 4162, Boulder CO 80306. Phone: 303-449-5412. Price: Call for current price.

•063• *Access USA News* is for all Americans with disabilities. The bimonthly magazine focuses on the disability lifestyle and culture. Access USA News, P.O. Box 1134, Crystal Lake IL 60039. Phone: 815-363-0900. Price: Call for current price.

Travel Companions is filled with tips and helpful travel information for singles in all age groups. If you want to meet a compatible travel partner this service matches solo travelers with like minded travelers so you never have to travel alone. Each issue has money-saving articles, travel tips and hundreds of listings of members looking for compatible partners, travel companions, new friends or travel-minded dates. Travel Companion Exchange Inc., P.O. Box 833, Amityville NY 11701-0833. Phone: 516-454-0880. Price: Several options are available for new members with prices ranging from $24.00 for just the newsletter to $66.00 for a six month VIP Membership. You may also request the most recent issue of the newsletter for $4.00 postpaid.

•066• *International Travel Card* has a program called *ITC-50* that entitles members to savings of up to 50% at over 2,500 hotels, motels and restaurants throughout the U.S. and at over 60 popular overseas destinations. Members also receive discounts on car rentals through Avis, Hertz, and National. New members receive a current directory listing all participating hotels, motels and restaurants. International Travel Card, 6001 North Clark Street, Chicago IL 60660. Phone: 800-342-0558. Dues: $36.00 per year.

•067• The *Extra Miler Club* is for all who love to travel the open road. The members goal is to visit every U.S. county, every State Capitol building, all National Parks, and points of the highest and lowest elevation in each state. The club bestows awards for visiting all 3,140 counties, 2,000 counties and 1,000 counties. All members also receive The *Extra Miler* newsletter on a periodic basis. Extra Miler Club, P.O. Box 61771, Boulder City NV 89006. Phone: 702-294-2617. Dues: Call for current price.

GENERAL TRAVEL
ASSOCIATIONS AND CLUBS

•064• The *Federation of American Consumers and Travelers* (F.A.C.T.) offers a wide variety of services and benefits for its members. F.A.C.T. is a not-for-profit corporation whose members represent "Mainstream America" and who want to improve their quality of life. F.A.C.T. supports programs, legislation and other organizations whose purpose is to enlighten, educate or otherwise help the American Consumer. Some of the benefits members enjoy are accident insurance, amusement park discounts, car purchase savings, car rental discounts, consumer hotline, consumer library, disaster aid program, eye wear savings, floral discounts, hotel/motel discounts, medical insurance, savings on office products & services, prescription drug discounts, scholarship programs, shopping discounts, telephone long distance savings, and travel savings including free road maps. Members also receive the quarterly newsletter *Fact-Finder* filled with things you should know about legislative changes that affect you, new F.A.C.T. benefits, health tips, tax and financial advice, and much more are all covered in detail. F.A.C.T., 318 Hillsboro Avenue, Edwardsville IL 62025. Phone: 800-USA-FACT. Dues: $30.00 per year.

•065• The *Travel Companions Exchange* offers a match-up service and newsletter for solo travelers. The bimonthly newsletter

GENERAL TRAVEL
BOOKS AND DIRECTORIES

•068• *The Travel & Vacation Discount Guide* lists discount travel clubs, air travel and cruise line discounts, lodging savings plus various other travel discounts. Senior citizen, student and specialized discounts are also covered as well as various exchange programs. Pilot Books, 103 Cooper Street, Babylon NY 11702. Phone: 516-422-2225. Price: $5.95 plus $1.00 S&H.

•069• *The Directory Of Low-Cost Vacations With A Difference* is a comprehensive guide of alternatives to the ordinary vacation. Covers bed and breakfast, farm vacations, home exchanges, senior citizen programs, vacation work programs, and more. Provides name, address, and a brief description of the organizations offering these vacations. Pilot Books, 103 Cooper Street, Babylon NY 11702. Phone: 516-422-2225. Price: $5.95 plus $1.00 S&H.

•070• *Toll-Free Travel & Vacation Information Directory* lists free information sources for the traveler and vacationer. Covers airlines; apartment, home and condominium rentals; automobile rentals and leasing; bus lines and charters; discount travel services; hotel and motel chains, plus other helpful information. Pilot Books, 103 Cooper Street, Babylon NY 11702. Phone: 516-422-2225. Price: $5.95 plus $1.00 S&H.

•071• The *'800' & Fax Travel Directory* is published for travel professionals but can prove useful for anyone who likes to arrange their own travel. The directory is the only source you will need to place your hotel, travel and transportation bookings. Complete with company name, address, '800' & fax numbers plus the key contacts you will need to know for hotels/lodging, tour & travel, transportation, and other travel related companies. World Travel Communications Inc., 7380 South Eastern Avenue #124-142, Las Vegas NV 89123. Phone: 702-795-2411. Price: $20.00 postpaid.

•072• *The Phone Booklet* provides hundreds of toll-free phone numbers for travelers. Listings include resorts, hotels, motels, airlines, car rentals, buses, amusement and theme parks, auto and travel clubs, ski areas, cruise lines and numbers for state, regional, city, and international travel and tourism offices. Scott American Corp., P.O. Box 88, West Redding CT 06896. Price: $2.00 per copy postpaid.

•073• The *World Chamber of Commerce Directory* features over 13,000 listing of U.S. chambers of commerce, state boards of tourism, convention and visitors bureaus, Canadian chambers of commerce, and much more. The guide is a great source of information contacts to help you plan your vacation. Listings are by state and then alphabetically by city providing chamber name, address, and phone number. World Chamber of Commerce Directory, P.O. Box 1029, Loveland CO 80539. Phone: 303-663-3231. Price: $29.00 postpaid.

•074• The 208 page *FM Station Reference Guide* features 102 pages of maps to help pinpoint over 8,000 FM stations covering all of North America. The guide lists call letters, location, musical format and other helpful information like how to improve your FM reception. FM Atlas, P.O. Box 336, Esko MN 55733-0336. Phone: 218-879-7676. Price: $14.95 plus $1.05 S&H.

•075• *The Next Exit* is a complete interstate highway travel guide. All major routes and exits are covered. Provides specific listings for gas, food, lodging, shopping facilities, and tourist attractions along the interstates. The Next Exit Inc., P.O. Box 888, Franklin NC 28734. Phone: 800-NEX-EXIT. Price: $17.95 postpaid.

•076• The *Rest Area Guide To The United States And Canada* provides information on locations and facilities at over 2,100 rest areas along the nations roadways. The information is arranged in a state by state and highway to highway format. Includes information on picnic tables, rest rooms, drinking water, outside night lights, handicapped facilities, public telephone, RV sanitary dump station, and welcome / information center plus much more. American Travel Publications Inc., 6986 El Camino Real - Suite 104-199, Carlsbad CA 92009. Phone: 619-438-0514. Price: $11.95 postpaid.

GENERAL TRAVEL CATALOGS

For other related information see listing #: 142.

•077• The *Traveller's Bookstore* 50 plus page catalog features

travel books, guide books, fiction and non-fiction travel titles. They also carry a selection of road and city maps as well as travel accessories. The Traveller's Bookstore carries over 10,000 travel related books so if you can't find it listed in the catalog, chances are good one phone call will have the book on its way to your doorstep. If you are in New York you are invited to stop by their retail store. Traveller's Bookstore, 22 West 52nd Street, New York NY 10019. Phone:800-755-8728. Price: $2.00 one time fee, waived when you order.

•078• *The Complete Traveller Bookstore* offers a wide selection of travel books and guides as well as foreign language tapes. The titles offered cover foreign destinations and the United States including state and regional titles. You will also find a few travel accessories listed in the catalog. The main catalog is supplemented twice a year with a newsletter to keep you informed of new titles. You are also welcome to stop by their retail store in New York. The Complete Traveller Bookstore, 199 Madison Avenue, New York NY 10016. Phone 212-685-9007. Price $1.00 includes the two newsletters.

•079• The *Book Passage* annual catalog has something to offer all traveler's. Whether you are traveling in the States or overseas you will find a book to make your journey more enjoyable. The catalog features hundreds of travel books and guides, armchair reading, foreign language books and tapes, maps, and travel accessories. If you can't find what you want listed in the catalog you are invited to call or stop by their retail store in California to discover the thousands of titles available. Book Passage, 51 Tamal Vista Blvd., Corte Madera CA 94925. Phone: 800-999-7909. Price: Free catalog.

•080• *The Family Travel Guides* 32 page catalog offers over 200 family-oriented travel guides and children's travel activity books. You will find the selection of titles offered to be a great help in planning that perfect family vacation. Carousel Press, The Family Travel Guides Catalog, P.O. Box 6061, Albany CA 94706-0061. Price: $1.00 S&H or a long, stamped (.52 cents) self-addressed envelope.

•081• The *Forsyth Travel Library* offers an extensive selection of travel guides and maps, international rail travel guides, maps and schedules including the Thomas Cook European Timetable. You can also order rail passes to Europe and Britain, join American Youth Hostels, and subscribe to over a dozen travel publications. They also offer travel accessories such as soft luggage, converters and adapters, security items, and miscellaneous accessories and essentials. You are also welcome to stop by their retail store located at 9154 West 57th Street, when in the area. Forsyth Travel Library Inc., P.O. Box 2975, Shawnee Mission KS 66201-1375. Phone: 800-FORSYTH. Price: Free information pack.

•082• The *Traveler's Checklist* catalog offers a nice selection of hard to find travel accessories. Items such as voltage converters, personal-care items, travel clocks, film shield pouch, plus other travel related products. Traveler's Checklist, 335 Cornwall Bridge Road, Sharon CT 06069. Phone: 203-364-0144. Price: Free.

•083• The *Magellan's* catalog is a good source for all your travel essentials. The catalog is full of products to make your trip safe and convenient. Just a few of the travel related items include alarm clocks, binoculars, books, compasses, computer accessories, dental care, first aid, games, hair dryers, hats, locks, luggage carts, maps, mirrors, photo gear, radios, repair kits, telephone accessories, water filters and treatments. When you are traveling in the area you will want to stop by their retail store located at 925 Calle Puerto Vallarta in Santa Barbara, CA. Magellan's, P.O. Box 5485, Santa Barbara CA 93150-5485. Phone: 800-962-4943. Price: Free catalog.

•084• The *Pelican Travel Catalog* offers several general interest travel books for the United States and locations around the world. The 15 page catalog provides brief descriptions and ordering information. Pelican Publishing Company, P.O. Box 3110, Gretna LA 70054. Phone: 800-843-1724. Price: Free catalog.

GENERAL TRAVEL NEWSLETTERS

•085• The *Travel Smart* newsletter provides travelers with tips and helpful information on travel. The monthly newsletter helps readers travel better for less. Includes information on the latest in travel deals, fares, package tours, sightseeing, hotels, restaurants, and much more. Features reviews of specific tours, travel guides and other related publications. Subscribers are also offered travel at discounts. Travel Smart, 40 Beechdale Road, Dobbs Ferry NY 10522-9989. Phone: 914-693-8300. Price: $37.00 per year.

•086• The *Consumer Reports Travel Letter* provides travelers with information and advice on travel goods and services to help you find the best travel values. Topics covered include air and rail passes, air fare, hotel rates, foreign exchange rates, car rental fees, and much more. The monthly newsletter also includes letters to the editor and book reviews. Consumer Reports, P.O. Box 51366, Boulder CO 80321. Phone: 800-999-7959. Price: $37.00 per year.

•087• Nationwide Intelligence publishes the *Personal Travel Report* to help the individual business or leisure traveler get the best value while avoiding the rip-offs and over-rated products and services. The monthly newsletter includes comprehensive city reports, recommended best buys, "10 Best" list, their favorite resorts and city hotels, what others are recommending, and a summary of the featured stories in the major consumer travel magazines along with some insider tips. Nationwide Intelligence, P.O. Box 1922, Saginaw MI 48605. Phone: 800-333-4130. Price: $25.00 per year.

•088• The *Unique & Exotic Travel Reporter* is a monthly newsletter providing travelers with an easy method of learning what's new in the world of out-of-the-ordinary travel. If you are looking for extraordinary travel experiences including remote treks, learning vacations, adventure travel expeditions, and special interest destinations the newsletter will keep you current on what is new and available. Unique & Exotic Travel Reporter, 6716 Eastside Drive NE - Suite 12, Tacoma WA 98422. Phone: 206-927-1688. Price: $39.00 per year.

•089• The *Travelore Report* carries worldwide travel news for people who love to vacation and travel. Provides information on tours, transportation, shops, accommodations, restaurants, and other valuable travel news to help you save money. The monthly newsletter also features book reviews and travel tips. T.R. Report, 1512 Spruce St., Philadelphia PA 19102-4524. Phone: 215-545-0616. Price: $30.00 per year.

•090• *Planet Talk* is a free quarterly newsletter for the benefit of anybody interested in travel. The articles cover a wide variety of subjects including letters written by readers of Lonely Planet Guides and from the guide authors. Lonely Planet Publications, 155 Filbert Street - Suite 251, Oakland CA 94607-2531. Phone: 510-893-8555. Price: Free.

•091• The *Photo Traveler Newsletter* provides practical information on places, subjects and events with photographic potential. The bimonthly newsletter includes comprehensive photo guides to national parks, outstanding scenic areas and little known places, written from a photographers point of view. You will know the best season, optimal time of day, and what equipment you might want to take along, and specific locations where you can find the best photos, including maps directing you to the best photo spots. The newsletter also list hundreds of upcoming photo tours and travel workshops, seasonal happenings, events around the country with photo potential, unusual places, and hard-to-find informational resources such as travel books written for photographers. Photo Traveler Publications, P.O. Box 39912, Los Angeles CA 90039. Phone: 213-660-0473. Price: $29.95 per year.

•092• The *Photograph America* newsletter is for those who love nature photography as a hobby or as a profession. The bimonthly newsletter provides solid information, opinions, and details, as well as suggestions on where to find the best locations for nature, landscape, scenic, and wildlife photography. You will also learn about the places to avoid and where to stay in each area with information on hotels, lodges, campgrounds, and RV parks. Photograph America Newsletter, 1333 Monte Maria Avenue, Novato CA 94947. Phone: 415-898-3736. Price: $30.00 per year.

•093• *Out West: America's On The Road Newspaper* is a quarterly tabloid newspaper the explores the back roads and small towns of the rural West. Chuck and Rodica Woodbury roam the back roads by motor home and write about the people and places they encounter along the way. They reexperience the old roads bypassed by the interstates, mom and pop cafes and general stores, roadside tourist attractions, little known state and national parks, interesting museums and attractions. Out West, 408 Broad Street - Suite 11, Nevada City CA 95959. Phone: 800-274-9378. Price: $11.95 a year or $3.00 for a sample issue.

GENERAL TRAVEL MAGAZINES

•094• *Adventure West* the bimonthly magazine focuses on travel and adventure in western North America. Geared toward those who look forward to experiencing travel for themselves, those who seek the unusual and provocative, and for those who visualize their next trip before the last one is over. Adventure West Subscription Dept., P.O. Box 461270, Escondido CA 92046-1270. Phone: 800-846-8575. Price: $11.97 for one year.

•095• *American Heritage* provides the reader with information concerning various facets of the American past and present. The magazine is published 8 times a year and provides in-depth articles on history, art, literature, politics, travel and the changing lifestyles of Americans. American Heritage, Forbes Inc., 60 Fifth Avenue, New York NY 10011-8890. Phone: 800-777-1222. Price: $32.00 per year.

•096• *Conde Nast Traveler* is a travel and lifestyle magazine for the frequent traveler with a sense of style and quality all its own. The monthly magazine serves as a guide to travel and travel related lifestyles and provides information on destinations, hotels, transportation, shopping and dining. Conde Nast Traveler, 360 Madison Avenue, New York NY 10017-3136. Phone: 212-880-8800. Price: $15.00 per year.

•097• *Discovery* is a quarterly magazine that gives the reader a better look at the world through travel. Features personalized stories to help you experience America and the world beyond. Discovery, Aegis Group Publishers, 30400 Van Dyke Avenue, Warren MI 48093. Phone: 313-574-9100. Price: Call for current price.

•098• The *Diversion* magazine is published monthly for physicians seeking ideas for leisure time activities. The articles feature popular travel spots, special events, dining, sports, finance, and profiles of key personalities. Diversion, Hearst Business Publications, 60 East 42nd Street - #2424, New York NY 10165. Phone: 212-297-9600. Price: $48.00 per year.

•099• The *Great Expeditions* magazine covers adventure travel to unusual destinations. The quarterly publication features essays and photos of destinations along with economically sound travel tips. Great Expeditions, P.O. Box 18036, Raleigh NC 27609. Phone: 919-846-3600. Price: Call for current price.

•100• The *National Geographic Traveler* is for those who enjoy to travel. The bimonthly magazine features articles on destinations to interesting places in the U.S. and abroad. Provides information to help in the planning and making of trips. Offers detailed maps, dining and lodging recommendations along with additional travel insights. National Geographic traveler, National Geographic Society, 17th & M Streets NW, Washington DC 20036. Phone: 202-857-7000. Price: $18.00 per year.

•101• *Northwest Travel* features articles from the wilderness to the city life in the northwest United States. The bimonthly magazine covers history, the people, architecture, geology and other facets of northwestern life. Northwest Travel Magazine Inc., P.O. Box 18000, Florence OR 97439-0103. Phone: 503-997-8401. Price: $14.95 per year.

•102• *Outdoor Photographer* is published 10 times per year covering scenic outdoor wildlife and sports photography. Outdoor Photographer, Werner Publishing, 12121 Wilshire Blvd. - #1220, Los Angeles CA 90025-1175. Phone: 310-820-1500. Price: $18.00 per year.

•103• *Outdoor Traveler* covers the mid-Atlantic region of the United States. The quarterly publication features outdoor activities, events, places to visit, and nature along the back roads as well as the main routes. Outdoor Traveler, WMS Publications, P.O. Box 1788, Charlottesville VA 22902. Phone: 804-984-0655. Price: $12.00 per year.

•104• *Touring America* features articles on destinations throughout the United States, Canada and Mexico. The bimonthly magazine covers travel, photography, calendar of events, travel tips and more. Touring America, Fancy Publications, P.O. Box 6050, Mission Viejo CA 92690. Phone: 714-855-8822. Price: $15.00 per year.

•105• *Travel America* provides information on tours all across the United States. The bimonthly publication covers tours on land and by sea plus resorts and special destinations. Travel America, World Publishing, 990 Grove Street, Evanston IL 60201. Phone: 708-491-6440. Price: $18.00 per year.

•106• *Travel Holiday* is published 10 times a year for the frequent pleasure traveler. Provides information on where to go, what to do and see for destinations in the United States and abroad. Each issue also covers food & wine, photography, travel news items, upcoming events and new travel products. Travel Holiday, Reader's Digest Publications, 28 West 23rd Street, New York NY 10010. Phone: 212-366-8700. Price: $11.00 per year.

•107• *Travel & Leisure* features articles on travel and pleasurable leisure time activities. The monthly magazine provides information on hotels, dining, hobbies, entertainment, and more to enhance the travel experience of pleasure and business traveler's. Travel & Leisure, American Express Publishing Corp., 1120 Ave. of the Americas, New York NY 10036-6770. Phone: 212-382-5600. Price: $15.00 per year.

•108• The *Travel News* magazine is published monthly for the leisure traveler. Offers advice on domestic and international travel destinations. The articles feature the latest information on tours and airfares along with guidelines to help you make the best vacation decision. Travel News, Travel Agents International Inc., 111 Second Avenue NE - 15th Floor, St. Petersburg FL 33701. Phone: 813-895-8241. Price: Free.

•109• *Travelin' Magazine* helps travelers explore the backroads of the west. The bimonthly magazine takes you off the beaten path to discover hidden places most tourists don't know about. Covers the 11 western states, western Canada, and Hawaii. Travelin' Magazine, P.O. Box 23005, Eugene OR 97402-0424. Phone: 503-485-8533. Price: $14.95 per year.

•110• *Vacations* is a quarterly publication designed as a practical money oriented guide to help you plan successful vacations around the United States and around the globe. Vacations, Vacations Publications Inc., 1502 Augusta Drive - #415, Houston TX 77057-4803. Phone: 713-974-6903. Price: $12.00 per year.

LODGING
HOTELS / MOTELS

For other related information see listing #: 066.

•111• The ***National Directory Of Budget Motels*** is a nationwide guide to over 2,200 low-cost chain motel accommodations. Many of the motels are conveniently located along major highways. The guide also lists the motel chain headquarters where you can get additional information. Pilot Books, 103 Cooper Street, Babylon NY 11702. Phone: 516-422-2225. Price: $5.95 plus $1.00 S&H.

•112• The ***State By State Guide To Budget Motels: Your national guide to the best low-cost lodgings*** is the largest guide to the budget motels throughout the United States and Canada. The 420 page guide lists more than 4,000 motels that offer overnight accommodations for $45.00 or less for two people. The listings include addresses, prices, and discounts, and toll-free numbers for reservations. Marlor Press Inc., 4304 Brigadoon Dr., St. Paul MN 55126. Phone: 612-484-4600. Price: $10.95 plus $2.50 S&H.

•113• ***America's Wonderful Little Hotels and Inns: U.S.A. and Canada*** lists more than 1,000 distinctive places to stay in major cities, resort areas, and out-of-the-way towns from coast to coast. Each listing includes hotel or inn name, location, prices, comments from guests, description of facilities, and background information. St. Martin's Press Inc., 175 Fifth Avenue, New York NY 10010-7848. Phone: 212-674-5151. Price: $19.99 plus S&H.

•114• The ***Small Hotel Directory*** helps travelers find the best small hotels in 101 cities around the world. These hotels are often landmarks, frequently quaint, and always special. A key factor in selecting the hotels was charm and that they be absolutely safe. Most of the hotels also offer facilities for the business traveler. The guide lists the outstanding feature of each hotel, telephone number, price category, and whether or not breakfast is included in the room rate. Communications House Inc., Dobbs Ferry NY 10522. Phone: 914-693-8300. Price: $9.95 postpaid.

•115• ***The Hotel/Motel Special Program and Discount Guide*** lists hotels and motels in the United States and Canada that offer special discounts and other money-saving programs. Presents the various special offers and gives you the address and phone numbers you can contact for free directories, updated information, enrollment information for the various programs and current rates. There are special deals for seniors, business travelers, frequent visitors, children, and club memberships plus other incentives. Pilot Books, 103 Cooper Street, Babylon NY 11702. Phone: 516-422-2225. Price: $5.95 plus $1.00 S&H.

•116• Many of the ***chain hotels/motels*** offer a free directory to their locations across the country. Below is a select list of some of the larger chains with a phone number for reservations and additional information. Be sure to ask them about any discount programs that they might offer.

Best Western International, 800-528-1234.
Budget Host Inns, 800-283-4678.
Choice Hotels, 800-221-2222.
     Clarion Hotels
     Comfort Inns
     Econo Lodges
     Friendship Inns
     Quality Inns
     Roadway Inns
     Sleep Inns
Courtyard By Marriott, 800-321-2211.

Days Inns Of America, 800-325-2525.
Doubletree Hotels, 800-222-8733.
Embassy Suites, 800-362-2779.
Fairfield Inns, 800-228-2800.
Hampton Inns, 800-426-7866.
Hilton Hotels, 800-445-8667.
Holiday Inn, 800-465-4329.
Homewood Suites, 800-225-5466.
Hospitality International, 800-251-1962.
     Downtowner Motor Inns
     Master Host Inns
     Passport Inns
     Red Carpet Inns
     Scottish Inns
Howard Johnson, 800-446-4656.
Hyatt Hotels, 800-233-1234.
ITT Sheraton Hotels, 800-325-3535.
La Quinta Inns, 800-531-5900.
Marriott Hotels, 800-228-9290.
Motel 6, 505-891-6161.
Omni Hotels, 800-843-6664.
Park Inns International, 800-437-7275.
Preferred Hotels, 800-323-7500.
Radisson Hotels, 800-333-3333.
Ramada Inn, 800-272-6232.
Red Roof Inns, 800-843-7663.
Residence Inns By Marriott, 800-331-3131.
Stouffer Hotels, 800-468-3571.
Super 8 Motels, 800-800-8000.
Travelodge, 800-578-7878.
Westin Hotels And Resorts, 800-228-3000.
Wyndham Hotels and Resorts, 800-996-3426.

LODGING
BED AND BREAKFAST

•117• The ***Bed & Breakfast North America*** features comprehensive listings for historic Victorian inns, intimate urban hotels, country inns, guesthouses and reservation services. The listings include location, price, facilities, amenities, and area tourist attractions. The 696 page guide provides access to over 10,000 accommodations. Betsy Ross Publications, 24406 S. Ribbonwood Drive, Sun Lakes AZ 85248. Phone: 602-895-2795. Price: $15.95 plus $2.50 S&H.

•118• ***The Official Bed and Breakfast Guide for the United States, Canada and the Caribbean*** features more than 1,600 listings of the finest bed and breakfasts homes and family-run inns, including many historical dwellings. Each entry includes name of B&B, address, phone number, rates, and all amenities offered. Each property is personally described by the owner and many include pictures. The 534 page guide also includes a *Reservation Service* section listing reservation specialists with access to more than 7,000 additional bed and breakfasts accommodations and a *Restaurant* section listing restaurants recommended for lunch and dinner by the bed and breakfasts proprietors. The National Bed & Breakfast Association, P.O. Box 332, Norwalk CT 06852.

Phone: 203-847-6196. Price: $ 16.95 plus $3.00 S&H. Mention you read about it in Road Trip USA and they will give you a 15% discount.

•119• The *Inspected, Rated, and Approved Bed & Breakfast and Country Inns* guide book lists over 400 B&Bs and inns throughout North America that meet national standards. Each property featured agrees to an annual on-site inspection and is awarded a consumer rating which appears in the book. Each entry in the 350 page guide includes name, address, phone, type of accommodations, rates, and more. The American Bed & Breakfast Association, 10800 Midlothian Tpke. Suite 254, Richmond VA 23235. Phone: 800-769-2468. Price: $16.95 plus S&H. Also available in most major book stores.

•120• *The National Trust Guide to Historic Bed & Breakfasts, Inns and Small Hotels* containing more than 600 listings, is a connoisseur's guide to historic bed & breakfasts. Travelers can choose historic destinations ranging in size from one-room guests houses to 100-room, family-run resorts. From rustic mountain lodges and plain, rural farmhouses to gingerbread seaside cottages and elaborate, high-style dwellings. Each listing in the 512 page guide includes name, address, phone, and a complete description of the accommodations. Attention Order Dept., The Preservation Press, 1785 Massachusetts Avenue NW, Washington DC 20036. Phone: 800-766-6847. Price: $15.95 plus $4.00 S&H.

•121• *The Annual Directory of American and Canadian Bed and Breakfasts* is an extensive directory of bed and breakfasts in the United States, Canada, Puerto Rico, and the Virgin Islands. Includes more than 6,000 entries organized alphabetically by state and by cities within each state. Each listing in the 1,440 page book includes a description, prices, meals included in the price, address, phone number, nearby activities, and much more. Rutledge Hill Press, 211 Seventh Avenue, North Nashville TN 37219-1823. Phone: 800-234-4234. Price: $18.95 plus S&H.

•122• *The Non-Smokers' Guide to Bed and Breakfasts* contains more than 3,000 entries whose guests rooms and indoor common areas are smoke-free. The 704 page guide is organized alphabetically by state and then by city. Each entry includes a description, number of rooms, prices, meals included in the price, address, phone number, nearby activities, and much more. Rutledge Hill Press, 211 Seventh Avenue, North Nashville TN 37219-1823. Phone: 800-234-4234. Price: $14.95 plus S&H

•123• The *Great Affordable Bed & Breakfast Getaways* describes B&B's located in popular tourist areas or in a historic, rustic, seaside, mountain or other special setting. The B&B's were chosen for their uniqueness and value with prices not to exceed $55.00 per day for two persons, including breakfast. The 312 page guide describes the B&B or historic inn and tells about the unique features visitors can enjoy in the area. Marlor Press Inc., 4304 Brigadoon Dr., St. Paul MN 55126. Phone: 612-484-4600. Price: $12.95 plus $2.50 S&H.

•124• The *Bed & Breakfast Locator* is a monthly publication that provides current information on Bed and Breakfast establishments for travelers. Eagle Publications, P.O. Box 471006, Fort Worth TX 76147-1006. Phone: 817-377-1991. Price: $24.00 per year or $3.00 for a sample issue.

•125• The *Gracious Stays And Special Places* is a quarterly publication that focuses on Bed & Breakfasts, Country Inns, Guest Houses, Plantations, and unique accommodations in the United States and abroad. Designed to promote the appreciation of historical and architecturally significant buildings, museums, and accommodations. Gracious Stays And Special Places, 2856 Hundred Oaks, Baton Rouge LA 70808-1533. Phone: 504-343-0672. Price: Call for current price.

•126• *Country Inns Bed & Breakfast* a bimonthly magazine for the traveler, features inns and bed and breakfast establishments throughout the United States, Canada and the world. Articles cover antiques, gourmet cuisine, books, art, and regional attractions. Country Inns Bed & Breakfast, P.O. Box 182, South Orange NJ 07079-0182. Phone: 201-762-7090. Price: $17.95 per year.

LODGING
CAMPGROUNDS

For other related information see listing #: 267.

•127• *Woodall's Campground Directory: The North American Edition* list over 15,000 campgrounds, RV parks, attractions, and RV dealership/service centers throughout the United States, Canada and Mexico. Woodall's rating system guides campers and RVers to the park that best suits their camping needs. The guide is also available in a *East* or *West* edition as well as eight regional editions. Every edition includes a copy of *Discover the Cultural Heritage of North America* - a 128 page magazine section about several of the many cultures which make up North America. Includes villages, attractions, and settlements where North America's cultural heritage can be discovered and enjoyed by travelers; events and festivals; recipes and more. Every edition also includes *Woodall's Guide to Seasonal Sites in RV Resorts/Campgrounds* which helps you choose campgrounds and resorts that offer a place to camp for a month or season. Fulfillment Department #1950, Woodall Publishing Company, 28167 North Keith Drive - Box 5000, Lake Forest IL 60045-5000. Phone: 800-323-9076. Price: North American Edition $16.95 plus $3.00 S&H. The Eastern Edition (31 eastern states and eastern Canada) $10.95 plus $2.50 S&H. The Western Edition (19 western states, western Canada, and Mexico) $10.95 plus $2.50 S&H. Each of the 8 Regional Editions are $5.50 plus $2.50 S&H.

•128• The *Trailer Life Campground, RV Park & Services Directory* covers campgrounds, RV service centers and tourist attractions in America. The directory provides over 15,000 listings and a special national section which includes a comprehensive road atlas, rules of the road and towing laws for each state along with other information of primary reference value to the RVer. Also includes a guide to more than 4,000 Good Sam Discount locations. See listing #339 for more information on the Good Sam Club. TL Enterprises, 3601 Calle Tecate, Camarillo CA 93012. Phone 805-389-0300. Price: $19.95 plus S&H.

•129• *Wheelers RV Resort & Campground Guide* includes listings for 16,000 publicly and commercially operated parks, resorts and campgrounds in the United States, Canada and Mexico.

The 800 page guide provides camp name, directions, facilities available, and season open. Wheelers Guide, 1310 Jarvis Ave., Elk Grove IL 60007. Phone: 800-323-8899. Price: $12.95 plus $2.50 S&H.

•130• The Christian Camping International / USA (CCI/USA) *Guide Pak* provides a state-by-state listing and description of Christian Camps and conference centers throughout the country. The directories are divided into four regions: Western, Rocky Mountain, Central, and Eastern. CCI/USA, P.O. Box 62189, Colorado Springs CO 80962-2189. Phone: 719-260-9400. Price: $5.95 for one region, $6.95 for two, $7.95 for three, or $8.95 for all four regions. Add $2.00 for S&H.

•131• The *KOA Directory, Road Atlas And Camping Guide* includes complete facilities and services listings for over 70,000 campsites at hundreds of KOA Kampgrounds across America. The guide shows the individual locations both on color atlas-style maps and in detailed locator diagrams. Many of the KOA Kampgrounds also offer *Kamping Kabins* - one or two room log cabins that rent for about $20.00 to $35.00 per night. Locations and cabin sizes are listed in the guide. KOA also offers a *KOA Value Kard* which entitles you to a 10% discount on all daily registration fees. The card is good for a period of two years and can be purchased for $8.00 at any KOA Kampground. KOA Directory, P.O. Box 30162, Billings MT 59107. Phone: 406-248-7444. Price: Available free of charge at any KOA Kampground or you may send $3.00 to cover S&H.

•132• *Guide To Free Campgrounds* provides campers with the locations of 5,500 U.S. campgrounds where no overnight fees are charged. The 434 page guide lists locations alphabetically by state and city, providing detailed directions to each campground as well as information about facilities and activities available. Cottage Publications Inc., 24396 Pleasant View Dr., Elkhart IN 46517. Phone: 219-293-7553. Price: $16.95 plus $2.95 S&H.

•133• *Save-A-Buck Camping* lists thousands of campsites where overnight fees of $4 and under are charged. Contains never-before-listed public fishing lakes where camping is available, hunting camps, wildlife area camps, fishing camps, utility company property campsites, off-season camps, fairground sites and boondock camps. Cottage Publications Inc., 24396 Pleasant View Dr., Elkhart IN 46517. Phone: 219-293-7553. Price: $14.95 plus $2.95 S&H.

•134• The *Best Holiday Trav-L-Park* directory list about 77 of the best parks across the nation, which have joined together for the purpose of guaranteeing the camping/RVing public the highest quality possible in accommodations. Best Holiday Parks, 1310 Jarvis Avenue, Elk Grove IL 60007. Phone: 800-323-8899. Price: Free directory.

•135• The following list includes *State Campground and RV Park Associations*. You can contact them for a list of campgrounds in their respective state. Most of the directories are available free of charge but some will charge a fee to cover the postage cost.

Alaska Campground Owners Association, c/o McKinley KOA Kampground, P.O. Box 340, Healy AK 99743. Phone: 907-683-2379

Arizona Travel Parks Association, 1130 East Missouri - Suite 530, Phoenix AZ 85014-2717. Phone: 602-230-1126.

California Travel Parks Association, P.O. Box 5648, Auburn CA 95604. Phone: 916-885-1624.

Colorado Association of Campgrounds Cabins & Lodges, 5101 Pennsylvania Avenue, Boulder CO 80303. Phone: 303-499-9343.

Connecticut Campground Owners Association, 14 Rumford St., West Hartford CT 06107. Phone: 203-521-4704

Delaware Campground Owners Association, c/o Seasons Camping Resort, P.O. Box 156, Rehoboth Beach DE 19971-0156. Phone: 302-227-2564.

Florida Association of RV Parks & Campgrounds, 1340 Vickers Drive, Tallahassee FL 32303-3041. Phone: 904-526-7151.

Idaho RV Campgrounds Association, 11101 Fairview Ave., Boise ID 83704. Phone: 208-345-5755.

Illinois Campground Association, P.O. Box 7471, Springfield IL 62791. Phone: 217-546-2794.

Recreation Vehicle Indiana Council, 3210 Rand Road, Indianapolis IN 46241. Phone: 317-247-6258.

Iowa Association of Campground Owners, c/o Timberline Best Holiday Trav-L-Park, 3165 Ashworth Rd., Waukee IA 50263. Phone: 515-987-1714.

Kansas Campground Association, c/o Malm's Smoky Valley Plazza, Box 175, Lindsborg KS 67456. Phone: 913-227-2932.

Campground Owners of Kentucky, Pioneer Playhouse, Rt. 2, Box 12, Danville KY 40422. Phone: 606-236-2747.

Louisiana Campground Owners Association, P.O. Box 4003, Baton Rouge LA 70821. Phone: 504-346-1857.

Maine Campground Owners Association, 655 Main St., Lewiston ME 04240. Phone: 207-782-5874.

Maryland Association of Campgrounds, 9800 Cherry Hill Road, College Park MD 20740-1210. Phone: 301-937-7116.

Massachusetts Association of Campground Owners, RR 1 - Box 3040, Kennebunk ME 04043-0998. Phone: 207-985-4864.

Michigan Association of Private Campground Owners, P.O. Box 68, Williamsburg MI 49690-0068. Phone: 616-267-5089.

Minnesota Association of Campground Operators, 1000 E. 146th Street - Suite 121, Burnsville MN 55337. Phone: 612-432-2228.

Misissippi Campground Owners Association, c/o Biloxi Beach Campground, 1816 Beach Blvd., Biloxi MS 39531. Phone: 601-432-2755.

Missouri Association of RV Parks & Campgrounds, 3020 South National - Suite 149, Springfield MO 65804. Phone: 314-564-2551.

Montana Campground Owners Association, c/o El-Mar KOA, 3695 Tina Avenue, Missoula MT 59801. Phone: 406-549-0881.

Nebraska Association of Private Campgrounds, c/o Fort McPherson Campground, RR. Box 142, Maxwell NE 69151. Phone: 308-582-4320.

New Hampshire Campground Owners Association, P.O. Box 141, Twin Mountain NH 03595. Phone: 603-846-5511.

New Jersey Campground Owners Association, 29 Cook's Beach Road, Cape May Court House NJ 08210. Phone: 609-465-8444.

Campground Owners of New York, P.O. Box 497, Dansville NY 14437. Phone: 716-335-2710.

North Carolina Campground Owners Association, 1002 Vandora Springs Road - Suite 101, Garner NC 27529. Phone: 919-779-5709.

Ohio Campground Owners Association, 3386 Snoufer Road - Suite B, Columbus OH 43235. Phone: 614-764-0279.

Oklahoma Association of RV Parks & Campgrounds, c/o MarVal Trout Campground, Rt. 1 - Box 314M, Gore OK 74435. Phone: 918-489-2295.

Oregon Lodging Association, 12724 SE Stark St., Portland OR 97233. Phone: 503-255-5135.

Pennsylvania Campground Owners Association, P.O. Box 5, New Tripoli PA 18066. Phone: 610-767-5026.

Rhode Island Campground Owners Association, Box 141, Hope Valley RI 02832.

South Carolina Campground Owners Association, c/o Ocean Lakes Campground, 6001 South Kings Highway, Myrtle Beach SC 29575. Phone: 803-238-5636.

South Dakota Campground Owners Association, P.O. Box 620, Black Hawk SD 57718-0620. Phone: 605-787-6836.

Tennessee Association of Campground Owners, c/o Little River Village Campground, 8533 State Hwy. 73, Townsend TN 37882. Phone: 615-448-2241.

Texas Association of Campground Owners, P.O. Box 14055, Austin TX 78761. Phone: 512-459-8226.

Utah Campground Owners Association, c/o Temple View RV Resort, 975 South Main, St. George UT 84770. Phone: 801-673-8400.

Vermont Association of Private Campground Owners, c/o Homestead Campground, RD 3 - Box 3454, Milton VT 05488. Phone: 802-524-2356.

Virginia Campground Association, 2101 Libbie Avenue, Richmond VA 23230-2621. Phone: 804-288-3065.

Washington Association of RV Parks & Campgrounds, c/o Minerva Beach Campground, 23215 76th West, Edmonds WA 98026. Phone: 206-283-5210.

West Virginia Recreational Vehicle Association, 205 First Avenue, Nitro WV 25143. Phone: 304-727-7431.

Wisconsin Association of Campground Owners, c/o Bass Lake Campground, N 1497 Southern Road, Lyndon Station WI 53944. Phone: 715-839-9226.

Wyoming Campground Association, c/o Foothills Motel & Campground, P.O. Box 174, Dayton WY 82836. Phone: 307-655-2547.

LODGING SPECIALITY

•136• *Farm, Ranch & Country Vacations* guides vacationers to rural destinations. The rural hosts provide guests the chance to go on hayrides, help with the harvest, try milking a cow, fish mountain streams, learn to horseback ride, and take in the local rodeos, fairs and auctions. Guests also enjoy relaxing at the pool, rocking on the porch, and kicking up their heels at a square dance. The 224 page book describes about 400 rural hideaways with information on who to contact, how to get there, the rates, activities, season open and how many guests can be accommodated. Adventure Guides Inc., 7550 E. McDonald Drive-Suite M, Scottsdale AZ 85250. Phone: 800-252-7899. Price: $19.00 postpaid.

•137• *The Dude Ranchers Magazine / Directory* provides descriptive listings of the 111 members of The Dude Ranchers' Association. Includes ranches located primarily in the Rocky Mountain West with a few in other Western States. The 32 page directory provides information on ranch name, address, season, description of area and facilities, activities, type of food and meals, and rates. The Dude Ranchers' Association, P.O. Box R471, Laporte CO 80535. Phone: 303-223-8440. Price: $5.00 postpaid.

•138• *Ranch Vacations: The Complete Guide to Guest and Resort, Fly-Fishing, and Cross-Country Skiing Ranches* contains more than 200 ranch listings. The 516 page guide includes information on accommodations, location, phone, activities, rates, reservations, dining, and nearby attractions. John Muir Publications, P.O. Box 613, Santa Fe NM 87504. Phone: 505-982-4078. Price: $19.95 plus S&H.

•139• The *Cabin Guide to Wilderness Lodging* lists over 500 cabins located in national and state forests, preserves, and other wildlife areas. The 260 page guide provides a description of the facilities and services, location, phone number, and more. Hammond Publishing, 1500 E. Tropicana Avenue-Suite 110, Las Vegas NV 89119. Phone: 904-378-8780. Price: $14.95 plus S&H.

OUTDOOR RECREATION
GENERAL INTEREST

•140• *Adventure Travel North America* provides specific information for vacationers wanting to arrange guided adventure trips. Information is provided on fly fishing, sea kayaking and trail riding, river rafting, biking, rock climbing, horseback trips, canoeing, covered wagon trips, llama treks, cattle roundups, hiking and wilderness exploring. Also featured in the 288 page book are trips especially for people fifty or over, as well as excursions ideal for families with young children. Adventure Guides, Inc., 7550 E. McDonald Drive Suite M, Scottsdale AZ 85250. Phone: 800-252-7899. Price: $19.00 postpaid.

•141• *Wilderness Press* offers a wide variety of outdoor books and maps for the United States and Baja California. Books to help you explore the backcountry of Yosemite, canoe the lakes and streams of the Boundary Waters Canoe Area, kayak in Baja Mexico, hike the volcanoes of Hawaii, and much more. Wilderness Press, 2440 Bancroft Way, Berkeley CA 94704. Phone: 510-843-8080. Price: Free catalog

•142• The *Backcountry Bookstore* catalog features a large selection of outdoor and travel books, maps, and videos. A few of the outdoor activities covered include backpacking, bicycling, climbing, fly fishing, nature & environment, paddlesports, skiing, travel, and women outdoors. You will also find books on families & children, first aid & safety, fitness & training, food and cooking. Whatever your interest, you are sure to find some helpful books from the 2,800 plus titles they have in-stock. Backcountry Bookstore, P.O. Box 6235, Lynnwood WA 98115. Phone: 206-290-7652. Price: Free catalog.

•143• Brigade's *Action Gear Catalog* is the sourcebook for tried and tested outdoor gear. The 84 page catalog features gear for hunting, adventuring, survival, law enforcement, or just roughing it in the great outdoors. You will also receive with the catalog a coupon good for 10 to 20% off your first order. Brigade Quartermasters, 1025 Cobb International Blvd., Kennesaw GA 30144-4360. Phone: 800-338-4327. Price: Free catalog.

•144• The *Cabela's* catalog offers a large selection of products for the outdoor enthusiast. You can choose from a wide assortment of gear for fishing, hunting, and camping. Cabela's, 812 13th Avenue, Sidney NE 69160. Phone: 308-254-5505. Price: Free catalog.

•145• The *Gander Mountain* catalog offers namebrand gear and equipment for the serious outdoor sportsman. Products include gear for hunting, fishing, boating, and camping as well as clothing. Gander Mountain Inc., P.O. Box 6, Wilmot WI 53192. Phone: 414-862-2331. Price: Free catalog.

•146• *Chevy Outdoors* covers the world of outdoor recreation for the enthusiast. The quarterly issues cover such topics as camping, boating, fishing, backpacking, recreational vehicles and much more. Chevy Outdoors, Aegis Group Publishers, 30400 Van Dyke Avenue, Warren MI 48093-2316. Phone: 313-574-9100. Price: Call for current price.

•147• The *Field & Stream* magazine is published monthly for the outdoor enthusiasts. Features articles on fishing, hunting, camping, boating, conservation and other outdoor pursuits. Also includes new product reviews, vehicles, and regional sections specifically tailored to the outdoorsmen in five geographic regions. Field & Stream, Times Mirror Magazines Inc., 2 Park Avenue, New York NY 10016. Phone: 212-779-5000. Price: $16.00 per year.

•148• *Outdoor Life* is for the active outdoor sports individual. The quarterly magazine covers camping, boating and fishing, hunting, conservation, and other related outdoor activities. Reviews new products such as clothing, boats, trucks, books, and camping equipment. Outdoor Life, Times Mirror Inc., 2 Park Avenue, New York NY 10016. Phone: 212-779-5000. Price: $14.00 per year.

•149• *Outside* covers a wide range of outdoor activities such as running, rock climbing, rafting, skiing, camping and much more. The monthly magazine features personality profiles, equipment evaluations, travel, adventure and news of the outdoor scene. Outside, Mariah Publications, 1165 North Clark Street, Chicago IL 60610. Phone: 312-951-0990. Price: $18.00 per year.

•150• *Sierra* provides information for the individual concerned with the natural world and its preservation. The bimonthly publication features articles on outdoor adventure, energy, wildlife, books, sports, and political reports. Sierra, 730 Polk Street, San Francisco CA 94109-7897. Phone: 415-923-5656. Price: $35.00 per year.

•151• *Sports Afield Magazine* focuses on a variety of outdoor activities for the outdoor sports enthusiast. The monthly publication covers fishing, boating, camping, hunting, outdoor adventure, conservation, personal experiences, and new product reviews. Sports Afield Magazine, The Hearst Corporation, 250 West 55th Street, New York NY 10019. Phone: 212-649-4000. Price: $14.00 per year.

•152• *Treasure Magazine* covers the world of metal detecting and prospecting. The monthly magazine provides information on relic hunting, diving, historical research and more. Treasure Magazine, Double Eagle Publishing, 31970 Yucaipa Blvd., Yucaipa CA 92399. Phone: 714-794-4612. Price: $35.00 per year.

•153• *Trilogy* magazine is devoted to a balance between outdoor recreation and conservation issues. The bimonthly issues focus on outdoor adventures, travel, responsible hunting and fishing and reviews of the latest equipment for the environmentally-conscious sportsman. Trilogy, 310 Old East Vine Street, Lexington KY 40507. Phone: 606-231-8522. Price: $15.00 per year.

•154• The *Wilderness* magazine is for individuals and groups interested in conservation and the protection of the environment. The quarterly issues focus on the preservation of wildlife species and their habitats as well as plants. Wilderness, 900 17th Street NW - 2nd Floor, Washington DC 20006. Phone: 202-833-2300. Price: $30.00 per year. $15.00 per year for students and seniors.

OUTDOOR RECREATION BOATING

Power Boats

For other related information see listings #: 173, 179, and 270.

•155• The *Boat Owners Association of the United States* is the nation's largest organization of recreational boaters with 500,000 members. They provide over 20 services for boater's including yacht charters, travel and cruise planning, an on-the-water towing network, lobbying for boaters rights, a consumer protection bureau, discounts on boating equipment and accessories, group-rate boat insurance, and boat loans. Members receive, 6 times per year, the *BOAT/U.S.-Reports* newsletter that features newly issued navigational publications, book reviews, and consumer news. They also publish the *Boater's Source Directory* which covers government, private, and non-profit groups that offer free services and publications on recreational boating. The Boater's Source Directory is available free of charge. BOAT/U.S. Membership Services, 880 South Pickett St., Alexandria VA 22304. Phone: 800-937-9307. Dues: $17.00 per year.

•156• The *Boating Accessories* catalog from Overton's offers a large selection of high quality products and accessories. Items for all your boating needs including boat seats and covers, safety equipment, electronics, hardware, apparel, boat covers, lubricants, wetsuits, and much more. Overton's, P.O. Box 8228, Greenville NC 27835. Phone: 800-334-6541. Price: Free catalog.

•157• The *E & B Marine Supply* catalog provides a complete selection of accessories for recreational boaters and fishermen. E & B Marine Supply, 201 Meadow Road, Edison NJ 08817. Phone: 908-819-7400. Price: Free catalog.

•158• *Sources of Public Boat Access Information* is a 39 page directory containing listings of pamphlets, brochures, maps, guides or atlases available from state and government agencies, most of it free for the asking, which locates government-owned boat launching ramps, marinas, and other recreational boating facilities throughout the United States. States Organization for Boating Access, P.O. Box 25655, Washington DC 20007. Phone: 202-944-4987. Price: $3.00 postpaid.

•159• The *Marine Buyer's Guide* contains 376 pages of detailed product specifications and discounted prices for over 60,000 products for boating, camping, fishing, RV's and watersports. You will find inflatable boats, rods and reels, extensive electronics, binoculars, solar panels, automotive and marine stereo equipment, 12v appliances, and much more. Defender Industries Inc., P.O. Box 820, New Rochelle NY 10801-0820. Phone: 914-632-3001. Price: Free catalog ($2.00 for postage is appreciated but not required)

•160• The National Marine Manufactures Association (NMMA) has a new publication entitled *Water Watch: What Boaters Can Do To Be Environmentally Friendly*. The booklet covers the choice and correct use of marine sanitation systems, low impact painting, cleaning and maintenance routines, litter control, sensible fueling practices, engine care recommendations, and a ten-point checklist serves as a quick reference to important environmental concerns. NMMA Water Watch, 401 N. Michigan Avenue #1150, Chicago IL 60611. Phone: 312-836-4747. Price: Free.

•161• The *Boating* magazine includes industry news in their monthly publication on powerboat accessories, seamanship, buying and financing, maintenance, racing and cruising, and sportfishing. Boating, Hachette Filipacchi Magazines, 1633 Broadway - 43rd Floor, New York NY 10019. Phone: 212-767-6000. Price: $24.00 per year.

•162• *Boating World* is for those who enjoy powerboats up to 30 feet long. The magazine is published 9 times a year with articles on cruising adventures, watersports, electronics, maintenance, new products, and fishing. Boating World, Trans World Publishing Inc., 2100 Powers Ferry Road, Atlanta GA 30339. Phone: 404-955-5656. Price: $23.00 per year.

•163• The *Hot Boat Magazine* is devoted to those who enjoy speed boats, racing, and the more adventuresome water activities. The monthly issues feature news on prop and jet driven boats, high-performance craft, and related activities. Hot Boat Magazine, 9171 Wilshire Blvd. - #300, Beverly Hills CA 90210. Phone: 310-858-7155. Price: $22.95 per year.

•164• *Houseboat Magazine* is published bimonthly with news and information on all aspects of houseboating. Features reviews of houseboats, travel opportunities, and maintenance. Houseboat Magazine, Harris Publications Inc., 520 Park Avenue, Idaho Falls ID 83402. Phone: 208-524-7000. Price: $17.00 per year.

•165• *Motor Boating & Sailing* is geared towards the owners of powerboats and sailboats. The monthly issues feature articles on technological developments, new products, calendar of events, and general advice on getting the most enjoyment from boating. Motor Boating & Sailing, Hearst Business Publications, 250 West 55th Street, New York NY 10019. Phone: 212-649-3068. Price: $16.00 per year.

•166• *Powerboat* magazine helps fulfill the information needs of individuals involved in powerboating. The monthly issues cover equipment reviews, performance evaluations, new product updates, personality profiles, and technical information. Powerboat, Nordskog Publishing Inc., 15917 Strathern Street, Van Nuys CA 91406. Phone: 818-989-1820. Price: $27.00 per year.

•167• The *Soundings* magazine is published monthly for pleasure boat owners. Regular features include news of business and legislative decisions and the impact on boating. Provides calendar of events, new product reviews, and coverage of national and international boating events. Soundings, 35 Pratt Street, Essex CT 06426. Phone: 203-767-3200. Price: $19.00 per year.

•168• *Trailer Boats* is for the owner and prospective owner of water craft transported by trailer. The monthly publication covers new products, safety, how-to technical features, maintenance, electronics, fishing, camping and travel opportunities. Trailer Boats, Poole Publications Inc., 20700 Belshaw Avenue, Carson CA 90746. Phone: 310-537-6322. Price: $20.00 per year.

•169• *The Water Skier* is published 7 times a year to encourage the safe enjoyment of water skiing. Provides information and news on ski competition, new products, and tips. The Water Skier, American Water Ski Association, 799 Overlook Drive, Winter Haven FL 33884. Phone: 813-324-4341. Price: $20.00 per year.

•170• **Waterski Magazine** is published 10 times a year providing news and information about the sport of water skiing. Waterski Magazine, World Publications Inc., 330 West Canton Avenue, Winter Park FL 32789. Phone: 407-628-4802. Price: $19.00 per year.

Sailboats

For other related information see listing #: 165.

•171• The **Sailboat Buyers Guide** provides over 300 pages of boat and gear information, as well as a complete listing of the names and addresses of manufactures and distributors. The guide features details on hundreds of boats, including photographs, specifications, prices, and manufacturer's commentary. The guide also fully covers sails, rig and hardware, engines, electronic and navigational equipment, apparel and sporting accessories, and dozens of other sailing essentials. Cahners Publishing Company, Sailboat Buyers Guide, P.O. Box 7820, Torrance CA 90504-9220. Phone: 800-362-8433. Price: $4.95 plus $2.00 S&H. (1995 edition available January 1st)

•172• The **JSI Discount Sailing Source** catalog offers a full range of sailboat equipment and supplies. They can also provide expert advice on all aspects of sailing. Johnson Sails Inc., 3000 Gandy Blvd., St. Petersburg FL 33702. Phone: 800-234-3220. Price: $3.00 refundable with first order.

•173• The **West Marine** catalog offers a large selection of sail and powerboat accessories. West Marine, 500 Westridge Dr., Watsonville CA 95076. Phone: 408-728-2700. Price: Free catalog.

•174• The **American Sailor** magazine is published 10 times a year for members of the U.S. Sailing Association. Designed for individuals who are active in the sport of sailing the magazine provides news of the organization, sailing, new products, calendar of events and services of interest to sailors. American Sailor, U.S. Sailing Association, P.O. Box 209, Newport RI 02840. Phone: 401-849-5200. Dues: $35.00 per year, includes the magazine.

•175• The **Cruising World** magazine is published monthly for sailing enthusiasts. Issues include safety tips, sailing experiences, new product reviews, and information on acquiring new skills for safer sailing. Cruising World, New York Times Magazine Group, 5 John Clarke Road, Newport RI 02840. Phone: 401-847-1588. Price: $24.00 per year.

•176• **Sail** magazine is published monthly for devoted sailors. Provides information on boat designs, racing events, technical, book reviews, and other developments in the boating world. Sail, Cahners Publishing Company Inc., 275 Washington Street, Newton MA 02158. Phone: 617-964-3030. Price: $19.00 per year.

•177• **Sailing** magazine is published monthly for experienced sailors. Issues feature technical information and news on gear, sailboats, racing, cruising, and tips to help you improve your sailing

performance. Sailing, Port Publications Inc.,125 East Main Street, Port Washington WI 53074. Phone: 414-284-3494. Price: $25.00 per year.

•178• **Sailing World** provides information for the pleasure sailor interested in performance craft and racing. The monthly issues feature news of racing events, personality profiles, equipment evaluations, techniques, and new products. Sailing World, New York Times Magazine Group, 5 John Clarke Road, Newport RI 02840. Phone: 401-847-1588. Price: $24.00 per year.

•179• The **Yachting** magazine is written for the pleasure boat enthusiasts. The monthly issues feature articles for both the sail and power boat owner. Provides information on boating events, new products and equipment, clothing, and other related news. Yachting, Times Mirror Magazines Inc., 2 Park Avenue, New York NY 10016. Phone: 212-779-5000. Price: $20.00 per year.

Canoes / Kayaks / Rafts

For other related information see listing #: 282.

•180• The **National Organization for River Sports** (NORS) caters to individuals interested in white water river sports including kayaking, rafting, and canoeing. NORS is dedicated to keeping rivers open to the public and to ensuring that access to rivers is available commercially as well as noncommercially. All members receive the *Currents* magazine that informs river enthusiasts about the conservation, access, and regulation challenges, as well as other aspects of the current river running scene. NORS members also receive discounts on everything in the NORS Resource Center which includes virtually every river book, map, and video available, and discounts from river equipment sources and services. NORS, 212 W. Cheyenne Mountain Blvd., Colorado Springs CO 80906. Phone: 719-579-8759. Dues: $15.00 per year.

•181• The **American Whitewater Affiliation** (AWA) promotes whitewater sports and the preservation of whitewater rivers nationwide. The AWA stays on top of all the latest trends and runs and passes the information along to the members. All members receive the bimonthly *American Whitewater* magazine which provides the latest news in safety equipment and rescue technique, whitewater expeditions, and news of the organization. American Whitewater Affiliation, P.O. Box 85, Phoenicia NY 12464. Phone: 914-688-5569. Price: $20.00 for individuals or $30.00 for family/household.

•182• The **We-no-nah Canoe** catalog is for those who know and love canoeing. The catalog features a complete line of fiberglass and kevlar canoes and a selection of accessories relating to canoes and canoeing. We-no-nah Canoe Inc., P.O. Box 247, Winona MN 55987. Phone: 507-454-5430. Price: Free catalog.

•183• The **Northwest River Supplies** catalog offers equipment and supplies for the paddle sports enthusiasts. Includes accessories, hardware, and literature for rafts, kayaks, and canoes. Northwest River Supplies, P.O. Box 9186, Moscow ID 83843. Phone: 208-882-2383. Price: $2.00 for S&H.

•184• *Boundary Waters Catalog* offers a complete selection of essentials for the canoeist. Includes books, tripping gear, maps, canoes and accessories, clothing, and information for Boundary Waters canoeing. Piragis Northwoods Co., 105 North Central Avenue, Ely MN 55731. Phone: 218-365-6745. Price: Free catalog.

•185• The *American Rowing* bimonthly magazine provides information and news on all aspects of the sport of rowing. Includes coverage of competition, recreation, clubs and other related news. American Rowing, 201 South Capitol Avenue - #400, Indianapolis IN 46225. Phone: 317-237-5656. Price: $35.00 per year.

•186• *Canoe* magazine is for enthusiasts of all paddlesports. The bimonthly publication covers canoeing, kayaking, safety, techniques, camping, fishing, new products, equipment profiles, and destinations. Canoe, Canoe America Association, 10526 NE 68th - #3, Kirkland WA 98083. Phone: 206-827-6363. Price: $18.00 per year.

•187• The *Paddler* magazine is for the intermediate to advanced paddler. The bimonthly publication provides news and information on rafting, kayaking, and canoeing including articles on destinations. Paddler, P.O. Box 775450, Steamboat Springs CO 80477. Phone: 303-879-1450. Price: $15.00 per year.

•188• *Sea Kayaker* provides information for the experienced and novice kayaker. The quarterly magazine features articles on safety, techniques, navigation, destinations, history, and the environment. Sea Kayaker, 6327 Seaview Avenue NW, Seattle WA 98107. Phone: 206-789-1326. Price: $13.00 per year.

OUTDOOR RECREATION
FISHING

For other related information see listings #: 159, 217, 223, 270, 278, and 282.

•189• The *Westbank Anglers Fly Fishing* catalog includes fly fishing tackle and accessories for fresh and salt water fishing. Westbank Anglers also offers world-wide travel destinations for fly fishing and operates a retail shop and guide service. Westbank Anglers, 3670 North Moose-Wilson Rd., Teton Village WY 83025. Phone: 307-733-6483. Price: Free catalog.

•190• The *Mepp's Fishing Guide* is a 48 page catalog filled with useful how-to information, including tricks of the trade from some of the finest outdoor writers in the world. It will show you new tactics for trout, bass, walleye, panfish, salmon and much more. Features the entire line-up of more than 45-hundred Mepps spinners and spoons. Mepp's, 626 Center Street, Antigo WI 54409-2496. Phone: 715-623-2382. Price: Free catalog.

•191• The *Orvis Fishing and Outdoor Catalog* offers a complete line of fishing gear and accessories for the serious fisherman. Orvis also operates 12 retail stores across the country. Orvis, P.O. Box 798, Manchester VT 05254-0798. Phone: 800-815-5900. Price: Free catalog.

•192• The *Capt. Harry's Fishing Supply* catalog offers a large selection of saltwater fishing and fly fishing tackle and accessories. Capt. Harry's Fishing Supplies, 100 NE 11th Street, Miami FL 33132. Phone: 305-374-4661. Price: Free catalog.

•193• *Bob Marriott's Flyfishing Store* catalog provides a complete selection of fly fishing and fly tying materials. You will also find a selection of outdoor clothing and books as well as a full service travel department. Bob Marriott's Flyfishing Store, 2700 West Orangethorpe, Fullerton CA 92633. Phone: 714-525-1827. Price: $3.00 a copy.

•194• The *Fly Shop* catalog offers one of the largest selections of gear including rods, reels, travel cases, tackle boxes, boots, clothing, and other related accessories as well as travel packages. Fly Shop, 4140 Churn Creek Road, Redding CA 96002. Phone: 916-222-3555. Price: Free catalog.

•195• The *American Angler* contains fly fishing information for the recreational angler. The bimonthly magazine includes how-to information and how-to reports. American Angler, Abenaki Publishers Inc., P.O. Box 4100, Bennington VT 05201. Phone: 802-447-1518. Price: $20.00 per year.

•196• *Angling America Magazine* features articles on freshwater fishing in America. The bimonthly publication covers bass, walleye, crappie, and bluegill. Angling America Magazine, P.O. Box 961, Madison IN 47250. Phone: 812-273-1612. Price: $13.00 per year.

•197• The *American Bass News* is the official publication of the American Bass Association. The bimonthly magazine covers tournament news, events, and association news. American Bass News, American Bass Association Inc., 2810 Trotters Trail, Wetumpka AL 36092. Phone: 205-567-6035. Price: Call for more information and dues on the association.

•198• *B.A.S.S. Times* is published monthly for the beginner as well as the expert bass angler. Covers new product reviews, tournament coverage, tips and tricks, and interviews with expert fishermen. B.A.S.S. Times, B.A.S.S. Publications, 5845 Carmichael Road, Montgomery AL 36117. Phone: 205-272-9530. Price: $12.00 per year.

•199• *Bassin* magazine is published 8 times a year and provides the sport fisherman with information to help enhance the enjoyment of the sport. Covers equipment, travel books, tips and technique. Bassin, Natcom Inc., 15115 South 76th E. Avenue, Bixby OK 74008. Phone: 918-366-4441. Price: $24.00 per year.

•200• The *Bassmaster Magazine* is for the beginner or expert freshwater bass fisherman. Published 10 times a year the articles feature advice from the pros, how-to and where-to, boats, motors, tournament reports, new product reviews, and accessories. Bassmaster Magazine, B.A.S.S. Publications, P.O. Box 17900, Montgomery AL 36141. Phone: 205-272-9530. Price: $15.00 per year.

•201• The *Fishing & Hunting News* provides information for the outdoor enthusiast on the latest hunting and fishing news. The biweekly magazine covers equipment selection, tips to improve your hunting and fishing technique, new products, and news on trade shows and events. Fishing & Hunting News, Outdoor

Empire Publishing Inc., 511 Eastlake Avenue East, Seattle WA 98109. Phone: 206-624-3845. Price: $50.00 per year

•202• *Fishing Facts* magazine is published 7 times a year for the avid fisherman. Issues include news on methods and techniques, calendar of events, new products, and step-by-step lessons. Fishing Facts, Quad Graphics, 312 East Buffalo, Milwaukee WI 53202. Phone: 414-273-1101. Price: $15.00 per year.

•203• *Fishing World* provides the beginner and expert fisherman with news on the best places to fish. The magazine is published bimonthly with coverage of tackle ideas, how-to information, and reviews of fishing literature. Fishing World, Allsport Publishing Co., 51 Atlantic Avenue, Floral Park NY 11001. Phone: 516-352-9700. Price: $12.00 per year.

•204• *Fly Fisherman Magazine* is for anglers who primarily fish with a fly rod. The bimonthly issues feature articles on where to go for both fresh and salt-water fishing, new products, rod making, fly tying and other news of interest to the fly fisherman. Fly Fisherman Magazine, Cowles Magazines, 6405 Flank Drive, Harrisburg PA 17112. Phone: 717-657-9555. Price: $21.00 per year.

•205• *Fly Rod & Reel* is a bimonthly magazine geared towards the fly fisherman. Issues provide in-depth articles on travel, new products, conservation, fly fishing how-to and related news on the sport of fly fishing. Fly Rod & Reel, Down East Enterprise Inc., P.O. Box 370, Camden ME 04843. Phone: 207-594-9544. Price: $15.00 per year.

•206• The *North American Fisherman* is for all fishing enthusiasts. The bimonthly magazine covers both fresh and salt-water fishing with tips on technique, new products and equipment, and fishing destinations. North American Fisherman, North American Fishing Club, 12301 Whitewater Drive - Suite 260, Minnetonka MN 55343. Phone: 612-936-0555. Price: $18.00 per year.

•207• *Salt Water Sportsman* caters to the devoted salt water fisherman. The monthly issues feature fishing spots, boating equipment, technology updates, fishing news and forecasts. Salt Water Sportsman, Times Mirror Magazines, 280 Summer Street, Boston MA 02210. Phone: 617-439-9977. Price: $20.00 per year.

•208• The *Sport Fishing* magazine is published 9 times a year for the offshore fishing enthusiasts. Each issue covers how-to articles, new products, boating tips, travel and entertainment news. Sport Fishing, World Publications Inc., 330 West Canton, Winter Park FL 32789. Phone: 407-628-4802. Price: $15.00 per year.

•209• *The In-Fisherman* is published 7 times a year for freshwater anglers at all experience levels. Covers fishing hot spots, best time to fish, and reviews of great fishing lakes. The In-Fisherman, 2 In-Fisherman Drive, Brainerd MN 56401. Phone: 218-829-1648. Price: $16.00 per year.

•210• *Trout* magazine is the official publication of Trout Unlimited. The quarterly issues cover trout, salmon and steelhead fishing tips and techniques, famous streams, and conservation issues. Trout, Trout Unlimited Inc., 800 Follin Lane SE - Suite 250, Vienna VA 22180. Phone: 703-281-1100. Price: $25.00 a year for membership.

OUTDOOR RECREATION
HUNTING

For other related information see listings #: 201, and 270.

•211• The *North American Hunting Club* promotes the enjoyment of bird and game animal hunting. Their bimonthly publication *Keeping Track* keeps members updated on club news, activities and programs, calendar of events, and reports on hunting techniques and equipment. North American Hunting Club, P.O. Box 3401, Minnetonka MN 55343. Phone: 612-936-9333. Dues: $12.00 per year.

•212• The *Directory of Hunting Resorts* lists about 350 member hunting preserves open to the public. Each listing includes the name of preserve, address, phone number, season, license requirements, and species of game available. North American Gamebird Association, c/o Walter S. Walker, P.O. Box 2105, Cayce-West Columbia SC 29171. Phone: 803-796-8163. Price: $2.00 postpaid.

•213• The National Shooting Sports Foundation (NSSF) *Directory of Public Shooting Ranges* provides a nationwide listing of shooting facilities open to the public. The directory lists more than 1,000 ranges, on a state-by-state basis, that are open to the general public or have memberships available. The directory is a valuable reference guide for traveling shooters. A series of 20 universal symbols illustrate the kinds of shooting facilities available at each club, indicates special services such as handicapped access and clubhouse facilities, directions to clubs and phone numbers. NSSF, 11 Mile Hill Road, Newton CT 06470-2359. Phone: 203-426-1320. Price: $2.00 postpaid.

•214• *Fox Ridge Outfitters* specializes in unique, quality items for the outdoorsman and outdoorswoman. They offer outdoor apparel, hunting and shooting accessories, knives and camping related tools, survival equipment, books, gift items, and firearms related accessories. Shop by mail or at their retail store in Rochester. Fox Ridge Outfitters Inc., 400 N. Main St., Rochester NH 03867. Phone: 800-243-4570. Price: Free catalog

•215• The *Wing Supply* catalog offers quality equipment for the hard core hunter at discount prices. The 36 page catalog features a large selection of game calls and accessories, treestands, decoys, boots, and a large selection of Camo clothing. Wing Supply is a department of "Uncle Lee's" store located at highway 62 east in Greenville, Kentucky and you are welcome to stop by when in the area. Fauntleroy Supply Inc., P.O. Box 367, Greenville KY 42345. Phone: 800-388-9464. Price: Free catalog.

•216• The *Orvis Hunting* catalog is for the serious hunter. The 80 page catalog features a large selection of hunting gear and accessories. Orvis also operates 12 retail stores across the country. Orvis, P.O. Box 798, Manchester VT 05254-0798. Phone: 800-815-5900. Price: Free catalog.

•217• The *Dunn's* Catalog specializes in top quality merchandise for the hunter and fisherman. Products include clothing, boots and waders, guns, videos and books, and other related gear for the hunting and fishing sportsman. They also provide a special service for scheduling outdoor adventure hunting. Dunn's Inc., 1

Madison Avenue, Grand Junction TN 38039. Phone: 901-764-6503. Price: Free catalog.

•218• The *American Hunter* is the monthly magazine of the National Rifle Association for the sport hunter. Issues include articles on technique, sportsmanship, safety, equipment, and legislative news of the association. American Hunter, National Rifle Association, 470 Spring Park Place - Suite 1000, Herndon VA 22070. Phone: 703-481-3340. Price: $25.00 per year.

•219• *Bowhunter* is a bimonthly magazine providing news and information for the bowhunter. Covers seasonal hunting forecasts, hunting and survival tips. Bowhunter, Cowles Magazines, P.O. Box 8200, Harrisburg PA 17112. Phone: 717-657-9555. Price: $24.00 per year.

•220• The *Bowhunting World* magazine is published 8 times a year with information for the bowhunter and recreational archer. Provides articles on hunting equipment, target archery, and bowfishing. Bowhunting World, Ehlert Publishing Group Inc., 601 Lakeshore Parkway - Suite 600, Minnetonka MN 55305. Phone: 612-476-2200. Price: $20.00 per year.

•221• *Buckmaster Whitetail Magazine* is for avid hunters of whitetail deer. The bimonthly publication covers new products, equipment, safety procedures, regulations, and tips on technique. Buckmaster Whitetail Magazine, 1020 Monticello Court, Montgomery AL 36117. Phone: 205-271-3337. Price: $20.00 per year.

•222• *Deer & Deer Hunting* provides hunters with information on hunting white-tailed deer. Published 8 times a year, articles focus on hunting ethics, deer history, techniques, destinations and instructions on dressing the deer. Deer & Deer Hunting, Krause Publications Inc., 700 East State Street, Iola WI 54945. Phone:715-445-2214. Price: $18.00 per year.

•223• The *Fur-Fish-Game* magazine provides the amateur and expert outdoorsman with news and information on hunting, fishing, trapping, and camping. The monthly issues cover the United States and Canada with tips on improving technique and skill. Fur-Fish-Game, Harding Publishing Co., 2878 East Main Street, Columbus OH 43209. Phone: 614-231-9585. Price: $16.00 per year.

•224• *Gun World* covers all phases of small arms for recreational use. The monthly magazine features new product news, reloading techniques, law enforcement, and various other gun related news. Gun World, Gallant/Charger Publications Inc., 34249 Camino Capistrano, Capistrano Beach CA 92624. Phone: 714-493-2101. Price: $20.00 per year.

•225• The *North American Whitetail* magazine is for the serious deer hunting enthusiast. Published 8 times a year, the articles cover where to hunt, the best time, technique and tips, and general news on deer management and their biology. North American Whitetail, Game & Fish Publications Inc., 2250 Newmarket Parkway - Suite 110, Marietta GA 30067. Phone: 404-953-9222. Price: $15.00 per year.

•226• *Petersen's Hunting* is a monthly magazine devoted exclusively to the sport of recreational hunting. Provides news and information on gear, new products, guns, gun dogs, plus other hunting related information. Petersen's Hunting, Petersen Publishing Co., 6420 Wilshire Blvd., Los Angeles CA 90048. Phone: 213-782-2184. Price: $20.00 per year.

OUTDOOR RECREATION
SKIING

For other related information see listing #: 246.

•227• The *White Book of Ski Areas* contains information on ski area facilities, statistics, travel, and services available at all ski areas in the United States and most of those in Canada. Provides name of ski area, location, snow condition phone number, season and rates, lodging availability and other recreational facilities in the vicinity. Inter-Ski Services Inc., P.O. Box 9595, Washington DC 20016. Phone: 202-342-0886. Price: $16.95 plus shipping.

•228• *The Best of Cross Country Skiing* lists hundreds of ski areas across the United States. The 16 page guide provides ski area name, address, phone, description of facilities, and services like lessons, rentals, lodging, and food service. Cross Country Ski Areas Association, 259 Bolton Road, Winchester NH 03470. Phone: 603-239-4341. Price: $3.00 postpaid.

•229• *Skiing With Children* provides information on approximately 85 ski resorts in the United States and Canada and is devoted to helping families plan successful family ski vacations. Includes all the information one needs to know before hitting the slopes. All the hard-to-find facts on infant nurseries and baby-sitting to teenage ski programs, how to get there, where to stay, plus things to do other than ski. TWYCH, Travel With Your Children, 45 West 18th Street, 7th Floor Tower, New York NY 10011. Phone: 212-206-0688. Price: $29.00 postpaid.

•230• The *Ski & Snowboard Tuning Tools* catalog will show you how to tune your skies or snowboard at home with the tools, wax, and helpful tips offered in the fully-illustrated catalog. The Third Hand, P.O. Box 212, Mt. Shasta CA 96067. Phone: 916-926-2600. Price: Free catalog.

•231• The *Cross Country Skier* magazine enables the reader to receive more enjoyment from the sport. The bimonthly issues include information and reviews of skiing spots, clothing and equipment as well as coverage on technique. Cross Country Skier, Collins Chase Publications Inc., 1823 Fremont Avenue South, Minneapolis MN 55403. Phone: 612-377-0312. Price: $15.00 per year.

•232• *Powder* magazine is written for the intermediate to advanced skiing enthusiast. The seven issues per year provide coverage of the whole United States with feature stories on ski resorts, equipment, and skiing techniques. Powder, Surfer Publications Inc., P.O. Box 1028, Dana Point CA 92629. Phone: 714-496-5922. Price: $16.00 per year.

•233• *Ski America* is for all skiers from the beginner to the advanced. The quarterly magazine provides ski resort reviews, travel features, ski personality profiles, equipment buyers guide, and calendar of events for national and international skiing events.

Ski America, P.O. Box 1140, Pittsfield MA 01202. Phone: 413-443-9200. Price: $2.00 per copy.

•234• *Ski Magazine* is published 8 times a year and provides information for skiers in every stage of expertise. Covers equipment and technique, travel, clothing, downhill competition and features on the ski life-style. Ski Magazine, Times Mirror Magazines Inc., 2 Park Avenue, New York NY 10016. Phone: 212-779-5000. Price: $12.00 per year.

•235• *Skiing Magazine* is published 7 times a year for the active skier determined to learn everything about the sport. Regular features include in-depth reporting on equipment, ski instruction, fashion, and travel. Also reports on the world's best ski areas. Skiing Magazine, Times Mirror Magazines, 2 Park Avenue, New York NY 10016. Phone: 212-779-5100. Price: $12.00 per year.

•236• *Snow Country* provides year-round coverage on the ski lifestyle. The monthly magazine provides news on the sport of skiing as well as mountain living. Snow Country, New York Times Inc., 5520 Park Avenue, Trumbull CT 06611. Phone: 203-373-7000. Price: $15.00 per year.

•237• *Snow Goer* serves the super active snowmobiler. The quarterly publication provides in-depth articles on machines, clothing, aftermarket products and performance items. Snow Goer, Ehlert Publishing Group, 601 Lakeshore Parkway - Suite 600, Minnetonka MN 55305. Phone: 612-476-2200. Price: $12.00 per year.

•238• *Snowmobile* is published 4 times a year during the winter for active snowmobilers. The issues cover all aspects of recreational snowmobiling with articles on trails, vacation hotspots, new machines and equipment, 4 x 4 trucks, and calendar of events. Snowmobile, Ehlert Publishing Group Inc., 601 Lakeshore Parkway - Suite 600, Minnetonka MN 55305. Phone: 612-476-8065. Price: $8.00 per year.

OUTDOOR RECREATION
HIKING-BACKPACKING-WALKING

For other related information see listings #: 246, 270, 271, 272, 278, and 282.

•239• The *American Hiking Society* (AHS) is dedicated to protecting the interest of hikers and preserving America's trails. The AHS maintains a public information service to provide hikers and other trail users with facts regarding facilities, organizations, and how to make the best use of trails while protecting the environment. All members receive the *American Hiker Magazine* and the *American Hiker Newsletter* both published quarterly. The two publications keep you informed on the issues and events around the country of interest to hikers and other trail users. American Hiking Society, P.O. Box 20160, Washington DC 20041-2160. Phone: 703-255-9304. Dues: Individual $25.00, family $35.00 plus several other options. You may also request a sample issue of the magazine and additional information on the club.

•240• The *Hiking Holidays* catalog offers guided inn-to-inn walking and hiking vacations in the United States, Canada, and Europe. Tour prices include lodging, breakfasts, lunches, taxes, guide services and accompanying support van. The catalog provides all the specifics for each tour. Hiking Holidays, P.O. Box 750, Bristol VT 05443. Phone: 802-453-4816. Price: Free catalog.

•241• The *500 Great Rail-Trails* provides information on old segments of abandoned railroad track that has been converted into trails for bicycling, hiking, walking, and other recreational purposes. Entries include the trail name, location and length, surface material and other pertinent information. Living Planet Press, 1400 16th Street NW - Suite300, Washington DC 20036. Phone: 800-888-7747. Price: $9.50 plus S&H.

•242• *Backpacker* magazine is published 9 times a year for the outdoor enthusiast. Articles are devoted to backpacking with emphasis on equipment and services. Provides reviews of new products, destinations, tips on survival techniques, and news of the current market covering wilderness sports activities. The March issue contains the *Buyers Guide* which is a compilation of manufacturer supplied information on what's new and hot for the season covering backpacking, boots, tents, water filters, sleeping bags, pack stoves and related outdoor equipment. Backpacker Magazine, Rodale Press Inc., 33 E. Minor Street, Emmaus PA 18098. Phone: 215-967-8296. Price: $24.00 for a one year subscription or $3.50 for the March Buyers Guide issue.

•243• The *Walking Magazine* is edited for the recreational and fitness walker. The bimonthly publication features news on health, nutrition, food, travel, equipment, and clothing. The Walking Magazine, 9-11 Harcourt Street, Boston MA 02116. Phone: 617-266-3322. Price: $15.00 per year.

OUTDOOR RECREATION
BICYCLING

For other related information see listing #: 241.

•244• The *Adventure Cycling Association* is America's largest recreational cycling association serving bicycle tourists, fitness riders, and mountain bikers. Adventure Cycling has developed a National Bicycle Route Network encompassing 20,000 miles of North American back roads and mountain bike trails, which are depicted on high-quality route maps. Members receive *Adventure Cyclist* magazine and the annually revised *Cyclist's Yellow Pages*, the most comprehensive cycling resource guide available. Members also qualify for discounts on maps and cycling gear through the Adventure Cycling catalog. Adventure Cycling Association, P.O. Box 8308, Missoula MT 59807. Phone: 406-721-1776. Dues: $25.00 per year.

•245• The *League of American Bicyclists* is an association for all bicyclists including recreational riders, tourists, commuters, racers and bicycle clubs. They sponsor national and regional rallies to bring members together from all over the United States. The rallies include daily workshops that provide information on safety, advocacy, cycling techniques, and more. All members also receive the *Bicycle USA* magazine eight times a year. Each issue covers riding techniques, touring schedules, legislation, and calendar of events. Members also receive the *TourFinder* and *Cyclist's Almanac* which includes information on affiliated bicycle clubs and bicycling contacts for all 50 states. Includes information on sources of maps, tour guides, films, periodicals on cycling, cycling events, and over 100 cycling instructors. The *Hospitality Homes* network allows members to stay in the homes of more than 1,600 fellow members, free of charge, while touring. League of American Bicyclists, 190 West Ostend Street - #120, Baltimore MD 21230-3755. Phone: 410-539-3399. Dues: $25.00 per year.

•246• The ***Backroads*** catalog offers distinctive touring and mountain bike vacations for all ability levels to 67 destinations in 24 states and provinces in 20 countries around the world. The trips follow some of the most scenic routes in the country. Each Backroads vacation is unique in that guest travel from one place to another under their own power and a Backroads van supports each trip, carrying luggage and supplies. Traveler's stay in the finest accommodations available and dine on freshly prepared, regional fare. Backroads also offers guided walking & hiking, running, and cross-country skiing vacations. Backroads, 1516 5th Street, Berkeley CA 94710-1740. Phone: 800-462-2848. Price: Free catalogs.

•247• The ***Vermont Bicycle Touring*** catalog features 45 deluxe worldwide bicycling vacations. Tours range from two to seventeen days for beginner, intermediate and advanced level cyclists. Tour prices include lodging, breakfasts, most dinners, services of two VBT leaders, taxes, cycling maps, and a fully-equipped support van. Vermont Bicycle Touring, P.O. Box 711, Bristol VT 05443. Phone: 802-453-4811. Price: Free catalog.

•248• The ***Bicycle Toolz*** catalog offers over 1000 bicycle tools from several manufacturers in their fully illustrated catalog. The Third Hand, P.O. Box 212, Mt. Shasta CA 96067. Phone: 916-926-2600. Price: Free catalog.

•249• The ***Performance Bicycle Catalog*** is for the serious cyclists. Their catalog features a full line of high-end road and mountain bikes along with a large selection of cycling clothing and equipment. Performance Inc., P.O. Box 2741, Chapel Hill NC 27514. Phone: 800-727-2453. Price: Free catalog.

•250• The ***Bike Nashbar*** 80 plus page catalog is a great source of affordable, top quality cycling equipment, apparel, and accessories. Features a complete line of products for the road or mountain cyclist. Bike Nashbar, 4111 Simon Road, Youngstown OH 44512-1323. Phone: 800-NASHBAR. Price: Free catalog.

•251• The ***TourFinder*** directory lists nearly 200 sponsors of bicycle tours. Entries include name of sponsor, address and phone number, price range of tours offered, length of tours in miles per day, total miles per tour, number of days or weeks, level of difficulty, location, accommodations, age limits, and much more. League of American Bicyclists, 190 West Ostend Street - Suite 120, Baltimore MD 21230. Phone: 410-539-3399. Price: $5.00 postpaid or free to members, see listing #245 for more information.

•252• ***Bicycling Magazine*** is published 11 times a year for the bicycling enthusiast. Covers key racing events and new product developments. Each issue also offers ideas for family bicycle vacations, buying & repairing bicycles, equipment reviews, health and fitness tips, and reports of bicycle adventures. Bicycling Magazine, Rodale Press Inc., 33 East Minor Street, Emmaus PA 18098. Phone: 215-967-5171. Price: $20.00 per year.

•253• ***Bicycle Guide*** magazine is published 10 times a year with coverage of cycle-racing, training, travel, equipment and technique. Each issue also provides product reviews, road tests, technology reviews and more for bicycling enthusiasts. Bicycle Guide, Petersen Publishing Co., 1415 Third Street - #303, Santa Monica CA 90401. Phone: 310-394-1321. Price: $18.00 per year.

•254• ***Velo-News*** is published 18 time a year with coverage of national, regional and international bike races, track meets, and other major rides for bicycle riders, coaches, fans and members of the bicycle trade. Each issue also covers technical features, training articles, nutrition and the history of bicycling. Velo-News, Inside Communications, 1830 North 55th Street, Boulder CO 80301. Phone: 303-440-0601. Price: $33.97 per year.

•255• ***Mountain Bike*** is published 11 times a year and covers every aspect of mountain biking for the adventurous. Includes new products, technology and design concepts, riding techniques, destinations, racing, health and fitness. Mountain Bike, Rodale Press, 33 East Minor Street, Emmaus PA 18098. Phone: 215-967-5171. Price: $20.00 per year.

•256• ***Mountain Bike Action*** is a monthly publication covering the off-road bicycle market. Features articles on testing, technical tips, race coverage, and buying tips for the trail rider, commuter, and ATB competitor. Mountain Bike Action, Daisy/Hi-Torque Publishing Co., 10600 Sepulveda Blvd., Mission Hills CA 91345. Phone: 818-365-6831. Price: $19.98 per year..

•257• ***Mountain Biking*** is published 9 times per year for the mountain bike enthusiast. Covers new products, technique, riding tips and more. Mountain Biking, Challenge Publications Inc., 7950 Deering Avenue, Canoga Park CA 91304-5007. Phone: 818-887-0550. Price: $20.00 per year.

OUTDOOR RECREATION
OFF-ROAD

•258• The ***United Four Wheel Drive Association*** promotes legislation beneficial to vehicle recreation and provides education in responsible land use and safe vehicle operation. The association also helps protect our natural resources through conservation practices, encourages Federal, State and Provincial land managing agencies to develop more areas and trails for outdoor use, promotes 4WD activities for all members, and unifies local, regional and state clubs. Members also receive the *United's Voice* newspaper four times a year that updates the club activities. United Four Wheel Drive Association, 4505 W. 700 S., Shelbyville IN 46176. Phone: 800-44-UFWDA. Dues: $20.00 per year.

•259• The ***Blue Ribbon Coalition*** is for individuals and organizations involved in the use of all types of recreational vehicles.

Seeks to preserve access to recreational areas for snowmobiles, motorcycles, mountain bikes, ATVs and other similiar off-road vehicles. Members also receive the *Blue Ribbon* newsletter every month covering motorized recreation and club activities. Blue Ribbon Coalition, P.O. Box 5449, Pocatello ID 83202. Phone: 208-237-1557. Dues: $20.00 per year.

•260• *4 Wheel & Off-Road* magazine is for the connoisseur of four wheel drive vehicles. The monthly publication focuses on off-road events, new products, repair tips, driving techniques and tips. 4 Wheel & Off-Road, Petersen Publishing Co., 6420 Wilshire Blvd. - 11th Floor, Los Angeles CA 90048. Phone: 213-782-2360. Price: $20.00 per year.

•261• The *4 Wheel Drive & Sport Utility* magazine offers information for the automotive enthusiasts who enjoys 4X4 and off-road sports. The monthly publication features technical articles from simple how-to's to detailed analysis with special emphasis on testing new vehicles and accessories. 4 Wheel Drive & Sport Utility, McMullen & Yee Publishing Inc., 774 South Placentia Avenue, Placentia CA 92670. Phone: 714-572-2255. Price: $12.00 per year.

•262• *Dirt Bike* magazine offers the off-road motorcyclist information on major racing events and tips on improving your dirt riding skills. The monthly publication also covers tests of new machines, product evaluations, and technical articles. Dirt Bike, Daisy/Hi-Torque Publishing Company Inc., 10600 Sepulveda Blvd., Mission Hills CA 91345. Phone: 818-365-6831. Price: $18.98 per year.

•263• *Dirt Rider* is published monthly for the off-road motorcycle enthusiast. Each issue features testing and evaluations of equipment and bikes, sportswear, trail tips, and new electronic gear. Dirt Rider, Petersen Publishing Company, 8490 Sunset Blvd., Los Angeles CA 90069. Phone: 310-854-2390. Price: $19.94 per year.

•264• The *Four Wheeler Magazine* features news and information for the four wheel drive and off-road recreational vehicle user. The monthly publication offers technical how-to stories, road tests, competition events, travel destinations, new products, and calendar of off-road events. Four Wheeler Magazine, 6728 Eton Avenue, Canoga Park CA 91303. Phone: 818-992-4777. Price: $18.00 per year.

•265• *On-Dirt Magazine* focuses on news and events for off-road and dirt racing enthusiasts. The monthly publication covers motorcycles, four wheel drives, trucks and coverage of racing and personality profiles. On-Dirt Magazine, Alta Publishing Inc., P.O. Box 6246, Woodland Hills CA 91365. Phone: 818-340-5750. Price: $35.00 per year.

•266• The *Off-Road* magazine is published monthly for the four wheel pickup and sport utility owner. Includes information on competition, new product reviews, technical tips, and news of the industry. Off-Road, Argus Publishers Corp., 12100 Wilshire Blvd. - Suite 250, Los Angeles CA 90025. Phone: 310-820-3601. Price: $15.00 per year.

OUTDOOR RECREATION
CAMPING

For other related information see listings #: 027, 127, 128, 129, 130, 131, 132, 133, 134, 135, 159, 214, 353, and 358.

•267• The *Plan-It • Pack-It • Go: Great Places to Tent • Fun Things to Do* is the only book of its kind which provides tenting families with great places to tent and fun things to do. Includes selected campgrounds welcoming tenters throughout the U.S., Canada, and Mexico. Listings feature complete information about both public and private campgrounds including directions, open/close dates, phone numbers, rates, and complete listings of facilities and recreational opportunities. The alphabetical quick-reference charts are featured at the front of each state along with a map of the state showing location of campgrounds, travel information sources, annual events and more. Fulfillment Department #1950, Woodall Publishing Company, 28167 North Keith Drive - Box 5000, Lake Forest IL 60045-5000. Phone: 800-323-9076. Price: $11.95 plus $2.75 S&H.

•268• *Family Campers And RVers* (FCRV) is for families who enjoy camping and the outdoors. The association promotes family and group camping/RVing, conservation, and campers' rights. Members also receive a 10% discount at more than 2,000 campgrounds, RV service centers and tourist attractions nationwide. Sponsors an annual *Campvention* hosted by a different state or province each year. Assists in establishing local chapters where members meet to exchange information on campsites, equipment, and related issues. Establishes regional information centers to give campers reports on local roads, trails, campsites, and outdoor recreation. All members receive the *Camping Today* magazine, 10 times a year, which keeps members updated on club news and activities, calendar of events, new products, and travel destinations. Family Campers And RVers, 4804 Transit Road - Bldg. 2, Depew NY 14043. Phone: 800-245-9755. Dues: $20.00 per year.

•269• The *Camping Women* association helps develop women's camping abilities and leadership skills. Created for women who like to camp, backpack, hike, canoe, bike, ski, and other outdoor activities. Members receive the *Camping Women Trails* newsletter 10 times a year to keep you informed on the club activities and upcoming events. Camping Women, 7623 Southbreeze Drive, Sacramento CA 95828. Phone: 916-689-9326. Price: Inquire for more information and current club dues.

•270• The *Bass Pro Shops* catalog offers a wide variety of camping and backpacking equipment for campers, fishermen, hunters, and boating enthusiasts. Bass Pro Shops, 1935 South Campbell, Springfield MO 65807. Phone: 800-BASS-PRO. Price: $3.00.

•271• The *Bay Archery* catalog provides equipment and accessories for the camping and backpacking outdoorsman. Bay Archery Sales, 1001 North Johnson Street, Bay City MI 48708. Phone: 517-894-0777. Price: Free catalog.

•272• The *Campmor* catalog offers outdoor clothing, biking, climbing, hiking and backpacking equipment. Campmor, P.O. Box 998, Paramus NJ 07653. Phone: 201-445-5000. Price: Free catalog.

•273• **Coleman Outdoor Products** offers backpacks, dining utensils, camping tools, sleeping bags, and other related outdoor camping products. Coleman Outdoor Products Inc., P.O. Box 2931, Wichita KS 67201. Phone: 800-835-3278. Price: Free Information.

•274• The **Colorado Tent Company** offers a full line of tents and sleeping bags. Colorado Tent Company, 2228 Blake Street, Denver CO 80205. Phone: 303-294-0924. Price: Free catalog.

•275• The **Eastern Mountain Sports** catalog offers a wide selection of outdoor clothing, camping gear and equipment. Eastern Mountain Sports Inc. One Vose Farm Road, Peterborough NH 03458. Phone: 603-924-9571. Price: Free catalog.

•276• The **Flaghouse Camping Equipment** catalog offers a full line of outdoor equipment and accessories. Flaghouse Camping Equipment, 150 Macquesten Parkway, Mt. Vernon NY 10550. Phone: 800-221-5185. Price: Free catalog.

•277• The **Igloo Products** catalog offers a complete line of outdoor cookers and ice chests. Igloo Products Corporation, P.O. Box 19322, Houston TX 77024. Phone: 713-465-2571. Price: Free catalog.

•278• The **L.L. Bean** catalog provides a nice selection of clothing for hiking, camping, fishing, and other outdoor activities. L.L. Bean Inc., Freeport ME 04033. Phone: 800-221-4221. Price: Free catalog.

•279• The **REI Recreational Equipment** catalog offers quality outdoor equipment including clothing, tents, knives, camping foods, rain gear, and other related items. REI Recreational Equipment Company, Sumner WA 98352. Phone: 800-426-4840. Price: Free catalog.

•280• **Sims Stoves** offers folding camp stoves, books, tents, and other related outdoor equipment. Sims Stoves, P.O. Box 21405, Billings MT 59104. Phone: 800-736-5259. Price: Free information.

•281• The **U.S. Cavalry** catalog offers a complete line of camping and outdoor gear and equipment. U.S. Cavalry, 2855 Centennial Avenue, Radcliff KY 40160. Phone: 800-777-7732. Price: $3.00.

•282• The **Wyoming River Raiders** catalog offers gear and equipment for camping, fishing, river expeditions, hiking, and outdoor related books. Wyoming River Raiders, 601 Wyoming Blvd., Casper WY 82609. Phone: 800-247-6068 ; 307-235-8624 in Wyoming. Price: Free catalog.

AUTOMOBILE
ASSOCIATIONS AND CLUBS

•283• The **National Motorists Association** (NMA) is an organization founded to represent and protect the interests of American motorists. NMA is dedicated to protecting the rights of motorists, enhancing personal mobility, implementing rational traffic laws, and improving driver skills and driver courtesy. Members receive many valuable benefits and services including a legal resource kit, attorney referral service, traffic justice program, special alerts about legislation or a regulation being considered, State chapter coordinators, public official directory, electronic bulletin board, and much more. All members also receive the bimonthly *NMA News* newsletter that keeps members informed about motorists issues, and your rights as a driver. When you join NMA you will also receive a copy of the *NMA Motorist's Guide to State and Provincial Traffic Laws*. This book covers traffic laws, insurance requirements, safety mandates, and speed traps in all fifty states and 12 Canadian Provinces. National Motorists Association, 6678 Pertzborn Road, Dane WI 53529. Phone: 608-849-6000. Dues: $29.00 per year.

•284• The following list of **Travel and Auto Clubs** offer a variety of services for the road traveler. Club benefits include emergency road service, tow service, discounts on lodging and car rentals, trip routing service, plus various other benefits available through membership. For more detailed information on each club contact the following:

Allstate Travel Club. Phone: 800-347-8880.

Allstate Motor Club. Phone: 800-255-2582 ext 333.

American Automobile Association. Phone: 800-765-4222.

Amoco Motor Club. Phone: 800-334-3300.

Chevron Travel Club. Phone: 800-222-0585.

Exxon Travel Club. Phone: 800-833-9966.

Mobil Auto Club. Phone: 800-621-5581.

Monoco Motor Club. Phone: 503-998-1068.

Montgomery Ward Motor Club. Phone: 800-621-5151.

Sears Discount Travel Club. Phone: 800-331-0257.

Shell Motor Club. Phone: 800-852-0555.

Sun Travel Club. Phone: 800-562-2238.

Texaco Travel Club. Phone: 800-526-6786.

AUTOMOBILE
BOOKS AND DIRECTORIES

•285• The **NMA Motorist's Guide to State and Provincial Traffic Laws** published by the National Motorists Association covers traffic laws, insurance requirements, safety mandates, and speed traps in all fifty states and 12 Canadian Provinces. National Motorists Association, 6678 Pertzborn Road, Dane WI 53529. Phone: 608-849-6000. Price: $9.95 plus $2.00 S&H. Free to new members of NMA, see listing #283.

•286• The *Edmund's Driver Companion: The A - Z Reference Guide To Be Kept In Your Car* provides comprehensive coverage of more than 300 up-to-date topics about all aspects of driving and automobiles. Designed to help make your driving experiences more enjoyable, economical, and safe, the 368 page book provides instant information and know-how while on the road. Edmund Publications Corp., 300 N. Sepulveda Blvd. - Suite 2050, El Segundo CA 90245. Phone: 310-640-7840. Price: $6.99 plus S&H.

AUTOMOBILE CATALOGS

For other related information see listing #: 310.

•287• The *EWA & Miniature Cars U.S.A* catalog offers a full line of automotive books, videos, and foreign automobile magazines. The 144 page catalog also includes model cars. EWA & Miniature Cars U.S.A., P.O. Box 188, Berkeley Heights NJ 07922. Phone: 908-665-7810. Price: $2.00 for S&H.

•288• The *Classic Motorbooks* catalog offers one of the largest selections of automotive books and videos available. The 120 page catalog is filled with books on racing, restoration, street rods, motorcycles, trucks, tractors, owner's manuals and much more. Classic Motorbooks, P.O. Box 1 / RTAREQ, Osceola WI 54020. Phone: 800-826-6600. Price: $3.00 for S&H.

•289• The *Dragich Discount Auto Literature* 48 page catalog offers a large selection of books and manuals for collectable American cars and trucks. Dragich Discount Auto Literature, 1660 93rd Lane NE, Minneapolis MN 55449. Phone: 800-328-8484. Price: Free catalog.

•290• The *J.C. Whitney Automotive* catalog offers over 65,000 items for all makes, years and models of American and imported vehicles. Includes items for cars, vans, trucks, motorcycles, and recreational vehicles. J.C. Whitney & Co., 1104 S. Wabash Avenue, Chicago IL 60605-2328. Phone: 312-431-6102. Price: Free catalog.

•291• The *Automobile Quarterly* catalog features publications for automobile enthusiasts and collectors. Also available is a collection of select readings on fine automobiles and history as well as listings of merchandise. Automobile Quarterly Publications, P.O. Box 348, Kutztown PA 19530-0348. Phone: 800-523-0236. Price: $3.00 per copy postpaid.

AUTOMOBILE MAGAZINES AND NEWSLETTERS

•292• *Adventure Road* is for everyone interested in travel and motoring for recreational enjoyment. The quarterly magazine covers maintenance tips, sporting events, camping, new products and book reviews, general travel tips, travel ideas and destinations. Adventure Road, M&A Publishing Ltd., 122 East 25th Street - 2nd Floor, New York NY 10010. Phone: 212-673-8930. Price: $15.00 per year.

•293• *Automobile Magazine* is published monthly for the sophisticated young car enthusiast. Focuses on the novelty as well as the tradition of all things automotive. Includes road tests, new product reviews, and travel destinations. Automobile Magazine, K-III Communications, 120 East Liberty, Ann Arbor MI 48104. Phone: 313-994-3500. Price: $18.00 per year.

•294• *AutoWeek* provides weekly news and features for the automotive enthusiasts. Provides coverage of major sporting events, latest automotive designs, nostalgia and collector's cars, travel destinations, and new product information. AutoWeek, Crain Communications Inc., 1400 Woodbridge Ave., Detroit MI 48207. Phone: 313-446-6000. Price: $28.00 per year.

•295• *Car & Driver* provides the latest news and information for automobile enthusiasts. The monthly magazine covers cars, trucks, vans, and accessories. Includes road tests, technical reports, new product and book reviews. Car & Driver, Hachette Filipacchi Magazines, 2002 Hogback Road, Ann Arbor MI 48105. Phone: 313-971-3600. Price: $20.00 per year.

•296• *Motor Trend* contains information on domestic, import and exotic cars. The monthly magazine features new car driving impressions, road tests, racing reports, design and engineering trends, auto repair, new product reviews, and service tips. Motor Trend, Petersen Publishing Co., 6420 Wilshire Blvd., Los Angeles CA 90048. Phone: 213-782-2222. Price: $20.00 per year.

•297• *Motor World* is published quarterly and features advice in basic automobile maintenance with reviews of the trends in the automobile industry. Motor World, Publishing & Business Consultants, 951 South Oxford - Suite 109, Los Angeles CA 90006. Phone: 213-732-3477. Price: $27.00 per year.

•298• *Road & Track* is a monthly magazine featuring news and developments in the automotive field. Topics covered include design, road tests, racing, technical information, profiles of personalities, auto travel, new products, and book reviews. Road & Track, Hachette Filipacchi Magazines, 1499 Monrovia Avenue, Newport Beach CA 92663. Phone: 714-720-5300. Price: $20.00 per year.

MOTORCYCLE ASSOCIATIONS AND CLUBS

For other related information see listing #: 283.

•299• The *American Motorcyclist Association* (AMA) was founded to promote and protect the sport of motorcycling. The AMA sanctions about 1,000 road riding events each year like dual sport events, rallies, poker runs, field meets, and tours. There are also over 3,000 racing events each year including motorcross, enduro, trails and road racing. Some of the other benefits available to members include, AD&D insurance, official road riding and AMA amateur competition rule books, motorcycle transport, form a member club, AMA products, law information, rider education program, theft recovery help, and much more. All members also receive the monthly *American Motorcyclist* magazine that provides news about the latest products and services, tips on technique and safety, features of the best places to tour, calendar of events, and news about all kinds of competition. American Motorcyclist Association, P.O. Box 6114, Westerville OH 43081-6114. Phone: 800-AMA-JOIN. Dues: $29.00 per year.

•300• The *International Brotherhood of Motorcycle Campers* (IBMC) is for families and individuals who enjoy motorcycling and camping. Members sponsor all the campouts, decide the time and place and send in the information so the details can be listed in the member newsletter, *The Campfire Ring.* Anyone who rides and camps is welcome. Members receive the bimonthly newsletter containing reports, stories, experiences and notices of future campouts. The IBMC, P.O. Box 2395, Chandler AZ 85244-2395. Phone: 602-963-6992. Dues: $8.00 per year.

•301• The *American Sport-Touring Rider's Association* (ASTRA) is for the sport-touring enthusiast of all makes and models of motorcycles. ASTRA is dedicated to the enhancement of comfort, convenience, and enjoyment of sport-touring. Membership benefits include tours, prospect cards, 20% discount on ASTRA merchandise / event fees, and motorcycle touring information. All members also receive the ASTRA Newsletter full of tips and ideas, reviews of products, and current club activities. ASTRA, P.O. Box 672051, Marietta GA 30067-0035. Phone: 404-443-2614. Dues: $20.00 per year or write for more free information.

•302• The *Women On Wheels* organization was founded to unite all women motorcyclists - whether they ride their own, are passengers on someone else's, or are future motorcyclists. Member benefits include the annual mileage contest, individual cumulative mileage recognition program, recruitment program, and the annual Women On Wheels International Ride-In, a rally held in July of each year at various locations throughout the United States. All members also receive the *Women On Wheels* bimonthly magazine which is a compilation of stories and articles written by and for the members. It also contains information about new products and happenings throughout the motorcycle industry. Women On Wheels, P.O. Box 081454, Racine WI 53408-1454. Phone: 800-322-1969. Dues: $25.00 per year or send for a free information pack that includes sample magazine, application, and other information.

•303• The *Women In The Wind* association is for women motorcyclists and enthusiasts. Sponsors a summer and winter national rally and meeting each year at various locations. All members also receive the *Shootin' the Breeze* newsletter 9 times per year. The newsletter provides current information on membership activities, news, calendar of events, and features articles on motorcycle safety and maintenance. Women in the Wind, P.O. Box 8392, Toledo OH 43605. Dues: $6.00 per year.

•304• The *Christian Motorcyclists Association* (CMA) is a national organization of motorcyclists representing over 48,000 members. Some activities include motorcycle rallies and tours, motorcycle games, fellowship services, gospel and other singing events. The goal is to promote Christian fellowship among motorcyclists. Members also receive the monthly *CMA Newsletter* which keeps them current on the clubs activities. CMA, P.O. Box 9, Hatfield AR 71945. Phone: 501-389-6196. Dues: Free. Donations accepted

•305• The BAM organization was started for motorcyclists and motorcycling organizations to help reduce the number of motorcycle accidents and fatalities in the U.S. The organization of over 300,000 volunteer members is available to aid motorcyclists with emergency repairs, housing, and transportation. When a member breaks down or needs assistance they call 800-4-BIKERS so another member that is close by can be contacted to help you out. BAM, 5455 Wilshire Blvd. - Suite 1600, Los Angeles CA 90036. Phone: 213-932-1277. Dues: Free.

MOTORCYCLE BOOKS AND DIRECTORIES

For other related information see listings #: 018, and 290.

•306• The *Motorcycle Touring and Travel: A Handbook of Travel by Motorcycle* is the book for anyone interested in travel by motorcycle. Every aspect of planning a trip is covered from picking the right bike and equipment, camping, and safety to just plain having fun. The 128 page guide includes 227 illustrations. Whitehorse Press, 154 West Brookline Street, Boston MA 02118. Phone: 800-531-1133. Price: $24.95 plus S&H.

•307• *A Rider's Guidebook* is a handy little book to make life a little easier for all motorcycle rider's. The 28 page book is filled with practical tips for making motorcycling more fun and enjoyable. Even if you have been riding for 30 years, you'll learn something from this book. Whitehorse Press, 154 West Brookline Street, Boston MA 02118. Phone: 800-531-1133. Price: $4.95 plus S&H.

•308• The *Motorcycle Log Book* allows rider's to recall their riding adventures. The book contains places to record mileage, lodging, fuel and food expenses, names and addresses. You can select from a choice of BMW, Honda Gold Wing, Harley-Davidson, or Kawasaki Voyager for the front cover. Custom orders are also available for clubs. R.N. Headley, P.O. Box 8286, Reno NV 89507. Price: $5.95 plus $1.20 S&H.

•309• *Dealernews - Buyers Guide & Statistical Issue* is an annual publication (December) that lists manufacturers, distributors, and service organizations serving the motorcycle, ATV, and watercraft industry. Entries include company name, address, phone number, brand names of products, and more. Advanstar Communications Inc., 7500 Old Oak Blvd., Cleveland OH 44130. Phone: 800-225-4569. Price: $25.00 plus $5.00 S&H.

MOTORCYCLE CATALOGS

For other related information see listings #: 288, and 290.

•310• **Whitehorse Press** offers a complete selection of motorcycling books, videos, and accessories in their free catalog. You will find hundreds of titles to choose from covering every aspect of motorcycling. Includes general interest, history, maintenance & technical, maps & atlases, performance, racing, safety, restoration, touring, travel guides, and titles by make of bike. Though geared toward the motorcyclist, automobile and RV travelers will find several travel titles of interest including maps & atlases. A must have catalog for all road traveler's. Whitehourse Press, 154 West Brookline St., Boston MA 02118. Phone: 800-531-1133. Price: Free catalog.

•311• The **Rider Wearhouse** catalog features top quality apparel and accessories for the motorcycle riding enthusiast. The 80 page catalog offers protective clothing, electronics, gloves, boots, helmets, tents, storage bags, and other riding associated products. They are one of the world's leading companies in advanced technology rider's clothing and related accessories. Rider Wearhouse, Eight South 18th Avenue West, Duluth MN 55806. Phone: 218-722-1927. Price: Free catalog.

•312• The **White Brothers Street Catalog** offers over 100 pages of products for sport bikes, cruisers, and touring motorcycles. Features performance oriented products designed to improve the performance, handling, serviceability, and appearance of your machine. They also offer a limited line of casual wear, special tools, and transporting products. White Brothers, 24845 Corbit Place, Yorba Linda CA 92687. Phone: 714-692-3404. Price: $4.00 postpaid.

•313• The **White Brothers Harley-Davidson Catalog** offers a wide selection of products for the Harley-Davidson rider. The 116 page catalog features products to improve the performance, handling, serviceability, and appearance of your bike. They also offer a limited line of casual wear, special tools, and transporting products. White Brothers, 24845 Corbit Place, Yorba Linda CA 92687. Phone: 714-692-3404. Price: $4.00 postpaid.

•314• The **Motoport USA** 40 page catalog offers a full line of leather clothing, riding suits, helmets, and bike accessories. Motoport USA, 6110 Yarrow Drive, Carlsbad CA 92009. Phone: 800-777-6499. Price: Free catalog.

•315• The **Thurlow Leather World** 20 page catalog offers deerskin riding gloves and garments. Thurlow offers ready-made wear or will custom handcraft and individually tailor to your measurements providing you with the perfect fit. Thurlow Leather World, 4807 Mercury Street, San Diego CA 92111. Phone: 619-279-9004. Price: $3.00 postpaid.

•316• The **Star Cycle Accessories** 70 page catalog includes a complete line of motorcycle accessories, apparel, and parts. Star Cycle Accessories, 7437 Van Nuys Blvd., Van Nuys CA 91405. Phone: 818-782-7223. Price: $2.00 for S&H.

MOTORCYCLE
MAGAZINES AND NEWSLETTERS

•317• **American Iron Magazine** is dedicated to those who love Harley-Davidsons. The monthly magazine covers all aspects of owning, enjoying and improving your motorcycle, new product reviews, travel destinations, and book reviews. American Iron Magazine, TAM Communications, 6 Prowitt Street, Norwalk CT 06855-1204. Phone: 203-855-0008. Price: $25.00 per year.

•318• The **American Motorcyclist** magazine is the official publication of the American Motorcyclist Association. The monthly publication covers all areas of motorcycling including national, regional, and district championships. See listing #299 for more information on the magazine and the association. American Motorcyclist, 33 Collegeview, Westerville OH 43081. Phone: 614-891-2425.

•319• **American Rider** is a quarterly magazine for today's Harley-Davidson rider. Written to capture the very essence of the Harley-Davidson experience. Covers Harley-Davidson accessories and apparel, tips and how-to articles. Includes travel stories about where to go and what to do, news about club events and other gatherings. American Rider, P.O. Box 59636, Boulder CO 80322. Phone: 800-926-0484. Price: $15.80 per year.

•320• **Cycle** magazine is published monthly for street bike enthusiasts. Features tests and evaluations of motorcycles, new product reviews, tips and technique. Cycle, Hatchette Filipacchi Magazines Inc., 1633 Broadway - 42nd floor, New York NY 10019-6741. Phone: 212-767-6677. Price: $16.00 per year.

•321• The **Cycle News** weekly magazine is geared toward the experienced motorcycle rider. Features articles on motorcycle competition, new products, touring, road tests, and general news on the latest developments in motorcycling. Cycle News, Cycle News Inc., P.O. Box 498, Long Beach CA 90801. Phone: 310-427-7433. Price: $35.00 per year.

•322• **Cycle World** is published for cycle enthusiasts with coverage of American and world racing events. The monthly issues feature personality profiles, technical developments, apparel, accessories and new product reviews. Cycle World, Hatchette Filipacchi Magazines Inc., 1499 Monrovia Ave., Newport Beach CA 92663-2752. Phone: 714-720-5300. Price: $16.00 per year.

•323• **Easyriders** is a monthly publication featuring examples of custom and personalized American bikes. Articles include road tests, ideas and helpful suggestions including how-to-do-it instructions for customizing a bike. Easyriders, Paisano Publications Inc., P.O. Box 3075, Agoura Hills CA 91376-3075. Phone: 818-889-8740. Price: $35.00 per year.

•324• **Enthusiast** is published quarterly for Harley-Davidson motorcycle enthusiasts. Features stories on touring, racing, nostalgia, and history. Enthusiast, Harley-Davidson Motor Co., P.O. Box 653, Milwaukee WI 53201-0653. Phone: 414-342-4680. Price: Free.

•325• **Hack'd** is a publication for motorcycle sidecar combinations. The quarterly publication features new products, book reviews, and touring along with news and information of interest to the sidecar biker. Hack'd, J & C Enterprises, P.O. Box 813, Buckhannon WV 26201. Phone: 304-472-6146. Price: $21.00 per year.

•326• **Harley Women** is edited for the female motorcycle rider and passenger. The bimonthly publication highlights family-oriented stories with information on new products, events, safety, maintenance, and travel destinations. Harley Women, Asphalt Angels Publications Inc., P.O. Box 374, Streamwood IL 60107. Phone: 708-888-2645. Price: $15.00 per year.

•327• The *Hot Bike* magazine is published 10 times a year for the high performance rider. Covers both street and track with stories on technical how-to and competition coverage of events around the country. Hot Bike, McMullen & Yee Publishing Inc., 774 South Placentia CA 92670. Phone: 714-572-2255. Price: $20.95 per year.

•328• *In the Wind* provides a pictorial look at American motorcycles and their riders. The quarterly magazine features stories on rallies and events with recommendations on the best places for bikers to explore along with news of interest for all motorcycle riders. In The Wind, Paisano Publications Inc., P.O. Box 3075, Agoura Hills CA 91376-3075. Phone: 818-889-8740. Price: $15.00 per year.

•329• The *Iron Works* magazine is dedicated to the mature and educated Harley-Davidson owner and enthusiast. The bimonthly publication covers riding and travel destinations, new product reviews, tips and how-to information for the home mechanic, and stories on custom - vintage - and performance American motorcycles. Iron Works, Dennis Stemp Publishing Inc., 235 North Versailles, Pittsburg PA 15137. Phone: 412-243-3940. Price: $20.00 per year.

•330• The *Motorcycle Shopper* magazine offers thousands of parts and accessories for all makes and models of bikes. The listings in the monthly publication are classified as *Buy, Sell, and Trade*. Motorcycle Shopper Magazine, 1353 Herndon Avenue, Deltona FL 32725. Phone: 407-860-1989. Price: $19.95 per year.

•331• *Motorcycle Tour & Travel* features great tours across the U.S. and Canada for motorcycle traveler's. Articles include planning tips, exchange of travel experiences, events listings, new product reviews, and more in eight big issues per year. Motorcycle Tour & Travel, T A M Communications Inc., P.O. Box 610, Mt. Morris IL 61054. Phone: 815-734-1101. Price: $17.97 per year.

•332• *Motorcyclist* covers every aspect of motorcycle riding with special emphasis on touring, sport riding, and competition. The monthly issues feature articles on road tests, new product reviews, maintenance tips, race coverage and information, and travel destinations. Motorcyclists, Petersen Publishing Co., 6420 Wilshire Blvd., Los Angeles CA 90048. Phone: 213-782-2230. Price: $14.00 per year.

•333• *Motorcyclist's Post* covers motorcycle activities, legislation, and events for the motorcycle rider active in sport riding. The monthly publication covers touring, competition, new products, news and information for the serious rider. Motorcyclist's Post, 21 Stiles Lake Ave., Spencer MA 01562. Phone: 508-752-5221. Price: $15.00 per year.

•334• *Rider* is a monthly magazine devoted to the touring enthusiast. Articles feature coverage of travel, performance, weekending, equipment, new products and accessories, and riding techniques. Rider, T L Enterprises Inc., P.O. Box 51901, Boulder CO 80321. Phone: 800-678-2279. Price: $15.98 per year.

•335• *Road Bike Action* is a monthly publication featuring product reviews, interviews, and how-to's for the avid road biker. Road Bike Action, Daisy/Hi-Torque Publishing Company Inc., 10600 Sepulveda Blvd., Mission Hills CA 91345-1936. Phone: 818-365-6831. Price: $19.98 per year.

•336• *Road Rider Motorcycle Consumer News* is published monthly for the dedicated motorcycle touring enthusiast. The monthly magazine covers motorcycle test results, new products, riding gear, travel destinations, safety tips, and news of events around the country. RRMC, Fancy Publications Inc., P.O. Box 6050, Mission Viejo CA 92690. Phone: 714-855-8822. Price: $21.97 per year.

•337• *Sport Rider* magazine is for the street riding enthusiasts. The bimonthly publication reports on new developments in technology, riding performance tips, safety, modifications, new products and accessories. Sport Rider, Petersen Publishing Company, 8490 Sunset Blvd., Los Angeles CA 90069. Phone: 800-800-5667. Price: $13.95 per year.

•338• *Supercycle* magazine focuses on custom, antique, and performance motorcycles. The monthly publication provides the news of interest to today's adult motorcycle enthusiast with a splash of humor, cartoons, and fiction. Supercycle, LFP Inc., 9171 Wilshire Blvd. - Suite 300, Beverly Hills CA 90210. Phone: 310-858-7155. Price: $27.95 per year.

RECREATIONAL VEHICLE ASSOCIATIONS AND CLUBS

For other related information see listings #: 026, 268, and 283.

•339• The *Good Sam Club* is an organization of over 940,000 families who enjoy the RV lifestyle. The club provides benefits and programs to enhance the members way of life. Members receive a 10% discount on overnight camping fees at thousands of Good Samparks all over the country. Good Samers also receive 10% off RV parts and accessories at their discount locations, and 10% off LP gas purchased at Amerigas locations. Other benefits include free mail forwarding, credit card loss protection, free trip routing, fee-free travelers cheques, a club merchandise line, an AT&T telephone card, vehicle insurance plan, discount rates on health and life insurance plans, RV financing through their Good Sam finance center, and an emergency road service program. Members also receive discounts on RV books and publications like the *MotorHome* and *Trailer Life* magazines. The Good Sam Club also plans six or more Samborees (rallies) per year at various locations. There are also 2,300 local Good Sam chapters all over the country that plan local activities, campouts, pot lucks, and caravans. All members receive the *Highways* magazine 11 times per year. *Highways* features great RV destinations, the latest RV product information, maintenance tips, and news about fellow Good Samers, plus much more. The Good Sam Club, P.O. Box 6060, Camarillo CA 93011. Phone: 800-234-3450. Dues: $12.00 per year.

•340• The **Family Motor Coach Association** (FMCA) is for own-ers of motor homes that use their vehicles for travel, recreation, and camping. Qualifying vehicles must be self-propelled and self-contained. The association offers many benefits for its members including motor coach insurance, trip routing service, accidental death coverage, free classified advertising, emergency driver avail-ability, emergency message service, membership directory, youth activities, anti-theft program, motor coach financing, emergency air ambulance program, national conventions, emergency road service, mail forwarding, credit card program, and discounts that include savings at campgrounds across the country, on motor coach components and accessories, and on car rentals. All members also receive the monthly *Family Motor Coaching* magazine that brings you the latest information on association activities, rally sched-ules and committee activities, travel and entertainment articles, the latest developments in motor coach design, new products, technical information, products and supplies. Family Motor Coach Association Inc., Dept. RP, 8291 Clough Pike, Cincinnati OH 45244. Phone: 800-543-3622. Dues: $35.00 for the first year and $25.00 for renewal. The *Family Motor Coaching* magazine is also available by subscription for $24.00 per year.

•341• The **National RV Owners Club** provides service and tech-nical information for those involved with the use or manufacture of recreational vehicles. Provides information on RV camping and traveling for the entire family. Conducts volunteer instruction programs and recreational vehicle use workshops. Organizes ral-lies, tours, and caravans. Membership includes the club news-letter *The Recreation Advisor* which features the latest happen-ings in recreation, leisure and travel. Other benefits include credit card protection, mail forwarding, free classified advertising in the club newsletter, discounts on auto rentals, RV and self help books. National RV Owners Club, P.O. Drawer 17148, Pensacola FL 32522-7148. Phone: 904-477-7992. Dues: $15.00 per year.

•342• **Escapees** is a club dedicated to providing a support net-work for RVers. Whether you live full time in your RV or use it to take trips, Escapees can provide you with some valuable ben-efits. Some of the benefits include one month free RV storage in Texas, lost pet service, short-term parking places, educational escapades, rallies, mail & message service, discounts on emer-gency road service, RV insurance, RV parts and products, and discounts at designated campgrounds. All members also receive the bimonthly newsletter *Escapees* where you will find informa-tion to help save you money and enrich your travels. The newslet-ter features technical articles on maintenance and customizing your RV for maximum self-sufficiency, RV products and services as well as many other RV related subjects. Escapees Inc., 100 Rainbow Drive, Livingston TX 77351. Phone: 409-327-8873. Dues: $50.00 first year and $40.00 renewal.

•343• The **RVing Women** association provides a forum through which women can communicate, share information and link up for traveling together and/or caravaning. Sponsors several rallies and events each year all across the United States. Members reveive a bimonthly newsletter full of technical and travel information, safety, maintenance, and letters from members. RVing Women, 201 E. Southern Ave., Apache Junction AZ 85219. Phone: 602-983-4678. Dues: $39.00 per year or write for a complimentary sample newsletter.

•344• The **Loners of America** organization is for single individu-als pursuing the RV lifestyle who enjoy camping and traveling.

All members receive the monthly newsletter *Loners of America News* that provides current information on campouts and rallies, club news and activities. Loners of America, Route 2 - Box 85E, Ellsinore MO 63937-9520. Phone: 314-322-5548. Price: Call for current price.

•345• The **Special Military Active Retired Travel Club** (S•M•A•R•T) is for recreational vehicle enthusiasts with a mili-tary background. Sponsors annual rally, seminars and workshops, assist military installations with the improvement and expansion of their campgrounds, and provides group travel opportunities. Members also receive the quarterly *Traveler* magazine which pro-vides news and information on the clubs activities. S•M•A•R•T• Inc., 600 University Office Bldg. - Suite 1A, Pensacola FL 32504. Phone: 904-478-1986. Dues: $35.00 for the first year and $25.00 annually.

•346• The following organizations are for **owners of particular brands of recreational vehicles**. You can contact the following addresses for additional club information and membership dues.

Alpenlite Travel Club, P.O. Box 9152, Yakima WA 98909-0152. Phone: 509-452-3524.

American Clipper Owners Club, 514 Washington St., Marina Del Rey CA 90292. Phone: 310-823-8945.

Avion Travelcade Club, 101 East Sioux Road - #1078, Pharr TX 78577-1719. Phone: 402-895-1850.

Barth Ranger Club, State Road 15 South, Milford IN 46542. Phone: 219-658-9401.

Beaver Ambassador Club, 20545 Murray Road, Bend OR 97701. Phone: 503-389-1144.

Bounders United Inc., 178 Schooner Lane, Modesto CA 95356. Phone: 209-523-7445.

Carriage Travel Club Inc., P.O. Box 246, Millersburg IN 46543-0246. Phone: 219-642-3622.

Champion Fleet Owners Association, 5573 E. North Street, Dryden MI 48428.

Cortez National Motorhome Club, 11022 E. Daines Drive, Temple City CA 91780. Phone: 818-444-6030.

ElDorado Caravan, P.O. Box 266, Minneapolis KS 67467. Phone: 913-392-2171.

Fan Trailer Club, 4-7653-10, Delta OH 43515. Phone: 419-822-3495.

Firan Owners Association, P.O. Box 482, 58277 S.R. 19 South, Elkhart IN 46515. Phone: 219-293-6581.

Fireball Caravaner, 302 W. Walnut Avenue, El Seguno CA 90245. Phone: 818-892-8634.

Foretravel Motorcade Club, 1221 NW Stallings Drive, Nacogdoches TX 75961. Phone: 409-564-8367.

Georgie Boy Owners Club, P.O. Box 44209, Cincinnati OH 45244. Phone: 219-258-0591.

Gulf Streamers International RV Club, P.O. Box 168, Osceola IN 46561-0168. Phone: 219-773-7761

Hitch Hiker of America International (NuWa), P.O. Box 180, Osceola IN 46561-0180. Phone: 219-258-0591.

Holiday Rambler RV Club, East 600 Wabash Street, Wakarusa IN 46573. Phone: 219-862-7330

International Coachmen Caravan Club, P.O. Box 30, Hwy. 13 North, Middlebury IN 46540. Phone: 219-825-8245.
International CC Country Club, P.O. Box 207, Junction City OR 97448. Phone: 503-998-3712.

International Skamper Camper Club, P.O. Box 338, Bristol IN 46507. Phone: 219-848-7411.

Jayco Jafari, P.O. Box 44209, Cincinnati OH 45244. Phone: 219-258-0591.

Lazy Daze Caravan Club, 4303 East Mission Blvd., Pomona CA 91766. Phone: 909-627-1219.

National Collins RV Club, 12122 SE 105th Drive, Portland OR 97266. Phone: 503-698-4461.

Newmar Kountry Klub, P.O. Box 30, Nappanee IN 46550-0030. Phone: 219-773-7791.

Rockwood Travel Club, 1700 Claybank Road, Logan OH 43138.

Serro Scotty Club, 450 Arona Road, Irwin PA 15642-9512. Phone: 412-863-3407.

Silver Streak Trailer Club, 226 Grand Avenue #207, Long Beach CA 90803. Phone: 213-433-0539.

Sportscoach Owners International, 3550 Foothill Blvd., Glendale CA 91214. Phone: 818-249-4175.

Starcraft Camper Club, 4159 Woodington Drive, Mississauga Ontario, Canada L4Z 1K2. Phone: 416-275-4848.

Streamline Royal Rovers, 808 Clebud Drive, Euless TX 76040. Phone: 817-267-2167.

Wally Byam Caravan Club (Airstream), 803 East Pike Street, Jackson Center OH 45334. Phone: 513-596-5211.

Wings RV Club (Shasta), P.O. Box 631, Middlebury IN 46540. Phone: 219-825-8555.

Winnebago Itasca-Travelers, P.O. Box 268, Forest City IA 50436. Phone: 515-582-6874.

•347• The following organizations offer *membership and ownership camping resorts*. The campground facilities generally offer a wide range of indoor and outdoor activities. For additional information and membership requirements contact the following organizations.

Avila Resorts Investments LTD, 7075 Ontario Road, San Louis Obispo CA 93405. Phone: 805-595-7111.

Best Holiday Trav-L-Park, 1310 Jarvis Avenue, Elk Grove IL 60007. Phone: 800-323-8899.

Camper Clubs of America, 2338 South McClintock Dr., Tempe AZ 85282. Phone: 800-243-2267.

Coast to Coast Resorts, 64 Inverness Drive East, Englewood CO 80112. Phone: 303-790-2267.

Leisure Systems Inc., 6201 Kellogg Avenue, Cincinnati OH 45230. Phone: 800-626-3720.

Outdoor Resorts of America Inc., 2400 Crestmoor Road, Nashville TN 37215. Phone: 615-244-5237.

Resort Parks International, P.O. Box 7738, Long Beach CA 90807. Phone: 800-635-8498.

Thousand Trails NACO West, 12301 NE 10th Place, Bellevue WA 98005. Phone: 206-455-3155.

RECREATIONAL VEHICLES BOOKS AND DIRECTORIES

For other related information see listings #: 127, 128, 129, 131, 134, 135, and 285.

•348• The *Who's Who in RV Rentals* lists over 200 RV rental locations. The information includes the location, type of units available (motorhome, mini-motorhome, travel trailer, fifth wheel, tent camper, or truck camper), price per week, mileage cost, airport pick-up and drop off, tow vehicle availability, and deposit or security fees. You will also receive the *Rental Ventures* publication that tells you how to rent an RV and get the maximum enjoyment out of it. RVRA, 3251 Old Lee Highway - Suite 500, Fairfax VA 22030. Phone: 800-336-0355. Price: $7.50 postpaid for both publications.

•349• *Woodall's RV Buyers Guide* contains all the information RV buyers need to make an intelligent buying decision. Over 300 vehicles are profiled for easy comparison with many shown in full-color. Includes all types of motor homes, travel trailers, pickup campers, van campers, tow vehicles and a special Yellow Page Directory of RV Dealers. Fulfillment Department #1950, Woodall Publishing Company, 28167 North Keith Drive - Box 5000, Lake Forest IL 60045-5000. Phone: 800-323-9076. Price: $5.50 plus $2.00 S&H.

•350• *Woodall's RV Owner's Handbook* is a 3 volume set of guides to RV maintenance & repair. *Volume 1* is an introduction to RV basics. It sets the groundwork for successful RV driving, towing, packing, trip planning, and seasonal maintenance. *Volume 2* explains the operation and relationship of major RV systems. *Volume 3* covers emergency and money-saving repairs as well as preventive maintenance for plumbing, power converters, and other RV systems. Fulfillment Department #1950, Woodall Publishing Company, 28167 North Keith Drive - Box 5000, Lake Forest IL 60045-5000. Phone: 800-323-9076. Price: $7.95 plus $2.00 S&H for each volume. Two volumes for $12.95 plus $2.75 S&H or all three volumes for $19.00 plus $3.00 S&H.

•351• The *Trailer Life RV Buyers Guide* provides one-stop RV shopping for prospective owners. Features detailed specifications and prices on nearly 400 motorhomes, travel trailers, fifth-wheel trailers, folding camping trailers, van conversions and truck campers. Each listing includes information on weight, construction, appliances, insulation, bed sizes and more along with photographs and floorplans. RV Buyers Guide, P.O. Box 10204, Des Moines IA 50336. Phone: 800-541-1010 ext. 1726. Price: $9.95 postpaid.

•352• The *Mountain Directory* for RV and motor home drivers provides information on over 250 mountain passes and steep grades in the 11 western states. Includes locations and description of length and grade, allowing you to plan ahead. Mountain Directory, P.O. Box 941, Baldwin City KS 66006. Phone: 800-594-5999. Price: $12.95 postpaid.

RECREATIONAL VEHICLES CATALOGS

For other related information see listings #: 159, 290, and 310.

•353• The *Coast Connection: RV Parts & Accessories* catalog offers a large selection of products for all road travelers. The 500 page catalog features items such as camping equipment, antennas, awnings and covers, electrical and plumbing, major appliances, hardware and tools, towing and safety items, and much more. Request part #: 90751. Pikes Peak Traveland Inc., 4815 E. Platte Avenue, Colorado Springs CO 80915-7905. Phone: 800-458-9622. Price: $4.95 postpaid. Catalog comes with a $5.00 discount coupon for your first order.

•354• The *RV Travel Adventure Library* catalog contains dozens of camping and travel books, all selected especially for adventuresome RV travelers. Cottage Publications Inc., 24396 Pleasant View Dr., Elkhart IN 46517. Phone: 219-293-7553. Price: Free catalog.

•355• The *Publications & Videos about the RV Lifestyle* catalog published by the Recreation Vehicle Industry Association features many books of interest to RVers. The areas covered include information/reference sources, camping, buying an RV, traveling and full-timing in an RV, and more. Publications Division, RVIA - Dept. RBT, P.O. Box 2999, Reston VA 22090-0999. Phone:714-532-1688. Price: Free catalog and information packet.

•356• For a free list from *NRVOC* of various articles pertaining to RV's and the different forms of recreation, leisure and travel, send a self addressed, stamped enveloped to: #1 Member Services - NRVOC, P.O. Drawer 17148, Pensacola FL 32522-7148.

•357• The *Isley's RV Centers* offers a 160 page catalog with over 2,000 parts and accessories for recreational vehicles. Items available through the catalog include appliances, camping and travel, electrical and plumbing, toilets, windows, and more. Isley's RV Centers, 2225 West Main Street, Mesa AZ 85201. Phone: 800-962-5547. Price: Free catalog.

•358• The *Campers Choice* 55 page catalog offers a wide selection of RV parts and accessories as well as items for camping. Some of the items include air conditioners, awnings and accessories, bedding, bikes and carriers, books, chairs, cleaning products, fans and vents, grills, heaters, jacks and stabilizers, stoves, TVs and VCRs, tables, and much more. Camper's Choice, P.O. Box 1546, Red Bay AL 35582. Phone: 800-833-6713. Price: Free catalog.

•359• *Camping World* offers a large selection of camping accessories and supplies for RV owners. Products are available through their mail-order catalog or at any of the 22 retail locations across the country. Some of the items carried include air conditioners, awnings, bathroom supplies, chairs, directories, electrical devices, engine performance, fans and vents, furnishings, generators, heaters, mirrors, outdoor items, repair and maintenance products, TVs and antennas, travel comforts, and much more. Camping World, P.O. Box 90017, Bowling Green KY 42102. Phone: 800-626-5944. Price: Free catalog.

RECREATIONAL VEHICLES MAGAZINES AND NEWSLETTERS

•360• The *Workamper News: The Guide to Working-While-Camping in America* is a bimonthly newsletter featuring thousands of current job listings for recreational vehicle travelers. Each issue also includes profiles of people who are enjoying this lifestyle, book reviews, and information about full-time RVing. All subscribers are also eligible to participate in their *Workamper Referral System* which greatly improves your chances of finding the right job for you. Workamper News, 201 Hiram Road, Heber Springs AR 72543-8747. Phone: 501-362-2637. Price: $23.00 per year.

•361• *Camperways* provides news and information on the recreational vehicle lifestyle. The monthly publication provides maintenance tips, travel destinations, campground information, new product reviews, and other information relating to RVs. Camperways, Woodall Publishing Company, 28167 North Keith Drive, Lake Forest IL 60045. Phone: 708-362-6700. Price: $15.00 per year.

•362• The *Camping & RV Magazine* contains news and information for camping and RV enthusiasts. The monthly publication covers new products, campgrounds, tips on repair and maintenance, book reviews, and other news of interest to the camper and RVer. Camping & RV Magazine, P.O. Box 458, Washburn WI 54891. Phone: 715-373-5556. Price: $17.95 per year.

•363• The *Coast To Coast Magazine* is published 8 times a year for members of Coast to Coast Resorts. The publication features travel destinations, membership information, book reviews, new product reviews, and other RV related articles. For additional information on membership see listing #347. Coast To Coast Magazine, Coast to Coast Resorts, 64 Inverness Drive E., Englewood CO 80112. Phone: 800-368-5721. Price: $51.00 to $54.00 per year depending on membership option.

•364• The *Family Motor Coaching* magazine is for members and prospective members of the Family Motor Coach Association, see listing #340 for more information. The monthly publication provides news and information for owners of self-contained motor homes. Articles cover travel planning, recreation, equipment reviews, maintenance tips, book reviews, new product reviews, and information on the associations activities. Family Motor Coaching, Family Motor Coach Association Inc., Dept. RP, 8291 Clough Pike, Cincinnati OH 45244. Phone: 800-543-3622. Price: $24.00 per year for the magazine.

•365• The *Highways* magazine is published 11 times a year for the members of the Good Sam Club, see listing #339 for more information on the club. Features news of the club, travel stories, maintenance articles, new product and book reviews. Highways, TL Enterprises Inc., P.O. Box 6060, Camarillo CA 93011. Phone: 800-234-3450. Price: Only available to members of the club.

•366• *MotorHome* magazine is for owners and prospective owners of motorized recreational vehicles. The monthly publication features tests and evaluations of motorhomes and mini-motorhomes, travel destinations, new product reviews, maintenance tips, book reviews, and other news of interest to all RV traveler's. Motorhome, TL Enterprises, 3601 Calle Tecate, Camarillo CA 93012. Phone: 805-389-0300. Price: $26.00 per year.

•367• The *Northeast Outdoors* provides news and information for the camper and RVer in the Northeastern states. The monthly publication features travel destinations, new product and book reviews, and other general information on the northeastern region. Northeast Outdoors, P.O. Box 2180, Waterbury CT 06722. Phone: 203-755-0158. Price: $8.00 per year.

•368• The *RV Times* magazine covers the mid-Atlantic region of the U.S. for outdoor enthusiasts. Published 11 times per year with information on travel destinations and points of interest, outdoor activities, family recreational activities, and a calendar of events. RV Times, Royal Productions Inc., P.O. Box 6294, Richmond VA 23230. Phone: 804-288-5653. Price: $15.00 per year.

•369• *RV West* is published monthly for owners and future owners of recreational vehicles. Features news and information on travel and adventure trips, RV care and maintenance, safety, cooking & recipes, and calendar of events for western regional activities. RV West, Prescomm Media Inc., 4133 Mohr Avenue - Suite 1, Pleasanton CA 94566-4750. Phone: 510-426-3200. Price: $12.00 per year.

•370• The *Southern RV* publication provides the recreational vehicle owner in the southeastern United States with travel and vacation destinations. The monthly magazine offers equipment reports, camping tips, and a calendar of events. Southern RV, Woodall Publishing Company, 28167 North Keith Drive, Lake Forest IL 60045. Phone: 708-362-6700. Price: $15.00 per year.

•371• The *Trailblazer* magazine is published 10 times a year for members of the Thousand Trails organization, a group comprised of recreational vehicle owners and campers. Features articles on the latest developments in equipment and products for outdoor activities, new product reviews, shows and meetings along with membership information. For more information on the organization see listing #347. Trailblazer, Thousand Trails Inc., 12301 NE 10th Place, Bellevue WA 98005. Phone: 206-455-3155. Price: Available to members only.

•372• The *Trailer Life* magazine provides news and information for the recreational vehicle owner. The monthly publication features travel destinations, how-to articles, RV tests, campground information, technical articles, and entertainment. Trailer Life, TL Enterprises Inc., 3601 Calle Tecate, Camarillo CA 93012. Phone: 805-389-0300. Price: $22.00 per year.

•373• The *Trails-A-Way* magazine is published for the camping and RV enthusiasts in the mid-west. The monthly publication provides news and information on RV destinations, technical reviews, and a calendar of events. Woodall Publishing Company, 28167 North Keith Drive, Lake Forest IL 60045. Phone: 708-362-6700. Price: $15.00 per year.

STATE TOURISM OFFICES AND THEIR PUBLICATIONS

Following is a list of the State Tourism Offices and the main publications they offer free of charge. Please note that many of these offices offer other publications on various activities, attractions and communities and many other specific areas of interest, also available free of charge. When you call or write for the listed publications be sure to inquire about the specific areas of interest to you.

Alabama Bureau of Tourism and Travel, P.O. Box 4309, Montgomery AL 36103-4309. Phone: 800-ALABAMA. / Alabama Vacation Guide; Alabama Lodging Guide; Golf Alabama; Alabama Calendar of Events; Alabama's Black Heritage.

Alaska Division of Tourism, P.O. Box 110801, Juneau AK 99811-0801. Phone: 907-465-2010. / Alaska State Vacation Planner; North! To Alaska (Highway travel planner); Alaska Map and Campground Guide; Alaska Calendar of Events; Alaska All Things Wild and Wonderful.

Arizona Office of Tourism, 1100 West Washington, Phoenix AZ 85007. Phone: 800-842-8257. / Arizona Traveler; Arizona Accommodations Directory; Arizona Calendar of Events. The *Arizona Highways* magazine is available for $17.00 for a one year subscription. The magazine offers a wide variety of books, maps and calendars about Arizona. For more information call 800-543-5432.

Arkansas Dept. of Parks and Recreation, One Capitol Mall, Little Rock AR 72201. Phone: 800-Natural. / Arkansas Tour Guide;

Arkansas Calendar of Events; Arkansas Campers Guide; Arkansas State Parks; Arkansas State Highway Map.

California Office of Tourism, P.O. Box 9278, Van Nuys CA 91409. Phone: 800-862-2543. / Golden California Visitor's Guide; Golden California Special Events; Discover the Californias' Accommodations; California State Parks; California Visitor Map.

Colorado Tourism Board, P.O. Box 7407, Denver CO 80207-7407. Phone: 800-265-6723. / Colorado State Vacation Guide; Colorado Accommodations Guide.

Connecticut Tourism Division, 865 Brook Street, Rocky Hill CT 06067-3405. Phone: 800-CT-BOUND. / Connecticut Vacation Guide.

Delaware Tourism Office, P.O. Box 1401, Dover DE 19903. Phone: 800-441-8846. / Delaware Vacation Guide; Delaware State Highway Map.

Florida Division of Tourism, 126 West Van Buren, Tallahassee FL 32399-2000. Phone: 904-487-1462. / Florida Vacation Guide; Florida Events Calendar; Florida Value Activities Guide; Florida Official Transportation Map.

Georgia Dept. of Industry, Trade and Tourism, 285 Peachtree Center Avenue NE - Suite 1100, Atlanta GA 30303-1230. Phone: 800-VISIT-GA. / Georgia On My Mind.

Hawaii Visitors Bureau, Information Office, 2270 Kalakaua Ave. - Suite 801, Honolulu HI 96815. Phone: 808-923-1811. / Islands of Aloha; Hawaii Accommodations Guide; Hawaii Entertainment & Restaurant Guide.

Idaho Dept. of Commerce, 700 West State Street, Statehouse Mail, Boise ID 83720-2700. Phone: 800-VISIT-ID. / Idaho State Travel Guide; Idaho Campground Directory; Idaho Highway Map.

Illinois Bureau of Tourism, 1000 Business Center Drive, Mount Prospect IL 60056. Phone: 800-ABE-0121 ext 18. / Illinois Visitors Guide; Illinois Activity Guide; Illinois Highway Map.

Indiana Division of Tourism, One North Capitol - Suite 700, Indianapolis IN 46204-2288. Phone: 800-289-6646. / Indiana Attractions; Indiana Festivals and Events; Indiana Lodging; Indiana Camping; Indiana Recreation Guide; Indiana Travel Guide; Indiana State Highway Map.

Iowa Division of Tourism, 200 East Grand Ave., Des Moines IA 50309. Phone: 800-345-IOWA. / Iowa Visitor Guide; Iowa Calendar of Events; Iowa Vacation Value Directory; Iowa Scenic Byways Brochure.

Kansas Travel and Tourism, 700 SW Harrison - Suite 1300, Topeka KS 66606-3712. Phone: 913-296-2009. / Kansas Travel Guide; Kansas Campgrounds and RV Parks; Fishing Guide to Kansas; Guide to Kansas Public Hunting; Golf on Course in Kansas; Kansas Fall Foliage Tours; Kansas Outdoor Review.

Kentucky Dept. of Travel Development, 500 Mero Street - Suite 2200, Frankfort KY 40601. Phone: 800-225-8747. / Kentucky Official Vacation Guide; Kentucky Outdoors; Kentucky Heritage Tours; Kentucky Travel Guide.

Louisiana Office of Tourism, P.O. Box 94921, Baton Rouge LA 70804-9291. Phone: 800-633-6970. / Louisiana Tour Guide; Louisiana Official Highway Map.

The *Maine* Publicity Bureau, P.O. Box 2300, Hallowell ME 04347. Phone: 800-533-9595. / Maine Invites You Vacation Guide; Maine Map And Travel Guide.

Maryland Office of Tourism Development, 217 E. Redwood Street, Baltimore MD 21202. Phone: 800-543-1036. / Destination Maryland; Maryland Calendar of Events; Maryland State Highway Map; Maryland Golf Guide.

Massachusetts Office of Travel and Tourism, 100 Cambridge Street - 13th Floor, Boston MA 02202. Phone: See Below. Massachusetts Getaway Guide - 800-447-MASS; Seasonal Calendar of Events - 800-632-8038 in the Northeast and 617-727-3201 elsewhere.

Michigan State Board of Tourism, P.O. Box 3393, Livonia MI 48151. Phone: 800-543-2937. / Michigan Travel Ideas; Michigan Travel Guide & Calendar of Events; Michigan Transportation Map.

Minnesota Office of Tourism, 100 Metro Square, 121 7th Place East, Saint Paul MN 55101-2112. Phone: 800-657-3700. / Northcentral & West Travel Directory; Southern Travel Directory; Northeastern Travel Directory; Minnesota Fishing; Minnesota Explorer; Minnesota Resorts; Minnesota Restaurants; Minnesota Bed and Breakfast and Historic Inns; Minnesota Hotel & Lodging Guide; Minnesota Campgrounds and RV Parks.

Mississippi Division of Tourism, P.O. Box 1705, Ocean Springs MS 39566-1705. Phone: 800-WARMEST. / Mississippi Travel Planner; Mississippi State Parks; Picture It - The Civil War; Picture It - History; Picture It - Natchez Trace Parkway; Mississippi Bed & Breakfast Guide; Mississippi Hotel / Motels Directory; Mississippi Calendar of Events; Mississippi Official Highway Map.

Missouri Division of Tourism, P.O. Box 1055, Jefferson City MO 65102. Phone: 800-877-1234. / Missouri Getaway State Travel Guide; Missouri Highway Map; Missouri Calendar of Events; Fun Money - Coupon Book.

Travel *Montana*, P.O. Box 200533, Helena MT 59620-0533. Phone: 800-VISIT-MT. / Montana Vacation Guide; Montana Travel Planner; Montana Winter Guide; Montana Snowmobile Guide; Montana Indian Reservations Brochure; Montana Fishing Guide; Montana Highway Map.

Nebraska Division of Travel and Tourism, P.O. Box 94666, Lincoln NE 68509-4666. Phone: 800-228-4307. / Nebraska Visitors Guide; Nebraska Accommodations Guide; Nebraska Catalog of Events; Nebraska State Highway Map.

Nevada Commision on Tourism, Capitol Complex, Carson City NV 89710. Phone: 800-NEVADA-8. / Nevada Visitors Guide; Nevada Official State Map; Nevada's Highway 50 Survival Guide Book; Discover Nevada Bonus Book.

New Hampshire Office of Travel and Tourism, P.O. Box 856, Concord NH 03302-0856. Phone: 800-FUN-IN-NH. / Official

New Hampshire Guidebook; New Hampshire Events Calendar; New Hampshire Highway Map.

New Jersey Division of Travel and Tourism, CN826, Trenton NJ 08625-0826. Phone: 800-JERSEY-7. / New Jersey Travel Guide; New Jersey Cultural & Historic Guide; Facts and Fun Brochure; New Jersey Outdoor Guide; New Jersey Calendar of Events; New Jersey Travel Planner.

New Mexico Dept. of Tourism, Room 751 - Lamy Bldg., 491 Old Santa Fe Trail, Santa Fe NM 87503. Phone: 800-545-2040 ext 751. / New Mexico Vacation Guide; New Mexico Magazine Catalog; *New Mexico* magazine also available for $21.95 for a one year subscription.

New York State Dept. of Economic Development, One Commerce Plaza, Albany NY 12245. Phone: 800-CALL-NYS. / I Love New York Travel Guide; The New York Hotel Guide; New York Calendar of Events; The Big Apple Movie ($3.00 S&H)

North Carolina Travel and Tourism Division, 430 North Salisbury Street, Raleigh NC 27611. Phone: 800-VISIT-NC. / North Carolina Vacation Guide; North Carolina State Transportation Map.

North Dakota Tourism, Liberty Memorial Bldg., 604 E. Boulevard, Bismark ND 58505-0820. Phone: 800-HELLO-ND. / North Dakota Vacation Guide; North Dakota Hunting & Fishing Guide; Outdoor Adventure Guide; North Dakota Official Highway Map.

Ohio Division of Travel and Tourism, P.O. Box 1001, Columbus OH 43266. Phone: 800-BUCKEYE. / State of Ohio Travel Planner; Ohio Calendar of Events; Ohio Pass Coupon Book; Ohio State Highway Map.

Oklahoma Tourism and Recreation Dept., P.O. Box 60789, Oklahoma City OK 73146-0789. Phone: 800-652-6552. / Oklahoma Vacation Guide; Oklahoma Calendar of Events; Oklahoma Highway Map; Oklahoma Fall Foliage Guide; Oklahoma Parks & Resorts Guide; Oklahoma Vacation Planner; Oklahoma Historic Route 66 Brochure; Oklahoma Bicycle Route Map.

Oregon Tourism Division, P.O. Box 14070, Portland OR 97214. Phone: 800-547-7842. / Oregon Travel Guide; Oregon Events Calendar; Oregon Accommodations Guide; Oregon Attractions Guide; Oregon Winter Activities Guide; Driving Tour Guide - Discovering Our Routes; Oregon Campground Guide.

Pennsylvania Office of Travel Marketing, 453 Forum Bldg., Harrisburg PA 17120. Phone: 800-VISIT-PA. / Pennsylvania Visitors Guide.

Rhode Island Tourism Division, 7 Jackson Walkway, Providence RI 02903. Phone: 800-556-2484. / Rhode Island Visitor's Map; Rhode Island Visitor's Guide; Rhode Island Camping Guide; Rhode Island Boating & Fishing.

South Carolina Division of Tourism, P.O. Box 71, Columbia SC 29202. Phone: 803-734-0122. / South Carolina Travel Guide; South Carolina Highway Map.

South Dakota Tourism, 711 E. Wells Ave., Pierre SD 57501-3369. Phone: 800-S-DAKOTA. / South Dakota Vacation Guide;

South Dakota State Map.

Tennessee Tourist Development, P.O. Box 23170, Nashville TN 37202. Phone: 615-741-2158. / Travel Tennessee: The Official Vacation Guide; Tennessee Official Highway Map; Tennessee Annual Events; Tennessee Seasonal Events; The Roots of Tennessee: An African-American Guide.

Texas Division of Travel and Information, P.O. Box 5064, Austin TX 78763-5064. Phone: 800-8888-TEX. / Texas State Travel Guide; Texas Accommodations Guide; Texas Official Travel Map.

Utah Travel Council, Council Hall / Capitol Hill, Salt Lake City UT 84114-1396. Phone: 800-200-1160. / Utah Travel Guide.

Vermont Dept. of Travel and Tourism, 134 State Street, Montpelier VT 05602. Phone: 802-828-3236. / Vermont Traveller's Guidebook; Vermont Official State Map; Vermont Attractions Brochure; Vermont Historic Sites Brochure; Vermont Outdoor Experience.

Virginia Division of Tourism, 1021 East Cary Street, Richmond VA 23219. Phone: 800-VISIT-VA. / Virginia Travel Guide.

State of *Washington* Tourism Division, P.O. Box 42500, Olympia WA 98504-2500. Phone: 800-544-1800. / Washington State Lodging & Travel Guide; Washington State Field Guide.

Washington DC Convention and Visitors Assn., 1212 New York Avenue NW - Suite 600, Washington DC 20005-3992. Phone: 202-789-7000. / Discover Washington, DC; Washington, DC Guide; Washington's Calendar of Events; Washington Visitor Map.

West Virginia Division of Tourism and Parks, P.O. Box 50312, Charleston WV 25305. Phone: 800-CALL-WVA. / West Virginia Vacation Guide; West Virginia Highway Map.

Wisconsin Division of Tourism, P.O. Box 55, Dodgeville WI 53533-0055. Phone: 800-432-8747 ext 42T. / Wisconsin Auto Tours; Wisconsin Recreation Guide; Wisconsin Calendar of Events; Summer Go To It Guide; Wisconsin's Historic Sites Visitor's Guide; Wisconsin Attractions Guide; Wisconsin Innkeeper's Guide; Directory of Wisconsin Bed & Breakfast Homes & Historic Inns; Wisconsin State Parks Visitors Guide; Wisconsin Golf Course Directory; Wisconsin Bike Trails Map; Wisconsin Highway Map.

Wyoming Division of Tourism, I-25 at College Drive, Cheyenne WY 82002. Phone: 800-CALL-WYO. / Wyoming Vacation Guide; Wyoming Official Highway Map.

NATIONAL PARKS

The National Park System of the United States consists of over 350 areas covering more than 80 million acres. More than half of the areas preserve places and commemorate people, events, and activities important in the Nation's history. Historical areas are usually preserved or restored to reflect their appearance during the period of their greatest historical significance.

Following is a state-by-state list of the National Park areas in alphabetical order. A brief description of the park has been included to help explain the importance of the park. The descriptions were obtained from the *National Parks Index* book mentioned below.

For more detailed information about the National Parks see the listing for *The Complete Guide to America's National Parks* described below. You can also contact the individual park of your interest for additional free information.

The *National Parks Index* provides a brief summary of over 350 areas in the National Park System including a listing of the regional offices for the National Park Service. The book also contains a descriptive listing of the National Park areas by state, an alphabetical listing of the Wild and Scenic River system, a listing of the National Trails system, and an index to the areas comprising the National Park system. Publications Service Section, U.S. Government Printing Office, STOP: SSOS, Washington DC 20402-9329. Phone: Inquiries 202-512-2457, Orders 202-783-3238. Price: $5.00 postpaid.

The Complete Guide to America's National Parks remains the most comprehensive travel/reference book available on the National Parks. The 540 page guide provides information on the 367 National Park areas and features a 2-page National Park System map, state and city maps, a 2-page map of scenic and historic trails, and separate sections on trails and wild and scenic rivers. The state-by-state listings begin with a description of each park's attractions and includes directions, camping and lodging information, access information for persons with disabilities, seniors and families with young children, and visitor activities. Sales of the guide also helps support the National Parks. National Park Foundation, 1101 17th Street NW - Suite 1102, Washington DC 20036. Phone: 800-533-6478. Price: $14.95 plus $3.00 S&H. Also available in bookstores.

ALABAMA

Horseshoe Bend National Military Park, Route 1, Box 103, Daviston AL 36256. Phone: 205-234-7111. On March 27, 1814, at the "horseshoe bend" in the Tallapoosa River, Gen. Andrew Jackson's forces broke the power of the Upper Indian Confederacy and opened large parts of Alabama and Georgia to settlement.

Little River Canyon National Preserve, P.O. Box 45, Fort Payne AL 35967. Phone: 205-997-9239. This preserve was created to protect 35 miles of the Little River flowing on top of Lookout Mountain.

Russell Cave National Monument, Route 1, Box 175, Bridgeport AL 35740. Phone: 205-495-2672. An almost continuous archeological record of human habitation from at least 7000 BC to about AD 1650 is revealed in this cave.

Tuskegee Institute National Historic Site, P.O. Drawer 10, Tuskegee AL 36087-0010. Phone: 205-727-6390. Booker T. Washington founded this college for black Americans in 1881.

Preserved here are the brick buildings the students constructed themselves, Washington's home, and the George Washington Carver Museum.

ALASKA

Aniakchak National Monument and Preserve, Box 7, King Salmon AK 99613-0007. Phone: 907-246-3305. The Aniakchak Caldera covers 30 square miles and is one of the great dry calderas in the world. The crater includes lava flows, cinder cones, and explosion pits, as well as Surprise Lake, source of the Aniakchak River, which cascades through a 1,500-foot gash in the crater wall.

Bering Land Bridge National Preserve, Box 220, Nome AK 99762-0220. Phone: 907-443-2522. Located on the Seward Peninsula in northwest Alaska, the preserve is a remnant of the land bridge that once connected Asia with North America.

Cape Krusenstern National Monument, P.O. Box 1029, Kotzebue AK 99752. Phone: 907-442-3760. Archeological sites located along a succession of 114 lateral beach ridges illustrate Eskimo communities of every known cultural period in Alaska.

Denali National Park and Preserve, P.O. Box 9, Denali Park AK 99755. Phone: 907-683-2294. The park contains North America's highest mountain, 20,320 foot Mount McKinley. Large glaciers of the Alaska Range, caribou, Dall sheep, moose, grizzly bears, and timber wolves are other highlights of this national park and preserve.

Gates of the Arctic National Park and Preserve, P.O. Box 74680, Fairbanks AK 99707-4680. Phone: 907-456-0281. This park is characterized by jagged peaks, gentle arctic valleys, wild rivers, and numerous lakes.

Glacier Bay National Park and Preserve, P.O. Box 140, Gustavus AK 99826-0140. Phone: 907-697-2230. Great tidewater glaciers, a dramatic range of plant communities from rocky terrain recently covered by ice to lush temperate rain forest. A large variety of animals, including brown and black bear, mountain goats, whales, seals, and eagles can be found within the park.

Katmai National Park and Preserve, P.O. Box 7, King Salmon AK 99613. Phone: 907-246-3305. Lakes, forests, mountains, and marshlands all abound in this national park and preserve. The Alaska brown bear thrives here, feeding upon red salmon that spawn in the many lakes and streams.

Kenai Fjords National Park, Box 1727, Seward AK 99664-1727. Phone: 907-224-3175. The park includes one of the four major ice caps in the United States, the 300 square mile Harding Icefield and coastal fjords. Here a rich, varied rain forest is home to tens of thousands of breeding birds and adjoining marine waters support a multitude of sea lions, sea otters, and seals.

Klondike Gold Rush National Historical Park, P.O. Box 517, Skagway AK 99840. Phone: 907-983-2921. Historic buildings in Skagway and portions of Chilkoot and White Pass Trails, all prominent in the 1898 gold rush, are within the park.

Kobuk Valley National Park, P.O. Box 1029, Kotzebue AK 99752. Phone: 907-442-3760. A rich array of arctic wildlife can be found here, including caribou, grizzly and black bear, wolf, and fox. The 25 square mile Great Kobuk Sand Dunes lie just south of the Kobuk River against the base of the Waring Mountains.

Lake Clark National Park and Preserve, 4230 University Drive, Suite 311, Anchorage AK 99508. Phone: 907-271-3751. The park-preserve contains great geologic diversity, including jagged peaks, granite spires, and two symmetrical active volcanoes.

Noatak National Preserve, P.O. Box 1029, Kotzebue AK 99752. Phone: 907-442-3760. The Noatak River basin is the largest mountain-ringed river basin in the Nation still virtually unaffected by man. The preserve contains the 65 mile long Grand Canyon of the Noatak.

Sitka National Historical Park, P.O. Box 738, Sitka AK 99835. Phone: 907-747-6281. The site of the 1804 fort and battle that marked the last major Tlingit Indian resistance to Russian colonization is preserved here.

Wrangell - St. Elias National Park and Preserve, P.O. Box 29, Glennallen AK 99588. Phone: 907-822-5234. The Chugach, Wrangell, and St. Elias mountain ranges converge here in what is often referred to as the "mountain kingdom of North America." The park-preserve includes the continent's largest assemblage of glaciers and the greatest collection of peaks above 16,000 feet.

Yukon - Charley Rivers National Preserve, P.O. Box 167, Eagle AK 99738. Phone: 907-547-2233. The preserve protects 115 miles of the 1,800 mile Yukon River and the entire Charley River basin. Numerous old cabins and relics are reminders of the importance of the Yukon River during the 1898 gold rush.

ARIZONA

Canyon de Chelly National Monument, P.O. Box 588, Chinle AZ 86503. Phone: 602-674-5500. At the base of sheer red cliffs and in canyon wall caves are ruins of Indian villages built between AD 350 and 1300. Modern Navajo Indians live and farm here.

Casa Grande National Monument, 1100 Ruins Drive, Coolidge AZ 85228. Phone: 602-723-3172. Ruins of a massive four story building, constructed of high lime desert soil by Indians who farmed the Gila Valley 600 years ago.

Chiricahua National Monument, Dos Cabezas Route, Box 6500, Willcox AZ 85646. Phone: 602-824-3560. The varied rock formations here were created millions of years ago by volcanic activity, aided by erosion. Faraway Ranch, an early dude ranch, has been restored.

Coronado National Memorial, 4101 East Montezuma Canyon Road, Hereford AZ 85615. Phone: 602-366-5515. Our Hispanic heritage and the first European exploration of the Southwest are commemorated hear.

Fort Bowie National Historic Site, P.O. Box 158, Bowie AZ 85605. Phone: 602-847-2500. Established in 1862, this fort was the focal point of military operations against Geronimo and his band of Apaches. The ruins can be reached only by trail.

Glen Canyon National Recreation Area. See Utah for address and description.

Grand Canyon National Park, P.O. Box 129, Grand Canyon AZ 86023. Phone: 602-638-7888. The park encompasses nearly 178 miles of the Colorado River. Forces of erosion have exposed an immense variety of formations which illustrate vast periods of geological history.

Hubbell Trading Post National Historic Site, P.O. Box 150, Ganado AZ 86505. Phone: 602-755-3475. This still active trading post, established in 1878, illustrates the influence of reservation traders on the Indians' way of life.

Lake Mead National Recreation Area. See Nevada for address and description

Montezuma Castle National Monument, P.O. Box 219, Camp Verde AZ 86322. Phone: 602-567-3322. One of the best preserved cliff dwellings in the United States, this 5 story, 20 room castle is 90% intact.

Navajo National Monument, HC71, Box 3, Tonalea AZ 86044. Phone: 602-672-2366. Betatakin, Keet Seel, and Inscription House (closed since 1968 due to its fragility) are three cliff dwellings of the Kayenta Anasazi.

Organ Pipe Cactus National Monument, Route 1, Box 100, Ajo AZ 85321. Phone: 602-387-6849. Sonoran Desert plants and animals found nowhere else in the United States are protected here as are traces of a historic trail, Camino del Diablo.

Petrified Forest National Park, P.O. Box 2217, Petrified Forest National Park AZ 86028. Phone: 602-524-6228. Trees that have petrified, or changed to multicolored stone, Indian ruins and petroglyphs, and portions of the colorful Painted Desert are features of the park.

Pipe Spring National Monument, HC65, Box 5, Fredonia AZ 86022. Phone: 602-643-7105. The historic fort and other structures, built here by Mormon pioneers, memorialize the exploration and settlement of the Southwest.

Saguaro National Monument, 3693 South Old Spanish Trail, Tucson AZ 85730-5699. Phone: 602-296-8516. Giant saguaro cacti, unique to the Sonoran Desert, sometimes reach a height of 50 feet in this cactus forest.

Sunset Crater Volcano National Monument, 2717 N. Steves Blvd. - #3, Flagstaff AZ 86004. Phone: 602-556-7042. This volcanic cinder cone with summit crater was formed just before AD 1100. Its upper part is colored as if by a sunset.

Tonto National Monument, HC02 - Box 4602, Roosevelt AZ 85545. Phone: 602-467-2241. These well preserved cliff dwellings were occupied during the 13th and 14th centuries by Salado Indians who farmed in the Salt River Valley.

Tumacacori National Historical Park, P.O. Box 67, Tumacacori AZ 85640. Phone: 602-398-2341. This historic Spanish Catholic mission building stands near the site first visited by Jesuit Father Kino in 1691.

Tuzigoot National Monument, P.O. Box 219, Camp Verde AZ 86322. Phone: 602-634-5564. Ruins of a large Indian pueblo that flourished in the Verde Valey between AD 1100 and 1450 have been excavated here.

Walnut Canyon National Monument, Walnut Canyon Road, Flagstaff AZ 86004-9705. Phone: 602-526-3367. These cliff dwellings were built in shallow caves under ledges of limestone by Pueblo Indians about 800 years ago.

Wupatki National Monument, 2717 N. Steves Blvd. - #3, Flagstaff AZ 86004. Phone: 602-556-7040. Ruins of red sandstone pueblos built by farming Indians about AD 1065 are preserved here.

ARKANSAS

Arkansas Post National Memorial, Route 1 - Box 16, Gillett AR 72055. Phone: 501-548-2207. The park commemorates the first permanent French settlement founded in 1686, in the Lower Mississippi Valley.

Fort Smith National Historic Site, P.O. Box 1406, Fort Smith AR 72902. Phone: 501-783-3961. This was one of the first U.S. military posts in the Louisiana Territory and served as a base of operations for enforcing federal Indian policy from 1817 to 1896.

Hot Springs National Park, P.O. Box 1860, Hot Springs AR 71902. Phone: 501-321-1433. Although the 47 thermal springs fluctuate in flow from 750,000 to 950,000 gallons a day, the temperature remains near 143 degrees year round. Persons suffering from illness or injury often seek relief in the ancient tradition of thermal bathing.

Pea Ridge National Military Park, Highway 62E, Peak Ridge AR 72751. Phone: 501-451-8122. The Union victory here on March 7-8, 1862, in one of the major engagements of the Civil War west of the Mississippi, led to the Union's total control of Missouri.

CALIFORNIA

Cabrillo National Monument, P.O. Box 6670, San Diego CA 92116. Phone: 619-557-5450. Juan Rodriguez Cabrillo, Portuguese explorer who claimed the West Coast of the United States for Spain in 1542, is memorialized here.

Channel Islands National Park, 1901 Spinnaker Drive, Ventura CA 93001. Phone: 805-658-5700. The park consists of five islands off southern California. Nesting sea birds, sea lion rookeries, and unique plants inhabit the area.

Death Valley National Monument, Death Valley CA 92328. Phone: 619-786-2331. This large desert, nearly surrounded by mountains, contains the lowest point in the Western Hemisphere.

Devils Postpile National Monument, P.O. Box 501, Mammoth Lakes CA 93546. Phone: 619-934-2289 summer and fall, 209-565-3341 winter and spring. Hot lava cooled and cracked some 900,000 years ago to form basalt columns 40 to 60 feet high resembling a giant pipe organ.

Eugene O'Neill National Historic Site, P.O. Box 280, Danville CA 94526. Phone: 510-838-0249. Tao House, near Danville, California, was built for Eugene O'Neill, who lived here from 1937 to 1944. Several of his best known plays, including "The Iceman Cometh" and "Long Day's Journey Into Night," were written here.

Fort Point National Historic Site, P.O. Box 29333, Presidio of San Francisco CA 94129. Phone: 415-556-1693. This classic brick and granite mid 19th century coastal fort is the only one of its style on the west coast of the United States.

Golden Gate National Recreation Area, Building 201, Fort Mason San Francisco, CA 94123. Phone: 415-556-0560. The park encompasses shoreline areas of San Francisco, Marin, and San Mateo counties, including ocean beaches, redwood forest, lagoons, marshes, military properties, a cultural center at Fort Mason, and Alcatraz Island, site of the penitentiary.

John Muir National Historic Site, 4202 Alhambra Ave., Martinez CA 94553. Phone: 510-228-8860. The home of John Muir, adjacent Martinez Adobe, and his gravesite commemorate Muir's contributions.

Joshua Tree National Monument, 74485 National Monument Drive, Twentynine Palms CA 92277. Phone: 619-367-7511. A representative stand of Joshua trees and a great variety of plants and animals exist in this desert region.

Kings Canyon National Park, Three Rivers CA 93271. Phone: 209-565-3341. Two enormous canyons of the Kings River and the summit peaks of the High Sierra dominate this mountain wilderness.

Lassen Volcanic National Park, P.O. Box 100, Mineral CA 96063-0100. Phone: 916-595-4444. Lassen Peak erupted intermittently from 1914 to 1921. Active volcanism includes hot springs, steaming fumaroles, mud pots, and sulfurous vents.

Lava Beds National Monument, P.O. Box 867, Tulelake CA 96134. Phone: 916-667-2282. Volcanic activity spewed forth molten rock and lava here creating an incredibly rugged landscape.

Manzanar National Historic Site, Death Valley CA 92328. Phone: 619-786-2331. This site preserves 1 of the 10 World War II relocation camps where Japanese-American and aliens were interned from 1942 through 1945.

Muir Woods National Monument, Mill Valley CA 94941. Phone: 416-388-2595. This virgin stand of coastal redwoods was named for John Muir, writer and conservationist.

Pinnacles National Monument, Paicines CA 95042. Phone: 408-389-4485. Spirelike rock formations 500 to 1,200 feet high, with caves and a variety of volcanic features, rise above the smooth contours of the surrounding countryside.

Point Reyes National Seashore, Point Reyes Station CA 94956. Phone: 416-663-8522. This peninsula near San Francisco is noted for its long beaches backed by tall cliffs, lagoons and esteros, forest ridges, and offshore bird and sea lion colonies.

Port Chicago Naval Magazine National Memorial, Attention: Public Affairs Officer, Concord Naval Weapons Station, 10 Delta St., Concord CA 94520-5100. Phone: 415-744-3968. Site of an explosion that occurred on July 17, 1944 as ships were being loaded with munitions to supply the Pacific Theater.

Redwood National Park, 1111 Second St., Crescent City CA 95531. Phone: 707-464-6101. Coastal redwood forests with virgin groves of ancient trees, including the world's tallest, thrive in the foggy and temperate climate.

San Francisco Maritime National Historical Park, Hyde Street Pier, Fisherman's Wharf, San Francisco CA 94123. Phone: 416-556-3002. The square rigged sailing ship *Balclutha*, steam schooner *Wapama*, three masted schooner *C.A. Thayer*, walking beam ferry *Eureka*, scow schooner *Alma*, steam tug *Hercules*, paddle wheel tug *Eppleton Hall*, and numerous smaller craft are preserved here.

Santa Monica Mountains National Recreation Area, 30401 Agoura Road - Suite 100, Agoura Hills CA 91302. Phone: 818-597-9192. This park, a large, rugged landscape covered with chaparral, fronts on the sandy beaches north of Los Angeles.

Sequoia National Park, Three Rivers CA 93271. Phone: 209-565-3341. Great groves of giant sequoias, Mineral King Valley, and Mount Whitney are spectacular attractions here in the High Sierra.

Whiskeytown - Shasta - Trinity National Recreation Area, P.O. Box 188, Whiskeytown CA 96095. Phone: 916-241-6584. Whiskeytown Unit provides a multitude of outdoor recreation opportunities as well as remains of buildings built during the Gold Rush.

Yosemite National Park, P.O. Box 577, Yosemite National Park CA 95389. Phone: 209-372-0200. Granite peaks and domes rise high above broad meadows in the heart of the Sierra Nevada; groves of giant sequoias dwarf other trees; and mountains, lakes, and waterfalls are found here.

COLORADO

Bent's Old Fort National Historic Site, 35110 Highway 194 East, La Junta CO 81050-9523. Phone: 719-384-2596. As an Anglo-American outpost on the Southern Plains, the fort was an Indian trading center and a center of civilization on the Santa Fe Trail.

Black Canyon of the Gunnison National Monument, 2233 E. Main - Suite A, Montrose, CO 81401. Phone: 303-249-7036. Shadowed depths of this sheer-walled canyon accentuate the darkness of ancient rocks of obscure origin.

Colorado National Monument, Fruita CO 81521. Phone: 303-858-3617. Sheer-walled canyons, towering monoliths, weird formations, dinosaur fossils, and remains of prehistoric Indian cultures reflect the environment and history of this colorful sandstone country.

Curecanti National Recreation Area, 102 Elk Creek, Gunnison CO 81230. Phone: 303-641-2337. Three lakes extend for 40 miles along the Gunnison River. When full, Blue Mesa Lake is the largest lake in Colorado.

Dinosaur National Monument, P.O. Box 210, Dinosaur CO 81610. Phone: 303-374-2216. Spectacular canyons were cut by the Green and Yampa Rivers through upfolded mountains. A quarry contains fossil remains of dinosaurs and other ancient animals.

Florissant Fossil Beds National Monument, P.O. Box 185, Florissant CO 80816. Phone: 719-748-3253. A wealth of fossil insects, seeds, and leaves are preserved here in remarkable detail. Here, also, is an unusual display of standing petrified sequoia stumps.

Great Sand Dunes National Monument, 11999 Highway 150, Mosca CO 81146. Phone: 719-378-2312. Among the largest and highest in the United States, these dunes were deposited over thousands of years by southwesterly winds blowing through the passes of the lofty Sangre de Cristo Mountains.

Hovenweep National Monument, McElmo Route, Cortez CO 81321. Phone: 303-529-4461. Pre-Columbian Indians built these 6 groups of towers, pueblos, and cliff dwellings.

Mesa Verde National Park, Mesa Verde National Park CO 81330. Phone: 303-529-4465. These pre-Columbian cliff dwellings and other works of early man are the most notable and best preserved in the United States.

Rocky Mountain National Park, Estes Park CO 80517. Phone: 303-586-2371, 303-586-8506 (TDD). The park's rich scenery is accessible by Trail Ridge Road, which crosses the Continental Divide.

CONNECTICUT

Weir Farm National Historic Site, 735 Nod Hill Road, Wilton CT 06897. Phone: 203-834-1896. J. Alden Weir, American impressionist painter, got his inspiration from the quiet, rural landscape that surrounded his farm, home, and studio. The same tranquil scenery is intact today.

DISTRICT OF COLUMBIA

Constitution Gardens, National Capital Parks - Central, 900 Ohio Drive SW, Washington DC 20242. Phone: 202-485-9880. This 40 acre park was constructed during the American Revolution Bicentennial. On an island in a lake is a memorial to the 56 Signers of the Declaration of Independence.

Ford's Theatre National Historic Site, National Capital Region - Central, 900 Ohio Drive SW, Washington DC 20242. Phone: 202-426-6924, 202-426-1749 (TDD). On April 14, 1865, President Lincoln was shot while attending a show here at 511 Tenth Street, NW. He was carried across the street to the Petersen house, where he died the next morning.

Frederick Douglass National Historic Site, National Capital Parks - East, 1900 Anacostia Drive SE, Washington DC 20020. Phone: 202-426-5961. From 1877 to 1895, this was the home of the Nation's leading 19th century black spokesman. Among other achievements, he was U.S. minister to Haiti in 1889.

John F. Kennedy Center for the Performing Arts, 2700 F St. NW, Washington DC 20566-0002. Phone: 202-416-7910, 202-416-7920 (TDD). Plays, concerts, films, opera, and ballet are presented in this structure designed by Edward Durell Stone.

Lincoln Memorial, National Capital Parks - Central, 900 Ohio Drive SW, Washington DC 20242. Phone: 202-485-9880. This classical structure of great beauty contains a marble seated statue 19 feet high of the Great Emancipator by sculptor Daniel Chester French.

Lyndon Baines Johnson Memorial Grove on the Potomac, c/o Turkey Run Park, McClean VA 22101. Phone: 703-285-2598. A living memorial to the 36th President, the park overlooks the Potomac River vista of the Capital.

Mary McLeod Bethune Council House National Historic Site, Bethune Museum and Archives, Inc., 1318 Vermont Ave. NW, Washington DC 20005. Phone: 202-332-1233. This is the headquarters of the National Council of Negro Women established by Mary McLeod Bethune in 1935.

National Capital Region, National Capital Region Headquarters, 1100 Ohio Drive SW, Washington DC 20242. Phone: 202-619-7222. The park system of the Nation's Capital comprises parks, parkways, and reservations in the District of Columbia, including such properties as the Battleground National Cemetery, the President's Parks, and a variety of military fortifications.

National Mall, National Capital Parks - Central, 900 Ohio Drive SW, Washington DC 20242. Phone: 202-426-6841. This landscaped park extending from the Capitol to the Washington Monument was envisioned as a formal park in the L'Enfant Plan for the city of Washington.

Pennsylvania Avenue National Historic Site, Pennsylvania Avenue Development Corp., 1331 Pennsylvania Ave. NW - Suite 1220N, Washington DC 20004-1703. Phone: 202-426-6720. This site includes a portion of Pennsylvania Avenue and the area adjacent to it between the Capitol and the White House encompassing Ford's theatre National Historic Site, several blocks of the Washington commercial district, the Old Post Office Tower, and a number of federal structures.

Rock Creek Park, Klingle Mansion, 3545 Williamsburg Lane NW, Washington DC 20008-1207. Phone: 202-426-6832. One of the largest urban parks in the United States, this wooded preserve contains a wide range of natural, historical, and recreational features in the midst of Washington.

Sewall - Belmont House National Historic Site, 144 Constitution Ave. NE, Washington DC 20002. Phone: 202-546-3989. Rebuilt after fire damage from the War of 1812, this red brick house is one of the oldest on Capitol Hill.

Theodore Roosevelt Island, George Washington Memorial Parkway, Turkey Run Park, McLean VA 22101. Phone: 703-285-2598. On this wooded island sanctuary in the Potomac River, trails lead to an imposing statue of Roosevelt, the conservation minded 26th President.

Thomas Jefferson Memorial, National Capital Parks - Central, 900 Ohio Drive SW, Washington DC 20242. Phone: 202-485-9880. This circular structure memorializes the author of the Declaration of Independence and President from 1801 to 1809. The interior walls present inscriptions from his writings.

Vietnam Veterans Memorial, National Capital Parks - Central, 900 Ohio Drive SW, Washington DC 20242. Phone: 202-485-9880. Located near the Lincoln Memorial at the west end of Constitution Gardens, the polished black granite wall is inscribed with the names of more than 58,000 persons who gave their lives or remain missing in the Vietnam war.

Washington Monument, National Capital Parks - Central, 900 Ohio Drive SW, Washington DC 20242. Phone: 202-485-9880. A dominating feature of the Nation's Capital, this 555 foot obelisk honors the country's first President, George Washington.

The White House, c/o National Park Service, 1100 Ohio Drive SW, Washington DC 20242. Phone: 202-755-7799. The White House has been the residence and office of the Presidents of the United States since November 1800. The cornerstone was laid October 13, 1792, on the site selected by George Washington.

FLORIDA

Big Cypress National Preserve, HCR61 - Box 110, Ochopee FL 33943. Phone: 813-695-4111. Subtropical plant and animal life abounds in this ancestral home of the Seminole and Miccosukee Indians.

Biscayne National Park, P.O. Box 1369, Homestead FL 33090-1369. Phone: 305-247-7275. Subtropical islands form a north-south chain, with Biscayne bay on the west and the Atlantic Ocean on the east. The park protects interrelated marine systems including mangrove shoreline, bay community, subtropical keys, and the northernmost coral reef in the United States.

Canaveral National Seashore, 308 Julia St., Titusville FL 32796. Phone: 407-267-1110. Twenty-five miles of undeveloped barrier island preserve the natural beach, dune, marsh, and lagoon habitats for a variety of wildlife.

Castillo de San Marcos National Monument, 1 Castillo Drive, St. Augustine FL 32084. Phone: 904-829-6505. Construction of this, the oldest masonry fort in the continental United States, was started in 1672 by the Spanish to protect St. Augustine.

De Soto National Memorial, P.O. Box 15390, Bradenton FL 34280-5390. Phone: 813-792-0458. The landing of Spanish explorer Hernando de Soto in Florida in 1539 and the first extensive organized exploration of what is now the southern United States by Europeans are commemorated here.

Dry Tortugas National Park, P.O. Box 6208, Key West FL 33041. Phone: 305-242-7700. A cluster of seven coral reefs, called the Dry Tortugas, are known for its bird and marine life, and its legends of pirates and sunken gold.

Everglades National Park, 40001 State Road 9336, Homestead FL 33034-6133. Phone: 305-242-7700. This largest remaining subtropical wilderness in the coterminous United States has extensive fresh and saltwater areas, open Everglades prairies, and mangrove forests.

Fort Caroline National Memorial, 12713 Fort Caroline Road, Jacksonville FL 32225. Phone: 904-641-7155. The present day fort overlooks the site of a French Huguenot colony of 1564-65. Here, the French and Spanish began two centuries of colonial rivalry in North America.

Fort Matanzas National Monument, 1 Castillo Drive, St. Augustine FL 32084. Phone: 904-471-0116. This Spanish fort was built to warn St. Augustine of British or other enemy approach from the south.

Gulf Islands National Seashore, 1801 Gulf Breeze Parkway, Gulf Breeze FL 32561. Phone: 904-934-2600. Offshore islands have sparkling white sand beaches, historic forts, and nature trails.

Timucuan Ecological and Historic Preserve, 13165 Mount Pleasant Road, Jacksonville FL 32225. Phone: 904-641-7155. Named for the Indians who once lived here and who may have been here for as long as 2,000 years, the preserve encompasses Atlantic coastal marshes, islands, tidal creeks, and the estuaries of the St. Johns and Nassau rivers.

GEORGIA

Andersonville National Historic Site, Route 1 - Box 80085, Andersonville GA 31711. Phone: 912-924-0343. This Civil War prisoner-of-war camp commemorates the sacrifices borne by American prisoners not only in the 1861-65 conflict but in all wars.

Chattahoochee River National Recreation Area, 1978 Island Ford Parkway, Dunwoody GA 30350. Phone: 404-399-8070. A series of sites along a 48 mile stretch of the Chattahoochee River is preserved so the public can enjoy recreation and visit historic spots.

Chickamauga and Chattanooga National Military Park, P.O. Box 2128, Fort Oglethorpe GA 30742. Phone: 706-866-9241. A major Confederate victory on Chickamauga Creek in Georgia, September 19-20, 1863, was countered by Union victories at Orchard Knob, Lookout Mountain, and Missionary Ridge in Chattanooga, Tennessee, November 23-25, 1863. This was the first national military park.

Cumberland Island National Seashore, P.O. Box 806, St. Marys GA 31558. Phone: 912-882-4338. Magnificent and unspoiled beaches and dunes, marshes, and freshwater lakes make up the largest of Georgia's Golden Isles.

Fort Frederica National Monument, Route 9 - Box 286C, St. Simons Island GA 31522. Phone: 912-638-3639. Gen. James E. Oglethorpe built this British fort in 1736-48 during the Anglo-Spanish struggle for control of what is now the southeastern United States.

Fort Pulaski National Monument, P.O. Box 30757, Savannah GA 31410-0757. Phone: 912-786-5787. Bombardment of this early 19th century for by rifled cannon in 1862 first demonstrated the ineffectiveness of old style masonry fortifications.

Jimmy Carter National Historic Site, Route 1 - Box 800, Andersonville GA 31711. Phone: 912-924-0343. The rural southern culture of Plains, Georgia, that revolves around farming, church, and school had a large influence in molding the character and in shaping the political policies of the 39th President of the United States. The site includes President Carter's residence, boyhood home, and high school.

Kennesaw Mountain National Battlefield Park, 900 Kennesaw Mountain Drive, Kennesaw GA 30144-4854. Phone: 404-427-4686. Two engagements took place here between Union and Confederate forces during the Atlanta Campaign, June 20 to July 2, 1864.

Martin Luther King, Jr. National Historic Site, 526 Auburn Ave. NE, Atlanta GA 30312. Phone: 404-331-5190. The birthplace, church, and grave of Dr. Martin Luther King, Jr., civil rights leader, are parts of this park.

Ocmulgee National Monument, 1207 Emery Hwy., Macon GA 31201. Phone: 912-752-8257. Traces of 10,000 years of Southeastern Confederacy prehistory from Ice Age Paleo Indians to the historic Creek Confederacy are preserved here.

HAWAII

Haleakala National Park, P.O. Box 369, Makawao HI 96768. Phone: 808-572-9306. The park preserves the outstanding features of Haleakala Crater on the island of Maui and protects the unique and fragile ecosystems of Kipahulu Valley, the scenic pools along 'Ohe'o gulch, and many rare and endangered species.

Hawaii Volcanoes National Park, P.O. Box 52, Hawaii Volcanoes National Park HI 96718. Phone: 808-967-7311. Active volcanism continues here, where at lower elevations, luxuriant and often rare vegetation provides food and shelter for a variety of animals.

Kalaupapa National Historical Park, Kalaupapa HI 96742. This park contains the site of the Molokai Island Hansen's disease settlement, areas relating to early Hawaiian settlement, scenic and geologic resources, and habitats for rare and endangered species.

Kaloko - Honokohau National Historical Park, P.O. Box 129, Honaunau HI 96726. This was the site of important Hawaiian settlements before arrival of European explorers. It includes coastal areas, 3 large fishponds, a house site, and other archeological remnants.

Pu'uhonua o Honaunau National Historical Park, P.O. Box 129, Honaunau HI 96726. Phone: 808-328-2326. Until 1819, vanquished Hawaiian warriors, noncombatants, and kapu breakers could escape death by reaching this sacred ground. Prehistoric house sites, royal fishponds, coconut groves, and spectacular shore scenery comprise the park.

Puukohola Heiau National Historic Site, P.O. Box 44340, Kawaihae HI 96743. Phone: 808-882-7218. Ruins of Puukohola Heiau ("Temple on the Hill of the Whale"), built by King Kamehameha the Great during his rise to power, are preserved.

U.S.S. Arizona Memorial, 1 Arizona Memorial Place, Honolulu HI 96818-3145. Phone: 808-422-2771. This floating memorial marks the spot where the USS Arizona was sunk in Pearl Harbor December 7, 1941, during the Japanese attack.

IDAHO

City of Rocks National Reserve, P.O. Box 169, Almo ID 83312. Phone: 208-824-5519. Scenic granite spires and sculptured rock formations dominate this landscape. Remnants of the California Trail are still visible in the area.

Craters of the Moon National Monument, P.O. Box 29, Arco ID 83213. Phone: 208-527-3257. Volcanic cones, craters, lava flows, and caves make this an astonishing landscape.

Hagerman Fossil Beds National Monument, P.O. Box 570, Hagerman ID 83332. Phone: 208-837-4793. Extraordinary fossils embedded in the banks of the Snake River have been exposed by the carving action of the river.

Nez Perce National Historical Park, P.O. Box 93, Spalding ID 83551. Phone: 208-843-2261. The history and culture of the Nez Perce Indian country are preserved, commemorated, and interpreted here.

ILLINOIS

Chicago Portage National Historic Site, c/o Forest Preserve District of Cook County, 536 N. Harlem Ave., River Forest IL 60305. Phone: 708-771-1335. A portion of the portage between the Great Lakes and the Mississippi River, discovered by French explorers Jacques Marquette and Louis Joliet, is preserved here.

Illinois and Michigan Canal National Heritage Corridor, 15701 S. Independence Blvd., Lockport IL 60441. Phone: 815-740-2047. Completed in 1848, this canal and the railroads that paralleled it were instrumental in opening up the west and in the growth of Chicago.

Lincoln Home National Historic Site, 413 South Eighth St., Springfield IL 62701-1905. Phone: 217-492-4150. Abraham Lincoln resided in this house for 17 years before he became President. The surrounding historic zone captures the atmosphere the Lincoln's knew.

INDIANA

George Rogers Clark National Historical Park, 401 South Second St., Vincennes IN 47591. Phone: 812-882-1776. This classic memorial building, located on the site of old Fort Sackville, commemorates the capture of the fort from the British by Lt. Col. George Rogers Clark, February 25, 1779, and the subsequent settlement of the region north of the Ohio River.

Indiana Dunes National Lakeshore, 1100 N. Mineral Springs Road, Porter IN 46304. Phone: 219-926-7561. Dunes rise 180 feet above Lake Michigan's southern shore with beaches, bogs, marshes, swamps, and prairie remnants as other natural features. Historic sites include an 1822 homestead and 1900 family farm.

Lincoln Boyhood National Memorial, P.O. Box 1816, Lincoln City IN 47552. Phone: 812-937-4541. On this southern Indiana farm, Abraham Lincoln grew from youth into manhood. His mother, Nancy Hanks Lincoln, is buried here.

IOWA

Effigy Mounds National Monument, RR 1 - Box 25A, Harpers Ferry IA 52146. Phone: 319-873-3491. The monument contains outstanding examples of prehistoric American Indian mounds, some in the shapes of birds and bears.

Herbert Hoover National Historic Site, P.O. Box 607, West Branch IA 52358. Phone: 319-643-2541. The birthplace, Friends Meetinghouse, and boyhood neighborhood of the 31st President, the gravesite of President and Mrs. Hoover, and the Hoover Presidential Library and Museum are within the park.

KANSAS

Fort Larned National Historic Site, RR 3, Larned KS 67550-9733. Phone: 316-285-6911. This military outpost was established midway along the Santa Fe Trail in 1859, to protect the mail and travelers.

Fort Scott National Historic Site, Old Fort Blvd., Fort Scott KS 66701. Phone: 316-223-0310. Established in 1842 as a base for the U.S. Army's peace keeping efforts along the "permanent Indian frontier," the fort was manned by U.S. Dragoons and infantry soldiers who served valiantly in the Mexican War.

KENTUCKY

Abraham Lincoln Birthplace National Historic Site, 2995 Lincoln Farm Road, Hodgenville KY 42748. Phone: 502-358-3137. An early 19th century Kentucky cabin, symbolic of the one in which Lincoln was born, is preserved in a memorial building at the site of his birth.

Big South Fork National River and Recreation Area. See Tennessee for address and description

Cumberland Gap National Historical Park, P.O. Box 1848, Middlesboro KY 40965. Phone: 606-248-2817. This mountain pass on the Wilderness Road, explored by Daniel Boone, developed into a main artery of the great trans-Allegheny migration for settlement of "the Old West" and an important military objective in the Civil War.

Mammoth Cave National Park, Mammoth Cave KY 42259. Phone: 502-758-2328. The park was established to preserve the cave system, including Mammoth Cave, the scenic river valleys of the Green and Nolin rivers, and a section of the hilly country north of the Green River.

LOUISIANA

Jean Lafitte National Historical Park and Preserve, 419 Rue Decatur, New Orleans LA 70130. Phone: 504-589-3882. The park consists of Barataria, Chalmette, the French Quarter, and the Acadia units. The Acadian Cultural Center at Lafayette interprets Cajun culture and history. Barataria, south of New Orleans, has trails and canoe tours through bottomland hardwood forests, swamp, and marsh. Chalmette, east of New Orleans, was the scene of the 1815 Battle of New Orleans. The French quarter unit interprets the ethnic population of the Delta.

Poverty Point National Monument, c/o Poverty Point State Commemorative Area, P.O. Box 248, Epps LA 71237. This park commemorates a culture that thrived during the first and second millennia, B.C.

MAINE

Acadia National Park, Box 177, Bar Harbor ME 04609. Phone: 207-288-3338. The sea sets the mood here, uniting the rugged coastal area of Mount Desert Island, picturesque Schoodic Peninsula on the mainland, and the spectacular cliffs of Isle au Haut.

Saint Croix Island International Historic Site, c/o Acadia National Park, Box 177, Bar Harbor ME 04609. Phone: 207-288-3338. The attempted French settlement of 1604, which led to the founding of New France, is commemorated on Saint Croix Island in the Saint Croix River on the Canadian border.

MARYLAND

Antietam National Battlefield, P.O. Box 158, Sharpsburg MD 21782-0158. Phone: 301-432-5124. Gen. Robert E. Lee's first invasion of the North was ended on this battlefield in 1862.

Assateague Island National Seashore, 7206 National Seashore Lane, Berlin MD 21811. Phone: 410-641-1441. This 37 mile barrier island, with sandy beach, migratory waterfowl, and wild ponies, includes the 9,021 acre Chincoteague National Wildlife Refuge.

Catoctin Mountain Park, 6602 Foxville Road, Thurmont MD 21788. Phone: 301-663-9330. Part of the forested ridge that forms the eastern rampart of the Appalachian Mountains in Maryland, this mountain park has sparkling streams and panoramic vistas of the Monocacy Valley.

Chesapeake and Ohio Canal National Historical Park, P.O. Box 4, Sharpsburg MD 21782. Phone: 301-739-4200. The park follows the route of the 184 mile canal along the Potomac River between Washington, D.C., and Cumberland, Maryland. The canal was built between 1828 and 1850.

Clara Barton National Historic Site, 5801 Oxford Road, Glen Echo MD 20812. Phone: 301-492-6245. This 38 room home of the founder of the American Red Cross was the headquarters of that organization for 7 years.

Fort McHenry National Monument and Historic Shrine, Baltimore MD 21230-5393. Phone: 410-962-4299. Successful defense of this fort in the War of 1812 inspired Francis Scott Key to write "The Star Spangled Banner."

Fort Washington Park, National Capital Parks - East, 1900 Anacostia Dr. SE, Washington DC 20020. Phone: 301-763-4600. This fort across the Potomac from Mount Vernon was built to protect Washington, D.C. Construction began in 1814 to replace an 1809 fort destroyed during the War of 1812.

Greenbelt Park, 6565 Greenbelt Rd., Greenbelt MD 20770. Phone: 301-344-3948. Just 12 miles from Washington, D.C., this woodland park offers urban dwellers access to many forms of outdoor recreation, including camping.

Hampton National Historic Site, 535 Hampton Lane, Towson MD 21286. Phone: 410-962-0688. This is a fine example of the lavish Georgian mansions built in America during the latter part of the 18th century.

Monocacy National Battlefield, 4801 Urbana Pike, Frederick MD 21701-7307. Phone: 301-662-3515. In a battle here July 9, 1864, Confederate Gen. Jubal T. Early defeated Union forces commanded by Brig. Gen. Lew Wallace. Wallace's troops delayed Early, however, enabling Union forces to marshal a successful defense of Washington, D.C.

Piscataway Park, National Capital Parks - East, 1900 Anacostia Dr. SE, Washington DC 20020. Phone: 301-763-4600. The tranquil view from Mount Vernon of the Maryland shore of the Potomac is preserved as a pilot project in the use of easements to protect park lands from obtrusive urban expansion

Thomas Stone National Historic Site, c/o George Washington Birthplace National Monument, RR 1 - Box 717, Washington's Birthplace VA 22443. Habre-de-Venture, a Georgian mansion built in 1771 near Port Tobacco, Maryland, was the home of Thomas Stone, a Signer of the Declaration of Independence and delegate to the Continental Congress.

MASSACHUSETTS

Adams National Historic Site, P.O. Box 531, Quincy MA 02269-0531. Phone: 617-773-1177. This was the home of Presidents John Adams and John Quincy Adams, of U.S. Minister to Great Britain Charles Francis Adams, and of the writers and historians Henry Adams and Brooks Adams.

Blackstone River Valley National Heritage Corridor, 15 Mendon St., Uxbridge MA 01569. Phone: 508-278-9400. The American Industrial Revolution had its roots here along some 46 miles of river and canals running from Worcester, Massachusetts, to Providence, Rhode Island.

Boston African American National Historic Site, 46 Joy St., Boston MA 02114. Phone: 617-742-5415. The site contains 15 pre-Civil War black history structures, linked by the 1.6 mile Black Heritage Trail. The meeting house is the oldest, standing, black church in the U.S.

Boston National Historical Park, Charlestown Navy Yard, Boston MA 02129. Phone: 617-242-5644. The events and ideas associated with the American Revolution and the founding and growth of the United States provide the common thread linking the sites that comprise this park.

Cape Cod National Seashore, South Wellfleet MA 02663. Phone: 508-349-3785. Ocean beaches, dunes, woodlands, freshwater ponds, and marshes make up this park on outer Cape Cod.

Frederick Law Olmsted National Historic Site, 99 Warren St., Brookline MA 02146. Phone: 617-566-1689. The great conservationist, landscape architect, and founder of city planning lived and worked here at Fairstead. An archival collection of drawings and plans is housed at the site.

John F. Kennedy National Historic Site, 83 Beals St., Brookline MA 02146. Phone: 617-566-7937. This house is the birthplace and early boyhood home of the 35th President.

Longfellow National Historic Site, 105 Brattle St., Cambridge MA 02138. Phone: 617-876-4491. Poet Henry Wadsworth Longfellow lived here from 1837 to 1882 while teaching at Harvard. George Washington used the house as his headquarters during the siege of Boston.

Lowell National Historical Park, 169 Merrimack St., Lowell MA 01852. Phone: 508-970-5000. The history of America's Industrial Revolution is commemorated here. The park includes mill complexes, a power canal system, and worker housing.

Minute Man National Historical Park, P.O. Box 160, Concord MA 01742. Phone: 508-369-6993. Scene of the fighting on April 19, 1775, that opened the American Revolution. The park includes North Bridge, the Minute Man statue by Daniel Chester French, a number of Colonial houses, and 4 miles of Battle Road between Lexington and Concord.

Salem Maritime National Historic Site, 174 Derby St., Salem MA 01970. Phone: 508-741-3648. Structures preserved here date from the era when Salem ships opened trade with ports of the Far East.

Saugus Iron Works National Historic Site, 244 Central St., Augus MA 01906. Phone: 617-233-0050. This is the site of the first integrated ironworks in North America. It includes the reconstructed blast furnace, the forge, the rolling and slitting mill, and a restored 17th century house.

Springfield Armory National Historic Site, One Armory Square, Springfield MA 01105-1229. Phone: 413-734-8551. From 1794 to 1968, Springfield Armory was a center for the manufacture of U.S. military small arms and the scene of many important technological advances. A large weapons museum is now housed in the original Main Arsenal Building.

MICHIGAN

Father Marquette National Memorial And Museum, 720 Church St., St. Ignace MI 49781. Phone: 906-643-9394. The memorial pays tribute to the life and work of Father Jacques Marquette, French priest and explorer.

Isle Royale National Park, 800 East Lakeshore Drive, Houghton MI 49931-1895. Phone: 906-482-0984. This forested island is distinguished by its wilderness character, timber wolves, moose herd, and pre-Columbian copper mines.

Keweenaw National Historical Park, P.O. Box 471, Calumet MI 49913-0471. Phone: 906-337-3168. This park commemorates the heritage of copper mining on the Keweenaw Peninsula.

Pictured Rocks National Lakeshore, P.O. Box 40, Munising MI 49862. Phone: 906-387-3700. Multicolored sandstone cliffs, broad beaches, sand bars, dunes, waterfalls, inland lakes, ponds, marshes, hardwood and coniferous forests, and numerous birds and animals comprise this scenic area on Lake Superior. The was the first national lakeshore.

Sleeping Bear Dunes National Lakeshore, P.O. Box 277, Empire MI 49630. Phone: 616-326-5134. This is a diverse land-scape with massive sand dunes, quiet birch lined streams, white sand beaches, dense beech maple forests, clear lakes, and rugged bluffs towering as high as 460 feet above Lake Michigan. Two offshore wilderness islands offer tranquility and seclusion.

MINNESOTA

Grand Portage National Monument, P.O. Box 668, Grand Marais MN 55604. Phone: 218-387-2788. This 9 mile portage was a vital link on one of the principal routes for Indians, explorers, missionaries, and fur traders heading for the Northwest.

Mississippi National River and Recreation Area, 175 5th St. East - Suite 418, St. Paul MN 55101-2901. Phone: 612-290-4160. For 69 miles, from Dayton to Hastings, Minnesota, the Mississippi flows through a variety of landscapes passing cultural, historical, and industrial features that tell the story of human activity in this area.

Pipestone National Monument, P.O. Box 727, Pipestone MN 56154. Phone: 507-825-5464. From this quarry, Indians obtained materials for making pipes used in ceremonies. The park includes the Upper Midwest Indian Cultural Center, which provides space for craftsmen to display their work and for demonstrations of traditional crafts to take place.

Voyageurs National Park, 3131 Highway 53, International Falls MN 56649-8904. Phone: 218-283-9821. Interconnected northern lakes, dotted with islands, once the route of the French-Canadian voyageurs, are surrounded by forest.

MISSISSIPPI

Brices Cross Roads National Battlefield Site, RR 1 / NT-143, Tupelo MS 38801. Phone: 601-680-4025. The Confederate cavalry was employed with extraordinary skill here during the battle of June 10, 1864.

Gulf Islands National Seashore, 3500 Park Rd., Ocean Springs MS 39564. Phone: 601-875-0821. Sparkling beaches, historic ruins, and wildlife sanctuaries, accessible only by boat, can be found on the offshore islands of this unit.

Natchez National Historical Park, P.O. Box 1208, Natchez MS 39121. Phone: 601-442-7047. In the decades before the Civil War, Natchez became a commercial, cultural, and social center of the South's "cotton belt," with power and wealth unmatched by other southern towns of comparable size. The city of Natchez today represents one of the best preserved concentrations of significant antebellum properties in the United States.

Tupelo National Battlefield, RR 1 / NT-143, Tupelo MS 38801. Phone: 601-680-4025. Here Lt. Gen. Nathan Bedford Forrest's cavalry battled a Union force of 14,000 sent to keep Forrest from cutting the railroad supplying Maj. Gen. William T. Sherman's march on Atlanta.

Vicksburg National Military Park, 3201 Clay St., Vicksburg MS 39180. Phone: 601-636-0583. Reconstructed forts and trenches evoke memories of the 47 day siege that ended in the surrender of the city on July 4, 1863. Victory gave the North control of the Mississippi River and cut the Confederacy in two.

MISSOURI

George Washington Carver National Monument, P.O. Box 38, Diamond MO 64840. Phone: 417-325-4151. The birthplace and childhood home of George Washington Carver, the famous black agronomist, includes the Carver family cemetery and the site where Carver was born.

Harry S. Truman National Historic Site, 223 North Main St., Independence MO 64050. Phone: 816-254-2720. Harry S. Truman, the 33rd President, called this Victorian structure home from 1919 until his death in 1972. Constructed by Mrs. Truman's grandfather, it was known as the "Summer White House" from 1945 to 1953.

Jefferson National Expansion Memorial, 11 North 4th St., St. Louis MO 63102. Phone: 314-425-4465. This park on St. Louis' Mississippi riverfront memorializes Thomas Jefferson and others who directed territorial expansion of the United States.

Ulysses S. Grant National Historic Site, 7400 Grant Rd., St. Louis MO 63123. Phone: 314-842-1867. Ulysses S. Grant lived on this St. Louis County estate in the years before the Civil War.

Wilson's Creek National Battlefield, Route 2 - Box 75, Republic MO 65738. Phone: 417-732-2662. The battle here on August 10, 1861, was the first major engagement west of the Mississippi. Confederates were not able to take advantage of their superior numbers, allowing Union troops to retreat and regroup; this was the turning point in keeping Missouri in the Union.

MONTANA

Big Hole National Battlefield, P.O. Box 237, Wisdom MT 59761. Phone: 406-689-3155. Nez Perce Indians and U.S. Army troops fought here in 1877 - a dramatic episode in the long struggle to confine the Nez Perce, and other Indians, to reservations.

Bighorn Canyon National Recreation Area, P.O. Box 7458, Yellow Tail MT 59035. Phone: 406-666-2412. Bighorn Lake, formed by Yellowtail Dam on the Bighorn River, extends 71 miles, including 55 miles through spectacular Bighorn Canyon.

Glacier National Park, West Glacier MT 59936. Phone: 406-888-5441. With precipitous peaks ranging above 10,000 feet, this ruggedly beautiful land includes nearly 50 glaciers, many lakes and streams, a wide variety of wildflowers, and wildlife.

Grant - Kohrs Ranch National Historic Site, P.O. Box 790, Deer Lodge MT 59722. Phone: 406-846-2070. This was the home ranch area of one of the largest and best known 19th century range ranches in the country.

Little Bighorn Battlefield National Monument, P.O. Box 39, Crow Agency MT 59022. Phone: 406-638-2621. The famous Battle of the Little Big Horn between twelve companies of the 7th U.S. Cavalry and the Sioux and Northern Cheyenne Indians was fought here on June 25-26, 1876.

NEBRASKA

Agate Fossil Beds National Monument, c/o Scotts Bluff National Monument, P.O. Box 27, Gering NE 69341. Phone: 308-436-4340. These renowned quarries contain numerous, well preserved Miocene mammal fossils and represent an important chapter in the evolution of mammals.

Chimney Rock National Historic Site, Nebraska State Historical Society, Box 82554, Lincoln NE 68508. Phone: 402-471-4758. As they traveled west, pioneers camped near this famous landmark, which stands 500 feet above the Platte River along the Oregon Trail.

Homestead National Monument of America, RR 3 - Box 47, Beatrice NE 68310. Phone: 402-223-3514. This park is a memorial to the pioneers who settled the Great West. Among the features are a typical homestead cabin, a restored frontier school, and more than 100 acres of tall grass prairie.

Scotts Bluff National Monument, P.O. Box 27, Gering NE 69341. Phone: 308-436-4340. Rising 800 feet above the valley floor, this massive promontory was a landmark on the Oregon Trail, associated with overland migration between 1843 and 1869 across the Great Plains.

NEVADA

Great Basin National Park, Baker NV 89311. Phone: 702-234-7331. A remnant icefield on 13,063 foot Wheeler Peak, an ancient bristlecone pine forest, 75 foot limestone Lexington Arch, and the tunnels and decorated galleries of Lehman Caves are the major features.

Lake Mead National Recreation Area, 601 Nevada Highway, Boulder City NV 89005. Phone: 702-293-8906. Lake Mead, formed by Hoover Dam, and Lake Mohave, by Davis Dam, on the Colorado River comprise this first national recreation area.

NEW HAMPSHIRE

Saint-Gaudens National Historic Site, RR 3 - Box 73, Cornish NH 03745. Phone: 603-675-2175. The park includes the home, studios, and gardens of Augustus Saint-Gaudens, America's foremost sculptor of the late 19th and early 20th centuries. Original sculpture is on exhibit.

NEW JERSEY

Edison National Historic Site, Main St. and Lakeside Ave., West Orange NJ 07052. Phone: 201-736-0550. Thomas Edison's laboratory and his residence were home to the inventor from 1887 until 1931. The complex includes his chemistry lab, machine shop and library.

Morristown National Historical Park, Washington Place, Morristown NJ 07960. Phone: 201-539-2016. Morristown was quarters for the Continental Army during two critical winters, January 1777 and 1779-80. The park includes the Ford Mansion, Jockey Hollow, and Fort Nonsense.

Pinelands National Reserve, The Pinelands Commission, P.O. Box 7, New Lisbon NJ 08064. This area, which is the largest essentially undeveloped tract on the Eastern seaboard, exceeds one million acres and is noted for its massive water resources with myriad marshes, bogs, ponds, and the dwarfed pines from which it gets its name.

NEW MEXICO

Aztec Ruins National Monument, P.O. Box 640, Aztec NM 87410. Phone: 505-334-6174 (Voice or TDD). Ruins of this large 12th century Pueblo Indian community have been partially excavated and stabilized.

Bandelier National Monument, Los Alamos NM 87544. Phone: 505-672-3861. On the canyon slashed slopes of the Pajarito Plateau are the ruins of many cliff houses of 13th century Pueblo Indians.

Capulin Volcano National Monument, P.O. Box 40, Capulin NM 88414. Phone: 505-278-2201. This symmetrical cinder cone is an interesting example of a geologically recent, inactive volcano.

Carlsbad Caverns National Park, 3225 National Parks Hwy., Carlsbad NM 88220. Phone: 505-785-2232. This series of connected caverns, with one of the world's largest underground chambers, has countless formations. The park contains 76 separate caves, including the Nation's deepest.

Chaco Culture National Historical Park, Star Route 4 - Box 6500, Bloomfield NM 87413. Phone: 505-786-7014. The canyon, with hundreds of smaller ruins, contains 13 major Indian ruins unsurpassed in the United States, representing the highest point of Pueblo pre-Columbian civilization.

El Malpais National Monument, P.O. Box 939, Grants NM 87020. Phone: 505-287-3407. El Malpais is a spectacular volcanic area, partially formed as recently as 1,000 years ago, featuring spatter cones, a 17 mile long lava tube system, and ice caves.

El Morro National Monument, Route 2 - Box 43, Ramah NM 87321. Phone: 505-783-4226. "Inscription Rock" is a soft sandstone monolith on which are carved hundreds of inscriptions. The monument also includes pre-Columbian petroglyphs and Pueblo Indian ruins.

Fort Union National Monument, Watrous NM 87753. Phone: 505-425-8025. Three U.S. Army forts were built on this site, a key supply point on the Santa Fe Trail. The largest visible network of Santa Fe Trail ruts can be seen here.

Gila Cliff Dwellings National Monument, Route 11 - Box 100, Silver City NM 88061. Phone: 505-536-9461. These well preserved cliff dwellings were inhabited from about AD 1280 to the early 1300s.

Pecos National Historical Park, P.O. Drawer 418, Pecos NM 87552. Phone: 505-757-6414. The park contains the ruins of the ancient 15th century Pueblo of Pecos and the remains of two Spanish missions.

Petroglyph National Monument, 4735 Unser Blvd. NW, Albuquerque NM 87120. Phone: 505-839-4429. More than 15,000 prehistoric and historic Native American and Hispanic petroglyphs and rock art carvings stretch 17 miles along Albuquerque's West Mesa escarpment.

Salinas Pueblo Mission National Monument, P.O. Box 496, Mountainair NM 87036. Phone: 505-847-2585. This park preserves and interprets the best remaining examples of 17th century Spanish Franciscan mission churches and conventos remaining in the United States.

White Sands National Monument, P.O. Box 1086, Holloman AFB NM 88330-1086. Phone: 505-479-6124. The park contains a significant portion of the world's largest gypsum dunefield. The glistening white dunes rise 60 feet high and cover 275 square miles.

NEW YORK

Castle Clinton National Monument, Manhattan Sites, 26 Wall St., New York NY 10003. Phone: 212-264-4456. Built 1808-11, this structure served as a defense for New York harbor, an entertainment center, and an immigration depot through which more than 8 million people entered the United States from 1855 to 1890.

Eleanor Roosevelt National Historic Site, 519 Albany Post Road, Hyde Park NY 12538. Phone: 914-229-7821. Mrs. Roosevelt used Val-Kill as a personal retreat from her busy life. Val-Kill Cottage is the focal point of the historic site.

Federal Hall National Memorial, Manhattan Sites, 26 Wall St., New York NY 10005. Phone: 212-264-8711. This graceful building is on the site of the original Federal Hall where the trial of John Peter Zenger, involving freedom of the press, was held in 1735; the stamp Act Congress convened, 1765; the Second Continental Congress met, 1785; Washington took the oath as first U.S. President, and the Bill of Rights was adopted, 1789.

Fire Island National Seashore, 120 Laurel St., Patchogue NY 11772. Phone: 516-289-4810. Ocean washed beaches, dunes, Fire Island Light, and the nearby estate of William Floyd, a signer of the Declaration of Independence, make this park a blend of recreation, preservation, and conservation.

Fort Stanwix National Monument, 112 East Park St., Rome NY 13440. Phone: 315-336-2090. The American stand here in August 1777 was a major factor in repulsing the British invasion from Canada.

Gateway National Recreation Area, Floyd Bennett Field, Brooklyn NY 11234. Phone: 718-338-3575. With beaches, marshes, islands, historic structures, military installations, airfields, a lighthouse, and adjacent waters in New York harbor, this park offers urban residents a wide range of recreational opportunities and historical perspectives.

General Grant National Memorial, Manhattan Sites, 26 Wall St., New York NY 10005. Phone: 212-264-4456. This memorial to Ulysses S. Grant, the Union commander who brought the Civil War to an end, includes the tombs of General and Mrs. Grant.

Hamilton Grange National Memorial, Manhattan Sites, 26 Wall St., New York NY 10005. Phone: 212-264-4456. The Grange, named after his grandfather's estate in Scotland, was the home of Alexander Hamilton, American statesman and first Secretary of the Treasury.

Home of Franklin D. Roosevelt National Historic Site, 519 Albany Post Road, Hyde Park NY 12538. Phone: 914-229-7821. Springwood was the birthplace, lifetime residence, and "Summer White House" of the 32nd President. The gravesites of President and Mrs. Roosevelt are in the Rose Garden.

Martin Van Buren National Historic Site, P.O. Box 545, Kinderhook NY 12106. Phone: 518-758-9689. Lindenwald was the retirement home of Martin Van Buren, eighth President of the United States, and one of the principal architects of the Democratic Party.

Sagamore Hill National Historic Site, 20 Sagamore Hill Rd., Oyster Bay NY 11771-1899. Phone: 516-922-4447. This estate was the home of Theodore Roosevelt from 1886 until his death in 1919.

Saint Paul's Church National Historic Site, Manhattan Sites, 26 Wall St., New York NY 10005. Phone: 212-264-4456. This 18th century church is associated with the trial of John Peter Zenger and the fight for freedom of the press. The church was completed in 1787.

Saratoga National Historical Park, 648 Rt. 32, Stillwater NY 12170. Phone: 518-664-9821. The American victory here over the British in 1777 was the turning point of the Revolution and one of the decisive battles in world history.

Statue of Liberty National Monument, Liberty Island NY 10004. Phone: 212-363-7770. The famous 152 foot copper statue bearing the torch of freedom was a gift of the French people in 1886 to commemorate the alliance of the two nations in the American Revolution.

Theodore Roosevelt Birthplace National Historic Site, Manhattan Sites, 26 Wall St., New York NY 10005. Phone: 212-264-4456. The 26th President was born in a brownstone house here on October 27, 1858. Demolished in 1916, it was reconstructed and rededicated in 1923 and furnished by the President's widow and sisters.

Theodore Roosevelt Inaugural National Historic Site, 641 Delaware Ave., Buffalo NY 14202. Phone: 716-884-0095. Theodore Roosevelt took the oath of office as President of the United States on September 14, 1901, here in the Ansley Wilcox House after the assassination of President William McKinley.

Vanderbilt Mansion National Historic Site, 519 Albany Post Road, Hyde Park NY 12538. Phone: 914-229-7821. This palatial mansion is a fine example of homes built by 19th century millionaires. This particular home was constructed by Frederick W. Vanderbilt, a grandson of Cornelius Vanderbilt.

Women's Rights National Historical Park, P.O. Box 70, Seneca Falls NY 13148. Phone: 315-568-2991. Located in Seneca Falls, this park commemorates women's struggle for equal rights and includes the Wesleyan Methodist Chapel, the Elizabeth Cady Stanton home, the M'Clintock House and other sites related to notable early women's rights activists.

NORTH CAROLINA

Cape Hatteras National Seashore, Route 1 - Box 675, Manteo NC 27954. Phone: 919-995-4474. Beaches, migratory waterfowl, fishing, and points of historical interest, including the Cape Hatteras Lighthouse overlooking the "graveyard of the Atlantic," are special features of the first national seashore.

Cape Lookout National Seashore, Harkers Island NC 28531. Phone: 919-728-2250. This series of undeveloped barrier islands extends 55 miles along the lower Outer Banks embracing beaches, dunes, historic Portsmouth Village, and Cape Lookout Lighthouse.

Carl Sandburg Home National Historic Site, 1928 Little River Rd., Flat Rock NC 28731. Phone: 704-643-4178. Connermara was the farm home of the noted poet-author for the last 22 years of his life. During his residence here, several of his books were published.

Fort Raleigh National Historic Site, c/o Cape Hatteras National Seashore, Route 1 - Box 675, Manteo NC 27954. Phone: 919-473-5772. The first English settlement in North America was attempted here. The fate of Sir Walter Raleigh's "Lost Colony" remains a mystery.

Great Smoky Mountains National Park. See Tennessee for address and description.

Guilford Courthouse National Military Park, P.O. Box 9806, Greensboro NC 27429-0806. Phone: 919-288-1776. The battle fought here on March 15, 1781, opened the campaign that led to Yorktown and the end of the Revolution.

Moores Creek National Battlefield, P.O. Box 69, Currie NC 28435. Phone: 919-283-5591. The battle on February 27, 1776, between North Carolina Patriots and Loyalists, is commemorated here. The patriot victory notably advanced the revolutionary cause in the South.

Wright Brothers National Memorial, c/o Cape Hatteras National Seashore, Route 1 - Box 675, Menteo NC 27954. Phone: 919-441-7430. The first sustained flight in a heavier-than-air machine was made here by Wilbur and Orville Wright on December 17, 1903.

NORTH DAKOTA

Fort Union Trading Post National Historic Site, RR 3 - Box 71, Williston ND 58801. Phone: 701-572-9083. The trading post that stood here was the principal fur trading depot in the Upper Missouri River region.

International Peace Garden, Route 1 - Box 116, Dunseith ND 58329. Phone: 701-263-4390. Peaceful relations between Canada and the United States are commemorated here.

Knife River Indian Villages National Historic Site, Box 9, Stanton ND 58571. Phone: 701-745-3309. The park contains remnants of historic and prehistoric American Indian villages, last occupied in 1845 by the Hidatsa and Mandan. The site contains an array of artifacts of Plains Indian culture.

Theodore Roosevelt National Park, Medora, ND 58645. Phone: 701-623-4466. The park includes scenic badlands along the Little Missouri River and part of Theodore Roosevelt's Elkhorn Ranch.

OHIO

Cuyahoga Valley National Recreation Area, 15610 Vaughn Rd., Brecksville OH 44141. Phone: 800-433-1986. This recreation area links the urban centers of Cleveland and Akron, preserving the rural character of the Cuyahoga River Valley.

David Berger National Memorial, Jewish Community Center, 3505 Mayfield Rd., Cleveland Heights OH 44118. Phone: 216-382-4000. This site honors the memory of the 11 Israeli athletes who were killed at the 1972 Olympic Games in Munich, Germany, one of whom was David Berger, an American citizen.

Dayton Aviation National Historical Park, P.O. Box 9280, Wright Brothers Station, Dayton OH 45409. Phone: 513-223-0020. The park preserves the area's aviation heritage associated with Orville and Wilbur Wright, their invention and the development of aviation.

Hopewell Culture National Historical Park, 16062 State Rt. 104, Chillicothe OH 45601. Phone: 614-774-1125. Twenty-three burial mounds of Hopewell Indians yielded copper breast-plates, tools, obsidian blades, shells, ornaments of grizzly bear teeth, and stone pipes carved as birds and animals. These provide insights into the ceremonial customs of these prehistoric people.

James A. Garfield National Historic Site, 8095 Mentor Ave., Mentor OH 44060. Phone: 216-255-8722. This site preserves property associated with the life of the 20th President.

Perry's Victory and International Peace Memorial, P.O. Box 549, Put-in-Bay OH 43456. Phone: 419-285-2184. Commodore Oliver H. Perry won the greatest naval battle of the War of 1812 on Lake Erie.

William Howard Taft National Historic Site, 2038 Auburn Ave., Cincinnati OH 45219-3025. Phone: 513-684-3262. William Howard Taft, the only person to serve as both President and Chief Justice of the United States, was born and raised in this restored home.

OKLAHOMA

Chickasaw National Recreation Area, P.O. Box 201, Sulphur OK 73086. Phone: 405-622-3165. The partially forested, rolling hills of south-central Oklahoma and its springs, streams, and lakes are the setting for swimming, boating, and fishing as well as picnicking, camping, and hiking.

OREGON

Crater Lake National Park, P.O. Box 7, Crater Lake OR 97604. Phone: 503-594-2211. Crater Lake is world known for its deep blue color. It lies within the caldera of Mt. Mazama, a volcano of the Cascade Range that erupted about 6,850 years ago. Its depth of 1,932 feet makes it the deepest lake in the United States.

Fort Clatsop National Memorial, Route 3 - Box 604-FC, Astoria OR 97103. Phone: 503-861-2471. Having reached the Pacific Ocean, the Lewis and Clark Expedition camped here in the winter of 1805-06.

John Day Fossil Beds National Monument, 420 West Main St., John Day OR 97845. Phone: 503-575-0721. Plant and animal fossils show four epochs, from Eocene to Pliocene.

McLoughlin House National Historic Site, 713 Center St., Oregon City OR 97045. Phone: 503-656-5146. John McLoughlin was famous for his efforts in securing most of the Oregon Country territory for Americans, earning him the title, "Father of Oregon."

Oregon Caves National Monument, 19000 Caves Hwy., Cave Junction OR 97523. Phone: 503-592-2100. Groundwater dissolving marble bedrock formed these cave passages and intricate flowstone formations.

PENNSYLVANIA

Allegheny Portage Railroad National Historic Site, P.O. Box 189, Cresson PA 16630. Phone: 814-886-6100. Traces of the first railroad crossing of the Allegheny Mountains can still be seen here.

Benjamin Franklin National Memorial, 20th St. and Benjamin Franklin Pky., Philadelphia PA 19103. Phone: 215-448-1329. In the Rotunda of the Franklin Institute, the seated statue of Franklin honors the inventor-statesman.

Delaware And Lehigh Navigation Canal National Heritage Corridor, 10 East Church St. P-208, Bethlehem PA 18018. Phone: 215-861-9345. These two 19th century canals and their associated early railroads opened up the rich anthracite coal fields of eastern Pennsylvania and fueled the Industrial Revolution.

Delaware Water Gap National Recreation Area, Bushkill PA 18324. Phone: 717-588-2435. This scenic area preserves relatively unspoiled land on both the New Jersey and Pennsylvania sides of the middle Delaware River. The river segment flows through the famous gap in the Appalachian Mountains.

Edgar Allan Poe National Historic Site, 313 Walnut St., Philadelphia, PA 19106. Phone: 215-597-8974, 215-597-1785 (TDD). The life and work of this gifted American author are portrayed in this three building complex where Poe lived.

Eisenhower National Historic Site, P.O. Box 1080, Gettysburg PA 17325. Phone: 717-334-1124, 717-334-1382 (TDD). This was the only home ever owned by Gen. Dwight D. Eisenhower and his wife, Mamie. It served as a refuge when he was President and as a retirement home after he left office.

Fort Necessity National Battlefield, RD #2 - Box 528, Farmington PA 15437. Phone: 412-329-5512. Colonial troops commanded by Col. George Washington, then 22 years old, were defeated here in the opening battle of the French and Indian War on July 3, 1754.

Friendship Hill National Historic Site, RD #2 - Box 149-A, Farmington PA 15437. Phone: 412-725-9190. This stone and brick home on the Monongahela River near Point Marion, Pennsylvania, belonged to Albert Gallatin, Secretary of the Treasury under Presidents Jefferson and Madison.

Gettysburg National Military Park, P.O. Box 1080, Gettysburg PA 17325. Phone: 717-334-1124. The great Civil War battle fought here July 1-3, 1863, repulsed the second Confederate invasion of the North.

Gloria Dei (Old Swedes) Church National Historic Site, c/o Independence National Historical Park, 313 Walnut St., Philadelphia PA 19106. Phone: 215-597-8974, 215-597-1785 (TDD). This is the second oldest Swedish church in the United States and was founded in 1677.

Hopewell Furnace National Historic Site, 2 Mark Bird Lane, Elverson PA 19520. Phone: 215-582-8773, 215-582-2093 (TDD). This is one of the finest examples of a rural American 19th century iron plantation. The buildings include a blast furnace, the ironmaster's mansion, and auxiliary structures.

Independence National Historical Park, 313 Walnut St., Philadelphia PA 19106. Phone: 215-597-8974, 215-597-1785 (TDD). The park includes structures and sites in central Philadelphia associated with the American Revolution and the founding and growth of the United States.

Johnstown Flood National Memorial, P.O. Box 355, Saint Michael PA 15951. Phone: 814-495-4643. A total of 2,209 people died in the Johnstown Flood of 1889, caused by a break in the South Fork Dam.

Steamtown National Historic Site, 150 South Washington Ave., Scranton PA 18503. Phone: 717-961-2033. The former Delaware, Lackawanna & Western Railroad yard, including the remains of the historic roundhouse, switchyard, associated building, 29 steam locomotives, 78 passenger, freight, and work cars are being restored and preserved to interpret the story of early 20th century steam railroading in America.

Thaddeus Kosciuszko National Memorial, c/o Independence National Historical Park, 313 Walnut St., Philadelphia PA 19106. Phone: 215-597-8974, 215-597-1785 (TDD). The life and work of this Polish born patriot and hero of the American Revolution are commemorated here.

Valley Forge National Historical Park, Box 953, Valley Forge PA 19481. Phone: 215-783-1077. Site of the Continental Army's winter encampment, the park contains Gen. Washington's headquarters, original earthworks, a variety of monuments and markers, and recreations of log buildings and cannon.

RHODE ISLAND

Roger Williams National Memorial, 282 N. Main St., Providence RI 02903. Phone: 401-528-5385. This memorial is a landscaped urban park on the site of the founding of Providence by Roger Williams in 1636.

Touro Synagogue National Historic Site, 85 Touro St., Newport RI 02840. Phone: 401-847-4794. One of the finest examples of colonial religious architecture, this synagogue is the present day place of worship of Congregation Jeshuat Israel.

SOUTH CAROLINA

Charles Pinckney National Historic Site, c/o Fort Sumter National Monument, 1214 Middle St., Sullivan's Island SC 29482. Phone: 803-883-3123. Charles Pinckney fought in the Revolutionary War and became one of the principal framers of the Constitution. Expected to be open to the public May 1995.

Congaree Swamp National Monument, 200 Caroline Sims Rd., Hopkins SC 29061. Phone: 803-776-4396. Congaree swamp contains the last significant tract of southern bottomland hardwood forest in the United States. It is home to a rich diversity of plant and animal species associated with an alluvial floodplain.

Cowpens National Battlefield, P.O. Box 308, Chesnee SC 29323. Phone: 803-461-2828. Brig. Gen. Daniel Morgan won a decisive Revolutionary War victory here over British Lt. Col. Banastre Tarleton on January 17, 1781.

Fort Sumter National Monument, 1214 Middle St., Sullivan's Island SC 29482. Phone: 803-883-3123. The first engagement of the Civil War took place here on April 12, 1861.

Historic Camden, Highway 521 South, P.O. Box 710, Camden SC 29020. Phone: 803-432-9841. This early colonial village was established in the mid 1730s and was known as Fredricksburg Township until it was renamed in 1768 in honor of Charles Pratt, Lord Camden.

Kings Mountain National Military Park, P.O. Box 40, Kings Mountain NC 28086. Phone: 803-936-7921. American frontiersmen defeated the British here on October 7, 1780, at a critical point during the Revolution.

Ninety Six National Historic Site, P.O. Box 496, Ninety Six SC 29666. Phone: 803-543-4068. This important colonial back country trading village is the scene of Nathanael Greene's siege in 1781. The site contains earthwork embankments of a 1781 fortification, the remains of two historic villages, a colonial plantation complex, and numerous prehistoric sites.

SOUTH DAKOTA

Badlands National Park, P.O. Box 6, Interior SD 57750. Phone: 605-433-5361. Carved by erosion, this scenic landscape contains animal fossils of 40 million years ago. Prairie grasslands support bison, bighorn sheep, deer, and antelope.

Jewel Cave National Monument, RR 1 - Box 60AA, Custer SD 57730. Phone: 605-673-2288. Limestone caverns consist of a series of chambers connected by narrow passages, with fine calcite crystal encrustations.

Mount Rushmore National Memorial, P.O. Box 268, Keystone SD 57751. Phone: 605-574-2523. Colossal heads of Presidents George Washington, Thomas Jefferson, Abraham Lincoln, and Theodore Roosevelt were sculpted by Gutzon Borglum on the face of a granite mountain.

Wind Cave National Park, RR 1 - Box 190 WCNP, Hot Springs SD 57747. Phone: 605-745-4600. This limestone cave in the scenic Black Hills is decorated by beautiful boxwork and calcite crystal formations.

TENNESSEE

Andrew Johnson National Historic Site, P.O. Box 1088, Greeneville TN 37744. Phone: 615-638-3551. The site includes two homes and the tailor shop of the 17th President and the Andrew Johnson National Cemetery, where the President is buried.

Big South Fork National River and Recreation Area, Route 3 - Box 401, Oneida TN 37841. Phone: 615-569-3625. The free flowing Big South Fork of the Cumberland River and its tributaries pass through 90 miles of scenic gorges and valleys containing a wide range of natural and historical features and offering a broad range of recreational opportunities.

Cumberland Gap National Historical Park. See Kentucky for address and description.

Fort Donelson National Battlefield, P.O. Box 434, Dover TN 37058. Phone: 615-232-5348. The first major victory for the Union Army in the Civil War occurred here in February 1862 under the leadership of Ulysses S. Grant.

Great Smoky Mountains National Park, 107 Park Headquarters Rd., Gatlinburg TN 37738. Phone: 615-436-1220. The loftiest range east of the Black Hills and one of the oldest uplands on Earth, the Smokies have a diversified and luxuriant plant life, often of extraordinary size.

Shiloh National Military Park, Route 1 - Box 9, Shiloh TN 38376. Phone: 901-689-5275. The bitter battle fought here April 6-7, 1862, prepared the way for Maj. Gen. U.S. Grant's successful siege of Vicksburg.

Stones River National Battlefield, 3501 Old Nashville Hwy., Murfreesboro TN 37129-3095. Phone: 615-893-9501. The fierce midwinter battle, which began the federal offensive to trisect the Confederacy, took place here December 31, 1862 to January 2, 1863.

TEXAS

Alibates Flint Quarries National Monument, c/o Lake Meredith National Recreation Area, P.O. Box 1438, Fritch TX 79036. Phone: 806-857-3151. For more than 10,000 years, pre-Columbian Indians dug agatized dolomite from quarries here to make projectile points, knives, scrapers, and other tools.

Amistad National Recreation Area, P.O. Box 420367, Del Rio TX 78842-0367. Phone: 210-775-7491. Boating, water sports, and camping highlight activities in the U.S. section of Amistad Reservoir on the Rio Grande.

Big Bend National Park, Big Bend National Park TX 79834. Phone: 915-477-2251. Mountains contrast with desert within the great bend of the Rio Grande, whose grit-laden waters rasp through deep cut canyon walls for 118 miles.

Big Thicket National Preserve, 3785 Milam, Beaumont TX 77701. Phone: 409-839-2689. A great number of plant and animal species coexist in this "biological crossroads of North America."

Chamizal National Memorial, 800 S. San Marcial, El Paso TX 79905. Phone: 915-532-7273. The peaceful settlement of a 99 year boundary dispute between the United States and Mexico is memorialized here. The Chamizal Treaty, ending the dispute, was signed in 1963.

Fort Davis National Historic Site, P.O. Box 1456, Fort Davis TX 79734. Phone: 915-426-3224. A key post in West Texas, soldiers from Fort Davis assisted in opening the area to settlement and protected travelers and merchants along the San Antonio - El Paso Road from 1864 to 1891.

Guadalupe Mountains National Park, HC60 - Box 400, Salt Flat TX 79847. Phone: 915-828-3251. Rising from the desert, this mountain mass contains portions of the world's most extensive and significant Permian limestone fossil reef. Also featured are a tremendous earth fault, lofty peaks, unusual flora and fauna, and a colorful record of the past.

Lake Meredith National Recreation Area, P.O. Box 1460, Fritch TX 79036. Phone: 806-857-3151. Man-made Lake Meredith on the Canadian River is a popular water activity center in the Southwest.

Lyndon B. Johnson National Historical Park, P.O. Box 329, Johnson City TX 78636. Phone: 210-868-7128. The park consists of the birthplace, boyhood home, and ranch of the 36th President, his grandparents' log cabin, and the Johnson family cemetery.

Padre Island National Seashore, 9405 S. Padre Island Dr., Corpus Christi TX 78418-5597. Phone: 512-937-2621. Noted for its wide sand beaches, excellent fishing and abundant bird and marine life, this barrier island stretches along the Gulf Coast for 80.5 miles.

San Antonio Missions National Historical Park, 2202 Roosevelt Ave., San Antonio TX 78210. Phone: 210-229-5701. Four Spanish frontier missions, part of a colonization system that stretched across the Spanish Southwest in the 17th, 18th, and 19th centuries, are commemorated here.

UTAH

Arches National Park, P.O. Box 907, Moab UT 84532. Phone: 801-259-8161. Extraordinary products of erosion in the form of giant arches, windows, pinnacles, and pedestals change color constantly as the sun moves overhead.

Bryce Canyon National Park, Bryce Canyon UT 84717. Phone: 801-834-5322. Innumerable highly colored and bizarre pinnacles, walls, and spires, perhaps the most colorful and unusual eroded forms in the world stand in horseshoe shaped amphitheaters along the edge of the Paunsaugunt Plateau in southern Utah.

Canyonlands National Park, 125 W. 200 S., Moab UT 84532. Phone: 801-259-7164. In this geological wonderland, rocks, spires, and mesas dominate the heart of the Colorado Plateau cut by canyons of the Green and Colorado rivers. Prehistoric Indian rock art and ruins dot the redrock landscape.

Capitol Reef National Park, HC70 - Box 15, Torrey UT 84775. Phone: 801-425-3791. Narrow high walled gorges cut through a 70 mile uplift of sandstone cliffs with highly colored sedimentary formations.

Cedar Breaks National Monument, P.O. Box 749, Cedar City UT 84720. Phone: 801-586-9451. A huge natural amphitheater has eroded into the variegated Pink Cliffs, 2,000 feet thick at this point.

Dinosaur National Monument. See Colorado for address and description.

Glen Canyon National Recreation Area, P.O. Box 1507, Page AZ 86040. Phone: 602-645-8200. The park lies in the midst of the Nation's most rugged canyon country. Lake Powell stretches for 186 miles along the old Colorado River channel with a shoreline of 1,960 miles.

Golden Spike National Historic Site, P.O. Box 897, Brigham City UT 84302. Phone: 801-471-2209. Completion of the first transcontinental railroad in the United States was celebrated here where the Central Pacific and Union Pacific Railroads met in 1869.

Hovenweep National Monument. See Colorado for address.

Natural Bridges National Monument, P.O. Box 1, Lake Powell UT 84533. Phone: 801-259-5174. Three natural bridges carved out of sandstone, including the second and third largest in the world, are protected here. Under one bridge are ancient Anasazi rock art and ruins.

Rainbow Bridge National Monument, c/o Glen Canyon National Recreation Area, Box 1507, Page AZ 86040. Phone: 602-645-8200. Greatest of the world's known natural bridges, this symmetrical, salmon pink sandstone span rises 290 feet above the floor of Bridge Canyon. Once remote and difficult to reach, the bridge is now accessible by boat from Lake Powell.

Timpanogos Cave National Monument, RR 3 - Box 200, American Fork UT 84003. Phone: 801-756-5239. The colorful limestone cavern on the side of Mount Timpanogos is noted for helicites - water created formations that grow in all directions and shapes, regardless of the pull of gravity.

Zion National Park, Springdale UT 84767. Phone: 801-772-3256. Colorful canyon and mesa scenery includes erosion and rock-fault patterns that create phenomenal shapes and landscapes.

VIRGINIA

Appomattox Court House National Historical Park, P.O. Box 218, Appomattox VA 24522. Phone: 804-352-8987. Here on April 9, 1865, Gen. Robert E. Lee surrendered the Confederacy's most successful field army to Lt. Gen. Ulysses S. Grant.

Arlington House, The Robert E. Lee Memorial, c/o George Washington Memorial Parkway, Turkey Run Park, McLean VA 22101. Phone: 703-557-0613. This antebellum home of the Custis and Lee families overlooks the Potomac River and Washington, D.C.

Assateague Island National Seashore. See Maryland for address and description.

Booker T. Washington National Monument, Route 3 - Box 310, Hardy VA 24101. Phone: 703-721-2094. This site was the birthplace and early childhood home of the famous black leader and educator.

Colonial National Historical Park, P.O. Box 210, Yorktown VA 23690. Phone: 804-898-3400. This park encompasses most of Jamestown Island, site of the first permanent English settlement; Yorktown, scene of the culminating battle of the American Revolution in 1781; a 23 mile parkway; and Cape Henry Memorial, which marks the approximate site of the first landing of Jamestown's colonists in 1607.

Cumberland Gap National Historical Park. See Kentucky for address and description.

Fredericksburg and Spotsylvania County Battlefields Memorial National Military Park, 120 Chatham Lane, Fredericksburg VA 22405. Phone: 703-373-4461. Portions of four major Civil War Battlefields, Chatham Manor, Salem Church, and the historic building in which Stonewall Jackson died comprise the park.

George Washington Birthplace National Monument, RR 1 - Box 717, Washington's Birthplace VA 22443. Phone: 804-224-1732. Birthplace of the first United States President, the park includes a memorial mansion and gardens and the tombs of several generations of Washingtons.

Great Falls Park, c/o George Washington Memorial Parkway, Turkey Run Park, McLean VA 22101. Phone 703-285-2598. This park is part of a riverfront parkway that links landmarks in the life of George Washington.

Green Springs Historic District, P.O. Box 1838, Louisa VA 23093. Phone: 703-967-9671. This portion of Louisa County in Virginia's Piedmont is noted for its concentration of fine rural manor houses and related buildings in an unmarred landscape.

Jamestown National Historic Site, c/o Colonial National Historical Park, P.O. Box 210, Yorktown VA 23690. Phone: 804-898-3400. Part of the site of the first permanent English settlement in North America and scene of the first representative legislative government on this continent.

Maggie L. Walker National Historic Site, c/o Richmond National Battlefield Park, 3215 E. Broad St., Richmond VA 23223. Phone: 804-780-1380. This rowhouse was the home of an ex-house slave's daughter who became a bank president and a leading figure in the Richmond black community.

Manassas National Battlefield Park, 12521 Lee Highway, Manassas VA 22110. Phone: 703-361-1339. The Battles of First and Second Manassas were fought here July 21, 1861, and August 28-30, 1862.

Petersburg National Battlefield, P.O. Box 549, Petersburg VA 23804. Phone: 804-732-3531. The Union Army waged a 10 month campaign here in 1864-65 to seize Petersburg, center of the railroads supplying Richmond and Gen. Robert E. Lee's army.

Prince William Forest Park, P.O. Box 209, Triangle VA 22172. Phone: 703-221-4706. The pine and hardwood forests of the Quantico Creek watershed shelter hiking trails, campgrounds, playing fields, and five Civilian Conservation Corps era cabins.

Red Hill Patrick Henry National Memorial, Route 2 - Box 127, Brookneal VA 24528. Phone: 804-376-2044. The law office and grave of the fiery Virginia legislator and orator are preserved at this small plantation, along with a reconstruction of Patrick Henry's last home, several dependencies, and a museum.

Richmond National Battlefield Park, 3215 East Broad St., Richmond VA 23223. Phone: 804-226-1981. The park commemorates several battles to capture Richmond, the Confederate capital.

Shenandoah National Park, Route 4 - Box 348, Luray VA 22835. Phone: 703-999-2266. Skyline Drive winds through hardwood forests along the crest of this outstanding portion of the Blue Ridge Mountains, with spectacular vistas of the Shenandoah Valley and the Piedmont.

Wolf Trap Farm Park for the Performing Arts, 1551 Trap Rd., Vienna VA 22182. Phone: 703-255-1800. At this first national park for the performing arts, Filene Center can accommodate an audience of 6,786, including 3,000 on the sloping lawn in a setting of rolling hills and woods.

WASHINGTON

Coulee Dam National Recreation Area, 1008 Crest Drive, Coulee Dam WA 99116. Phone: 509-633-9441. Formed by Grand Coulee Dam, 130 mile long Franklin D. Roosevelt Lake is the principal recreation feature here.

Ebey's Landing National Historical Reserve, P.O. Box 774, Coupeville WA 98239. Phone: 206-678-6084. This area of central Whidbey Island protects important natural and historic features.

Fort Vancouver National Historic Site, 612 E. Reserve St., Vancouver WA 98661. Phone: 206-696-7655. From 1825 to 1849, Fort Vancouver was the western headquarters of the Hudson's Bay Company's fur trading operations.

Klondike Gold Rush National Historical Park, 117 South Main St., Seattle WA 98104. Phone: 206-553-7220. News of the gold strike in Canada's Yukon Territory spread from Seattle across the country, and from here most prospectors left for the gold fields.

Lake Chelan National Recreation Area, 2105 Highway 20, Sedro Woolley WA 98284. Phone: 206-856-5700. Here the beautiful Stehekin Valley, with a portion of fjord-like Lake Chelan, adjoins North Cascades National Park.

Mount Rainier National Park, Tahoma Woods, Star Route, Ashford WA 98304. Phone: 206-569-2211. This greatest single peak glacial system in the United States radiates from the summit and slopes of an ancient volcano, with dense forests and sub-alpine flowered meadows below.

North Cascades National Park, 2105 Highway 20, Sedro Woolley WA 98284. Phone: 206-856-5700. High jagged peaks intercept moisture-laden winds, producing glaciers, icefalls, waterfalls, and other water phenomena in this wild alpine region where lush forests and meadows, plant and animal communities thrive in the valleys.

Olympic National Park, 600 East Park Ave., Port Angeles WA 98362. Phone: 206-452-0330. This mountain wilderness contains the finest remnant of Pacific Northwest rain forest, active glaciers, rare Roosevelt elk, and 50 miles of wild, scenic ocean shore.

Ross Lake National Recreation Area, 2105 Highway 20, Sedro Woolley WA 98284. Phone: 206-856-5700. Ringed by mountains, this national recreation area offers many outdoor recreation opportunities along the upper reaches of the Skagit River, between the north and south units of North Cascades National Park.

San Juan Island National Historical Park, P.O. Box 429, Friday Harbor WA 98250. Phone: 206-378-2240. This park marks the events on the island from 1853 to 1872 in connection with final settlement of the Oregon Territory's boundary, including the so-called Pig War of 1859.

Whitman Mission National Historic Site, Route 2 - Box 247, Walla Walla WA 99362. Phone: 509-529-2761. The mission of Marcus and Narcissa Whitman at Waiilatpu was an important way station in the early days of the Oregon Trail.

WEST VIRGINIA

Gauley River National Recreation Area, P.O. Box 246, Glen Jean WV 25846. Phone: 304-465-0508. The 25 miles of free flowing Gauley River and the 6 miles of the Meadow River pass through scenic gorges and valleys containing a wide variety of natural and cultural features.

Harpers Ferry National Historical Park, P.O. Box 65, Harpers Ferry WV 25425. Phone: 304-535-6223. Because of its strategic location at the confluence of the Shenandoah and Potomac rivers, this town changed hands eight times during the Civil War. John Brown's raid took place here in 1859.

WISCONSIN

Apostle Islands National Lakeshore, Route 1 - Box 4, Bayfield WI 54814. Phone: 715-779-3397. Twenty-one picturesque islands and an 11 mile strip of adjacent Bayfield Peninsula along the south shore of Lake Superior comprise this park.

Ice Age National Scientific Reserve, Wisconsin Dept. of Natural Resources, P.O. Box 7921, Madison WI 53707. Phone: 608-266-2181. This first national scientific reserve contains nationally significant features of continental glaciation. State parks in the area are open to the public.

WYOMING

Bighorn Canyon National Recreation Area, 20 Highway 14A East, Lovell WY 82431. See Montana for description.

Devils Tower National Monument, P.O. Box 8, Devils Tower WY 82714. Phone: 307-467-5283. This 865 foot tower of columnar rock, the remains of a volcanic intrusion, is the Nation's first national monument.

Fort Laramie National Historic Site, Fort Laramie WY 82212. Phone: 307-837-2221. A fur trade post once stood here, but the surviving buildings are those of a major military post that guarded wagon trails to the West.

Fossil Butte National Monument, P.O. Box 592, Kemmerer WY 83101. Phone: 307-877-4455. The most noteworthy record of freshwater fossil fish ever found in the United States is preserved here.

Grand Teton National Park, P.O. Drawer 170, Moose WY 83012. Phone: 307-733-2880. The most impressive part of the Teton Range, this series of blue-gray peaks rising more than a mile above the sagebrush flats was once a noted landmark for Indians and "mountain men."

Yellowstone National Park, P.O. Box 168, Yellowstone National Park WY 82190. Phone: 307-344-7381. Old Faithful and some 10,000 other geysers and hot springs make this the Earth's greatest geyser area. Here, too, are lakes, waterfalls, high mountain meadows, and the Grand Canyon of the Yellowstone - all set apart in 1872 as the world's first national park.

NATIONAL FOREST SERVICE

The National Forest system consists of 156 forest in 44 states. The 190 million acres of public lands provide access to many outdoor activity areas including:

- 10,000 recreation areas.
- Over 6,000 campgrounds and picnic areas.
- 102,500 miles of trails.
- 128,000 miles of rivers and streams.
- Over 1,100 boating sites.
- 2.2 million acres of lakes and reservoirs.
- 329 wilderness areas totaling 32.4 million acres.
- About 50 percent of the nation's big game animals.
- 307 winter sport areas with 157 ski areas providing over 40 percent of all downhill skiing opportunities in the U.S.

There are no entrance fees for the National Forest, although many of the developed recreational sites charge a user fee. To receive additional free information on logding, camping, and recreational opportunities contact the National Forest office for the area you are interested in..

REGIONAL HEADQUARTERS

National Forest - Washington D.C. Headquarters, 12th St. and Independence Avenue SW, P.O. Box 96090, Washington D.C. 20090. Phone: 202-447-3957.

National Forest - Alaska Region, P.O. Box 21628, Juneau AK 99802-1628. Phone: 907-586-88632. States: AK.

National Forest - Southern Region, 1720 Peachtree Rd. NW - Suite 951, Atlanta GA 30367-9102. Phone: 404-347-4191. States: AL, AR, FL, GA, KY, LA, MS, NC, OK, PR, SC, TN, TX, VA.

National Forest - Pacific Southwest Region, 630 Sansome St., San Francisco CA 94111. Phone: 415-705-2874. States: CA.

National Forest - Rocky Mountain Region, 740 Simms Street, Golden CO 80401. Phone: 303-275-5050. States: CO, NE, SD, WY.

National Forest - Northern Region, Federal Building 200 E. Broadway St., P.O. Box 7669, Missoula MT 59807. Phone: 406-329-3511. States: ID, MT.

National Forest - Southwestern Region, Federal Building 517 Gold Avenue SW, Albuquerque NM 87102. Phone: 505-842-3292. States: AZ, NM.

National Forest - Pacific Northwest Region, 333 SW First Ave., P.O. Box 3623, Portland OR 97208-3623. Phone: 503-221-2877. States: OR, WA.

National Forest - Intermountain Region, Federal Building 324 25th St., Odgen UT 84401-2310. Phone: 801-625-5354. States: ID, NV, UT, WY.

National Forest - Eastern Region, 310 W. Wisconsin Ave., Milwaukee WI 53203. Phone: 414-297-3693. States: IL, IN, OH, MI, MN, MO, NH, ME, PA, VT, WV, WI.

ALABAMA

Bankhead National Forest
Conecuh National Forest
Talladega National Forest
Tuskegee National Forest
National Forests in Alabama, 2950 Chestnut, Montgomery AL 36107-3010. Phone: 205-832-4470.

ALASKA

Chugach National Forest, 201 East 9th Avenue - Suite 206, Anchorage AK 99501. Phone: 907-271-2500.
Tongass National Forest, Federal Building, Ketchikan AK 99901. Phone: 907-225-3101.

ARIZONA

Apache-Sitgreaves National Forest, 309 S. Mountain Avenue, U.S. Hwy 180, P.O. Box 640, Springerville AZ 85938. Phone: 602-333-4301.
Coconino National Forest, 2323 E. Greenlaw Lane, Flagstaff AZ 86004. Phone: 602-527-7400.
Coronado National Forest, Federal Building 300 West Congress, Tucson AZ 85701. Phone: 602-670-6483.
Kaibab National Forest, 800 S. 6th St., Williams AZ 86046. Phone: 602-635-2681.
Prescott National Forest, 344 S. Cortez St., Prescott AZ 86303. Phone: 602-445-1762.
Tonto National Forest, 2324 E. McDowell Rd., P.O. Box 5348, Phoenix AZ 85010. Phone: 602-225-5326.

ARKANSAS

Ouachita National Forest, 100 Reserve St., P.O. Box 1270, Hot Springs AR 71902. Phone: 501-321-5202.

Ozark - St. Francis National Forest, 605 W. Main St., P.O. Box 1008, Russellville AR 72801. Phone: 501-968-2354.

CALIFORNIA

Angeles National Forest, 701 N. Santa Anita Ave., Arcadia CA 91006. Phone: 818-574-5200.

Cleveland National Forest, 10845 Rancho Bernardo Road - Suite 200, San Diego CA 92127-2107. Phone: 619-674-2901.

Eldorado National Forest, 100 Forni Rd., Placerville CA 95667. Phone: 916-622-5061.

Inyo National Forest, 873 N. Main St., Bishop CA 93514. Phone: 619-873-5841.

Klamath National Forest, 1312 Fairlane Rd., Yreka CA 96097. Phone: 916-842-6131.

Lassen National Forest, 55 S. Sacramento St., Susanville CA 96130. Phone: 916-257-2151.

Los Padres National Forest, 6144 Calle Real, Goleta CA 93117. Phone: 805-683-6711.

Mendocino National Forest, 420 E. Laurel St., Willows CA 95988. Phone: 916-934-3316.

Modoc National Forest, 441 N. Main St., Alturas CA 96101. Phone: 916-233-5811.

Plumas National Forest, 159 Lawrence St., P.O. Box 11500, Quincy CA 95971-6025. Phone: 916-283-2050.

San Bernardino National Forest, 1824 S. Commercenter Cir., San Bernardino CA 92408-3430. Phone: 714-383-5588.

Sequoia National Forest, 900 W. Grand Ave., Porterville CA 93257-2035. Phone: 209-784-1500.

Shasta-Trinity National Forests, 2400 Washington Ave., Redding CA 96001. Phone: 916-246-5152.

Sierra National Forest, 1600 Tollhouse Rd., Clovis CA 93612. Phone: 209-487-5155.

Six Rivers National Forest, 1330 Bayshore Way, Eureka CA 95501. Phone: 707-442-1721.

Stanislaus National Forest, 19777 Greenley Rd., Sonora CA 95370. Phone: 209-532-3671.

Tahoe National Forest, P.O. Box 6003, Nevada City CA 95959-6003. Phone: 916-265-4531

COLORADO

Arapahoe & Roosevelt National Forest, 240 W. Prospect Rd., Fort Collins CO 80526-2098. Phone: 303-498-1100.

Grand Mesa - Uncompahgre & Gunnison National Forests, 2250 Highway 50, Delta CO 81416-8723. Phone: 303-874-7691.

Pike and San Isabel National Forests, 1920 Valley Drive, Pueblo CO 81008-1797. Phone: 719-545-8737.

Rio Grande National Forest, 1803 W. Highway 160, Monte Vista CO 81144 . Phone: 719-852-5941.

Routt National Forest, 29587 West U.S. Hwy. 40 - Suite 20, Steamboat Springs CO 80487. Phone: 303-879-1722.

San Juan National Forest, 701 Camino del Rio - Room 301, Durango CO 81301. Phone: 303-247-4874.

White River National Forest, 9th and Grand, P.O. Box 948, Glenwood Springs CO 81602. Phone: 303-945-2521.

FLORIDA

Apalachicola National Forest
Ocala National Forest
Osceola National Forest
National Forests In Florida, Woodcrest Office Park - Suite F-100, 325 John Knox Rd., Tallahassee, FL 32303. Phone: 904-681-7265.

GEORGIA

Chattahoochee & Oconee National Forests, 508 Oak St. NW, Gainsville GA 30501. Phone: 404-536-0541.

IDAHO

Boise National Forest, 1750 Front St., Boise ID 83702. Phone: 208-364-4100.

Caribou National Forest, Federal Building - Suite 282, 250 S. 4th Ave., Pocatello ID 83201. Phone: 208-236-7500.

Challis National Forest, Highway 93 N, HC63 - Box 1671, Challis ID 83226-1671. Phone: 208-879-2285.

Payette National Forest, 106 W. Park St., P.O. Box 1026, McCall ID 83638. Phone: 208-634-8151.

Salmon National Forest, Highway 93 N, P.O. Box 729, Salmon ID 83467. Phone: 208-756-2215.

Sawtooth National Forest, 2647 Kimberly Rd. E, Twin Falls ID 83301-7976. Phone: 208-737-3200.

Targhee National Forest, 420 N. Bridge St., P.O. Box 208, St. Anthony ID 83445. Phone: 208-624-3151.

Clearwater National Forest, 12730 Highway 12, Orofino ID 83544. Phone: 208-476-4541.

Nez Perce National Forest, Route 2 - Box 475, Grangeville ID 83530. Phone: 208-983-1950.

Idaho Panhandle National Forests, 1201 Ironwood Dr., Coeur d'Alene ID 83814. Phone: 208-765-7223.

ILLINOIS

Shawnee National Forest, 901 S. Commercial St., Harrisburg IL 62946. Phone: 618-253-7114.

INDIANA

Wayne-Hoosier National Forests, 811 Constitution Ave., Bedford IN 47421. Phone: 812-275-5987.

KENTUCKY

Daniel Boone National Forest, 100 Vaught Rd., Winchester KY 40391. Phone: 606-745-3100.

LOUISIANA

Kisatchie National Forest, 2500 Shreveport Highway, P.O. Box 5500, Pineville LA 71360. Phone: 318-473-7160.

MICHIGAN

Hiawatha National Forest, 2727 N. Lincoln Rd., Escanaba MI

49829. Phone: 906-786-4062.
Huron-Manistee National Forests, 421 S. Mitchell St., Cadillac MI 49601. Phone: 616-775-2421.
Ottawa National Forest, 2100 E. Cloverland Dr., Ironwood MI 49938. Phone: 906-932-1330.

MINNESOTA

Chippewa National Forest, Route 3 - Box 244, Cass Lake MN 56633. Phone: 218-335-8600.
Superior National Forest, 515 W. First St., P.O. Box 338, Duluth MN 55801. Phone: 218-720-5324.

MISSISSIPPI

Bienville National Forest
Delta National Forest
Desoto National Forest
Holly Springs National Forest
Homochitton National Forest
Tombigbee National Forest
National Forests in Mississippi, 100 W. Capitol St. - Suite 1141, Federal Building, Jackson MS 39269. Phone: 601-965-4391.

MISSOURI

Mark Twain National Forest, Public Affairs Office, 401 Fairgrounds Rd., Rolla MO 65401. Phone: 314-364-4621.

MONTANA

Beaverhead National Forest, 610 N. Montana St,. Dillon MT 59725. Phone: 406-683-3900.
Bitterroot National Forest, 1801 N. First St., Hamilton MT 59840. Phone: 406-363-3131.
Custer National Forest, 2602 First Ave. N., P.O. Box 2556, Billings MT 59103. Phone: 406-657-6361.
Deerlodge National Forest, Federal Building, P.O. Box 400, Butte MT 59703. Phone: 406-496-3400.
Flathead National Forest, 1935 Third Ave. East, Kalispell MT 59901. Phone: 406-755-5401.
Gallatin National Forest, 10 East Babcock St., P.O. Box 130, Bozeman MT 59771. Phone: 406-587-6701.
Helena National Forest, 301 S. Park, Drawer 10014, Helena MT 59626. Phone: 406-449-5201.
Kootenai National Forest, 506 U.S. Highway 2 West, Libby MT 59923. Phone: 406-293-6211.
Lewis and Clark National Forest, 1101 15th St. North, P.O. Box 869, Great Falls MT 59403. Phone: 406-791-7700.
Lolo National Forest, Bldg. 24-A - Fort Missoula, Missoula MT 59801. Phone: 406-329-3750.

NEBRASKA

Nebraska National Forest, 270 Pine St., Chadron NE 69337. Phone: 308-432-3367.

NEVADA

Humboldt National Forest, 976 Mountain City Hwy., Elko NV 89801. Phone: 702-738-5171.

Toiyabe National Forest, 1200 Franklin Way, Sparks NV 89431. Phone: 702-355-5302.

NEW HAMPSHIRE

White Mountain National Forest, 719 N. Main St., P.O. Box 638, Laconia NH 03247. Phone: 603-528-8722.

NEW MEXICO

Carson National Forest, Forest Service Building, 208 Cruz Alta Rd., P.O. Box 558, Taos NM 87571. Phone: 505-758-6200.
Cibola National Forest, 2113 Osuna Road NE. - Suite A, Albuquerque NM 87113-1001. Phone: 505-275-5207.
Gila National Forest, 2610 N. Silver St., Silver City NM 88061. Phone: 505-388-8201.
Lincoln National Forest, Federal Bldg., 1101 New York Ave., Alamogoroo NM 88310-6992. Phone: 505-437-6030.
Santa Fe National Forest, 1220 St. Francis Dr., P.O. Box 1689, Santa Fe NM 87504. Phone: 505-988-6940.

NEW YORK

Finger Lakes National Forest, P.O. Box W, Montour Falls NY 14865. Phone: 607-594-2750.

NORTH CAROLINA

Croatann National Forest
Nantahala National Forest.
Pisgah National Forest
Uwharrie National Forest
National Forests in North Carolina, 100 Post and Otis St., P.O. Box 2750, Asheville NC 28802. Phone: 704-257-4200.

OHIO

Wayne-Hoosier National Forests, 811 Constitution Ave., Bedrod IN 47421. Phone: 812-275-5987.

OKLAHOMA

Black Kettle National Grassland, Route 1 - Box 55B, Cheyenne OK 73628. Phone: 405-497-2143.

OREGON

Deschutes National Forest, 1645 Hwy. 20 East, Bend OR 97701. Phone: 503-388-8574.
Fremont National Forest, 524 North G Street, Lakeview OR 97630. Phone: 503-947-2151.
Malheur National Forest, 139 NE Dayton St., John Day OR 97845. Phone: 503-575-1731.
Mt. Hood National Forest, 2955 N.W. Division St., Gresham OR 97030. Phone: 503-666-0700.
Ochoco National Forest, 3000 East Third St., P.O. Box 490, Prineville OR 97754. Phone: 503-447-6247.
Rogue River National Forest, 333 West 8th St., P.O. Box 520, Medford OR 97501. Phone: 503-776-3684.
Siskiyou National Forest, 200 NE Greenfield Rd., P.O. Box 440, Grants Pass OR 97526. Phone: 503-471-6500.

Siuslaw National Forest, 4077 Research Way, P.O. Box 1148, Corvallis OR 97339. Phone: 503-757-4480.
Umatilla National Forest, 2717 S.W. Hailey Ave., Pendleton OR 97801. Phone: 503-278-3716.
Umpqua National Forest, 2900 N.W. Stewart Parkway, P.O. Box 1008, Roseburg OR 97470. Phone: 503-672-6601.
Wallow-Whitman National Forest, 1550 Dewey Ave., P.O. Box 907, Baker City OR 97814. Phone: 503-523-6391.
Willamette National Forest, 211 E. Seventh Ave., P.O. Box 10607, Eugene OR 97440. Phone: 503-465-6521.
Winema National Forest, 2819 Dahlia St., Klamath Falls OR 97601. Phone: 503-883-6714.

PENNSYLVANIA

Allegheny National Forest, 222 Liberty St., P.O. Box 847, Warren PA 16365. Phone: 814-723-5150.

SOUTH CAROLINA

Francis Marion & Sumter National Forests, 1835 Assembly St.- Room 333, Columbia SC 29201. Phone: 803-765-5222.

SOUTH DAKOTA

Black Hills National Forest, Route 2 - Box 200, Custer SD 57730. Phone: 605-673-2251.

TENNESSEE

Cherokee National Forest, P.O. Box 7, Unicoi TN 37692. Phone: 615-743-8000.

TEXAS

Angelina National Forest
Davy Crockett National Forest
Sabine National Forest
Sam Houston National Forest
National Forests In Texas, Homer Garrison Federal Building, 701 N. 1st St., Lufkin TX 75901. Phone: 409-639-8501

UTAH

Ashley National Forest, 355 N. Vernal Ave., Vernal UT 84078. Phone: 801-789-1181.
Dixie National Forest, 82 N. 100 East, P.O. Box 580, Cedar City UT 84721-0580. Phone: 801-865-3700.
Fishlake National Forest, 115 E. 900 North, Richfield UT 84701. Phone: 801-896-9233.
Manti-LaSal National Forest, 599 W. Price River Dr., Price UT 84501. Phone: 801-637-2817.
Uinta National Forest, 88 West 100 North, Provo UT 84601. Phone: 801-377-5780.
Wasatch-Cache National Forest, 8236 Federal Building, 125 S. State, Salt Lake City UT 84138. Phone: 801-524-5030.

VERMONT

Green Mountain National Forest, 151 West St., P.O. Box 519, Rutland VT 05702. Phone: 802-773-0300.

VIRGINIA

George Washington National Forest, Harrison Plaza, 101 N. Main St., P.O. Box 233, Harrisonburg VA 22801. Phone: 703-433-2491.
Jefferson National Forest, 5162 Valleypointe Parkway, Roanoke VA 24019-3050. Phone: 703-982-6270.

WASHINGTON

Colville National Forest, 765 S. Main St., Colville WA 99114. Phone: 509-684-3711.
Gifford Pinchot National Forest, 6926 E. Fourth Plan Blvd., P.O. Box 8944, Vancouver WA 98668. Phone: 206-750-5001.
Mt. Baker-Snoqualmie National Forest, 21905 64th Ave., West Mountlake Terrace WA 98043-2278. Phone: 206-744-3200.
Okanogan National Forest, 1240 S. Second Ave., P.O. Box 950, Okanogan WA 98840. Phone: 509-422-2704.
Olympic National Forest, 1835 Black Lake Blvd. SW, Olympia WA 98502-5623. Phone: 206-753-9534.
Wenatchee National Forest, 301 Yakima St., Wenatchee, WA 98807. Phone: 509-662-4367.

WEST VIRGINIA

Monongahela National Forest, 200 Sycamore St., Elkins WV 26241. Phone: 304-636-1800.

WISCONSIN

Chequamegon National Forest, 1170 S. Fourth Ave., Park Falls WI 54552. Phone: 715-762-2461.
Nicolet National Forest, 68 S. Stevens St., Rhinelander WI 54501. Phone: 715-362-3415.

WYOMING

Bighorn National Forest, 1969 S. Sheridan Ave., Sheridan WY 82801. Phone: 307-672-0751.
Medicine Bow National Forest, 2468 Jackson St., Laramie WY 82070-6535. Phone: 307-745-8971.
Shoshone National Forest, 225 W. Yellowstone Ave., P.O. Box 2140, Cody WY 82414. Phone: 307-527-6241.
Bridger-Teton National Forest, 340 North Cache, P.O. Box 1888, Jackson WY 83001. Phone: 307-739-5500.

UNITED STATES BUREAU OF LAND MANAGEMENT

The Bureau of Land Management administers the nation's largest and least explored system of public lands, about 272 million acres. The 67,000 miles of back country roads offer unlimited recreational opportunities including:

• Over 470 developed and 1,830 undeveloped recreation sites.

- 5,948 miles of general hiking trails.
- 85,000 miles of rivers and streams.
- Over 130 boating sites.
- 4.2 million acres of lakes and reservoirs.
- 125,000 historic and archeological sites, of which 350 are entered in the National Register of Historic Places.

There are no entrance fees for the BLM areas, although user fees are charged at many of the developed sites. To receive additional free information on the outdoor recreational opportunities contact the BLM office for the area you are interested in.

BLM Headquarters Office, U.S. Dept. of the Interior, 18th & C Streets NW, MIB 5600, Washington DC 20240. Phone: 202-343-5717.

BLM - Eastern States Office, 7450 Boston Ave., Springfield VA 22153-3121. Phone: 703-274-0190.(Jurisdiction for all states bordering the west bank of the Mississippi River and states east of the river.

ALASKA

BLM - Alaska State Office, 222 W. 7th Avenue #13, Anchorage AK 99513-7599. Phone: 907-271-5960.
BLM - Anchorage District Office, 6881 Abbott Loop Rd., Anchorage AK 99507. Phone: 907-267-1246
BLM - Arctic District Office, 1150 University Ave., Fairbanks AK 99709-3844. Phone: 907-474-2302.
BLM - Glennallen District Office, P.O. Box 42, Glennallen AK 99588. Phone: 907-822-3217.
BLM - Kobuk District Office, 1150 University Ave., Fairbanks AK 99709-3844. Phone: 907-474-2332.
BLM - Steese/White Mountain District Office, 1150 University Ave., Fairbanks AK 99709-3844. Phone: 907-474-2352.

ARIZONA

BLM - Arizona State Office, Siete Square Building, 3707 North 7th St., P.O. Box 16563, Phoenix AZ 85011. Phone: 602-640-5547.
BLM - Arizona Strip District Office, 390 North 3050 East, St. George UT 84770. Phone: 801-673-3545.
BLM - Phoenix District Office, 2015 W. Deer Valley Rd., Phoenix AZ 85027. Phone: 602-863-4464.
BLM - Safford District Office, 711 14th Avenue, Safford AZ 85546. Phone: 602-428-4040.
BLM - Yuma District Office, 3150 Winsor Ave., Yuma AZ 85365. Phone: 602-726-6300.

CALIFORNIA

BLM - California State Office, 2800 Cottage Way, Federal Building - Room E-2845, Sacramento CA 95825-1889. Phone: 916-978-4746.
BLM - Bakersfield District Office, 3801 Pegasus Avenue, Bakersfield CA 93308. Phone: 805-391-6000.
BLM - California Desert District Office, 6221 Box Springs Blvd., Riverside CA 92507-2497. Phone: 909-697-5204.
Susanville District Office, 705 Hall St., Susanville CA 96130-3730. Phone: 916-257-5381.
BLM - Ukiah District Office, 2550 N. State St., Ukiah CA 95482-5599. Phone: 707-468-4000.

COLORADO

BLM - Colorado State Office, 2850 Youngfield St., Lakewood CO 80215-7076. Phone: 303-239-3600.
BLM - Canon City District Office, 3170 E. Main St., P.O. Box 2200, Canon City CO 81215-2200. Phone: 719-275-0631.
BLM - Craig District Office, 455 Emerson St., Craig CO 81625. Phone: 303-824-8261.
BLM - Grand Junction District Office, 2815 H Rd., Grand Junction CO 81506. Phone: 303-244-3050.
BLM - Montrose District Office, 2465 S. Townsend Ave., Montrose CO 81401. Phone: 303-249-7791.

IDAHO

BLM - Idaho State Office, 3380 Americana Terrace, Boise ID 83706. Phone: 208-384-3000.
BLM - Boise District Office, 3948 Development Ave., Boise ID 83705. Phone: 208-384-3300.
BLM - Burley District Office, Route 3 - Box 1, Burley ID 83318. Phone: 208-678-5514.
BLM - Idaho Falls District Office, 940 Lincoln Rd., Idaho Falls ID 83401. Phone: 208-529-1020.
BLM - Salmon District Office, P.O. Box 430, Salmon ID 83467. Phone: 208-756-5400.
BLM - Shoshone District Office, 400 West "F" St., P.O. Box 2-B, Shoshone ID 83352. Phone: 208-886-2206.
BLM - Coeur d'Alene District Office, 1808 N. 3rd St., Coeur d'Alene ID 83814. Phone: 208-765-1511.

MONTANA

BLM - Montana State Office, 222 N. 32nd St., P.O. Box 36800, Billings MT 59107-6800. Phone: 406-255-2913.
BLM - Miles City District Office, P.O. Box 940, Miles City MT 59301-0940. Phone: 406-232-4331.
BLM - Butte District Office, 106 N. Parkmont, P.O. Box 3388, Butte MT 59702-3388. Phone: 406-494-5059.
BLM - Lewistown District Office, P.O. Box 1160, Lewiston MT 59457-1160. Phone: 406-538-7461.

NEVADA

BLM - Nevada State Office, 850 Harvard Way, Reno NV 89502-2055. Phone: 702-785-6500.
BLM - Carson City District Office, 1535 Hot Springs Road - Suite 300, Carson City NV 89706-0638. Phone: 702-885-6000.
BLM - Battle Mountain District Office, 50 Bastian Rd., P.O. Box 1420, Battle Mountain NV 89820-1420. Phone: 702-635-4000.
BLM - Elko District Office, 3900 E. Idaho St., P.O. Box 831, Elko NV 89803-0831. Phone: 702-753-0200.
BLM - Ely District Office, 702 North Industrial Way, HC33 - Box 33500, Ely NV 89301-9402. Phone: 702-289-4865.
BLM - Las Vegas District Office, 4765 W. Vegas Dr., Las Vegas NV 89108-2135. Phone: 702-647-5000.
BLM - Winnemucca District Office, 705 E. 4th St., Winnemucca NV 89445-2807. Phone: 702-623-1500.

NEW MEXICO

BLM - New Mexico State Office, P.O. Box 27115, Santa Fe NM 87502-0115. Phone: 505-988-6000.
BLM - Albuquerque District Office, 435 Montano Road NE, Albuquerque NM 87107-4935. Phone: 505-761-8911.
BLM - Las Cruces District Office, 1800 Marquess St., Las Cruces NM 88005-1420. Phone: 505-525-8228.
BLM - Roswell District Office, 1717 W. 2nd St., P.O. Box 1397, Roswell NM 88201-1397. Phone: 505-622-9042.

NORTH DAKOTA

BLM - Dickinson District Office, 2933 Third Ave. West, Dickinson ND 58601-2619. Phone: 701-225-9148.

OKLAHOMA

BLM - Tulsa District Office, 9522-H East 47th Place, Tulsa OK 74145. Phone: 918-581-6480.

OREGON

BLM - Oregon State Office, 1300 N.E. 44th Ave., Portland OR 97213. Phone: 503-280-7001.
BLM - Salem District Office, 1717 Fabry Rd., S.E., Salem OR 97306-1208. Phone: 503-399-5646.
BLM - Burns District Office, HC74-12533 Hwy. 20 West, Hines OR 97738. Phone: 503-573-5241.
BLM - Coos Bay District Office, 1300 Airport Lane, North Bend OR 97459-2000. Phone: 503-756-0100.
BLM - Eugene District Office, 2890 Chad Dr., P.O. Box 10226, Eugene OR 97440. Phone: 503-683-6600.
BLM - Lakeview District Office, 1000 Ninth St. South, P.O. Box 151, Lakeview OR 97630. Phone: 503-947-2177.
BLM - Medford District Office, 3040 Biddle Rd., Medford OR 97504. Phone: 503-770-2200.
BLM - Prineville District Office, 185 E. 4th St., P.O. Box 550, Prineville OR 97754. Phone: 503-447-4115.

BLM - Roseburg District Office, 777 NW Garden Valley Blvd., Roseburg OR 97470. Phone: 503-440-4930.
BLM - Vale District Office, 100 Oregon St., Vale OR 97918. Phone: 503-473-3144.

UTAH

BLM - Utah State Office, 324 S. State St. - Suite 301, Salt Lake City UT 84111-2303. Phone: 801-539-4001.
BLM - Salt Lake District Office, 2370 S. 2300 West, Salt Lake City UT 84119. Phone: 801-977-4300.
BLM - Cedar City District Office, 176 E. D.L. Sargent Dr., P.O. Box 724, Cedar City UT 84720. Phone: 801-586-2401.
BLM - Richfield District Office, 150 E. 900 N., Richfield UT 84701. Phone: 801-896-8221.
BLM - Moab District Office, 82 E. Dogwood, P.O. Box 970, Moab UT 84532. Phone: 801-259-6111.
BLM - Vernal District Office, 170 S. 500 East, Vernal UT 84078. Phone: 801-789-1362.

WASHINGTON

BLM - Spokane District Office, East 4217 Main Ave., Spokane WA 99202. Phone: 509-353-2570.

WYOMING

BLM - Wyoming State Office, 2515 Warren Ave., Cheyenne WY 82001-3198. Phone: 307-775-6256.
BLM - Rawlins District Office, 1300 N. 3rd St., P.O. Box 670, Rawlings WY 82301-0670. Phone: 307-324-7171.
BLM - Casper District Office, 1701 East E St., Casper WY 82601-2167. Phone: 307-261-7600.
BLM - Rock Springs District Office, Hwy. 191 N., P.O. Box 1869, Rock Springs WY 82902-1869. Phone: 307-382-5350.
BLM - Worland District Office, 101 S. 23rd, P.O. Box 119, Worland WY 82401-0119. Phone: 307-347-9871.

For additional copies of *Road Trip USA* - send check or money order for $18.95 plus $3.00 S&H to:
Roundabout Publications, 2767 South Parker Road - Suite 240, Aurora Colorado 80014-2701